HANDBOC __
OF LIFE IN
BIBLE TIMES

To my wife Marion who has assisted me
in a thousand ways over many years.

HANDBOOK
OF LIFE IN
BIBLE TIMES

J.A.Thompson

Inter-Varsity Press

INTER-VARSITY PRESS
38 De Montfort Street, Leicester LE1 7GP, England
Box 1400, Downers Grove, Illinois 60515, U.S.A.

Unless otherwise stated, quotations from the Bible are taken from the HOLY BIBLE: NEW INTERNATIONAL VERSION, 1978 by the International Bible Society, New York. Published in Great Britain by Hodder and Stoughton Ltd., and used in U.S.A. by permission of Zondervan Bible Publishers, Grand Rapids, Michigan.

First published 1986
Reprinted 1987, 1992

British Library Cataloguing in Publication Data
Thompson, J. A.
  Handbook of life in Bible times.
  1. Archaeology and history–Palestine
  2. Palestine–Social life and customs
  –Sources
933   DS112
ISBN 0–85110–633–1
ISBN 0–85110–977–2 (paperback)

Library of Congress Cataloging-in-Publication Data
Thompson, J. A. (John Arthur), 1913–
  Handbook of life in Bible times.
  1. Jews–Civilization–To 70 A.D.
  2. Palestine–Social life and customs–To 70 A.D.   3. Bible–Antiquities. I. Title.
DS112. T48 1986   220.9′5   86–3046
ISBN 0–87784–949–8
ISBN 0–8308–1755–5 (paperback)

Set in Bembo and Helvetica

Design, artwork and typesetting by Swanston Graphics Limited, Derby DE1 1NU, England

Printed in Great Britain by Bath Press Colourbooks, Glasgow

Inter-Varsity Press, England, is the book-publishing division of the Universities and Colleges Christian Fellowship (formerly the Inter-Varsity Fellowship), a student movement linking Christian Unions in universities and colleges throughout the United Kingdom and the Republic of Ireland, and a member movement of the International Fellowship of Evangelical Students. For information about local and national activities write to UCCF, 38 De Montfort Street, Leicester LE1 7GP.

InterVarsity Press, U.S.A., is the book-publishing division of InterVarsity Christian Fellowship, a student movement active on campus at hundreds of universities, colleges and schools of nursing in the United States of America, and a member movement of the International Fellowship of Evangelical Students. For information about local and regional activities, write Public Relations Dept., InterVarsity Christian Fellowship, 6400 Schroeder Rd., P.O. Box 7895, Madison, WI 53707–7895.

Distributed in Canada through InterVarsity Press, 860 Denison St., Unit 3, Markham, Ontario L3R 4H1, Canada.

Contents

Abbreviations

ABBREVIATIONS USED IN THE FURTHER READING LISTS

ASOR	*American Schools of Oriental Research*
BA	*Biblical Archaeologist*
BAR	*Biblical Archaeology Review*
BASOR	*Bulletin of the American Schools of Oriental Research*
IBD	*Illustrated Bible Dictionary*
IDB	*Interpreter's Dictionary of the Bible*
IEJ	*Israel Exploration Journal*
ISBE	*The International Standard Bible Encyclopedia*
JNES	*Journal of Near Eastern Studies*
PEQ	*Palestine Exploration Quarterly*
ZPEB	*The Zondervan Pictorial Encyclopedia of the Bible*

GENERAL ABBREVIATIONS

AV	Authorized Version of the Bible (King James' Version)
cc	cubic centimetre(s)
cm	centimetre(s)
ft	foot, feet
g	gram(s)
in	inch(es)
kg	kilogram(s)
km	kilometre(s)
LB	Living Bible
lb	pound(s)
m	metre(s)
NEB	New English Bible
oz	ounce(s)
RSV	Revised Standard Version of the Bible
yd	yard(s)

BIBLE REFERENCES

To avoid breaking up the text, Bible references have been printed in the margin at the appropriate point. A single arrowhead indicates that the reference applies to the column next to the margin: a double arrowhead points to the farther column.

Preface

This handbook has a three-fold purpose. The first is to make available, in non-technical and easily understood form, a selection of the discoveries of modern archaeology from the lands of the Bible. This idea is not new but the vigorous work of archaeologists today makes it necessary to keep up to date with their discoveries and the implications that follow.

The second purpose of this book is to bring the discoveries of archaeology *to life*. We are accustomed to think of life here and now as real and, by contrast, life in previous ages, including biblical times, as somehow unreal. This impression is heightened by much of the art of ancient time, especially from Assyria and Egypt, which often portrays people as flat and apparently wooden. Yet these very sources show us much of how people dressed and behaved, people every bit as real as we are. This book sets out to destroy the time-barrier, to compare life then with life now, and to show that not everything has changed: in fact in many important ways humankind has not changed at all.

The third purpose, and the most important, is to show how this reality of life underlies the narrative of the Bible from Genesis to Revelation. The message of God to his people is described very properly as timeless, appropriate to every age, but when we appreciate the everyday lives of those to whom it was first revealed, we can respond to that message much more richly and with more understanding and feeling.

The book is arranged by topics. This makes for ease of reference and makes it possible to understand the developments of, for instance, house-building from the earliest times through to the time of Jesus Christ in one chapter. There is an easy-to-use index and a wealth of biblical references. The references have been placed in the margin to avoid breaking up the text. A short reading list is provided at the end of each chapter for those wanting to investigate further.

A book of this size must be a team effort and this handbook is no exception. The author of the text, J. A. Thompson, provided a solid base and has worked tirelessly on amendments and updating. Derek Williams, as text editor, has brought a practical expertise to bear in rearranging and presenting the text. For picture research we are chiefly indebted to Caroline Masom and, at an earlier stage, to Tessa Clowney, who both worked on *The Illustrated Bible Dictionary* (IVP, 1980). We also warmly appreciate the work of John Bimson, Librarian and Lecturer in Old Testament and Hebrew at Trinity College, Bristol and Alan Millard, Rankin Reader in Hebrew and Ancient Semitic Languages at the University of Liverpool, for their invaluable and painstaking help in specialist matters of ancient history, archaeology and epigraphy.

The design and presentation of the handbook were undertaken by Swanston Graphics Limited of Derby who also designed the *New Bible Atlas* (IVP, 1985).

Our hope is that the pooling of these skills and resources will have produced a book that, under the guidance of the Holy Spirit, will help to bring the Bible to life.

SECTION I:
Introduction

The people and lands of the Bible

1

The Bible is primarily about people. It recalls the achievements and failures, the discoveries and beliefs of generations of people from Abraham 2,000 years before Christ to the apostles in the half-century or so after Christ. It glances behind Abraham to the mysterious dawn of human life and beyond the present world to the new age prefigured by Jesus. As its story unfolds, so too do its characters' awareness and understanding of God, culminating in his ultimate revelation through Jesus Christ: 'In the past God spoke to our forefathers through the prophets at many times and in various ways, but in these last days he has spoken to us by his Son.'

The people who feature in its pages – military and political heroes such as Joshua and David, prophetic leaders such as Moses and Isaiah, colourful characters such as Samson and fallible ones such as Peter – remain real and believable centuries after their brief lives. It is easy for people in every age to identify with the timidity of Moses the shepherd sent to defy the mighty king of Egypt, or with the brash but fragile boldness of Peter promising friendship to Jesus and then denying it within hours.

It is less easy, however, to picture the details of their lives and of their encounters with God, because they lived in a period of history which was unlike our own and in a part of the world which has few geographical parallels in the west. To get the most from the Bible, we modern readers need to do two things. We need to ask, what was this event like, or what did this teaching relate to, at the time in which it took place or was given? Then we are encouraged by the Bible itself to ask how its timeless truths relate to our differing outward circumstances: 'For everything that was written in the past was written to teach us, so that through endurance and the encouragement of the Scriptures we might have hope.'

◁ Romans 15:4

◁◁ Hebrews 1:1

The purpose of this book is to sketch the background picture into which the people and events of the Bible fit. It describes the kinds of places they lived in, what they ate and how they worked, warred and worshipped. It does not aim to explain each chapter or book of the Bible, but to provide a framework of information which will make the Bible clearer as you read it. Numerous Bible references are given to anchor and illustrate the facts being described (most of them are quoted so that you do not have to keep consulting the Bible as you read this book), but the references are by no means exhaustive.

Before we turn back the pages of history and walk through the streets of biblical cities and peer into the windows of the people's houses, we need in this introductory section to take a panoramic look at the places in which the events occurred so that we can visualize the scenes. Then we shall set the main biblical events in order, so that basic Bible history does not need to be spelled out in every chapter. And

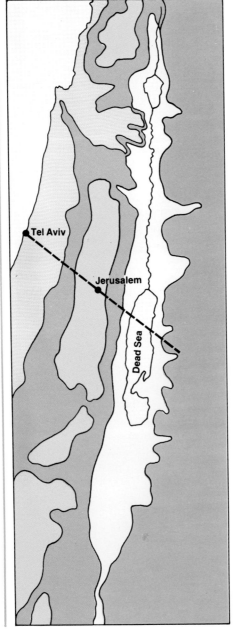

The Holy Land, showing, in simplified form, the five regions described in this chapter. The dotted line shows the line of the cross-section on the facing page.

Tel Aviv

Jerusalem

Dead Sea

we shall look briefly over the shoulders of the archaeologists who are largely responsible for the information in this book, to discover how they found it all out.

MOUNTAINS AND VALLEYS

The stage on which much of the Bible drama is played is small and compact. The biblical borders of Palestine, from Dan in the north to Beer-sheba in the south, are barely 240 km (150 miles) apart. The country is 86 km (54 miles) wide at the foot and a mere 44 km (28 miles) across at the top. In area it is slightly larger than the state of Vermont in North America; about 25% larger than Wales; and in Australia it would fit comfortably in length between Newcastle and Wollongong and in width between the Pacific and the Blue Mountains. It is divided down its length into five noticeably different regions (see map).

The coastal plain is a narrow, flat strip of sand and alluvium running down the shore of the Mediterranean Sea. It is almost unbroken by inlets or natural harbours although Joppa, Dor and Ashdod were ports in Old Testament times. King Herod built an artificial harbour at Caesarea shortly before the birth of Christ. The plain is fertile, apart from the coastal dunes, and has three sub-sections: the Plain of Acco (Acre) in the north; the Plain of Sharon in the centre (between Mount Carmel and Joppa) which was once covered in forest and swamp and was therefore rather inhospitable; and the more cultivable Philistine Plain (Philistia) from which the name 'Palestine' is derived.

The plain gives way eastwards to low-lying hills, the second natural region. They are referred to as the 'lowland' or 'foothills' in Bible translations. They are cut by wadis

1

Cross-section of the Holy Land at the line indicated on the map on page 12. The Dead Sea is on the right, Jerusalem on the highest point west of the rift valley.

(dry river courses) and by intermittent streams running down from the mountains. These wadis provided people with natural roads into the mountains, and fortified towns were sometimes built at their entrances to guard them.

The third region is the hill country; an outcrop of rough, rocky limestone. It is not easily cultivated, yet was the main area of Israelite occupation, and included Jerusalem, the capital of the south, and Samaria, the chief town of the north.

The Galilee area of the hill country reaches almost 1,200 m (4,000 ft) above sea level at Merom. Level plains north of Nazareth and around Capernaum have been extensively cultivated over the centuries. South of Galilee the hill country is broken by the valley of Jezreel (or Esdraelon) just south of

Olive grove in the hill country of Samaria.

The rugged hill country of Judaea near Hebron, showing terraced vineyards.

Nazareth. This makes a passage from the coast to the Jordan valley. The fortified town of Megiddo (the Armageddon of the book of Revelation) guarded important trade routes through the valley, which in the wet season often became swampy.

South of the valley the hill country of Samaria rises to over 1,000 m (3,300 ft) at Baal-hazor, close to Mount Ebal and Mount Gerizim, the latter being an important focus of Samaritan worship. Further south is the hill country of Judah, lower in height and cut by numerous wadis giving it a rugged appearance. The western slopes received adequate rainfall for cultivating crops but the eastern side near the Dead Sea is semi-desert. At the southernmost end the hill country descends to the Negeb below Beer-sheba This inhospitable desert area, for centuries the preserve of semi-nomadic Bedouin, is now occupied by people acutely conscious of the need to conserve water.

The fourth natural region is the Jordan valley, part of a huge geological fault which begins in Syria and runs south through the Dead Sea,

◁ John 4:20

The inhospitable desert area of the Negeb. A flock of sheep and goats survives in the harsh conditions.

The Sea of Galilee, looking east.

and on into the Red Sea and Africa. The river Jordan rises on the western slopes of Mount Hermon and falls quickly to 210 m (700 ft) below sea level by the time it enters the beautiful and mildly saline Sea of Galilee (sometimes called Chinnereth, Gennesaret or Tiberias). Grass-covered hills surround the lake, and the alluvial plain on the north-west side has been well cultivated over the centuries.

The river leaves Galilee and falls 195 m (650 ft) in the space of some 104 km (65 miles). Its winding course is hemmed in by mountains on both sides. In most parts of the valley crops are grown, until the river reaches the vicinity of the Dead Sea where rainfall is only 10 cm (4 in) each year.

The Dead Sea is so saline that tourists sometimes have themselves photographed as they sit floating in it and reading a newspaper. It is 80 km (50 miles) north–south and up to 17 km (11 miles) across at its widest point just north of En Gedi. Its northern portion is over 380 m (1,250 ft) deep, although in the south it is only 6 m (20 ft) deep.

The fifth region is the Transjordan plateau on the eastern side of the

The river Jordan, south of the Sea of Galilee, follows a winding course.

Jordan. It was here that the peoples of Edom, Moab and Ammon lived. It is subdivided into five sections by the streams which flow across it into the Jordan. One of the regions familiar to Bible readers is Gilead, between the rivers Yarmuk and Jabbok. It is mountainous in the north, gently sloping in the south. Forests covered the hill slopes in biblical times. Agriculture is possible in parts of Transjordan where the rising land causes rain to fall.

Psalm 1:1,3 ▷▷

People in Bible times were therefore familiar with rich agricultural plains and barren mountainous areas, the most common colours being the deep green of trees and crops and the yellow-brown of the dry and dusty hills. The life-giving rivers and the harsh hot deserts both contributed to the spiritual imagery of the Jews. The Psalmist voiced a sentiment often echoed in the Bible: 'Blessed is the man who does not walk in the counsel of the wicked.... He is like a tree planted by streams of water, which yields its fruit in season and whose leaf does not wither.'

The Dead Sea, looking north. The Judaean hills are on the left, the hills of Moab on the right.

1

Above: the hills of Moab to the east of the Jordan.

Below left: the sources of the river Jordan at Dan. Right: the river Kidron, south of Jerusalem, as it winds its way through the Judaean hills towards the Dead Sea.

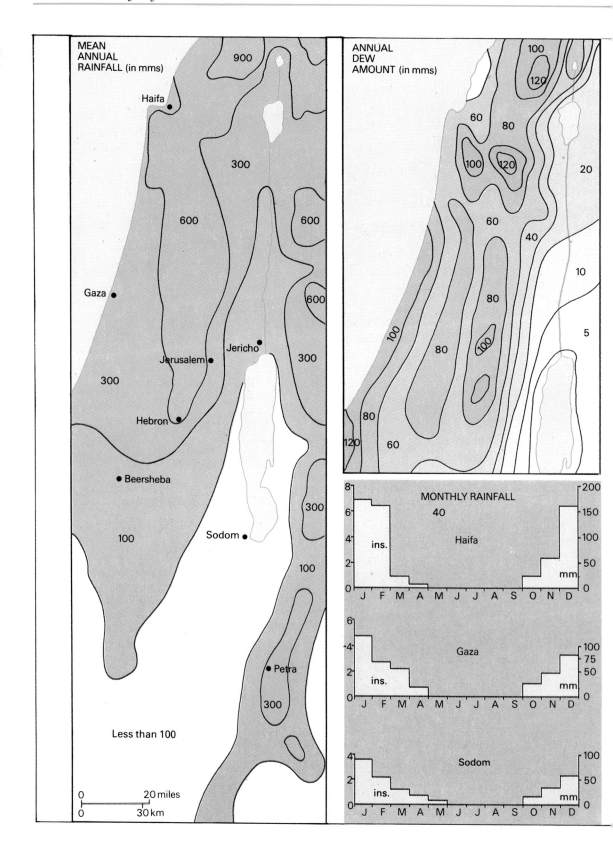

MEAN
ANNUAL
RAINFALL (in mms)

900

Haifa

300

600

600

Gaza

600

Jericho

Jerusalem

300

300

Hebron

Beersheba

300

100

Sodom

100

300

Petra

300

Less than 100

0   20 miles
0   30 km

ANNUAL
DEW
AMOUNT (in mms)

100

120

60   80

100   120   20

60

40

10

80

5

100

80

100

80

120   60

MONTHLY RAINFALL
40
Haifa

8   200
6   150
ins.   100
4   50
2   mm
0
J F M A M J J A S O N D

Gaza

6   100
4   75
ins.   50
2   mm
0   0
J F M A M J J A S O N D

Sodom

4   100
2   50
ins.   mm
0   0
J F M A M J J A S O N D

THE CLIMATE OF PALESTINE

The weather in Palestine normally follows a very regular pattern. For six months it is cool and wet, and for the rest of the year hot and dry.

The first rains of winter begin in mid-October, as moist sea air encounters the hot dry air rising from the earth's surface and causes thunderstorms which may be very local in their effect: 'I sent rain on one town, but withheld it from another. One field had rain; another had none and dried up.'

The heaviest rains fall in December, January and February, with some rain (called in the Bible the 'latter' rains) during March and April which is vital for bringing the growing grain to head. The harvest takes place after these rains in the beginning of the hot period.

Once the rains and the harvest are over, the hot winds blow in from the desert. The scorching sirocco wind dries out the vegetation and turns the land yellow. Daytime temperatures in some places can be in excess of 40°C (104°F), although in the hill country the evening temperature can fall sharply and the night can feel distinctly chilly. Snow is a rarity except on the high hills and even winter temperatures rarely drop below 10°C (50°F).

The climate varies according to the regions, of course, as the accompanying map indicates. The north and west tend to be wetter than the south and east. Heavy rain in the drier areas causes flash floods, and the wadis (intermittent streams) quickly fill up. Heavy dew is a source of additional moisture in many parts.

Has the climate changed since biblical times?

It is often asked whether the climate of the Bible lands has changed since biblical times. Accepting that *fluctuations* can and do occur, there is no archaeological evidence for significant change. Near the Gulf of Aqabah, for example, excavated Roman gutters still fit the springs for which they were constructed. It is therefore necessary to seek other reasons why a land notable for milk, honey and splendid

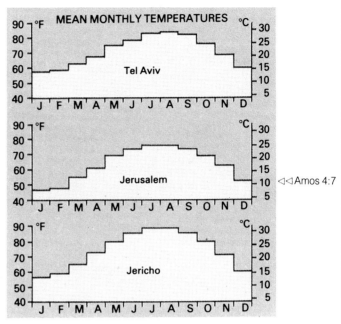

Aspects of the climate of the Holy Land are illustrated by the charts on these two pages. The rainfall pattern (facing page) includes dewfall, which is an important source of moisture in a dry land. Above: monthly temperatures.

◁◁Amos 4:7

fruit crops had become, by the early twentieth century, a barren and treeless land of little or no agricultural value.

Rather than infer change of climate, it is simpler to assume that the people of Israel were responsible for initiating processes which were then continued and intensified over succeeding centuries:

1. Because they never conquered and occupied the whole land assigned to them by God, the land became overcrowded, and overcrowding in dry lands usually brings with it soil erosion and loss of fertility.

2. Because they lacked trust in God, they repeatedly became entangled in regional alliances, seeking the help of powerful neighbours for their own protection, and so became involved in wars. War brought invasion, devastation, the loss of tree cover, and frequent war resulted in desertification. In these lands of the Bible, the ecological balance is a delicate one: human carelessness is all too promptly followed by national disaster.

◁Deuteronomy 20: 19
◁Jeremiah 6: 6

◁◁Numbers 13: 27

ANIMALS AND PLANTS OF PALESTINE

Palestine was never a thickly wooded area, although there were woods and forests in some of the hills. Lebanon to the north was a major source for wood, and Solomon imported Lebanese timber (mostly cedar) for the temple. Out in the desert spreading, thorny acacia trees provided some shade, as did the terebinth or turpentine tree which was sometimes used as a shady spot for sacrifices. Poplars grow by the Jordan, and oaks in the hills, while the sycamore-fig is a common, rather ugly spreading tree in many parts.

Large shrubs also form part of the landscape. Broom, which can grow to 4 m (13 ft) in height, sheltered Elijah from the sun. Wild flowers brighten up the spring landscape. Jesus referred to 'the lilies of the field' which could have been hyacinths or anemones, or even daisies. Out in the drier areas, only thorns and thistles survive the hot conditions.

Apart from the domesticated farm animals, which will be referred to in a later chapter, a number of wild animals were to be found in Palestine in Bible times. The dog was not domesticated and was regarded as a scavenger and a pest. Deer inhabited some of the more wooded areas, and these and domestic animals would be preyed on by wild cats (lions and possibly leopards) and bears, all of which are now extinct in the areas. Foxes, jackals and wolves were common, as were hares and rabbits.

Among the birds would have been small sparrows and huge storks, eagles and vultures. Swifts, swallows and martins are known to have lived in Palestine, and pigeons and doves were often used in sacrifices by poor people.

A wide range of snakes can be found in Palestine. Most of them are harmless but half a dozen species are potentially lethal. Locusts are a potential hazard to crops when they are blown on the wind in huge swarms. Among other small creatures there are several species of scorpion.

1 Kings 19:4–5 ▷

Matthew 6: 28 ▷

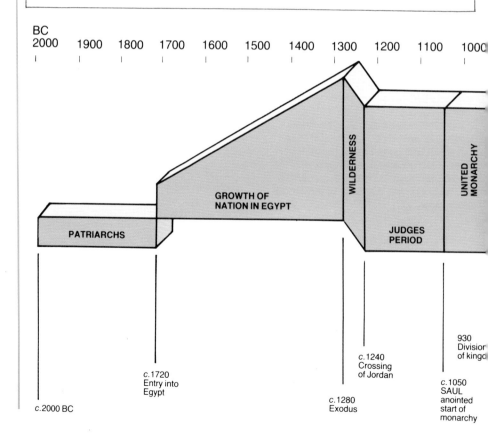

KINGS AND CONQUERORS

The sixty-six books of the Bible cover a period of over 2,000 years of recorded history; more, if the first eleven chapters of Genesis are included, which look back to the very dawn of time. The books are not collected in strict chronological order, so the reader new to the Bible often has difficulty in relating events and people to each other. For example, the historical narratives of Ezra and Nehemiah, which follow the books of Chronicles, refer to events contemporary with the minor prophets Malachi, Haggai and Zechariah at the end of the Old Testament; those events are foretold by Jeremiah, which in the Bible comes after Ezra and Nehemiah.

Simplified diagram showing the history of Israel from patriarchal times to the fall of Jerusalem in AD 70.

The accompanying diagram illustrates the order of biblical events visually, and relates them to the archaeological periods which are sometimes mentioned in the rest of this book. The following text is a brief summary of Bible history.

FROM PATRIARCHS TO PROMISED LAND

The patriarchs (Abraham, Isaac and Jacob) lived during the period about 2000-1700 BC, and their story is told in Genesis 12–50. There were many migrations of people at that time, so Abraham's journeys are not unique. These movements were partly caused by political turbulence following the collapse of the third dynasty (about 2060-1950 BC) of Ur in Southern Mesopotamia.

Egypt achieved stability at the time under the twelfth dynasty kings (1991–1786 BC) ruling from Memphis in

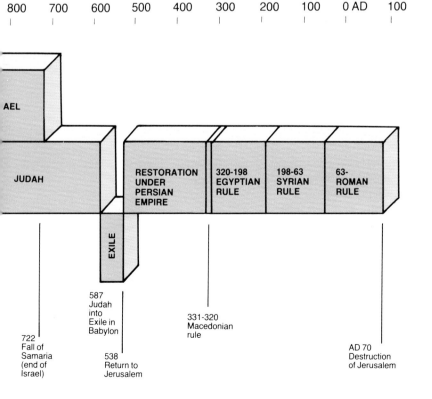

800	700	600	500	400	300	200	100	0 AD	100

AEL

JUDAH

RESTORATION UNDER PERSIAN EMPIRE

320-198 EGYPTIAN RULE

198-63 SYRIAN RULE

63- ROMAN RULE

EXILE

587 Judah into Exile in Babylon

331-320 Macedonian rule

722 Fall of Samaria (end of Israel)

538 Return to Jerusalem

AD 70 Destruction of Jerusalem

Genesis 37:27–36 ▷

Lower Egypt. During the last part of this period Joseph's family moved south to the full granaries of Egypt while Canaan starved in a famine (Joseph himself having already been in Egypt for some years). But by about 1750 BC Egyptian power had waned and a group of Asiatic people of Semitic stock, the Hyksos, controlled the country. In Palestine the Amorites probably took advantage of Egypt's weakness and may have integrated with the native Canaanites, so setting the cultural scene for Israel's invasion in the thirteenth century, the late Bronze Age.

The exact date of the exodus is unknown, but a document produced by Pharaoh Merenptah (1213-1204 BC) listed the people of Israel among those he defeated in his Palestine campaigns. That would probably set the exodus during the reign of Rameses II (about 1279–1213 BC). For details see the *New Bible Atlas* (IVP, 1985) pages 38–39.

FROM CONQUEST TO DEFEAT

The story of Israel's exodus from Egypt and their arrival in the 'promised land' is chronicled in the books of Exodus, Numbers, Deuteronomy and Joshua. The book of Judges describes how they settled down and recounts the skirmishes they had with the Philistines, or Sea Peoples, another group of invaders who occupied the southern coastal areas. Israel lacked any central leadership at this time, and the book of 1 Samuel describes how they asked for, and finally succeeded in getting, a king, Saul.

When Saul died in battle, David was appointed king (about 1010 BC), and a hereditary monarchy continued in Judah (the southern half of Israel) until 586 BC. This period, known as the Iron II period, or the days of the kings, saw considerable political, social and cultural changes. It is covered by the books of Samuel, Kings, Chronicles, Jeremiah, Ezekiel, Amos, Micah, Hosea, Zephaniah, Nahum, Habakkuk and parts of Isaiah. Many Psalms and the books of Proverbs and Ecclesiastes originated at this time too.

The kingdom faced pressures from outside, with occasional strong rulers in Egypt pushing northwards and the rising power of Assyria pushing southwards, turning Israel into a buffer zone. Rivalries within Israel led to the division of the kingdom after Solomon's death into Israel (north) and Judah (south). These were the days of the major pre-exilic prophets, who constantly rebuked the two nations for spiritual apostasy and foretold God's punishment in the form of political defeat and the exile of the people in a foreign land.

That punishment came first to the north as the Assyrians turned Israel into a subject state; the Black Obelisk of Shalmaneser, dated about 826 BC, shows Jehu king of Israel bowing in allegiance to the Assyrian king. Internal problems in Assyria prevented the situation from worsening for Israel for a century, but Shalmaneser V (726-722 BC) captured Samaria and brought the kingdom of Israel to an end in 722 BC. Sennacherib (704-681 BC) continued the invasion and besieged Jerusalem, the capital of Judah, in 701 BC. Her king submitted to him.

But Assyria was weakening and Jerusalem survived. On to the Near Eastern scene came Babylon to defeat Assyria, and under the leadership of Nebuchadrezzar sacked Jerusalem in 587 BC and carried off its more talented citizens to labour camps on the banks of the Euphrates.

FROM PERSIA TO ROME

Jeremiah, Ezekiel, Daniel and parts of

Isaiah all deal with events from the time Judah was in exile. Some Psalms come from this period, too, which was a time of consolidation for Israelite religion. The Babylonian Empire was short-lived, and was soon replaced by the Persians who allowed Judah (and other subject nations) to return home in 539 BC. The Bible books of Ezra, Nehemiah, Malachi, Haggai and Zechariah describe the ensuing period in which national identity and Jewish faith were recovered and the city and temple of Jerusalem rebuilt.

The biblical narrative then largely fades for three centuries, a time covered partly by the apocryphal books and especially by the books of Maccabees. The Greek Empire succeeded the Persian in 331 BC, and Palestine was ruled by the successors of the Greek general Ptolemy I (323-285 BC) until the descendants of another general, Seleucus I (312-280 BC), took power in a coup in 198 BC. One of these, Antiochus Epiphanes (175-163 BC), desecrated the temple in Jerusalem and provoked the Maccabean revolt of some Jews led by Mattathias and his three sons.

Having succeeded against huge odds in regaining religious liberty, the guerrilla fighters set their sights on political liberty. By 142 BC the Jews under Simon Maccabaeus had become an independent state ruled by high priests. But the prospect of a return to the old days of spiritual rule was short-lived. Political ambition corrupted and divided the people just as it had in the days of the kings. The Romans, who had replaced the Greeks as the dominant world power, took full advantage of the Jewish wranglings and stepped in to assume control. By 40 BC the Roman Senate had placed Herod the Great on the throne of Judah to reign as a puppet king. Herod was not really a Jew. His father was Idumaean and his mother Nabataean.

The Idumaeans (Edomites) had been forced to adopt Judaism by one of the Jewish high-priest kings, John Hyrcanus.

When Herod died in 4 BC his territory was divided between his three sons Archelaus, Antipas and Philip. Archelaus inherited Judah, Idumaea and Samaria but he was so incompetent that he was banished to Vienna in AD 6 to be replaced by Roman procurators based in Caesarea. Of them, Pontius Pilate (AD 26-36), Felix (AD 52-60) and Festus (about AD 60–62) make brief but significant appearances in the New Testament record; the first at the crucifixion of Jesus, and the others agreeing on the final banishment of Paul to Rome.

Herod Agrippa was made king by the Emperor Caligula in AD 37, and by AD 41 he ruled all Palestine except for Judaea. Despite a growing threat from Rome which, under Nero, was making sport of the Christians in the arena, the Jews rebelled against Rome in AD 66. It was a fatal move which cost them their nation and their temple. The temple was destroyed by the Romans in AD 70, and the last Jewish stronghold, Masada, overlooking the Dead Sea at its narrowest point, fell in AD 73. It was not until the modern era that the Jews once more had a land which they could call their own.

FROM OLD TO NEW

By the middle of the first century AD a new force was spreading like a bush fire across the Roman Empire. Non-political in nature, it was feared and opposed by politicians and religious leaders alike. Men and women everywhere were claiming that one Jesus Christ had risen from the dead and was the promised Jewish Messiah, the unique Son of God, through whom alone people could discover a fresh personal relationship with a loving

Matthew 5:17 ▷▷

heavenly Father–God.

In the space of some seventy years after their leader had been crucified for alleged blasphemy and treason, Christians had reached every corner of the Empire and were circulating documents about the life of Jesus and letters of encouragement and instruction from the apostles.

Acts 17:6 (RSV) ▷▷

2 Corinthians 5:17 ▷

Filled with a new confidence which came from God as his Spirit filled their lives, they asserted boldly that 'If anyone is in Christ, he is a new creation; the old has gone, the new has come!' They saw themselves not as a replacement of the old Judaism, but as its fulfilment. Jesus had told them, '"Do not think that I have come to abolish the Law or the Prophets; I have not come to abolish them but to fulfil them."'

And so began the Christian era. From its unlikely beginnings with the crying of a baby lying on straw in a Palestinian stable, to its justifiable reputation of having 'turned the world upside down'; it resulted in men having songs on their lips as they went to their graves, and injected into the world a new dynamic and a new attitude towards God and people which changed the course of history.

★ FOR FURTHER READING

GEOGRAPHY
Aharoni, Y., *Land of the Bible*, 2nd rev. ed. (Burns and Oates, 1979. US ed. Westminster Press).
Aharoni, Y. and Avi-Yonah, M., *The Macmillan Bible Atlas* (Macmillan, 1968).
Avi-Yonah, M., *The Holy Land from the Persian to the Arab Conquest. A historical geography*, rev. ed. (Baker Book House, 1977).
Baly, D., *Geographical Companion to the Bible* (Lutterworth, 1963).
Baly, D., *The Geography of the Bible* (Lutterworth, 1964).
Bimson, J.J. and Kane, J.P. (eds), *New Bible Atlas* (IVP, 1985).
May, H.G. (ed.), *Oxford Bible Atlas*, 3rd ed. rev. by J. Day (Oxford University Press, 1984).
Wright, G.E. and Filson, F.V., *The Westminster Smaller Bible Atlas* (SCM, 1957).

HISTORY
Bright, J., *A History of Israel*, 2nd rev. ed. (SCM, 1981).
Bruce, F.F., *Israel and the Nations*, rev. ed. (Paternoster, 1983).
Herrmann, S., *A History of Israel in Old Testament Times*, rev. ed. (SCM, 1981).
Kitchen, K.A., *The Bible in its World: the Bible and Archaeology Today* (Paternoster, 1977. US ed. IVCP).
Wiseman, D.J. (ed.), *Peoples of Old Testament Times* (Oxford University Press, 1973).

★ For a list of abbreviations used in this and the other book lists, see p.6.

Shedding light on the past

2

Each time a person opens the Bible and reads a passage, he or she forms some kind of image about the people, objects and ideas which are mentioned. Bringing a twentieth-century mind to the Bible has its problems.

When Jesus fed the great crowds with five loaves and two fishes, what did the loaves look like? They were certainly not white, sliced and wrapped in clear plastic! Or those lamps which the servant girls in Jesus' story forgot to prepare in case the bridegroom returned home early; were they like old-fashioned hurricane lamps?

What sort of clothes did Abraham wear? Was he really dressed like a Bedouin Arab, as many illustrations suggest? If some books are to be believed, Solomon's palace was rather like Buckingham Palace in London, but it was not. Goliath, the huge warrior whom David killed with a well-aimed stone, is too easily dressed in our minds like a mediaeval crusader encased in a heavy suit of armour.

Answers to these questions may not greatly affect our understanding of the Bible's teaching, but they do affect our approach to it. The more we can relate the Bible to accurate pictures in our minds, the more it will come alive as a

'We can find fragments ... and stick them together'.
A juglet in the Greek style, found at Tell el-Far'ah. It is about 20 cm (8 in) high. (See following page.)

record of real people's experiences of God. And the more that happens, the clearer is the way for the Holy Spirit to interpret the Bible's truths to our contemporary lives: 'when ... the Spirit of truth comes,' said Jesus, 'he will guide you into all truth.'

John 16: 13 ▷

This is the valuable contribution of archaeology. By patient research, excavation of ancient sites and interpretation of ancient inscriptions, we can satisfy our curiosity about some of the artefacts and events of everyday life in Bible times. We can guess the shape of bread loaves by examining the ovens in which they were baked. We can find fragments of oil lamps and glue them together. We can see contemporary paintings of people and discover what clothes they wore, and we can dig out the foundations of buildings and see for ourselves what was their shape and size.

In the tombs of kings and warriors we can unearth the furniture, pottery and weapons they used, and from their burial chambers learn more about their attitude to life and death. Graves in Jericho dating from about 1600 BC even had grains and seeds left in them, providing valuable evidence about the food eaten by the people of the time.

The study of the archaeology of the Near East is a relatively young science. Crusaders and other travellers in the Middle Ages took back to Europe drawings and accounts of life there as they saw it, and of some of the ancient sites. Scholarly expeditions began in earnest in the early nineteenth century, and in 1838 an American theologian, Edward Robinson, spent three months identifying many biblical places for the first time. In 1865 the Palestine Exploration Fund was established to finance excavations.

An aerial view of Lachish showing clearly the shape of the tell or ruin mound. Compare with the diagram on pages 30–31.

2

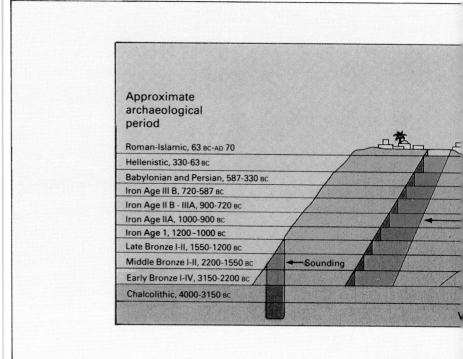

Approximate
archaeological
period

Period
Roman-Islamic, 63 BC-AD 70
Hellenistic, 330-63 BC
Babylonian and Persian, 587-330 BC
Iron Age III B, 720-587 BC
Iron Age II B - IIIA, 900-720 BC
Iron Age IIA, 1000-900 BC
Iron Age 1, 1200-1000 BC
Late Bronze I-II, 1550-1200 BC
Middle Bronze I-II, 2200-1550 BC
Early Bronze I-IV, 3150-2200 BC
Chalcolithic, 4000-3150 BC

←Sounding

Above: diagram of a tell (ruin mound) showing levels of occupation. In reality many of the periods shown here would be represented at most tells by more than one stratum (level), while some periods would not be represented at all because of breaks in occupation.
This diagram shows the archaeological periods, as generally known, and their dates, alongside the biblical period which corresponds to each.
The vertical is exaggerated for convenience.

Lack of finance and the periodic interruptions of war have hindered the exploration of the Near East. It is estimated that there are 5,000 tells (mounds hiding old settlements) in Palestine. Only a few hundred have been examined, and only about fifty have been excavated in any detail. Probably 90% of the ruins in Palestine still wait to be explored. But those which have been excavated have produced valuable information.

ANCIENT SITES

Many biblical towns occupied the same site for centuries. Others were abandoned and then returned to later.

2

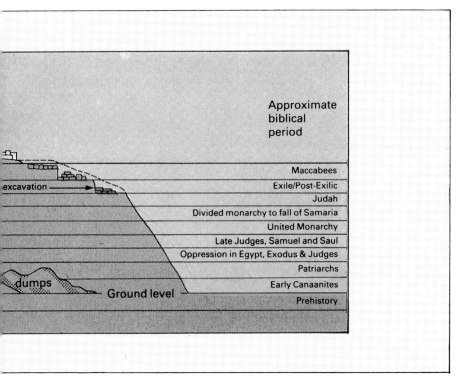

Approximate biblical period

excavation →	Maccabees
	Exile/Post-Exilic
	Judah
	Divided monarchy to fall of Samaria
	United Monarchy
	Late Judges, Samuel and Saul
	Oppression in Egypt, Exodus & Judges
	Patriarchs
dumps — Ground level	Early Canaanites
	Prehistory

Left: great care is needed in excavating the remains of ancient buildings. Machinery cannot be used. Here a pick-man, a shovel-man and a basket-carrier reveal the past shape of Fort Shalmaneser at Nimrud in Assyria.

Below: excavation in progress in Jerusalem below the temple wall.

Joshua 11: 13 ▷

Already in the time of Joshua the Bible refers to 'cities built on their mounds', that is, on the remains of previous cities.

The traveller in the Near East will see these mounds (or 'tells'). They look like small hills, often littered with pottery fragments which have come loose from the compacted debris.

When a town was rebuilt on the site of a previous settlement – perhaps because it had a good water supply or was a strategic site to be defended – the people made no attempt to clear the site first. The town was built on the ruins of the old one after filling holes and levelling, sometimes using some of the old walls, masonry and other materials. Over the centuries the remains of previous occupations accumulated. In some cases the old city walls held the remains together. They were left in place as the city expanded and new walls were built above or beyond them. Eventually the site was abandoned. Vegetation grew among the ruins and as it dried off and rotted year by year the process of obliterating the old town was completed until all that could be seen was a grassy mound with its tell-tale fragments of walls and artefacts visible on the surface of the ground.

The excavator digs down into the mound to discover the layers of debris, the remains of the towns that once flourished on the site. Not every site will have a layer of rubble for each known archaeological period, because not every site was inhabited continually through all the periods. So when each new layer is unearthed, it has to be dated. When a number of tells have been excavated, it is possible to correlate the remains and give to each layer a relative date (such as 'layer B at Tell X is later than layer b at Tell Y').

To find an accurate date, the excavator has to look for objects which can be dated such as coins or inscriptions in the layer, or in other tells which have a corresponding layer of pottery and other remains which can be dated. Sometimes imported items which can be dated in another land such as Egypt, are found in a particular stratum making dating possible. By building up the total archaeological picture for Palestine it becomes possible to date a particular stratum even if it does not contain coins or inscriptions itself.

FOR FURTHER READING

Aharoni, Y., *The Archaeology of the Land of Israel* (SCM, 1982. US ed. Philadelphia, Westminster, 1978).

Kenyon, K.M., *Archaeology in the Holy Land*, 4th ed. (Ernest Benn, 1979. US ed. New York, W.W. Norton).

Kenyon, K.M., *Beginning in Archaeology*, 2nd ed. (Phoenix, 1961. US ed. New York, Praeger).

Lapp, P.W., *The Tale of the Tell* (Pittsburgh, Pickwick, 1980).

Millard, A.R., *Treasures from Bible Times* (Lion Publishing, 1985).

Wheeler, M., *Archaeology from the Earth* (Oxford Press, 1954. New ed. Penguin).

Wiseman, D.J. *et al.*, 'Archaeology', *IBD*, 1 (IVP, 1980), pp.93-102.

SECTION II:
People at home

Towns and villages

3

Think of a modern city – say New York, London or Sydney. Picture the dense central areas full of tall offices and shops, and the more spacious leafy suburbs where many of the inhabitants live.

Look at the tourist map and see the sights. The soaring Empire State Building; the historic Houses of Parliament; centres of culture such as the Sydney Opera House.

And notice the people. There are several millions of them, scurrying through congested streets in cars and buses. They are generally healthy, they can read and write, and they have money to spare for food, clothes and mass-produced gadgets beyond the bare necessities. For the most part they are free, untroubled by the police speeding across the city in their wailing squad cars.

Transfer that image into the different culture of modern Jerusalem in Israel. It has much in common with western cities. There are shopping and commercial centres, tall apartment blocks and busy roads which could be almost anywhere. There are plenty of

Jerusalem ancient and modern: the Lion Gate, the Old City and modern buildings beyond, viewed from the Mount of Olives.

big hotels and tourist attractions, too.

It is, however, much smaller. With a population of just over 300,000 Jerusalem is similar to middle-sized places such as Louisville, Kentucky; Leicester, England; or Wellington, New Zealand. It also looks different; there is something 'eastern' about it.

Take a walk up the Mount of Olives and look back across the valley to the city. Instead of the blue-greys of concrete and glass, and the reds of brick and tile which dominate western cities, there is a predominance of beige and off-white from stone building blocks and plastered houses. Some roofs are flat, others are gently pitched, and there are domes of mosques as well as towers of churches. And, as in most countries bordering the Mediterranean Sea, clumps of olive-green trees and shrubs stand out like dark oases in a stony desert.

In the older parts of the city especially, made conspicuous by its wall, the streets are narrow and some are cobbled or paved rather than tarred. Here, traders haggle over prices

in little shops. The people thronging the streets are generally darker and a little shorter than those of northern European origin, and the cosmopolitan crowd includes many people dressed in Arab robes, and some tie-less orthodox Jews with their distinctive hats, beards and pig-tails.

Now, in your imagination, take away all the modern 'western' buildings. Shrink the city between the walls so that you can walk from one end to another in well under half an hour. Cram the flat-roofed beige houses into the narrow streets, and replace all the cars and buses with camels and mules – and the smell of diesel with that of dung.

Rub out the advertising signs, rip out the phone lines, tear down the TV aerials and switch off the electricity supply. Dress everyone in robes, but leave the market traders shouting and arguing, and the cosmopolitan mixture of pilgrims – the earliest tourists – and foreigners in town on business.

Remove the Dome of the Rock and replace it with Herod's temple. Take away the compulsory schooling and the health services, leave the blind and handicapped to beg in the streets, and reduce the general standard of living to a little above subsistence. Remember that running hot water and flush toilets as we know them will not become commonplace here or anywhere else for another 1,900 years. And instead of the police, send in a force of Roman soldiers armed with swords and spears, to be used they say on civilians at the slightest provocation.

You are now getting closer to the city of Jerusalem as it was when the New Testament was written; the Jerusalem in which Jesus Christ walked, taught and was crucified 2,000 years ago.

Streets are narrow and traders haggle over prices. A bazaar in Hebron.

JERUSALEM AS JESUS KNEW IT

It was, by all accounts, a beautiful place, even if to modern eyes it would have looked quaint and cluttered. Built on two hills some 760 m (2,500 ft) above sea level, it was surrounded on three sides by steep valleys. Just as modern Jerusalem is dominated from every angle by the golden-capped Dome of the Rock, a seventh-century Moslem shrine, so the first-century city was dominated by that spectacular Jewish temple built by King Herod where the Dome now stands.

Jesus and his friends once admired it, 'adorned with beautiful stones and with gifts dedicated to God'. Faced with cream marble and overlaid in places with gold, it was set in a courtyard about twice the area of St Paul's Cathedral in London.

The Madeba Mosaic, as described on the following page. This map formed part of the floor of the Church of St George at Madeba in Jordan.

Jerusalem was a place which had stirred affection and imagination for centuries. A modern Christian song has picked up the ancient Israelite pride of the psalmist: 'Great is the Lord, and greatly to be praised in the city of our God, in the mountain of his holiness. Beautiful for situation, the joy of the whole earth, is Mount Zion, on the sides of the north, the city of the great King.' The exact meaning is obscure, but the feeling of elation is clear.

◁ Psalm 48:1–2 (AV)

3

King Herod, who died shortly after Jesus was born, had been a prodigious builder. The city expanded under his rule, and some scholars have estimated that up to 200,000 people may have lived there; if so, it would have been very cramped, perhaps like one of the European mediaeval towns which still exist.

◁◁ Luke 21:5

The Jewish historian Josephus reported that Herod also built an amphitheatre for sports and a theatre for entertainment, and there was a splendid palace and a fort, too. But the

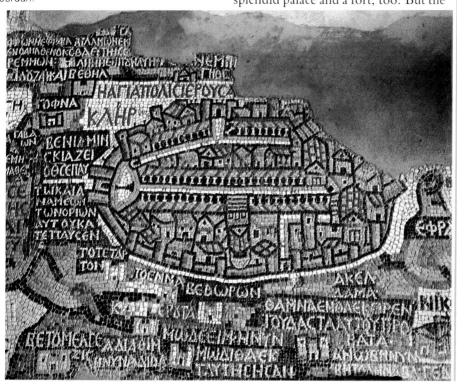

theatres have never been definitely located, so we can only guess that they were modelled on the rounded Roman pattern.

A mosaic found at Madeba in Jordan, dating from Byzantine times in the sixth century AD, shows that Luke 19:41–44 ▷▷ Jerusalem at that time had six gates in its walls, and that main streets crossed it in the Roman gridiron pattern – north-south, east-west. That may have been the street plan in the first century, too, but we cannot be sure. Two outstanding models of Herodian Jerusalem have been built (one is at the Holy Land Hotel in Jerusalem, the other is at the Bible Museum in Amsterdam), but the detail is largely a matter of guesswork.

All that remains of Herod's temple is part of the retaining wall which supported the huge platform the temple stood on, the Western Wall which was formerly known as 'the Wailing Wall', where Jews go to pray. Some traces of monumental stairways from the first century have been unearthed, together with part of a viaduct carrying a road leading to the Western Hill and some fine houses on the Hill itself, and such places as the Pool of Siloam and the Garden of Gethsemane can still be seen. Otherwise the Jerusalem, over which Jesus wept as he entered it like a king riding on a donkey, has been buried beneath successive building projects and kept alive only in the sometimes dubious traditions surrounding some of the tourist sites.

It is a fate which has overtaken many places named in the Bible. Even scanty remains can, however, give us some idea of what Bible characters saw when they looked from their doorways each day. Needless to say, in a period covering thousands of years, no static picture will emerge, but a progressive development.

FROM TENTS TO TOWNS

Some of the people whose stories are recorded early on in the Bible did not live in permanent settlements at all.

Nomad tents in the Negeb.

They were semi-nomads, pitching tents for a while before moving on to find fresh pasture and water for their sheep and goats.

Among these wanderers were the patriarchs – Abraham and Sarah, Lot, Jacob and many others. Centuries later, after the exodus from Egypt, the Israelites lived in tents in the desert for some forty years before entering Palestine. There were many thousands of people on that trek; when they pitched camp there must have been tents as far as the eye could see, with animals herded between them.

The nomadic life became an important religious symbol. The father of a house would recite, '"My father was a wandering Aramean…"' as he gave thanks for a settled home in the 'promised land'. One group, the Rechabites, lived in tents as a matter of principle right down to the sixth century BC. In the New Testament the image was taken up by Peter who reminded Christians that they were 'aliens and strangers in the world'. The writer to the Hebrews said, 'Here we do not have an enduring city, but we are looking for the city that is to come.' The picture is of the church, like Abraham and ancient Israel, moving forward to fresh things under God's guidance.

Of course, there were towns and villages long before the patriarchs. The tent-dwellers belonged to a world which was already well civilized. In Mesopotamia, for example, there is evidence from very early times that towns had ruling councils which organized the people and planned public building works – temples, palaces, storehouses, market places and fortified walls.

The fortifications, and the need for a local water source, would have especially marked these towns out from their modern counterparts where water can be pumped over long distances, and walls are no defence from aerial attack. The physical security of large stone walls too high to be climbed and too thick to be easily breached was very important to the people of the time.

In Palestine itself, about 8000 BC in the pre-pottery period, the city of Jericho was surrounded by a solid free-standing stone wall over 2 m (6 ft) wide. A great stone tower was built against the inside wall which still stands 9 m (30 ft) high.

At Arad, in the Negeb to the south of Canaan, there was a city occupied about 2850-2650 BC (the Early Bronze II period). Here there was a substantial wall. Every 20–25 m (65–80 ft) semi-circular towers about 3 m (10 ft) in diameter were set in it. Inside the walls were extensive living quarters divided by streets and squares.

Some of the larger towns had satellite villages in the countryside which were not so well protected. These are called 'daughters' in some Bible versions, or 'surrounding settlements'. They probably supplied the nearby town with food; just as today, the townspeople would have specialized in a variety of trades and professions, and were not self-sufficient.

One such unwalled village has been found about 1 km south-east of the fortified eighteenth-century BC site of Bethshemesh in Judah. Bethshemesh later became an important city set aside by Joshua for the Levites. The village, now known as Givat Sharett, had a dozen or so courtyard houses strung along an uphill path. The simple homes contained mostly domestic pottery, stone tools such as flint sickles for cutting grain and saddle-querns for grinding it. Perhaps because it was unprotected, the village was occupied only for a short while.

◁◁ Genesis 12:8; 13:5; 24:67; 25:27

3

◁◁ Deuteronomy 26:5

◁ *E.g.* Numbers 21:25; 2 Chronicles 28:18; Nehemiah 11:25–31

◁◁ 1 Peter 2:11

◁◁ Hebrews 13:14

◁ Joshua 21:16

WHAT THE ISRAELITES FOUND

Numbers 13:28 ▷

When Joshua, Caleb and ten others went to spy out the land of Canaan, they reported to Moses that 'the people who live there are powerful, and the cities are fortified and very large'. One of the best examples – and one which was to figure prominently in the conquest –

Deuteronomy 34:3 ▷

was Jericho. Known as the 'City of Palms' it was built on fertile land beside a constantly flowing spring in the shadow of the rugged and arid western highlands.

Joshua 6 ▷▷

Jericho was founded back in the Middle Stone Age (Mesolithic Age), between 10,000 and 7500 BC, when people moved from caves to small round houses and began cultivating crops. By the time of the patriarchs and Israel's slavery in Egypt (the Middle Bronze period) it was a well-established town and an important fortress on the

Joshua 10:38f. ▷▷
Judges 1:11–13 ▷▷

eastern border of Canaan.

Excavators have traced two of the streets about two metres wide up a steep slope in a series of broad cobbled steps, beneath which were well-built drains. Opening on to the streets were rows of closely-packed two-storey houses with small rooms. The ground floors seem to have been 'lock-up' shops and stores; each was a single room not connected with the rest of the building.

Many had large jars in them, filled with carbonized grain, the result of a fire which destoyed the town about 1550 BC and caused the upstairs rooms to collapse, showering their contents on the ground. People probably lived in the upper rooms, although as quantities of clay loom-weights were found they may also have based their weaving industry in them. One area yielded fifty-two saddle-querns and many rubbing stones* for grinding grain, far more than a private house needed, which suggests that people here specialized in milling corn, perhaps on behalf of those whose storage jars were found in the shops.

The remains of later periods of Jericho's turbulent history are scanty. A few tombs from the Late Bronze Age have been found, but nothing has come to light from the mid-thirteenth century BC when Joshua's attack finally took place and the walls, according to the scriptural record, fell down after the army had circled them for a week.

We obtain a better idea of the layout of typical Canaanite towns from the more southerly Tell Beit Mirsim. Some scholars think that it may have been the biblical Debir, which both Joshua and later Caleb attacked and defeated. There were narrow streets and lanes packed with houses in the Middle Bronze Age (up to 1550 BC). There were open spaces, too, although no-one is sure what they were for: were they market places, grazing areas or vegetable plots, or just spaces where the children might have played? Clearly there were differences between rich and poor, just as there have always been, because one house was found which was much more impressive and spacious, probably belonging to a nobleman.

Living in such crowded settlements, even if the population was only a few thousand, would have been noisy and very public; people would have known a lot about each other.

Aerial view of Tell es-Sultan, OT Jericho.

*These implements are described in chapter 10

3

Remains of the substantial wall and a semi-circular tower at Arad in the Negeb.

SETTLING IN THE PROMISED LAND

The Israelites had become an independent group by the late thirteenth century BC, although they were still more like a loose federation than a closely knit nation. When they had been moving into Palestine they had remained in tents or taken over existing settlements. As they spread out, however, they began to build their own. The earliest Israelite villages have been uncovered in previously unoccupied areas in the central highlands and the hills to the west of Galilee.

They are little more than unwalled hamlets. One, at a place now called Izbet Sartah, 3 km (2 miles) east of Tell Aphek, was a cluster of four-roomed houses occupied from about 1200 to 1000 BC. Nearby were large storage pits for grain or water, cut into the earth down to the bedrock, and presumably shared by the villagers.

It took some while for Israel to conquer the Canaanites, and the book of Judges records that they 'never drove them out completely'. The people who remained, such as Rahab from Jericho, would have influenced the way the Israelites rebuilt old settlements. The invaders would also have observed how their enemies had laid out their towns, whether or not they eventually demolished them, and this knowledge probably influenced their own later town planning.

◁ Joshua 6:25

◁ Judges 1:28

One Canaanite town they did occupy was Bethel. It had been a fine city in the Late Bronze Age, about 1550-1200 BC. It had large houses built round courtyards, flagstone pavements and even a stone-lined drainage system which took rainwater and sewage under the large houses and discharged them outside the city wall.

◁ Judges 1:22

But the town which meant much to Israel, in that it had been named by the patriarch Jacob as a memorial to his dream of a ladder connecting earth and heaven ('Bethel' means 'House of God'), was a ramshackle place under the first Israelite settlers. Houses were mere huts, and pottery was poor.

◁ Genesis 28:10–19

TOWNS OF THE PHILISTINES

The Philistines emigrated to the south-west corner of Palestine and to other areas from the Aegean coasts about 1200 BC. Early illustrations of them show that they wore distinctive feathered head-dresses. They established five towns – Gaza, Ashkelon, Ashdod, Gath and Ekron – which are all referred to in the Bible, and others not mentioned there have also come to light through excavations.

Ashod was occupied by the Philistines early in the twelfth century BC, just as Israel was also settling into Palestine. It was a strong and carefully planned town with streets, building-complexes and a wall with a fortress-tower. The city spread outside the wall about the middle of the eleventh century BC.

Judges 16:25–30 ▷▷

The best example, however, is Tell Qasile just north of the modern Tel Aviv. It was a port founded by the Philistines on the Yarkon Estuary in the twelfth century. It may have been the port where ships brought timber from Lebanon for Solomon's temple, and later for the temple Zerubbabel rebuilt after the Jews returned from exile in Babylon.

2 Chronicles 2:16 ▷

The excavation of the site is not complete, but the plans of an entire quarter can now be drawn, showing streets, houses and public buildings such as storehouses and industrial buildings. The city walls, if they ever existed, have not been found. The houses had narrow rooms along two sides of a square court, and some courts had a paved path along one side and a row of pillars which imply that they were roofed over.

One large building on the southern side of a street had two rows of pillars, and may have been a public gathering place. A Philistine temple with central pillars was also found, having been in use for a couple of centuries, although modified from time to time. One of the Old Testament's most colourful characters, the strong man Samson, died as he demolished a Philistine temple in Gaza by dragging down two of its central pillars.

Right: towns and villages mentioned in this chapter. The Philistine cities are printed in capitals.

Below: the remains of the Philistine temple found at Tel Aviv. The bases of the central pillars can be seen in the centre.

STRONGHOLDS FOR THE KINGS

3

When Israel asked for a king, they got warfare as well, as Samuel had warned them. The generally localized skirmishes of the days of the Judges gave way to longer and larger battles. Once again, towns needed to be well defended against attack. Most of those built by the Israelites had strong walls, gates and sometimes towers, and a water supply inside the town as a precaution against sieges as well as for sheer convenience. Their populations generally ranged from 1,000 to 3,000 (based on an estimate of 240 people per urban acre, with most of the sites being between five and twelve acres), although some would have been smaller and others larger.

Some of the towns dating from the time of Saul, David and Solomon have similar layouts. There is a strong wall, a belt of houses nestles just inside it, and then a ring road circles the central area. Three examples reflect these similarities.

◁1 Samuel 8:11f., 20

One is Beer-sheba, deep in the arid south, where Abraham dug a well and 'called upon the name of the Lord', as did his son Isaac. No remains of the patriarchal period have been found, but by the time of the kings it was an administrative centre on the trade route from southern Jordan to Egypt.

◁Genesis 21:30, 33

◁Genesis 26:25

The second is Tell En-Nasbeh, which was probably the biblical Mizpah, on a hill-top 13km (8 miles) north of Jerusalem, where Saul was chosen as king. The third is Hazor, one of Solomon's royal cities, rebuilt by workers conscripted from the non-Israelite groups which still remained in the land. It had been a large, flourishing Canaanite city, perhaps with some thousands of inhabitants, but had been destroyed by the Israelites under Joshua.

◁1 Samuel 10:17

◁1 Kings 9:15, 20, 21

◁Joshua 11:10–13

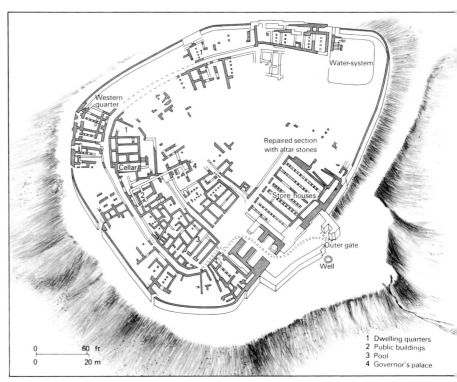

Western quarter

Cellar

Repaired section with altar stones

Store houses

Outer gate

Well

Water-system

1 Dwelling quarters
2 Public buildings
3 Pool
4 Governor's palace

0   60 ft
0   20 m

A plan of the Iron Age (Israelite) city at Tel Beersheba (about 950-about 700 BC). This plan clarifies the aerial photograph (below), showing excavations on the mound of Tel Beersheba. The modern excavators' camp (top right) gives some idea of the small size of an Iron Age 'city'. The plan shows clearly the double entrance and the casemate walls, both described on the facing page.

THE WALLS

At Tell En-Nasbeh a solid wall 660 m (722 yd) long and 4 m (13 ft) thick was built, possibly in Solomon's time, outside older walls. Projecting from it at irregular intervals were rectangular towers of varying sizes, and here the wall was 6–9 m (20–30 ft) across. The towers and many sections of the wall were strengthened by a sloping retaining wall called a glacis. To stop enemies climbing the wall, it was covered with plaster up to a height of about 5 m (16 ft), and a ditch (called a fosse) between two and five metres wide was dug beyond the walls as a further hindrance to invasion.

Some of these towns were surrounded by massive 'casemate' walls. Two walls, each at least 1 m thick and 2 or 3 m apart, were braced at intervals by cross-walls to create a broad defence.

At Beer-sheba, the spaces in the casemate walls were used as the back rooms of the outer circle of houses. Presumably they were occupied by either the very poor or the very brave, as they would have been first in the firing line in an assault on the town. The walls at Hazor, however, were free-standing, and the houses were all safely separated from the fortification.

THE GATES

Gates were potential weak spots in a town's defence, and so places like Beer-sheba and Tell En-Nasbeh had a double entrance. The outer gate led into a passageway running parallel to the main walls in which was set the main inner gate. It would have been a bottleneck if a large number of people ever wanted to get in or out very quickly – like a narrow entrance to a large modern sports arena – but it was, of course, intended to prevent invaders gaining easy access. Enemies could then be trapped between the walls.

The gateways were built of stone piers and had guard chambers in them. The gates themselves were double doors, wide enough to allow carts and chariots through. They were made of wood and in some cases covered with metal to prevent their being set on fire. They may have been either pulled back into sockets in the walls, or simply swung open on hinges. In some towns there may have been more than one set, as added protection.

Once they were closed, heavy beams were drawn across the gates to lock them. When David was on the run from Saul, he sheltered in 'a town with gates and bars'. In a list of Solomon's civil servants, one is said to have officiated over 'sixty large walled cities with bronze gate bars'. And by the time of the exile, well into the Iron Age, it is said of the Persian King Cyrus that he will 'break down gates of bronze and cut through bars of iron' –

◁ 1 Samuel 23:7

◁ 1 Kings 4:13

◁ Isaiah 45:2

Entrance to the citadel of Hazor. This reconstruction of the 9th-8th-century BC building is in the Israel Museum and gives some idea of its massive construction.

3

a graphic picture of a ruler no one could resist.

If that was being written in the twentieth century AD, perhaps the nearest equivalents would be the armour-plated strong-rooms of banks, with their time locks and electronic surveillance: safe, but never totally impregnable to a determined attacker. Or recall the fear that makes some western people heavily bolt and bar their homes, wire up their windows and doors with burglar alarms and refuse to go out or answer the doorbell at night. That kind of insecurity gripped whole towns from Old Testament times and beyond.

Joshua 12:21▷▷

Besides being a major line of defence, the gates were also a place where business and legal deals were clinched. At Tell En-Nasbeh there was an open square in front of the gate, 9 m · x 8 m (26 ft x 30 ft) with benches built around it, and there was a similar open space inside the gate. Absalom, David's rebellious son, used to wait at the gate of Jerusalem and discuss people's complaints. The eighth-century prophet Amos condemned injustice 'in the gates' ('courts', NIV).

2 Samuel 15:2–4 ▷

Amos 5:10, 12, 15▷

THE CENTRAL AREA

At Hazor, the central area combined monumental buildings, residential districts and administrative centres. It was rebuilt in the ninth century BC, by the time of Kings Omri and Ahab, probably following its destruction by the Syrians.

One of the most notable public buildings was the citadel on the western edge of the town. Roughly rectangular, 21 m x 25 m (70 ft x 80 ft), it had 2 m-thick walls and two long corridors in the centre surrounded by rooms on the north, south and east sides. Downstairs rooms were used for storage, while the main upstairs

THE CHANGING FACE OF MEGIDDO

Megiddo was one of those places which is always changing. People living there in Joshua's day would not have recognized it if they had been able to return to see Solomon's splendid buildings. And even that wise king would have been surprised at what one of his successors, Ahab, did with his provincial capital.

Megiddo stood in the north of Palestine commanding a strategic east-west pass through the scrub-covered limestone Carmel Hills from the coastal plain to the Valley of Esdraelon. It was also on an important north-south trading route. It was captured and subdued by Joshua, but it was not finally occupied by the Israelites until the time of King David.

It had always been a large city. The present-day remains cover some ten acres (about the area of seven football fields), and as that is the top of the mound, earlier settlements may have been larger. That is still small in comparison with modern standards, however.

A town wall has been unearthed dating from the time of the patriarchs. There were three large houses built against it and facing on to a street. These date from about 1750 to 1700 BC. No remains have been found in Megiddo from the next three centuries

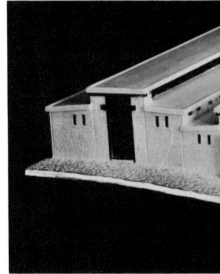

or so, but from the period 1450 to 1350 BC comes evidence of much new building and a broader town plan with many streets and houses.

It was Solomon, however, who changed it beyond recognition. He surrounded it with a casemate wall and erected a magnificent gateway. The outer gate, fortified with two towers, was approached up a long exposed slope. A narrow entrance led to the inner gate with three guardrooms either side, in what has become known as the 'Solomonic gateway'.

Turning left inside the town, the visitor would have seen a number of private houses, and further on a substantial building which was either a fortress or a palace. On the south side, opposite the gateway, was another substantial building some 23 m x 21 m (nearly 70 ft x 80 ft). It was surrounded by a large courtyard with a lime and plaster floor. Its walls were built of alternate pieces of dressed stone and rubble, and it had a large gate-like structure with two pairs of chambers standing in the north-east corner. Then, in the far right-hand corner (the south–west) lay a covered gallery and camouflaged passage leading outside the walls and down the hill to the spring.

In the days of Ahab, in the ninth century BC, the plan of Megiddo changed once more. The private dwellings were taken over and three blocks of storehouses were built over them, together with a governor's house set in a courtyard entered through a two-chambered gateway. Another block of storerooms was built on the south side. These storehouses have been the subject of considerable debate among researchers, because they were once thought to have been stables dating from Solomon's time. However, it is generally agreed now that they belong to Ahab's time.

Further to the west lay the entrance to the water system built in the vicinity of Solomon's gallery. Ahab sank a shaft below the city to reach a horizontal tunnel under the walls leading to the spring. The walls were no longer Solomon's casemate variety, but were solid, with sections jutting out at intervals. This method of wall-building is known as 'offset and inset'. They retained the Solomonic gateway, however. The offsets and insets helped to defend the town. By shooting from the protruding sections the defenders had a wider arc of fire.

Israelite Megiddo was destroyed by the Assyrians in 733 BC and rebuilt as the capital of an Assyrian province. With the decline of Assyria in the seventh century, it probably became part of the kingdom of Josiah, who died there in 609 BC, while engaged in conflict with Pharaoh Neco.

 ◁ 1 Kings 9:15–19

 ◁ 2 Kings 23:29–30

Model of the Megiddo store-rooms, dating from Ahab's time. These are the buildings once thought to be Solomon's stables. It is easy to see how such a mistake could be made.

2 Samuel 5:6–9 ▷▷

quarters were reached by an outside staircase. In the ruins lay two stone blocks which had served as the capitals of pillars. They are carved with a simple design copied from the top of a palm tree. More of these capitals have been found at other major cities (such as Megiddo, Samaria, Jerusalem). They are called 'proto-Aeolic' because they pre-figure the Aeolic style known from Greek temples of later date. The capitals from Hazor are now to be seen at the Israel Museum in Jerusalem in a reconstruction of the monumental entrance to the citadel.

2 Samuel 5:9 ▷▷
1 Kings 9:15 ▷▷

Among the other buildings in Hazor was a large storehouse about 21 m x 13 m (70 ft x 53 ft). It had two rows of pillars down the centre and two halls were attached to the north side. There were public stores at Beer-sheba, too, to the right of the gate, and other public buildings in front of the gate.

Both Hazor and Beer-sheba had good water supplies inside the city.★ At the latter, for example, stairs were cut into the ground in the north-east corner to tap the water table of a wadi (intermittent stream) which runs along the base of the mound. Some drainage channels under the streets collected rainwater which was stored in cisterns such as one 10 m (33 ft) deep just inside the gate. It was wise to save water for the summer months when there was no rain and the wadis were dry. To die of thirst was the last thing people shut up inside a besieged city wanted. Besides, in peace-time it was more convenient to fetch water from across the town than to climb down a steep hill for it and risk spilling it.

1 Kings 16:23f. ▷▷

JERUSALEM AND SAMARIA

1 Kings 5:13 – 7:51 ▷

Jerusalem was the most important of

★ Water-supply is described in detail in chapter 8.

Solomon's royal cities, housing the temple, royal palace and many public as well as domestic buildings. It had been a walled city in patriarchal times, and David captured it at the start of his reign. It then covered less than eleven acres, and was built on terraces supported by retaining walls on the slope leading to the Kidron Valley. David and Solomon both repaired it, but only Solomon expanded it.

Little is known about it in Solomon's time, however, which is tantalizing, given that it was Judah's capital during a vital part of biblical history. A few houses dating from the seventh century BC (two hundred years later than Solomon) have been found, and these were packed closely together. They were built of rough stones, possibly faced with plaster, and their rooms were small and irregularly planned. Part of the base of a wall dating back to the eighth or seventh centuries BC has also been found. It was 7 m (23 ft) wide and built of both rough and smooth (dressed) stones laid without any cementing agent.

Samaria, which was capital of the northern kingdom after the division of Israel, was built on a fresh site by King Omri. Like Jerusalem, it was on top of a hill, and it was surrounded by steep valleys on all sides. It was easy to defend and lay close to an important road which led north to Phoenicia. Omri built a series of terraces supported by retaining walls. The royal quarter was a broad terrace 145 m (158 yd) east-west and 76 m (82 yd) north-south, built on the western side of the hill open to the cool Mediterranean breezes.

The smooth dressed masonry was unequalled in the Near East at the time; its pattern of one stretcher (a block laid lengthways) to two headers (blocks laid widthways) give the remains, which can still be seen, a surprisingly

3

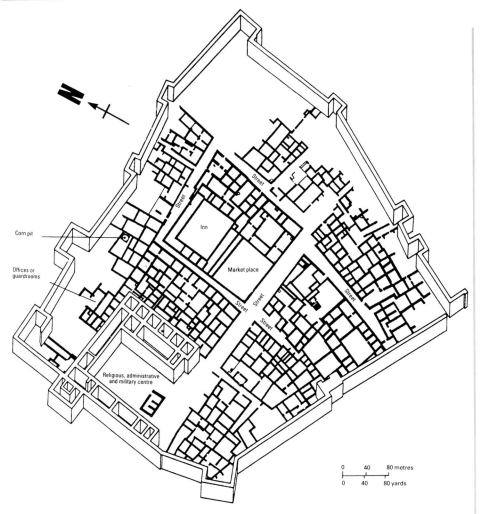

Corn pit

Offices or
guardrooms

Street

Street

Inn

Market place

Street

Street

Street

Street

Religious, administrative
and military centre

| 0 | 40 | 80 metres |
| 0 | 40 | 80 yards |

*Plan of Marisa (Mareshah) described on the
following page, showing the orderly planning of
the streets.*

modern look.

Omri began the building of Samaria,
but it was Ahab who finished it. Like
many other Israelite cities, it fell to the
Assyrians in 722 BC, an event which
ushered in a new era for the nation.

THE FIRST 'MODERN' CITIES

Some modern cities have been planned
like a gridiron or chequer-board;
streets criss-cross at right angles to
each other, enclosing blocks of
buildings. Parts of New York are like
this; so too is the new town of Milton
Keynes in England.

The plan has its root in Persian times
(the sixth century BC). In the next
century it was popularized in the Greek
Empire by a town planner called
Hippodamus, who came from Miletus
and gave his name to this plan. One of
the earliest examples of it is Megadim,
a rectangular town on the
Mediterranean coast, north of Strato's
Tower, (Caesarea), which had a built-
up area bisected by a wide, straight

road with narrow lanes running off it at right angles.

Greek towns usually had two distinct grids of uniform blocks of houses separated by an irregularly-planned zone of public buildings, all enclosed by a defensive wall. The streets ran exactly north-south and east-west, and one (usually the main east-west street) was wider than the others and led to the agora, or market place. Temples and public buildings were usually located near the market.

Mareshah (or Marisa), some 40 km (25 miles) south-west of Jerusalem, is one of the best examples in Palestine. It had been settled in Joshua's time, and was the scene of a battle between Asa and the Cushites during the period of the Kings. It was resettled in the Hellenistic period by Phoenicians from Sidon, and became an important cultural and trading centre.

Joshua 15:44 ▷

2 Chronicles ▷
14:8–13

2 Maccabees 12:35▷
(Apocrypha)

Mareshah was roughly square (158 m (172 yd) east-west and 152 m (166 yd) north-south), and surrounded by a wall built partly of limestone blocks cut like bricks. Two main streets ran east-west, and three north-south. They varied in width from 2 to 6 m, and were paved.

The main east-west street had a drain connected to the private houses beside it. In addition to many houses, Mareshah also boasted open areas, which were used perhaps for markets or public meetings. Fragments of majestic Ionic and Greek capitals (tops of columns) and panels decorated with rosettes have been discovered there, and indicate that it was a prosperous place.

Of course, this pattern of town planning could not be fully adopted on hill sites. Jerusalem, for example, was an expanding city during the days of the Hasmonaean rulers in the second century BC, and many remains have been found dating from that time, but

Harbour mole, or breakwater, at Herod the Great's port of Caesarea.

it could never be rebuilt on a strict gridiron pattern because of the uneven ground.

The Madeba Mosaic, however, which dates from the sixth century AD, shows that Jerusalem did have two main streets bisecting each other at that time (see page 37). This was probably due to Roman rather than Greek influence. Many Roman towns, often developed from military camps, had a main north-south street called the *cardo* and one east-west called the *decumanus*. Such towns were not usually rectangular, but had irregularly shaped walls.

Herod the Great built up a number of Palestinian towns on the Roman pattern. For example, he built the port of Caesarea with all the features of a Roman town: amphitheatre, market, harbour, temple to Augustus, fountains and fine streets and houses. Among his other achievements were theatres at Sidon and Damascus, gymnasia at Tripolis, Damascus and Ptolemais, baths at Ascalon and an aqueduct at Laodicea.

PLACES PAUL VISITED

Many of the places Paul visited during his three long journeys were strategic centres of culture, commerce and communications. The gospel planted in them would spread quickly to surrounding towns and villages, and further afield too as travellers took the good news home with them. Four of the most important places he visited were Athens, Corinth, Ephesus and Rome.

ATHENS: CITY OF LEARNING

Paul spent a short time in Athens, where he encountered the Epicureans and philosophers who 'spent their time doing nothing but talking about and listening to the latest ideas'. It was a

◁ Acts 17:16–34

The dramatic Acropolis at Athens.

magnificent city with many spectacular buildings.

Athens was 8 km (5 miles) inland from the port of Piraeus. Inside the gate, a visitor would find himself on a long avenue flanked by large buildings. It led to the agora (market place), the political, commercial and social centre surrounded by public buildings. It was close to the large rocky hill called the Acropolis where there were many temples to the gods.

The Acropolis was approached by a marble staircase lined with sculptured friezes and monuments. At the top there was the Parthenon built by Pericles in the fifth century BC, in honour of the city's goddess Athena, *Acts 18:4 ▷▷* and a magnificent statue of her stood to the left. Nearby was the Areopagus. Named after the god of war, Ares, this small hill was originally the meeting place for the most ancient court and council of Athens, though when Paul was called to explain his teaching the *Acts 18:12–17 ▷▷* court had moved to the 'Royal Porch' in the agora. The Areopagus was surrounded by altars and monuments. The synagogue where Paul preached was near the agora.

CORINTH: CITY OF SHOPKEEPERS

1 Corinthians 9:24 ▷▷

All ancient cities would have had their shops, but in Corinth the shopping centre has been excavated on three sides of the agora. A block found on *Romans 9:21 ▷▷* the north side was inscribed 'meat market with fish market', leading some scholars to suppose that this was the site of the meat market Paul referred to *1 Corinthians 10:25 ▷* in his first letter to Corinth. Some of *1 Corinthians 6:18 ▷▷* the meat sold there would have been part of the sacrifice offered in the great temple of Apollo, which had thirty-eight columns each about 2 m (6 ft) thick and 6 m (20 ft) high.

On the west side of the market there were thirty-three shops, and each had a well sunk into the rock to connect with one of the tunnels which fed water from the natural spring called the Fountain of Peirene. These wells may have been used as cold stores for perishable food, so the meat market may have been there. In fact, one block found there has the inscription 'Lucius the butcher'.

Corinth lay 3 km (2 miles) inland from the Gulf of Corinth at the foot of a rocky hill rising 574 m (1,886 ft) above sea level. The main road leading to the agora was 8 m (25 ft) wide and paved with hard limestone. The entrance to the agora was a broad staircase topped by a monumental gateway. Nearby a stone was found with part of the inscription 'synagogue of the Jews', presumably where Paul preached. In the centre of the agora was a well-built stone platform which probably had benches down each side. It may have been to this area that Paul was summoned when a tribunal was held to hear charges brought against him by the Jews.

Corinth also possessed two theatres and an amphitheatre which hosted gladiatorial shows and athletics, notably the Isthmian Games. Paul used the picture of an athlete stretching for the tape to encourage the Christians to press on with their faith. During his eighteenth-month stay in the city he must have watched the potters at work in their extensive quarter just inside the wall. In his letter to the Romans, probably written from Corinth, he refers to God as a potter moulding people for his good purposes. Dominating the city is a hill (Acrocorinth) where stood the temple of the goddess of love, Aphrodite, which encouraged the immorality Corinthian Christians had to resist.

EPHESUS: CITY OF ARTEMIS

When Paul left Corinth, he went on to

Ephesus, returning there later to find some disciples who had trusted in Jesus but who had not been taught about the Holy Spirit. For three months he preached in the synagogue, until a local silversmith decided he had heard enough. Paul's teaching had caused a slump in the trade of silver images of the goddess Artemis (or Diana).

Artemis had her temple a little way outside the city. After the one built by Croesus, King of Lydia (about 560 BC) had been destroyed by fire in 356 BC, the citizens gave their jewellery to rebuild it. The new temple became one of the seven 'Wonders of the Ancient World'. It was 110 m (361 ft) long and 55 m (180 ft) wide, four times the size of the Parthenon in Athens. Over one hundred pillars supported the roof, many of them carved and decorated with gold. The statue of Artemis, which stood behind the altar, was said to have fallen from heaven. In recognition of Ephesus' devotion to the goddess, the city was called 'temple keeper of Artemis'.

It was also an important trading centre at the junction of the Asiatic caravan route to the east and the sea route to Rome in the west. Its main street, the Arkadiane, was paved with marble and led from the harbour to the Great Theatre, with ornamental gateways at each end. The theatre could hold 24,000 people, and it was there that Paul's companions were dragged, apparently by the whole population, during the riot.

◁◁ Acts 18:18f.; 19:1f.

◁ Acts 19:29
◁◁ Acts 19:35

ROME: CITY OF SEVEN HILLS

Rome was a magnificent place when Paul arrived with an armed escort to spend the last years of his life under house arrest there. Built on the river Tiber around seven hills, and

◁ Acts 28:16

Rome: the Forum. In the middle foreground the temple of Castor and Pollux; behind that the Arch of Titus; and in the left background part of the Colosseum.

surrounded by a wall over 21 km (13 miles) in circumference, it was full of temples, theatres, forums, palaces, baths, administrative buildings, triumphal arches, colonnades and circuses. (Circuses were round buildings; one, the Circus Maximus, was an apartment block for 150,000 people.) There were fine roads and gardens, too, with chariot races, gladiatorial contests, athletics and plays to entertain the people.

At the heart of the city lay the Forum, the centre of civic activities bounded by four of the seven hills. On one of these, the Capitol, was the great Temple of Jupiter, while on another, the Palatine Hill, were the great houses and palaces of the emperors and very rich people.

But in contrast to this lavish splendour, the ordinary people lived in tenements often three or four storeys high and sometimes so badly built that they were liable to collapse or burn down. They were surrounded by narrow, dirty, dangerous and noisy streets with an incessant flow of traffic day and night. Many people were poor and unemployed, and the government was required to provide wheat for them.

FOR FURTHER READING

Avigad, N., *Discovering Jerusalem* (Blackwell, 1984. US ed. Nashville, Nelson, 1983).

Encyclopedia of Archaeological Excavations in the Holy Land, Vols. I-IV (Jerusalem, Masada Press, 1975-78).

IBD, Parts 1, 2 and 3 (IVP, 1980).

Kenyon, K.M., *Digging up Jericho* (Ernest Benn, 1957).

Kenyon, K.M., *Jerusalem, Excavating 3000 years of History* (Thames and Hudson, 1967).

Wright, G.E., *Shechem. The Biography of a Biblical City* (Duckworth, 1965. US ed. New York, McGraw-Hill, 1964).

Yadin, Y., *Hazor. The Rediscovery of a Great Citadel of the Bible* (Weidenfeld & Nicholson, 1975. US ed. New York, Random House).

Yadin, Y., *Hazor. The Schweich Lectures, 1970* (OUP for British Academy, 1972).

Yadin, Y., 'Megiddo of the Kings of Israel', *BA*, 33 (3), (1970), pp.66-96.

Yadin, Y., (ed.), *Jerusalem Revealed. Archaeology in the Holy City, 1968-1974* (Jerusalem, Israel Exploration Society, 1975).

House and home 4

Perhaps some of Jesus' most moving words were his warning about homelessness: "'Foxes have holes and birds of the air have nests, but the Son of Man has no place to lay his head.'"

Born in a borrowed cradle, buried in a borrowed tomb, Jesus spent much of his three-year public ministry living like a refugee in the world he had created. He renounced what in his time, as in every period of history, is considered normal and necessary: a place to call home, giving shelter from the weather and security to raise a family.

◁◁ Matthew 8: 20

Jesus was, of course, no stranger to home life. His first thirty years were spent in the obscurity of a carpenter's home in Nazareth. Later, during his

Homes in Bible times were not all nomad tents. There were overcrowded cities too. This model of Jerusalem shows an area of poor housing (left background) close to the temple, in this case 'Ezekiel's temple' (6th-1st centuries BC).

Luke 10: 38 ▷

Matthew 8: 14 ▷

public ministry, he seems to have found a home from home with Mary, Martha and Lazarus in Bethany. Peter, too, opened his home to Jesus on at least one occasion.

The home in Bible times was even more central to people's lives than it is in many countries today. Birth, marriage and death all took place in the home. Several generations might live under the same roof. Home was often a social centre and a workplace as well as somewhere to eat and sleep.

There were, of course, many changes in the physical appearance of houses from the time of the patriarchs to that of the apostles. They differed enormously from place to place and from period to period, just as

mediaeval cottages differ from twentieth-century apartment blocks, and suburban avenues from inner-city streets.

CAMP LIFE

The Bible writers were usually more concerned with who people were and what they did than with what they looked like or how they lived. But sometimes a single verse suddenly opens up a picture of their life and times.

Take, for example, this comparison between Jacob (elsewhere described as

A modern Bedouin tent probably gives a good idea of the construction of a tent in patriarchal times, though materials have changed.

a smooth-skinned man) and his brother Esau (called a 'hairy man'): 'The boys grew up, and Esau became a skilful hunter, a man of the open country, while Jacob was a quiet man, staying among the tents.'

Not only does that verse reinforce the personalities of the two brothers (Esau is rugged and adventurous, Jacob quiet and home loving, rather like the prodigal son and his brother in Jesus' story), but it also reveals how they lived at the time. It seems that there was a camp of tents where a number of families lived close together. There were enough of them for Jacob to live and work 'among' the tents; it would have been like a small village, or camp site.

The tents probably looked like modern Bedouin tents. These are long and almost flat, but slightly higher at the centre to enable rain to run off the roof. In Jacob's time the tent was probably made of animal skins. Later, handwoven strips of black or dark brown goat's hair about 90 cm (3 ft) wide were sewn together and reinforced. Leather loops were fixed to these covering strips so that the guy ropes could be tied to them. Goat's hair is resistant to both heat and water, and once washed it shrinks and becomes taut.

If the family increased in size, the tent could be easily extended. If the occupants wanted to divide up the inside, they hung curtains to create separate rooms. In the heat of the day, the sides of the tent could be folded back or even taken down to ventilate the interior. Members of the same household seem to have had their own separate tents. Jacob's two wives, Leah and Rachel, had their own tents, and their two maidservants shared another.

The tents were portable. The covering and the poles could be bundled up and taken to a new site

with relative ease. Jacob, like the other patriarchs, is said to have 'pitched his tent' in different places. He even bought a plot of land outside Shechem for his camp.

For many of the people introduced in Genesis, Exodus, Leviticus, Numbers and Deuteronomy, and for many Israelites in the early chapters of Joshua, home was a goatskin tent, dark, stuffy, but surprisingly comfortable. Even in the days of the judges, some people still lived in tents, although by then more permanent and solid homes were common.

Today the relatively simple, down-to-earth life of camping attracts many people for their holidays. The whole nation of Israel had an annual holiday which they spent in 'booths' made of tree branches. This 'Feast of Tabernacles' was a reminder of their tent-dwelling past and of God's goodness to them as they tramped through the desert after they had fled from Egypt.

The memory of those centuries seemed to linger almost nostalgically in the later religious writings of the Israelites. The psalmist saw God the creator 'stretching out the heavens like a tent'. Isaiah looked forward to a time when Jerusalem would be 'a tent that will not be moved; its stakes will never be pulled up, nor any of its ropes broken.' And Jeremiah laments the destruction of Jerusalem: 'My tent is destroyed; all its ropes are snapped. … no-one is left now to pitch my tent or to set up my shelter.'

One group of people, the Rechabites, remained tent dwellers and nomadic shepherds for centuries. They grew no crops, built no houses, and drank no wine as a matter of principle.

HOUSES IN CANAAN

While Abraham, Isaac, Jacob and their

◁ Genesis 31: 25
◁◁ Genesis 27: 11
◁◁ Genesis 25: 27
◁◁ Genesis 33: 19

◁ Deuteronomy 1: 27;
◁ Deuteronomy 5: 30;
◁ Joshua 7: 21-24

4

◁ Leviticus 23: 39-43

◁ Psalm 104: 2

◁ Isaiah 33: 20

◁ Jeremiah 10: 20

◁ Jeremiah 35: 6-10

◁◁ Genesis 31: 33

families were pitching camp in different parts of Palestine, they would have noticed that not everyone already in the land lived as they did. Some people had built permanent homes. Abraham, indeed, had left a brick-built city in his youth.

The Bible itself offers little information about the structure of these houses. As in many languages, the Hebrew word for house, *bayit*, which occurs over 2,000 times in the Old Testament, can refer to anything from a peasant cottage to a palace, or even a temple. The word also refers to the family who lived together in the house, and can even indicate the wider extended family or tribe. Expressions such as 'the house of David' or 'the house of Israel' include many generations of people.

E.g. Genesis 42:19 ▷

Joshua 7: 14 ▷
1 Kings 13: 2 ▷
Psalm 115: 12 ▷

The houses of people living in Palestine during the time of the patriarchs (the Middle Bronze Age, or the centuries after 2000 BC) were often built on one or more sides of a courtyard. The simplest house had a single room on the west side so that the prevailing wind blew the smoke from the fire in the courtyard away from the house. There was usually a silo (a circular stone-lined pit) for storing grain inside the house.

These homes were tiny, like the cramped bed-sits (boarding rooms) which students sometimes use today in western countries. Some houses excavated at Tell Nagila, south of Lachish and east of Gaza, dating from about 1700 BC, were 3 m x 2 m (10 ft x 7 ft). Three of them were built on a courtyard measuring 5 m x 3 m (16 ft x 10 ft). These were not single people's residences, but provided shelter for whole families.

Sometimes the single room was divided by a partition built from mud bricks and covered with mud plaster. Small houses were built close together,

and sometimes back-to-back. Whole terraces have been excavated with houses joined not only at the sides, but at the back as well, rather like a single storey apartment block. In such cases, one row of houses had to sacrifice the eastern outlook, and the occupants would have been plagued by smoke from the fires outside.

There were larger houses too, of course. One, excavated at Tell Beit Mirsim (according to some scholars the Debir which Joshua attacked, about 40 km (25 miles) south-west of Jerusalem), dating from about 1600 BC, had six rooms off a courtyard which measured 10.5 m x 6 m (35 ft x 19 ft). The stone walls were very thick, and it is therefore likely that there were two floors having some 140 sq m (1,500 sq ft) of living space. An average British three-bedroomed semi-detached house today would have 850 sq ft of space.

Some larger houses had rooms on two sides of the courtyard, and one found at Megiddo, dating from 1600 BC, had rooms on three sides. Each of its nine rooms had a door (a luxury for many people), and a lime-plastered courtyard. Also at Megiddo were three houses built against the city wall, separated by party (shared) walls and with a courtyard in the centre of each house.

While Joseph and his descendants were in Egypt during the Late Bronze Age (1500-1200 BC), the scene was being set for the Israelites' return to Palestine. The courtyard house seems to have remained the norm, although only a few have been unearthed from this period. One, at Bethshemesh, had rooms on two sides of the court and a stone staircase to the upstairs living quarters. In Megiddo, a large house with rooms on all four sides of the courtyard has been found. It probably belonged to a wealthy person or a government official.

THE FOUR-ROOMED HOUSE

Two rooms downstairs and two upstairs was the formula for many nineteenth-century houses in Europe, and is still the pattern for many relatively cheap 'starter homes'. It provides basic accommodation for single people or small families. Once the Israelites had moved back into Palestine after the conquests of Joshua, they too began building 'four-roomed houses' (usually on one floor only), and these remained the standard pattern of house building for many centuries.

The plan was simple. From the street you entered a courtyard. On one side were one or two rooms for storage; on the other, byres for cattle. At the end was a large living and sleeping room (see illustration on page 61).

The roof was flat, and strong enough for people to work, rest and play on it. An outside staircase or ladder gave access to the roof. Pillars rather than walls, often separated the side rooms from the courtyard, so these rooms would have been light and airy, little more than shelters from rain. Some houses were set in a larger walled courtyard where donkeys, sheep and goats may have been kept. The yard probably resembled a modern farmyard, cluttered with animals, people working, stores of fodder and piles of debris.

Some four-roomed houses were further subdivided to provide extra rooms. Others were more enclosed, with only a single line of pillars down the centre supporting the roof. For this reason, some writers prefer not to use the name 'four-roomed house' as a general description of Israelite houses. There were many variations on the theme.

In Hazor, for example, an almost square house dating from the days of the kings, about 750 BC, is almost twice the size of a normal dwelling. It may therefore have been the home of a wealthy landowner or official. The courtyard was flanked with three rooms on each side. A row of pillars in the yard may have supported a roof which created a covered portico, which acted as a kind of cloister, in front of the rooms on one side.

Each room had a door of its own, set in the corner of the room so that only one door post was needed. The rooms were roughly equal in size. The walls dividing them were roughly 70 cm (2 ft 3 in) thick while the northern exterior wall was 1.5 m (4 ft 9 in) thick and built of dressed stone; the corners and door jambs were built from larger ashlar blocks. (For a description and an illustration of how doors were made, see the following page.)

RICH AND POOR DISTRICTS

Towns in Bible times had their rich and poor districts, just like modern cities. Amos, the eighth-century BC prophet, was especially concerned that the rich landowners 'built stone mansions' but also 'trample on the poor and force him to give you corn'.

◁ Amos 5: 11

A good example of this social division illustrated by housing comes from Tell el Farah (Tirzah, between Samaria and the River Jordan). One section of the town had fine houses with thick walls and paved courtyards. The rest of the town was separated from this area by a wall; there, the houses were smaller, had thinner walls and virtually no paving.

The French excavator de Vaux commented on this stark comparison, 'Here is the reflection of the social transformation which in the course of the 9th - 8th centuries set the "possessing" class in opposition to the

HOW HOUSES WERE BUILT

The average home in biblical times would have been quite dark and draughty. Windows, if there were any, were small and high in the wall; they were without glass and so let in the cold air at night as well as the light of daytime. Wooden doors were fixed to heavy posts which turned on stone sockets by the doorsill and were held in the frame of the lintel. Hinges were unknown in Old Testament times. Inside the houses there might be only curtains to close the entrances to the rooms.

The floors were usually bare mud trodden hard or plastered. They were often covered with straw mats or, in wealthy homes, with carpets. Where water was in use the floors might be paved with stone slabs (easy to trip over!), and in New Testament times, the rich had mosaic floors in their bathrooms.

When the Israelites first moved into Palestine, most people would have built their own houses; there was no need for public buildings. But as society became more complex the need grew for administrative buildings and palatial homes for rulers. As techniques improved, men became specialists in different kinds of building work: stone building, brick-laying and carpentry.

STONE HOUSES
Many simple homes throughout the biblical period were built with a single thickness of large, undressed (rough) stones. Smaller stones were packed into the gaps and the rough wall was faced with a layer of mud plaster. There was usually a foundation below ground level, and sometimes wooden stakes were driven into the ground along the length of the wall to give it extra stability. A plumbline enabled builders to keep the wall vertical.

Amos 7: 7f. ▷

Larger houses often had a double thickness of stones. The corners and doorways were made of squared (dressed) stones. In large public buildings the now familiar pattern of stretchers and headers was used:

rectangular stones were laid alternately lengthways and widthways, to give greater strength to the wall and also to make it look more attractive. There are good examples from excavations in Megiddo and the royal palace in Samaria.

This drawing shows how doors, in biblical times, were hung without hinges. The door is fixed to a wooden post which turns with it. The bottom of the post is tipped with stone and turns on a hollowed stone below threshold level. The top is held between the beams of the lintel.

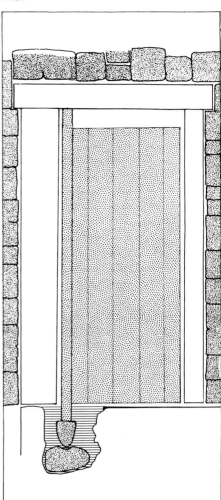

4

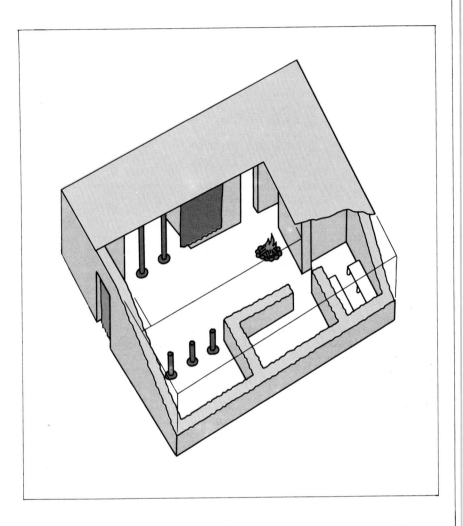

BRICK HOUSES

Most houses in Palestine were made from stone for the simple reason that there was plenty of it in the limestone mountain areas. But down in the Jordan valley, for example, which was covered with rich mud and bordered by chalk hills, it was easier to build houses with mud bricks rather than transport the stone long distances from the mountains.

The earliest bricks were moulded by hand and were oval in shape, but once wooden moulds were used they became rectangular. Made from baked mud, they would be white or pale red in

Reconstruction of a typical Israelite four-roomed house as described on page 59.

colour. In Canaan, before the Israelites appeared on the scene, houses were sometimes built with a stone foundation and a few stone courses above ground, before being finished off with mud bricks. This was normal in many areas, not only in the Jordan valley.

Roofs of houses were usually made by laying wooden beams across the walls and then covering them with brush and finally mud or clay. Long timbers were hard to obtain in Palestine, so most rooms were quite narrow.

proletariat thus illustrating the preaching of the prophets who condemned precisely the pride of Ephraim "who built houses of hewn stone".'

Another distinction between rich and poor has come to light where archaeologists have excavated large areas of a town. Usually the larger, better-built houses were in the western part where the westerly breezes cooled them in hot weather. The poorer houses were downwind in the eastern sector, catching the full force of dust and smells from the richer suburbs. In Tell en-Nasbeh (Mizpah) the better houses were on the east side; the prevailing wind blew straight up a valley to the east of the town.

Many of the houses which have survived the ravages of time sufficiently to help archaeologists piece together a picture of how people lived in them are the richer, better-built variety. Out in the country districts people who scratched a living from the land probably dwelt in simple homes constructed more roughly than the big town houses.

Some poorer homes have been excavated by Dr Kathleen Kenyon in Jerusalem. They were built on terraces running along the side of the Kidron valley to the east of the city, and date from the years shortly before Nebuchadrezzar destroyed Jerusalem in the sixth century BC. The rooms were small, and the walls were built of rough stones without any mortar, but **2 Kings 4: 8-10 ▷▷** probably faced with mud plaster. The house plans tended to be irregular, partly because of the uneven ground, but some followed the 'four-roomed' pattern.

The distinction between rich and poor became clearer during the eighth and seventh centuries BC. One example of how a rich person used her house for God's purposes and not just her own **Haggai 1: 4 ▷▷** comfort, however, is found in the

earlier story of Elisha. A wealthy Shunem woman built a roof chamber on to her house which she furnished for Elisha to use whenever he passed by. Small roof chambers were common at the time of the kings, too, and some good examples have been found in Hazor.

AFTER THE EXILE

According to the prophet Haggai, the

SHECHEM: TWO STOREY HOUSE AND EXTENSION

If you had lived in Shechem between 748 and 724 BC, the last years of Israel's independence before the nation was attacked by the Assyrians, you would have found this house behind a tall wall facing the street. In the street, just by the doorway, was a pebble-filled sump for drainage.

Going through the door into the central courtyard, you would have seen a storage bin on your right and in front of you an oval hearth about 2 m (6 ft 6 in) wide. The hearth was filled with stones, and those round the rim were covered in plaster or slaked lime, and stained black by the fire.

Also on the right of the courtyard was a heavy saddle-quern for crushing grain, and a large jar for the flour. Nearby were two hand crushers, one of black basalt, flat on one side and round on the other, and one of pink quartzite some 45 cm (18 in) long and weighing about 18 kg (40 lb).

At the back was the living room, with a small door in the rear wall, and a storage silo. There were four rooms either side of the courtyard and the two at the front, paved with cobblestones, may have sheltered the animals at night. The roof over these side rooms was supported partly by pillars and partly by walls. The walls at the back were solid enough to support a second

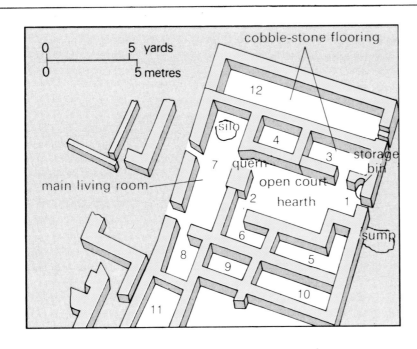

cobble-stone flooring

main living room

4

Plan of the house excavated at Shechem and dated from the 8th century BC. The numerals indicate: 1-7 the house as planned, 8-11 additions and 12 a paved passage.

floor, and plaster found on the ceiling beams (which were made of half logs) is a further indication that the house had upstairs rooms.

The walls were built up to a metre high with large stones 40 cm (15½ in) wide coated with mud plaster which increased the thickness to between 60 and 80 cm (2 ft and 2 ft 7 in). The upper part of the wall was built of bricks measuring 37 cm x 32 cm x 12 cm (14½ in x 12½ in x 4½ in). The roof was made from smoothed mud and straw.

The original house was later extended. A long annexe was built down the left-hand side (as you faced the house from the street). A corridor from the back living room led to this two-roomed extension. One of the additional rooms was probably a kitchen; grain-grinding tools were found in it, and there was a storage silo, too. Both new rooms had an underground stone-filled sump connected by an underground drain.

Jews who had returned to Jerusalem from Babylon after the exile were building themselves panelled or roofed houses. (The Hebrew word can mean either; it probably refers to the roof and indicates that the people had finished their homes but had not started the temple.) Many people had stayed in Judah and only the cream of the population had been deported, so it is likely that the houses continued to follow the pattern of those which had been built before the exile. Very few have been found dating from this period, however.

There is more evidence of what houses looked like in the Hellenistic period between the Old and New Testaments. At Marisa, for example, 40 km (25 miles) south-east of Jerusalem, the clear patterns of the Iron Age have gone and Hellenistic patterns have replaced them. Marisa was a Sidonian trading city which fell into

Jewish hands in the days of John Hyrcanus (134–104 BC).

The domestic houses had several rooms, but were not arranged in any clear plan. Some had hearths, basins and shelves, and some had staircases leading either to the second storey or down into the basement. One house in the south of the town had a granary, and the pottery in the houses has been claimed to be the richest find of the period.

Mark 2: 1-2 ▷▷
Luke 22: 12 ▷▷

NEW TESTAMENT HOMES

Roman houses bore a strong resemblance to those which already existed in Palestine. The typical classical dwelling had an unroofed courtyard surrounded by rooms, one of which may have been larger than the others. More expensive houses had colonnades (rows of pillars) around the courtyard.

Mark 5: 22 ▷▷

The main living room must have been quite large in some of the houses. When Jesus went to Capernaum a crowd packed the house where he was staying. He ate the last supper with his closest disciples in 'a large upper room, all furnished', in what was probably one of Jerusalem's wealthier homes.

Once again, it is the houses of the wealthier people which have been preserved; those of the poor gradually decayed and finally disappeared altogether. The Western Hill of Jerusalem, in what is now the Jewish quarter of the Old City, contains several well-preserved houses. They provide a unique window through which we can see how at least one group of people lived at the time of Jesus. They would have been the sort of houses occupied by 'the ruler of the synagogue', perhaps, or Zacchaeus the

The remains of an elaborate villa in Ephesus. The home of a wealthy family, this villa was built on five levels or terraces.

4

Painted plaster from Herod's palace at Masada.

tax gatherer, and the landowner in Jesus' parable of the vineyard workers, people of some substance who lived quite comfortably.

The first Christians seem to have met mostly in large houses. On the Day of Pentecost, 'they were all together in one place' – a house. The church in Rome met at Priscilla and Aquila's house, which would have been similar to the large houses found in Jerusalem, of which three stand as examples of the rest.

THE HERODIAN HOUSE

This spacious house had a series of rooms arranged round a central courtyard in which four cooking ovens were sunk. A large ritual bath (*mikve*) on the east side was approached by a broad stairway with a vaulted roof, and there was a second, smaller cistern as well in the house. Near the main *mikve* was a hollowed-out stone which may have been a foot bath.

The walls were built of both dressed and hewn stone, covered with a plain plaster. (Similar houses sometimes had painted plaster; one of the best examples has been found in Herod's fortress at Masada.) The western wall had three cupboards built into it, where pieces of broken pottery were found. Some of the floors also had a plain plaster covering, which suggests that they were once covered by mats or carpets – a comparative rarity at a time when most homes would have had plain mud floors or uncovered flagstones.

The house was demolished during or shortly after the reign of Herod the Great, when the area was replanned. A street paved with huge stone slabs was laid over the ruins, but the basic wall plan of the house was preserved beneath it. The street led to the temple

◁◁ Luke 19: 5
◁◁ Matthew 20: 1

◁◁ Acts 2: 1

◁◁ Romans 16: 5

area from Robinson's Arch, so called because it was discovered by Edward Robinson in 1838. The arch supported a stairway leading to the street.

THE MANSION

This house stood in a commanding position overlooking the Temple Mount. Two rows of interconnected rooms on the west side of the site are still visible to a height of 3 m (10 ft). The house covered a huge area (600 sq m or 6,450 sq ft), and had at least two storeys with rooms arranged around a central paved courtyard.

Reconstruction of the mansion described on this page.

The walls were decorated with colourful friezes, and in one room, perhaps a reception hall, the plaster was moulded so that it resembled Herodian masonry. Another room had a fine mosaic floor.

A unique feature of this house was the water-supply. Water from the wide roof and the courtyard was channelled into several pools and cisterns. On the eastern wing of the ground floor was a bathroom which had a small pool with steps leading into it, making a bath big enough to sit in. The floor there was paved with a mosiac six-petalled rose in black and red.

From the courtyard two stairways led to the lower level where several

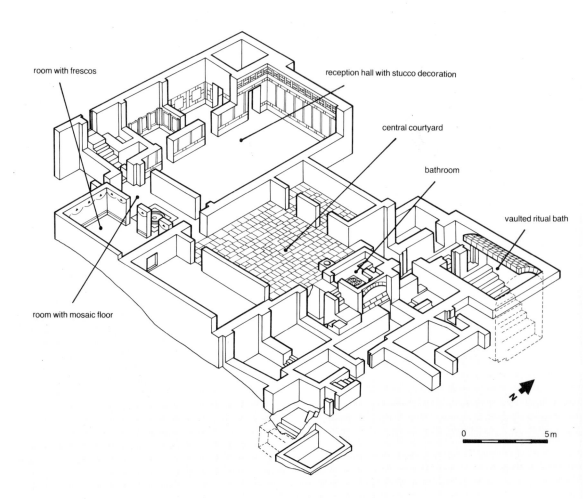

room with frescos

reception hall with stucco decoration

central courtyard

bathroom

vaulted ritual bath

room with mosaic floor

0   5m

LIFE ON THE ROOFTOPS

One of Jesus' best-known miracles occurred when he was teaching in a crowded home in Capernaum. Four people had brought their paralysed friend to be healed by Jesus, but the crowd was so dense that they could not carry the stretcher into the house. So they went upstairs to the roof, hacked a hole in it, and lowered their friend down on ropes to Jesus. Luke's account refers to tiles. Most roofs were of the normal flat variety, but the Romans had introduced the gabled, tiled roof, which perhaps explains the reference.

Most ordinary roofs were supported by wooden beams resting on the walls. Across these beams were laid smaller 'beams' (often just thick branches), sycamore in poorer houses, cedar or cypress in richer ones. Then came layers of brush, reeds, mud, grass and clay, levelled off with a roller. The roof would be rolled after heavy rain, too, to flatten it out.

Access to the roof would be by an outside staircase or even a wooden ladder propped against the wall. Jewish law required a roof to have a parapet, 'so that you may not bring the guilt of bloodshed on your home if someone falls from the roof'.

On the roof all kinds of domestic activities took place. Weaving and washing; drying out dates, figs and flax; and even prayer. Peter prayed on a roof in Joppa, where he received a vision of the inclusion of the Gentiles in God's kingdom.

One of the Mishna tracts refers to 'the road of the roofs'. A person who was running from danger could go from roof to roof along a street until he got to the stairs of the last house in the row. It is possible that Jesus had this in mind when he said that as the coming embodiment of evil approached, 'let no-one on the roof of his house go down to take anything out of the house' – he should just run along the roofs.

The roof was also the natural place to make public announcements: 'What is whispered in your ear, proclaim from the housetops', Jesus instructed the twelve. The booths for the Feast of Tabernacles were often set up on the roof, where there was ample space for the family to live and feast during the week-long celebrations.

Flat-roofed house with outside staircase in Cana, Gallilee.

◁◁ Mark 2: 1-12

◁◁ Luke 5: 17-26

4

◁◁ Deuteronomy 22: 8

◁ Matthew 24: 17

◁ Matthew 10: 27

◁◁ Joshua 2: 6

◁◁ Acts 10: 9-16

rooms were built on an east-facing terrace. Some pools here were vaulted over, and deep cisterns were sunk into the bedrock, providing a supply of fresh, cool water.

THE BURNT HOUSE

This was in the same street as the Mansion, about 150 m (400 ft) to the west of the temple area. Like many other houses in Jerusalem, it was badly burnt when the city was destroyed in AD 70, but part of the lowest floor level has been preserved with walls up to a metre high. It had an entrance corridor, four rooms, a kitchen and a small bath.

Heaped on the floor were smashed kitchen utensils, pots, weights and

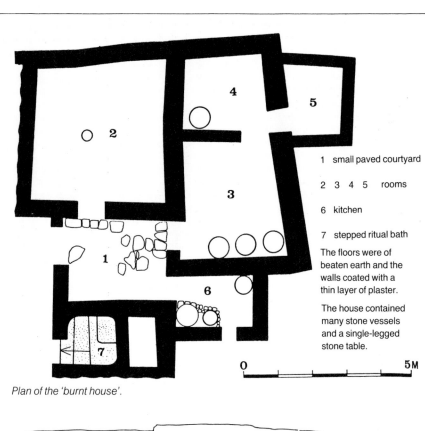

1 small paved courtyard

2 3 4 5 rooms

6 kitchen

7 stepped ritual bath

The floors were of beaten earth and the walls coated with a thin layer of plaster.

The house contained many stone vessels and a single-legged stone table.

0   5 M

Plan of the 'burnt house'.

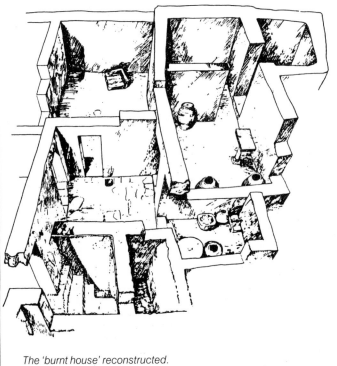

The 'burnt house' reconstructed.

coins, mostly coated with a heavy layer of sticky soot. The coins show that people lived in the house in the first century AD and the other finds agree with that date. Here are relics of people who were alive in the time of the New Testament events, and who were overwhelmed by the disaster Jesus foretold. They had fine pottery locally made and shiny red imported ware. They had a surprisingly large number of jars, jugs and bowls carved from the local limestone. While there were roughly finished ones for kitchen service, others were carefully turned and polished to grace a dining table. This stoneware was apparently a means employed by the well-to-do to avoid problems caused by the laws of ritual purity, for stone vessels could be cleansed whereas the porous pottery could not.

One of the stone weights was inscribed: 'belonging to Bar Kathros'. This man may have been a member of the Kathros family of priests who abused their status by exploiting others. The Jewish Talmud refers to it: 'Woe unto me from the House of Kathros ... who are high priests, and their sons are (temple) treasurers, and their sons-in-law are (temple) officers and their slaves beat the people with rods.'

4

FOR FURTHER READING

Aharoni, Y., *The Archaeology of the Land of Israel* (SCM, 1982. US ed. Philadelphia, Westminster Press, 1978).

Avigad, N., *Archaeological Discoveries in the Jewish Quarter of Jerusalem, Second Temple Period* (Jerusalem, Israel Exploration Society, 1976), pp.8-13.

Avigad, N., *Discovering Jerusalem*, chapter 3 (Blackwell, 1984. US ed. Nashville, Nelson, 1983).

Beebe, H.K., 'Ancient Palestinian Dwellings', *BA*, 31 (2), (1968), pp.38-58.

Kenyon, K.M., *Archaeology in the Holy Land*, 4th ed. (Ernest Benn, 1979).

Paul, S.M., and Dever, W.G., *Biblical Archaeology* (Jerusalem, Keter, 1973), pp.27-53.

Selman, M.J., 'House', *IBD*, 2 (IVP, 1980), pp.668-672.

Shiloh, Y., 'The Four Room House. Its situation and function in the Israelite city', *IEJ*, 20 (1970), pp.180-190.

Wright, G.E. *Shechem. The Biography of a Biblical City* (Duckworth, 1965), pp.158-162.

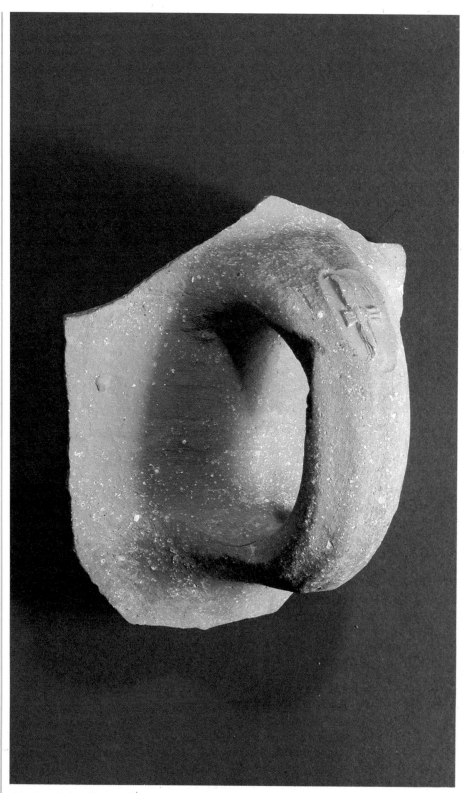

A jar handle from Hebron, bearing the royal seal.

Furniture and fittings

It is one thing to unearth buried houses in order to gain a picture of what they looked like. It is quite another to recover in any detail a picture of what it was like to live inside them.

Part of the problem, of course, is that clothing fabrics, leather, basketry and wooden furniture usually decayed soon after they fell into disuse. Pottery and stonework have often been well preserved, however. Written records from ancient times, the Bible, and carvings and paintings also inform us about objects in everyday use.

One of the most important archaeological finds to throw light on everyday life in the home was made at Jericho. Pottery relating to the Canaanite period (Middle Bronze Age) was discovered there, and in the tombs there was some wooden furniture. The illustration suggests what the main living room in an ordinary home may have looked like. The clothes are partly conjectural, although beads and dress

Reconstruction of the Middle Bronze Age living-room described on this page.

pins have been found in tombs.

The room probably had a low wooden table and chairs or stools with wicker-type seats. The beds were wooden-framed with a wicker covering. Large storage jars for grain and other foodstuffs stood in the room. There were bowls and jugs for eating and drinking, and small or valuable objects were kept in a decorated wooden box. Lamps stood in niches in the wall.

2 Kings 9: 30-33 ▷▷

2 Kings 1: 2 ▷▷

1 Samuel 19: 12 ▷

LIGHT TO SEE BY

Houses in Bible times had windows, but these were usually just holes in the wall. Sometimes they were big enough for people to climb through. Michal let her husband David out of the window when he had to escape from King Saul in a hurry. Queen Jezebel was looking out of a window when Jehu arrived in Jezreel. He called her servants to throw her out, which they did, killing her and fulfilling an earlier prophecy of Elijah.

Clear glass did not come into use until Roman times, and the only protection ever put across windows seems to have been some form of lattice. It presumably deterred intruders and kept out the larger birds, but it was not strong enough to prevent Ahaziah falling out of a window. The rooms which opened on to the central courtyard would get some light from it, and these may have

An ivory carving from Nimrud, showing a woman looking out of a window. Early 8th century BC.

5

A simple lamp with a pinched lip for the wick. Found at Gezer. Early Iron Age dated about 900 BC.

been where animals were stabled and daytime work was carried out.

In the dark corners of the main living room, and everywhere at night, oil lamps would be lit. The earliest lamps seem to have been the bases of broken jars. They were filled with olive oil and a wick of flax or wool was draped over the side.

More than a thousand years before the patriarchs, people in Palestine were making attractive lamps which looked rather like square saucers with pinched corners for the wick. By the time of the patriarchs (the Middle Bronze Age), the usual shape of lamps was oval with a single pinched lip for the wick. Later lamps often had flanges round the rim and a round base.

In the Persian period (586–330 BC) Greek influences led to a smaller, round lamp, which was covered at the top except for a filler hole and a protruding spout for the wick. In New Testament times the older open style had gone out of use, and lamps were being made more ornate. The upper half might be pressed in a mould,

decorated with flowers, or, outside the Jewish area, with scenes from daily life and pagan myths.

To ensure that the rather dim light from the oil lamp illuminated as large an area as possible, and perhaps to prevent lamps from being accidentally knocked over, they were often set in small niches in the walls about a metre and a half above floor level. They would have needed to be refilled regularly because they held only a small amount of oil – as the foolish servant girls in Jesus' parable found out to their cost. There were no safety matches to relight an empty lamp.

◁ Matthew 25: 1-13

Light became a symbol of the continuity of life for the Jews. David was promised that he would always have 'a lamp before me in Jerusalem', meaning that his family would always live there. 'The lamp of the wicked', however, according to the book of Proverbs, will be put out. In the New Testament, Jesus calls himself 'the light

◁ 1 Kings 11: 36

◁ Proverbs 13: 9

John 8: 12 ▷

of the world', and he promises 'the light of life' to all who follow him, meaning the reality of God's presence and power in this life and the next.

A much more elaborate lamp with places for seven wicks. This comes from Palestine in the 2nd century AD. It is 27 cm (about 10½ in) long.

TABLES, CHAIRS AND BEDS

1 Samuel 20: 29 ▷▷

Everyone needs tables and chairs. They may be plush or plain, polished or

2 Samuel 9: 7 ▷▷
1 Kings 10: 5 ▷▷

painted, but in most parts of the world homes will have some furniture for eating off and sitting on – much of it made from wood.

People in Bible times were no exception. The remarkable discovery of well-preserved wooden furniture in the wealthy Middle Bronze Age tombs of Jericho showed that the design and

Isaiah 21: 5 ▷▷

construction of furniture has changed little down the centuries. Accurately cut mortised and mitred joints also revealed that the hard-to-learn craft of the carpenter was already mastered some 2,000 years before Jesus Christ picked up the tools in Joseph's workshop.

Stools had holes bored in the frame so that woven cords could be threaded across the top to make something like the modern cane-bottomed or wicker chair.

John 2: 12-17 ▷▷

Just how much furniture existed in ordinary Israelite homes during the entire Old Testament period is unclear. There are numerous references to tables, but it is likely that these were mostly owned by the wealthy. David, for example, sat at Saul's table, and later had his own to which he invited Mephibosheth, the fearful grandson of Saul. The Queen of Sheba was impressed by the lavish spread on Solomon's table. While the word 'table' may mean only a person's hospitable provision for guests, as in Psalm 23, there was probably a physical piece of furniture upon which food was spread.

Isaiah hints that the tables were low. Rugs were spread on the floor when people ate, presumably for them to sit or recline on, instead of chairs at a higher table. Poor people may well have had only a skin or mat on the floor to use as a table, which they sat round for meals.

The New Testament word for table, *trapeza*, literally means an object with four feet. It was the Roman practice in more wealthy homes to recline on low couches in front of a low table. The tables of the traders in the temple, which Jesus tipped over, however, were probably higher. In the story of the rich man and Lazarus, Jesus referred to crumbs falling from the rich man's table, but while that suggests a table with legs, it gives no indication of its height.

Some stone tables have been found in the wealthy houses excavated on the Western Hill of Jerusalem, made in a style also found at Pompeii. One had a top 45 cm x 75 cm (18 in x 30 in) on a central pedestal about 75 cm (30 in) high. The edges of the table were carved with rosettes, egg and dart or floral patterns. It would have stood in a garden or reception room, and refreshments or objects of art would have been placed on it.

Chairs were probably a luxury in many ordinary homes. The same Hebrew word can mean chair, seat and throne, and most of its occurrences in the Old Testament refer to a king's throne. The elderly Eli sat on a chair in the temple doorway, perhaps a chair of office and so comparable to a throne. When Elijah went to stay in the house of a Shunammite woman, however, she provided him with a table, chair, bed and lamp in her upper room.

Beds in Old Testament times seem to have varied from a straw mat to the wooden-framed beds decorated with

ivory to which Amos in the eighth century took exception in his tirade against the idle rich. He also complained that during the day these people 'lounge on your couches', referring perhaps to an early version of the bed-settee, a dual purpose piece of furniture.

During the time of the kings, some beds seem to have been portable, and therefore made of a rigid wooden frame. Saul commanded his servants to bring David to him on his bed. Later, in Persian times (586–330 BC), some beds had bronze fittings for the legs and iron rods which held the legs together. In Hellenistic times Pharaoh Ptolemy II (Philadelphus, 285–246 BC) gave Eleazar the high priest ten couches with silver legs.

The Egyptians had wooden headrests on their beds. Jacob made do with a stone when he slept in the open air, while pillows of goats' hair were in use by the time David ran from Saul.

Jesus once told an invalid, '"Get up! Pick up your mat and walk."' The word for 'mat' is translated in some versions as 'bed', and it was clearly something thin and easily carried. Perhaps it was the first-century equivalent of the modern bed roll or even stretcher, for Mark records that when Jesus arrived at Gennesaret the people 'carried the sick on mats to wherever they heard he was'.

Even the couches on which people

◁ Amos 6: 4
◁◁ Luke 16: 21

5

◁ 1 Samuel 19: 13-15

◁ Genesis 28: 11
◁◁ 1 Samuel 1: 9
◁ 1 Samuel 19:13

◁ John 5: 8
◁◁ 2 Kings 4: 10

◁ Mark 6: 55

Bronze bedstead from Tel el-Farah. It is about 2 m (6 ft 6 in) long and dates from the Persian period (550-370 BC). The legs are held together with iron rods.

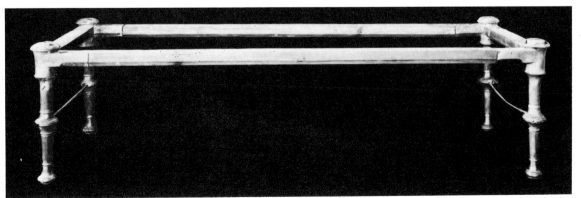

Mark 4: 21 ▷

reclined may not have been very substantial, although Jesus did once refer to the folly of putting a lamp under a bed, which implies that at least some were substantial pieces of furniture with legs.

POTS AND PANS

Most of the household utensils used by people in Bible times were made of earthenware or terracotta and would have been thicker and heavier than those in use today. Ordinary homes would have had plain brown or grey bowls, jugs and dishes. More expensive earthernware had decoration sculpted into it before it was fired, and some pots were also painted.

Unlike wooden and soft furnishings,

An Iron Age storage jar from Hazor (8th century BC). It measures about 68 cm (27 in) high. When full the jar would be too heavy to lift easily and its shape made it convenient to roll from place to place.

Isaiah 22: 24-25 ▷▷

Jeremiah 19: 1-15 ▷▷

Genesis 24: 14-18 ▷▷

1 Kings 18: 33 ▷▷

pottery can survive for centuries. In Abraham's time, people in Palestine were using flat-based bowls with gently rounded sides, and with 'profiled' rims which curved either inwards or outwards. Some bowls had a 'carination' or bulge rather like the prow of a ship (the Latin *carina* means prow) in the side. Some of the finest pottery found in Palestine belongs to this period.

The people also had a wide range of jugs. The most common were the 'dipper juglets', graceful vessels 12 – 18 cm (5 – 7 in) high. They had a round or pointed base, and were intended for ladling liquids out of large storage jars. The body of the jug was oval, and the neck widened out at the top. They usually had a handle from the rim to the shoulder.

By the time of the kings, some homes had a large mixing bowl or krater, with two or four handles. It was about 40 cm (16 in) in diameter and 20 cm (8 in) high. In Isaiah it is said to be one of the vessels which were hung on wall pegs, but which were so heavy that they might pull the peg from the wall and be smashed on the floor.

One of the most graceful of domestic vessels in the monarchy period was the decanter, which could be between 10 and 25 cm (4 – 10 in) high. It had a narrow neck, and liquid gurgled as it was poured out – so the Israelites called it *baqbuq*, which imitated the noise it made. It was this which Jeremiah smashed as a sign that God would destroy Judah and Jerusalem because of the people's sin: a beautiful and useful vessel broken beyond repair.

One Hebrew word describes both a flour container and a water jug. Rebekah was using one at the well when Abraham's servant, looking for a wife for Isaac, met her. Elijah used four of them to douse the sacrifice on

A Late Bronze Age flask from Hazor, of the type known as a 'pilgrim flask', used by travellers and soldiers.

Mount Carmel before calling for the fire of God to burn it up. It was the same kind of vessel which had contained the flour he and the widow of Zarephath had lived on during the drought. The reason the same kind of jar was used for both flour and water was probably that it had a narrow neck which could be stoppered easily, to prevent spillage and contamination.

Small bowls were used for soup and ordinary food, and bowls or cups were used for drinks. Amos records the fact that gluttons, however, drank wine from a large bowl. Another drinking vessel was the two-handled flask, usually used by travellers and soldiers. Archaeologists call it the pilgrim's flask. It had a round, almost wheel-like body, with a narrow neck which was easy to drink from and easy to stopper. The two handles ran from the neck to the shoulder, to which a strap or cord could be fixed. It was probably one of these which David took from the sleeping Saul, and which Elijah found beside him when he woke up one day in the desert during his escape from Ahab.

◁◁ Amos 6: 6

Pottery in New Testament times was usually harder and firmer than before. Those who could afford it used shiny-red ware imported from the

◁◁ 1 Samuel 26: 11

This collection of objects found in Jerusalem and dating from around the time of Jesus Christ includes stone tables and jars perhaps similar to those in use at the wedding at Cana (see John 2: 1-11).

◁ 1 Kings 19: 6

5

Roman glass bottles from Jerusalem (1st-2nd century AD).

Matthew 10: 42 ▷
Revelation 14: 10 ▷▷
Luke 22: 17, 20 ▷
Matthew 26: 23 ▷▷
Matthew 23: 25 ▷
Mark 10: 38; 14: 36 ▷
John 13: 5 ▷▷

Aegean. Cups were like small bowls without handles. There were many different shapes, just as there are today. Jesus spoke of giving a cup of water to a needy person, and passed a cup round during the last supper with his disciples. The Pharisees were careful about cleaning cups as part of their religious observance. The cup became a symbol of the suffering Jesus would have to endure, and in the book of Revelation it is a symbol of God's anger.

During the last supper, the disciples dipped their hands into a dish, which was probably a large but shallow bowl. When Jesus washed their feet, he probably used a large container like a krater.

FOR FURTHER READING

Amiran, R., *Ancient Pottery of the Holy Land* (Jerusalem, Masada Press, 1969. US ed. Rutgers UP, 1970).

Avigad, N., *Archaeological Discoveries in the Jewish Quarter of Jerusalem, Second Temple Period* (Jerusalem, Israel Exploration Society, 1976), pp.19–25.

Avigad, N., *Discovering Jerusalem* (Blackwell, 1984. US ed. Nashville, Nelson, 1983).

Kenyon, K.M., *Archaeology in the Holy Land*, 4th ed. (Ernest Benn, 1979. US ed. New York, W.W. Norton), pp.172–175.

Paul, S.M. and Dever, W.G., *Biblical Archaeology* (Jerusalem, Keter, 1973), pp.217–219.

Smith, R.H., 'The Household Lamps of Palestine in Old Testament Times', *BA*, 27 (1), (1964), pp.1–31.

Smith, R.H., 'The Household Lamps of Palestine in Intertestamental Times', *BA*, 27 (4), (1964), pp.101–124.

Smith, R.H., 'The Household lamps of Palestine in New Testament Times', *BA*, 29 (1), (1966), pp.2–27.

Family customs and roles

6

Family life was strong throughout Bible times. The family – grandparents, parents, children, perhaps together with other relatives or even servants – formed a unique social unit. Most family members lived near to each other. Work and religion were as much centred on the

This seal, shown alongside its imprint, dates from about 600 BC. It comes from Mizpah (Tell en-Nasbeh) and bears the name 'Jazzaniahu, servant of the king' in Old Hebrew script.

The name means 'Yahweh hears' and is usually written Ja'azaniah. The seal may even have belonged to the Judaean army commander mentioned in 2 Kings 25: 23 and Jeremiah 40: 8.

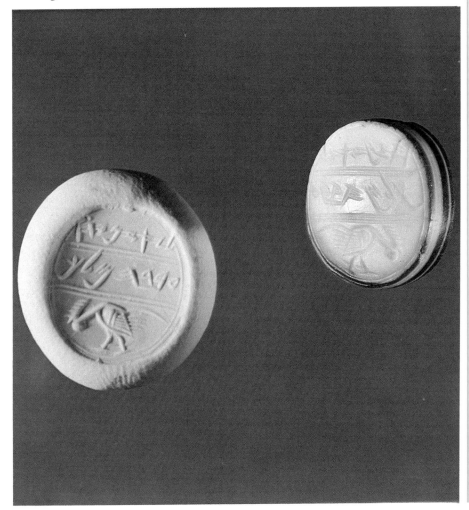

1 Samuel 1: 6-11 ▷▷

home as were rearing children, eating and sleeping. Each stage in a person's life was marked by appropriate religious ceremonies, and each family member had a well-defined role within the community.

Luke 2: 22-27 ▷▷

EARLY DAYS

The birth of a child is usually a joyful occasion, and not just because the pain of delivery is over. The emergence into the world of a perfectly formed miniature

Luke 1: 46-48 ▷

person rarely fails to evoke at least a passing sense of wonder and tenderness.

The Bible records that joy was felt by mothers centuries ago just as it is today,

Genesis 21: 3 ▷▷

especially because a woman grew in status in the community when she helped perpetuate the family line. That is

why childless women such as Hannah were not only sorrowful themselves but were also scorned by others. According to religious custom, the new mother was ritually 'unclean' for some days, after which she had to offer a pigeon or dove and a lamb (or a second bird if she was poor) as a sacrifice.

Children's names were chosen carefully because they were held to represent their character. Often the name had some reference to the circumstances of the birth, a national event, or the response of the parents to God's goodness. So, for example, Abraham called his second son Isaac ('he laughs') because Sarah had laughed when she was

A sight that will have changed little over the centuries: a Bedouin mother drawing water from a well near Bethlehem.

told she would become pregnant; she thought she was too old. Isaac's twin sons were called Esau (because he was hairy) and Jacob (because he grabbed his brother's heel as they were born). Eli's daughter-in-law called her son Ichabod ('there is no glory') because the Ark, the sacred box containing sacred items and representing God's presence, had been captured by the Philistines.

Other names referred to God. The name of Eliezer, Abraham's servant, means 'God is helper'. King Hezekiah's name meant 'God is strength', and the prophet Isaiah's 'God is salvation'. Some children were called after plants or animals: Jonah means 'dove' and Deborah 'bee'; Susannah is 'lily'. Leah ('wild cow') and Caleb ('dog') may not have been pleased with their parents' vivid but perceptive choices of names.

Some Bible characters changed their names when they began a new task for God. Abram became Abraham, Hoshea became Joshua. Paul in the New Testament had two names, which was not unusual: his Jewish name was Saul and his Roman name Paul. Names of children could be decided by either father or mother, and on one famous occasion it was the neighbours who made the choice: local women named the son of Ruth and Boaz 'Obed', meaning 'servant'.

When a boy was eight days old he was circumcized by his father. His foreskin was cut off with a flint knife. Israel was not the only nation to practise circumcision (Jeremiah mentions Egypt, Edom, Ammon and Moab), but it was essential if a person was to belong to Israel. It was seen as a sign of God's convenant with Abraham that he would be the father of many nations which would obey God's law.

In the later periods of the Old Testament, when Israel was confronted with alien cultures during the Babylonian, Persian, Greek and Roman incursions, the concept of God's convenant with Abraham, and its sign of circumcision, helped to preserve Israel's unity and distinctiveness. The Greeks actually tried to stamp out the practice, but they did not succeed.

Servants and resident aliens who formed part of the Israelite's household had to be circumcized, too, as did people of other races who wanted to become part of Israel. It was a painful operation for an adult.

The practice was so vivid that it became a powerful symbol of a person's relationship with God. An uncircumcized heart was unable to receive God's life and love; an uncircumcized ear was closed to what God had to say. If that which caused the barrier or hindrance was cut away, then the heart or ear would be 'circumcized' and open to God.

Paul took up the idea of circumcision of the heart in the New Testament, as the Christian church recognized that the physical act was no longer necessary to guarantee a person's acceptance by God; only faith in Jesus was needed. However, many of the early Christians, like Jesus himself, were Jews, and therefore had been circumcized. The subject remained controversial for some time; the more rigorous Jewish Christians wished to impose circumcision on Gentile converts.

If a boy was the first male child in a family, he was 'redeemed' when about a month old. His parents paid silver to the priest of the local sanctuary. Israelites believed that the first-born belonged specially to God. First-born animals were always sacrificed, but God had spared the first-born sons of Israel when their Egyptian counterparts died during the plagues in Egypt, and in any case he hated the human sacrifice which was practised by some nations. So they were 'redeemed' by five shekels of silver, which ultimately became a religious tax.

◁◁Genesis 25: 25f.
◁1 Maccabees 1: 48, 60 (Apocrypha)
◁◁1 Samuel 4: 19-21

◁ Genesis 17: 12-13

◁ Joshua 5: 8

6

◁Jeremiah 4: 4

◁Jeremiah 6: 10

◁ Galatians 5: 6

◁Philippians 3: 5

◁ Luke 2: 21

◁◁ Ruth 4: 17
◁*E.g.* Acts 15: 5-11
◁Galatians 2: 3-5, 12
◁ Numbers 3: 46-51
◁◁ Leviticus 12: 3

◁◁ Jeremiah 9: 25f.
◁ Exodus 22: 29-30

◁◁ Genesis 17: 10-14

◁ Exodus 13: 14-16
◁ Leviticus 20: 2-5

GROWING UP

Babies today are usually weaned from total dependence on breast or bottle milk to solid food (even if mashed) before their first birthday. In Israel a child was not usually weaned until it was at least two, and sometimes even three. Until then it was breast-fed by its mother or sometimes by a wet-nurse.

Weaning seems to have been marked by a family celebration; Abraham made a great feast when Isaac was weaned. He had good reason. To have brought a child through infancy in days of poor medicine and indifferent hygiene was a cause for rejoicing. It was also a moment of release for the mother.

Then, as they grew older, young Israelites, like children everywhere, took to the streets and squares of the town or the fields around the village to play with their friends. At home, the mother and father would teach them their first lessons, and the family would say prayers together and attend worship on sabbaths and festival days (see chapter 21). It was the duty of parents to teach their children the Israelite saga, the drama of the exodus and the meaning of God's law. At each annual Passover meal a child would ask 'What does this mean?' and the father would recount the story and explain its significance.

School did not exist for most children until a couple of centuries before Christ, when the rabbis at the synagogues took on the role of teachers. Their instruction would have been mostly religious and moral, based on the Torah, the first five books of the Bible, but it probably also included basic numeracy and literacy. Education started when boys were about six; girls were never educated. Pupils sat on the ground at their teacher's feet, and learned largely by repetition. There were

Opposite: an Athenian vase-painting showing a seated youth (left) studying the alphabet. About 400 BC.

no Christian schools in the early church, but there were Roman schools across the Empire with slaves as teachers, where pupils studied philosophy, maths, music, literature, rhetoric, and perhaps astronomy and architecture. (See also chapter 15.)

If school was rare, work was common. While children were not slaves in the sense that some were in nineteenth-century Britain before the factory laws were enacted, they would have learned skills from their parents and helped in fields, workshop or kitchen as soon as they could walk.

The growing child was therefore much more physically attached to its home than many western children today. Once a modern child is five years old (for some it is even younger), he or she has already discovered that there are two quite distinct worlds to live in – school and home. For Israelite children, and probably for most children in the New Testament period also, play, work, education and family activities were all closely integrated with the home. Even to this day, close bonding of Jewish families is legendary. The greater freedom and resultant variety now offered to most western children may be partly responsible for present-day rootlessness and disaffection of youth and the disintegration of marriages and once-unified social groups.

Surprisingly perhaps, in view of the late weaning and close family ties, Israelite boys were initiated into religious and legal maturity when they were only thirteen. Most men would also be married by their late teens, women even earlier.

The coming of age ceremony is now called the Bar Mitzvah. (One for girls aged twelve, the Bath Mitzvah, was devised in the nineteenth century.) It seems to have had a long history. An ancient rabbinic tractate, *Aboth*, 'The sayings of the Father', describes the following stages of life:

◁◁ 2 Maccabees 7: 27 (Apocrypha)

◁◁ Exodus 2: 7-9

◁◁ 2 Kings 11: 1-3

◁◁ Genesis 21: 8

6

◁◁ *E.g.* Jeremiah 9: 21

◁◁ Matthew 11: 16f.

◁◁ Deuteronomy 6: 20-25

At five years one is fit for the Scriptures, at ten years for the Mishna, at thirteen for the commandments, at fifteen for the Talmud, at eighteen for the bride-chamber, at twenty for pursuing a calling, at thirty for authority, at forty for discernment, at fifty for counsel,

Bar Mitzvah ceremonies at the Western Wall, Jerusalem. The close bonding of Jewish families is expressed dramatically.

at sixty to be an elder, at seventy for grey hairs, at eighty for special strength, at ninety for bowed back and at a hundred a man is as one that has already died and passed away and ceased from this world.

The significant words are 'at thirteen for the commandments', which are translated by some writers as 'for the fulfilling of the commandments'.

In the second century AD Rabbi Eleazar ben Simeon taught that a father was responsible for the deeds of his son until the age of thirteen. After that age the boy was regarded as a responsible member of Israel and could make vows, become a member of the synagogue and be recognized as legally responsible. It is perhaps significant that when Jesus was twelve years old he sat among the teachers, listening and asking them questions, when his parents went up to Jerusalem for the Passover. He may have been preparing himself for his imminent accession to manhood.

MARRIAGE

'Love and marriage go together like a horse and carriage' were the words of a once-popular twentieth-century song. They echoed a sentiment which is taken for granted, that marriage should be based on the couple's mutual love. That assumption would have sounded as strange to Abraham's or even Paul's ears as the concept of 'arranged marriages' sounds to ours, for in Bible times, bride and groom had little choice in the matter.

That may not have been quite as barbaric as it seems; if indeed most marriages were between teenagers, matchmaking parents might have a shrewder idea of compatibility than inexperienced adolescents. (From the book of Kings it seems that Jehoiachin was married at sixteen and Amon and Josiah at fourteen, although ordinary people may have waited a few years more in order to learn a trade and save up the marriage price paid to the bride's family.) By New Testament times rabbis had fixed the minimum age for marriage at twelve for girls and thirteen for boys.

The marriage was arranged by the couple's fathers; neither boy nor girl was usually consulted. Abraham sent his servant to choose a wife for Isaac, who drew up the contract with Rebekah's brother Laban; she was consulted only when the deal was complete.

⊲ Genesis 24: 34-58

This rather extreme example of an arranged marriage (the servant had to travel from Canaan to north Mesopotamia, a distance of some 1,600 km or 1,000 miles) illustrates the intense concern among Israelite families to choose wives for their sons from their own kith and kin. Samson grieved his father by not choosing a wife from his own people, however, and that somewhat wilful action indicates that some children did have a say in the matter. Isaac, it seems, chose a middle path by advising his son Jacob to marry one of his cousins, and Rachel was Jacob's own choice.

⊲⊲ Luke 2: 41-47

⊲ Judges 14: 3

⊲ Genesis 28: 1f.

Once the proposal was put, the couple's fathers began their financial negotiations. To lose or gain a daughter was to lose or gain a worker. The marriage price, or *mohar*, was compensation to the woman's father for his loss. The bride was not regarded as an object to be bought, and there is evidence that in time of personal need the woman received back the marriage price for her own use. The amount varied according to the social standing and wealth of the bride's father. In the case of compulsory marriage after a rape, the price was set at 50 shekels of silver. Jacob substituted an agreed period of work for the marriage price, and David was given his bride Michal by defeating

⊲ Deuteronomy 22: 28-29

⊲ Genesis 29: 15-30

⊲ I Samuel 18: 27

6

the Philistines at Saul's request.

When the marriage was agreed, the groom gave presents to the bride's family – the opposite of today's practice when the family gives all it can to the new couple. Some fathers did give their daughters presents: Othniel gave his daughter a piece of land, for example.

E.g. Hosea 2: 4f. ▷▷
Joshua 15: 18f. ▷

The couple were now engaged (or 'betrothed'), a stricter legal relationship than contemporary engagements. If the wedding was abandoned, a financial penalty would be imposed on the person responsible. They were not permitted to have sexual relations, however, which was what made Mary's pregnancy embarrassing and led Joseph to consider 'divorce', as they were not yet married.

Deuteronomy 24: 1▷▷

Matthew 1: 19 ▷

All that now remained in normal circumstances was for the celebrations to be arranged, so that, in the words of Genesis setting out God's purpose for men and women, 'a man will leave his father and mother and be united to his wife, and they will become one flesh'.

Deuteronomy 22: ▷▷
13-19

Genesis 2: 24 ▷

Deuteronomy 22: ▷▷
28f.

Hosea chapters 2 ▷▷
and 3

POLYGAMY AND DIVORCE

Marriage has two purposes: to provide companionship for the couple who complement each other, and to guarantee a secure environment for raising children. Those purposes were spelled out in the book of Genesis, and they assume that each person will have only one partner.

Matthew 19: 3-12▷▷

Polygamy soon emerged in Israelite society, however, beginning in the reprobate line of Cain's descendants when Lamech took two wives. Abraham had mistresses (or concubines) and secondary wives such as Hagar. Ancient inscriptions, notably Hammurabi's Code, indicate that the practice was widespread at the time. Bigamy is recognized as legal in the

Genesis 1: 28; 2: 18,▷
24

Genesis 4: 19▷

1 Corinthians 11:▷▷
2-16

Deuteronomy 21: ▷
15-17

book of Deuteronomy, which sets down strict rules to prevent family feuds over property between children of rival mothers. However, it seems likely to have been more common among kings than ordinary people; the Wisdom books never mention it and the Prophets present a picture of a monogamous society.

Divorce was possible for Israelites, and at times on apparently flimsy grounds. The prescription 'If a man marries a woman who becomes displeasing to him because he finds something indecent about her' has a familiarly modern ring to it. What was different in Bible times was that only men could divorce; women had no legal redress in court. Unfaithfulness by the wife was the main ground for divorce, but there were restrictions. A man who falsely accused his wife of not being a virgin when he married her could not divorce her, nor could a man divorce the woman he had to marry after raping her. A husband could take back an unfaithful wife if she had not remarried.

In the New Testament, Jesus looks back to God's original intention for strict monogamy, but does allow unfaithfulness as a reason for divorce. In Jewish, Greek and Roman society, it seems that adultery (that is, sexual relations between a married person and someone other than the marriage partner) was completely forbidden. Fornication (sexual relations outside marriage) was tolerated, but not among the Jews, and both Jesus and Paul emphasized that this, too, violated God's intention for human beings.

The apostles urged their readers to take care not to fall, or appear to fall, into sexual immorality. That is why women in the church were to have long hair; short hair was the mark of a woman found guilty of adultery. Jesus himself, and presumably the apostles, attracted social outcasts who included converted prostitutes. The sexual standards of the non-Christian culture were low.

So both Jesus and Paul emphasized that sexual union creates a new bond between two people and is therefore appropriate and lawful only in the context of a life-long marriage partnership. Jesus' teaching on divorce was intended to protect women. It was possible that they would be forced into prostitution if they were thrown out of their homes; they had no legal rights.

Paul's discussion of the sexual relationship of husband and wife in 1 Corinthians 7 is unparalleled in ancient thought, so profound is his insight and so sensitive his concern for the couple. He says that each partner's body belongs to the other; in saying that of women, as well as men, he was sowing the seeds of a social revolution.

WOMEN IN BIBLE TIMES

The modern struggle for the recognition of equality between men and women, which was given public impetus by the suffragettes campaigning for voting rights in the early twentieth century, may give the impression that women have always been regarded as inferior beings.

That was not wholly true in some periods covered by the Bible. In the later centuries of the Old Testament period, official Jewish teaching was certainly male-orientated, and women were regarded as second class in both social and spiritual terms. But in earlier times, and in the early church, they

◁◁Matthew 19: 5-6
E.g. 1 Corinthians 6: 12-20;
Ephesians 5: 21-23

6

This seal and its impression (compare with that on page 79) bears the name 'Hannah', evidence that women were sometimes considered important enough to have their own seal.

Exodus 2: 1-10 ▷▷

were granted a high degree of respect and status, although their practical role as mothers and housewives was not often changed. It was an ambiguous way of life which has no parallel in the twentieth century. Patriarchal, Israelite and early Christian family life was not always oppressive to the womenfolk.

Micah 6: 4 ▷▷
Numbers 12: 1-15 ▷▷

OLD TESTAMENT: EQUALITY IN HONOUR

Judges 4: 5 ▷▷

The woman's lot was not an easy one – nor, for that matter, was the man's. The woman, however, bore the brunt of the hard work around the home.

1 Samuel 25 ▷▷

But in the account of creation the woman is regarded as the man's

Genesis 2: 18 ▷

'helper', and the Hebrew word means his 'counterpart'. In other words, men and women as created by God were intended to complement each other, the strengths and abilities of one balancing the weaknesses and inabilities of the other.

Exodus 20: 17 ▷▷
Exodus 20: 12 ▷

The ten commandments called for equal honour to be shown to both parents, and the same punishment was laid down in the Levitical law for a

Leviticus 20: 9 ▷

person who cursed either mother or

Proverbs 23: 22;
30: 17   ▷
E.g. Genesis 18: 12 ▷▷

father. The Wisdom books insist on respect being paid to mothers. In the Old Testament there are glimpses of husbands who deeply loved their wives and treated them as equals, and this attitude would not have been unusual.

1 Samuel 1: 4-8, ▷
20–23

It is written of Elkanah, father of the prophet Samuel, for example, that he loved Hannah his wife, who for many years was unable to have children. When she decided to miss the annual

Numbers 27: 1-11 ▷▷

religious sacrifice until the baby was weaned, he said, 'Do what seems best to you'; there was no legalism and oppression there.

Daughters seemed to share in family life as much as sons. They are often grouped with sons as participating in

Job 42: 13-15 ▷▷

religious festivals and subject to the law with identical penalties for offenders of either sex.

Some women had a profound influence on national life. Miriam, Moses' elder sister, whose clever idea enabled her infant brother both to live and be reared by his own mother when neither seemed possible, was still honoured in the eighth century BC by Micah the prophet, who bracketed her with Aaron and Moses as Israel's 'leaders', even though at one point she had turned against Moses. Deborah was a prophetess and one of the judges or leaders of her time, while Abigail, wife of the churlish Nabal, knew, as only women do, how to avert the dangers of her husband's folly in snubbing David. Queen mothers are often mentioned, and they seem to have influenced their sons' rule.

Despite respect and even influence, women did not have the same rights as men, however. From the beginning there were signs that women were treated as possessions rather than people; a wife is listed along with a man's property, land, servants and animals in the commandments about covetousness, although a special word for coveting a wife is used which clearly distinguishes her from the rest. Wives seem to have called their husbands 'master' or lord, much as a slave would address a king.

A woman could not divorce her husband, nor could she make a vow unless her husband or father gave consent, and if he did not, the vow was null and void. Daughters and wives could not inherit property from their father or husband unless there was no male heir. In one famous case, Moses ruled that orphaned daughters who had no brother should be given some of their dead father's land, with the promise that they married men from their father's tribe. An exception to the rule seems to have been made in Job's case. His three daughters shared their inheritance with their seven brothers, but perhaps Job was not an Israelite or

WEDDING DAY

The daily grind in a world which generally lacked lavish entertainment or variety of foods threw religious feast days and family celebrations into sharp relief. Once in a while, people could have a really enjoyable time feasting together. Weddings were such an occasion, as Jesus explained in his parable of the king's wedding banquet.

It was a lavish meal. Oxen and fat calves were killed and cooked. Two sets of invitations were sent out; one, some time in advance and the second when everything was ready. For people to refuse the invitation was unpardonable, as was the appearance of a guest without the appropriate festive clothes.

Another of Jesus' parables describes the procession before the banquet. The groom would go with his friends to the bride's house in the evening. There they would collect the bride and her friends and process back to the groom's house with singing, music and dancing. She would be wearing a rich dress, with jewels if she could afford them, and her face would be veiled. (That explains how poor Jacob found he had been tricked into marrying the wrong woman.) The groom may have had garlands of flowers round his neck.

There would be love songs for the couple (Psalm 45 and the Song of Songs are examples), stories would be told, and the food and drink would be plentiful. One of the groom's friends would be the equivalent of 'best man', and perhaps also the 'master of the banquet'. The feasting could often last for a week; poorer people would meet together each evening for a celebratory meal, then go off to their normal occupations during the day. Finally, the bride and groom were taken to the nuptial chamber, a room set aside for them, and then left alone, when the party broke up.

◁Psalm 45: 13-15

◁Song of Songs 4: 1

◁Genesis 29: 23-25

◁◁Matthew 22: 1-14

◁Job 22: 9

6

◁◁John 2: 8f.; 3: 29

◁◁Matthew 25: 1-13

---

subject to Mosaic law.

Daughters could sometimes be sold as slaves and were unlikely to be released, as a son could be, unless the girl had become a concubine and then displeased her master, when she could be ransomed. A Levitical law forbade a man to sell his daughter as a prostitute, which implies that some fathers did indeed treat their daughters with contempt in this way, or were forced to by poverty.

Sexual unfaithfulness was regarded as equally serious whether committed by men or women. A married couple 'knew' each other in the sense that there was total commitment between them; sexual sins thus disrupted deep personal relationships, and at that point at least, Israelite men and women were equal before the law.

NEW TESTAMENT: ONE IN CHRIST

Jesus introduced into the legalistic and rather oppressive social climate of his time a wholly new attitude to women. He laid down no new rules, apart from a new commandment to love one another. Just as he never condemned the institution of slavery as such, so he never suggested that women should be given more social freedom and greater individual status. He simply led by example, and in so doing implied that social change was as much a matter of reforming personal opinion as it was of revising national law.

He astounded his disciples, for example, by talking alone with the woman at the well. She happened to be a foreigner as well as a female. Two of his close friends were women, Mary and Martha, the sisters of Lazarus; he clearly regarded them as affectionately as he did their brother.

He made no distinction between men and women in his teaching and healing ministry. Indeed, one woman who begged him to heal her daughter

◁◁Exodus 21: 7f.; Deuteronomy 15: 12-15

◁◁Leviticus 19: 29

◁◁Leviticus 20: 10
◁John 4: 4-30

◁John 12: 1-3

◁Mark 7: 24-30

Luke 7: 36-50 ▷

was also non-Jewish, like the woman at the well. Another woman, known locally as a prostitute, anointed his feet with perfume as a thank-you for the forgiveness of her sins, a sign which Jesus accepted; "'Your faith has saved you,'" he told her; "'go in peace.'"

Jesus was showing through such actions that he came especially to help those whom the world despised.

Besides Mary and Martha several women played an important role in his ministry. It was the women who stood by during the painful hours of his

rucifixion, who prepared spices for mbalming his body, and who were he first witnesses of his resurrection.

Moreover, Jesus honoured his own nother by ensuring, even as his own ife ebbed away, that she (presumably by then also a widow) should be looked after by John the apostle. Her cousin Elizabeth had ensured that Mary would be honoured for her

◁◁ Luke 23: 55 – 24: 8

◁◁ John 19: 26f.

Egyptian women mourners, depicted on a wall-painting from the tomb of Ramose at Thebes, about 1400 BC.

6

faithfulness to God in being the person who bore Jesus into the world: "'Blessed are you among women,'" Luke 1: 42 ▷ she had prophesied, "'and blessed is the child you will bear.'"

After Jesus died, women seem to have held important places in churches. Paul often greets them in his letters. E.g. Romans 16: 1, ▷ 3, 6, 12, 15 Some were gifted prophets, others Acts 21: 9 ▷ deacons, and the office of deacon seems to have remained open to women as well as to men for some time in the E.g. Genesis 37: 34 ▷▷ early church.

Paul does, however, place restrictions on women's ministry. A woman is not to teach or have 1 Timothy 2: 12 ▷ authority over men, he told Timothy. Women should keep silent, he told the 1 Corinthians 14: ▷ 34f. Corinthians (although this may have Deuteronomy 14: 1f.; ▷▷ referred to the habit of women gossiping, rather than listening to the Jeremiah 16: 6 ▷▷ readings and sermons, in the 1 Peter 3: 1-7 ▷ synagogues). Wives, said Peter, were to be submissive to husbands who in turn were to be considerate and to treat their wives as 'heirs with you of the gracious gift of life'. Paul also stresses Jeremiah 16: 7 ▷▷ the unity of men and women in Christ. Galatians 3: 28 ▷ There is neither male nor female in God's sight, he said. And on another occasion he told husbands to love their Ephesians 5: 25-30 ▷ wives self-sacrificially – as much, indeed, as they loved themselves.

This mixture of restriction and deep respect (probably unusual at a time when women were rarely well treated) John 11: 39 ▷▷ was another example of change from within rather than its being imposed Deuteronomy 21: ▷▷ 22f. from outside. Paul (like Jesus) was not prepared simply to sweep away the Genesis 50: 1-3, 26 ▷▷ culture in which his readers were steeped. The seeds of destruction were sown in it, however; if men really loved women as deeply as Paul and Peter said they should, women could Leviticus 20: 14 ▷▷ not remain second-class citizens for long. Unfortunately, self-giving love has never come easily to men or Amos 5: 16 ▷▷ women.

DEATH AND BURIAL

Death, in Bible times, was never hushed up. When a person died there was an open and public demonstration of grief by the close family, friends and neighbours. Feelings were never hidden; 'grown men don't cry' would have seemed a strange idea to people in Bible times.

People would cry, moan and beat their breasts. Some would tear their outer clothes and then don sackcloth, a coarse material worn round the waist next to the skin. Mourners usually took off their shoes and men often covered their heads. Sometimes they threw earth over their heads, rolled in the dust or sat among ashes. They gave up using perfumes or even washing; they fasted, and some shaved their hair or even cut their bodies – practices which were outlawed in Israel because of their association with pagan rites.

The mourning period usually lasted seven days, and during that time neighbours would bring the relatives mourning bread and 'the cup of consolation'.

The home of a dead person was ritually unclean, and food could not be prepared in it.

The interval between death and burial was probably quite short. Bodies decomposed quickly in the heat and would be a health risk if left exposed. Martha feared a stench after Lazarus had been dead for four days. The bodies of people executed had to be buried the same day. The seventy days' mourning before Jacob was buried was most unusual and reflected Egyptian practice rather than Israelite custom. Cremation was virtually unknown; burning a body was an outrage inflicted only on evildoers.

The funeral procession was not a silent affair. People sang or cried a lamentation, perhaps a repeated 'Alas!

Alas!' with the addition of a name or title, 'Alas! My brother!' It was an expressive burst of deeply-felt pain, providing a legitimate and socially acceptable outlet for emotion. Everyone joined in; indeed, lamentation was a duty for the close relatives. Sometimes these expressions of grief were developed into a longer poem or lament which was composed in a rhythm of three beats followed by two; the book of Lamentations is a very long example, mourning for Jerusalem and her people, slain, in effect, by the Babylonians. Laments were sometimes composed and sung by professional mourners, usually, but not exclusively, women.

Coffins were generally not used. Wealthy people had burial chambers cut into soft rock. They were usually big enough to accommodate several corpses and so became family tombs. Abraham and his family were all buried in the tomb of Machpelah. The common phrase 'to sleep with one's fathers' may have originated from the practice.

Burial places were usually marked in some way; Jacob set up a *stele* or tall stone over Rachel's tomb.

A practice of later years, particularly in the Herodian age, was to collect the bones and place them in a bone box, called an *ossuary*. There is a necropolis (literally 'city of the dead') for important people in the Kidron valley area near Jerusalem.

When bodies were buried in tombs they were embalmed, certainly by New Testament times, with linen cloths, spices, myrrh and aloes. This was how Jesus was buried. His friend Lazarus, whom he raised from the dead, emerged from the tomb 'his hands and feet wrapped with strips of linen, and a cloth around his face'. Jesus told the mourners to remove the grave clothes.

◁◁ 1 Kings 13: 30

◁ Genesis 35: 20

◁◁ *E.g.* 2 Samuel 1: 17-27

◁ John 19: 39-40

◁◁ *E.g.* Jeremiah 9: 17f.

◁ John 11: 44

◁◁ Genesis 23: 4-20

6

The interior of the tomb in Bethany, traditionally associated with the burial of Lazarus.

THOSE LEFT BEHIND

It was only after burial, of course, that the real problems began for the survivors, especially for women. There was no paid employment available for them, no social security. Their support had gone; they could be reduced to begging unless someone looked after them. This may put the incident of the widow of Nain, whose only son was raised from the dead by Jesus, into powerful perspective. She received back her only hope for personal survival.

Younger widows might remarry, and until then they may, like Tamar, have gone back to their fathers' house or even, as in the exceptional case of Ruth, to their mother-in-law. A man had a duty to marry his widowed sister-in-law if his brother (her husband) had died childless, in order to raise up a successor; this is now called 'Levirate marriage', from the Latin *levir*, 'husband's brother'.

Men were inclined to ignore widow and orphans, however, and the Psalms reminded them that God cared especially for them. The law allowed widows to glean grapes, grain and olives and receive part of the 'third year tithe'. Job describes wicked people who 'sent widows away empty-handed and broke the strength of the fatherless'. Some even took away the widow's ox (her only means of ploughing a plot of land) as a pledge for a loan. Jesus denounced the Pharisees who 'devour widows'

E.g. Psalm 146: 9 ▷▷
Deuteronomy 24: ▷▷ 19-21
Deuteronomy 14: ▷▷ 28f.
Job 22: 9 ▷▷
Luke 7: 11-17 ▷
Job 24: 3 ▷▷
Genesis 38: 11 ▷
Mark 12: 40 ▷▷
Ruth 1: 8 ▷
Genesis 38: 8-10 ▷

Coffins were not usually used in Jewish burials but this sarcophagus (stone coffin) in the Greek style dates from the late 1st century BC or early AD.

6

The tomb of Jesus has never been identified with certainty but this recently excavated tomb
t Nazareth shows clearly the type of stone which was rolled across the entrance.

John 14: 2f. ▷▷

Malachi 3: 5 ▷

Psalm 16: 10 ▷▷

Acts 6: 1 ▷
James 1: 27 ▷
Job 19: 26 ▷▷
1 Corinthians 15 ▷▷

Job 7: 9 ▷
E.g. Psalm 6: 5 ▷

houses'. According to the prophets, those who oppress widows will suffer God's judgment along with sorcerers, adulterers and dishonest employers.

The early Christians also took their responsibilities to widows seriously. They received help from a regular distribution of food and, according to James, caring for widows was a sign of true religion.

No charitable help and loving care could recompense for the loss of someone who was loved, of course. Yet until the coming of Jesus, belief in life after death was very hazy. The Old Testament often refers to Sheol, the abode of the dead, but it is a place which lacks the vitality of the heaven Jesus described and in which he prepared a place for those who follow him on earth. There are flashes of insight and faith, as when the psalmist cries, 'you will not abandon me to the grave, nor will you let your Holy One see decay', or when Job declares, 'After my skin has been destroyed, yet in my flesh I will see God.'

But Jesus' resurrection, according to Paul, drew the sting of death and robbed the grave of its ultimate victory over life. The Jewish life was anchored to the earth. Certainly the rabbis speculated a great deal on 'the world to come' but the Christian revelation saw life on earth in the perspective of time and space without limit or end.

FOR FURTHER READING

Baab, J.O., 'Marriage', *IDB*, 3 (New York, Abingdon, 1962), pp.278–287.

Edersheim, A., *Sketches of Jewish Life in the Days of Christ* (reprint 1876. Grand Rapids, Eerdmans, 1967), pp.103–181.

Kaster, J., 'Education in the Old Testament', *IDB*, 2 (New York, Abingdon, 1962), pp.27–34.

McCasland, S.V., 'Education in the New Testament', *IDB*, 2 (New York, Abingdon, 1962), pp.34–38.

Morris, L.L., 'Death', *IBD*, 1 (IVP, 1980), pp.374–377.

Motyer, J.A., 'Circumcision', *IBD*, 1 (IVP, 1980), pp.288–289.

Selman, M.J., 'Comparative customs and the Patriarchal Age', chapter 4 in *Essays on the Patriarchal Narratives* edited by A.R. Millard and D.J. Wiseman (IVP, 1980. US ed. Eisenbrauns, 1983).

Vaux, de R., *Ancient Israel: its Life and Institution* (Darton, Longman and Todd, 1962. US ed. New York, McGraw-Hill, 1961), pp.19–64. (New UK ed. 1973).

Wright, J.S. and Thompson, J.A., 'Marriage', *IBD*, 2 (IVP, 1980), pp.954–958.

Clothes and shoes

People wear clothes for three reasons. One is because they feel ashamed to be naked, as Adam and Eve did in the garden of Eden. Another is to protect themselves against sunburn, cold and rain. And the third is because they want to look attractive.

During the whole of Bible history, clothes could be merely functional or mainly fancy, just as they are today; the major difference from modern times was the lack of variety. Men and women dressed similarly, and special clothes were distinguished from ordinary ones by colour and embroidery rather than by style.

While there were stylistic differences between clothes of one period or place and another, people throughout Bible times would have worn some kind of tunic, usually from shoulder to knee or ankle. Trousers, socks and sweaters were unknown to them. There may be good reasons for this. One is that to sew material was a laborious hand process, and the more joins there are in a garment such as a pair of trousers, the longer it takes. Tunics are relatively simple to cut and sew; smocks were often worn by men even in western Europe down to the Middle Ages and since.

Indeed, clothes were regarded as valuable just because of the time and effort invested in making them. In early times the whole process from shearing the sheep or harvesting the flax to decorating the finished garment was done in the home. Sisera's mother dreamed of 'colourful garments embroidered, highly embroidered garments for my neck' as part of the spoils of war, presumably because she lacked the skills, means or sheer patience to make them herself.

But more important perhaps is the fact that tunics could be both cool and warm in a country where the temperature can vary considerably. The flowing tunic allows air to circulate around the body in the hot sunshine; at night it can be wrapped closely round the body like a blanket for warmth.

It should also be remembered that it is mostly in modern times that clothes have been designed to reveal and emphasize a person's features. In Israel, modesty was not only a virtue but a cultural characteristic; the skin-tight, see-through or skimpy garments of the twentieth century are themselves a reflection of a general attitude to the body and to sexuality. It is perhaps worth noting, however, that the women of other cultures, contemporary with the Israelites, knew little of such modesty, to judge from such evidence as Egyptian tomb paintings. The ancient Israelite attitude is perhaps best illustrated by the story of Noah. When he got drunk and lay down naked on his bed, his son Ham was condemned for not covering him up; Shem and Japheth, his other sons, were commended for covering him — and they kept their backs to him as they did it.

Women usually wore veils over their heads and faces, also a mark of

◁◁ Genesis 3: 7

◁ Genesis 9: 20-27

◁◁ Judges 5: 30

modesty. And everyone (except the poorest people) wore open leather sandals on their feet, which were little more than a flat sole held on by thongs across the instep and between the toes.

Most of the evidence for clothing comes from paintings, mosaics, statues and bas-reliefs, because woollen and linen material does not last for

'People throughout Bible times would have worn some kind of tunic'. This Assyrian relief of the 7th century BC shows Ashurbanipal on his chariot. The men are wearing long or short decorated tunics.

hundreds of years. There was one remarkable find, however, in the 1960s at Masada, the last Jewish fortress to be taken by the Roman invaders in the year AD 73.

Pieces of cloth which had once been bags and tunics were found in the casemate walls, and are the earliest textiles yet recovered from the Roman period. A few pieces of the woven woollen fabric suggest that some of the garments were exquisite rather than plain and merely functional. There were leather sandals there, too, which look almost modern in style.

One of the most amazing finds was hair still attached to a young woman's scalp. It was plaited, although as no head-dress has been found at Masada it is uncertain whether the women all wore their hair in plaits or whether they also followed the usual practice of wearing a veil.

Some palettes of eye paint, bronze eye-shadow sticks, baked-clay perfume phials, bronze mirrors and wooden combs were also found at Masada. Cosmetics are not a modern invention, and even the strict Jews at Masada clearly allowed their women to wear make-up.

A few fragments of clothing, dating from about 800 BC, have also been discovered at a desert site south of Beer-sheba. More have been found from the fourth century BC in a cave near Jericho, and others in the caves around the Dead Sea dating, like the Masada finds, from the first century AD.

CLOTHING IN OLD TESTAMENT TIMES

The best illustration of clothing in patriarchal times is found in a remarkable wall painting in the tomb of a noble, Khnum-hotep III, at Beni-Hasan on the Nile in Egypt. It dates from about 1890 BC. In one scene, a Semite is shown leading a group of thirty-seven Asiatics who came from Shutu, in Sinai or southern Palestine.

Men and women are all wearing tunics made of strips of cloth woven in brightly coloured patterns. The tunics are draped over one shoulder leaving the other bare, rather like the Roman toga much later. Women's tunics reached to the ankle, men's to the knee; some of the men and the one child in the group wore skirts from waist to knee. The men had sandals on their feet, and the women low boots. None wore head coverings.

Other pictures in the same set of wall paintings show Eygptian craftsmen at work. Some wore the short skirts, others the long tunic, but these clothes were not coloured; they were made of a white or off-white material like linen.

In tombs of the Eighteenth Dynasty period (c.1550-1300 BC) at Thebes there are paintings of people from the Syrian region. Their clothes vary from a fairly short loin cloth to an ankle-length tunic with sleeves. The off-white material was decorated with a few red and blue lines along the edges and down the front. Some of the long tunics seem to have had a sari-like band wrapped round the lower part. One long tunic shown in the tombs seems to have been a long undergarment which reached in folds to the ankles; a shoulder cape is worn over it.

The Bible does not describe the dress of its early characters in any detail. Abraham and his descendants probably wore a simple loin cloth made from wool, linen or even animal skin when working under the hot sun in the fields. At cooler times, or indoors, they would wear a longer tunic.

Joseph was given a special coat by his father Isaac but the usual translation 'coat of many colours', or even 'coat with sleeves', is simply guesswork. A similar word is used in 2 Samuel of a garment worn by the daughters of

◁Genesis 37: 3

◁2 Samuel 13: 18f.

7

kings, and inventories of clothes found on Babylonian lists suggest it was a richly embroidered tunic, clearly expensive and attractive.

When Joseph became assistant to the king of Egypt, he was dressed in 'robes of fine linen', and had a gold neck chain and signet ring. When he met his brothers again, he gave them each a new set of clothes, but they are not described. Indeed, it is often the special clothes which are mentioned in the biblical narrative, and not the ordinary ones. Samson offered thirty party garments and thirty linen ones (presumably for everyday wear) to anyone who could answer his riddle.

Different styles of women's clothing showed the wearer's status. Judah's daughter-in-law, Tamar, seduced him by changing her widow's garments and putting on those of a prostitute. Another Tamar, during the time of the Kings, wore 'a richly ornamented robe' as a sign of being a virgin

Genesis 41: 42 ▷
Genesis 45: 22 ▷

Isaiah 3: 18-23 ▷▷

Judges 14: 12f. ▷

Genesis 38: 13-15▷

2 Samuel 13: 18-19 ▷

Painting from the tomb of Khnum-hotep III at Beni-Hasan, as described on the previous page. The scene is reminiscent of the visit to Egypt of Jacob's sons (see Genesis 43: 11).

daughter of King David. After she had been raped by her half-brother Amnon, she tore it and went about as if she was mourning.

Isaiah describes – and denounces – the finery of the rich women in his day which was in marked contrast to the dress of poorer people. His list consists almost entirely of adornments which went far beyond the wearers' basic needs: 'the bangles and headbands and crescent necklaces, the ear-rings and bracelets and veils, the head-dresses and ankle chains and sashes, the perfume bottles and charms, the signet rings and nose rings, the fine robes and the capes and cloaks, the purses and mirrors, and the linen garments and tiaras and shawls.'

His description of the wearers was graphic. 'The women of Zion are haughty, walking along with outstretched necks, flirting with their eyes, tripping along with mincing steps, with ornaments jingling on their ankles.' There were clearly people in his generation, as in every other, who were more concerned with drawing attention to themselves than with doing God's will.

Some wall-sculptures from Assyria provide important evidence of what clothes looked like in the latter periods of the Old Testament. Reliefs left by three Assyrian rulers, Shalmaneser III (859-825 BC), Sargon II (721-705 BC) and Sennacherib (704-681 BC) show Israelites of that time mostly wearing the traditional long tunic.

◁◁ Isaiah 3: 16-17

'Robes of fine linen' were worthy of note in ancient times. Here Hunefer and his wife Nasha demonstrate the dramatic appearance of fine linen.
From the Papyrus of Hunefer, Book of the Dead (about 1310 BC).

7

Shalmaneser's Black Obelisk shows Jehu, King of Israel, or his representative kneeling in obeisance before the Assyrian ruler. Behind him is a row of Israelites carrying 'tribute' or gifts and taxes, and they are wearing long tunics with embroidered fringes at the bottom. They seem to have a second, sleeved garment thrown over the tunic, open at the side and embroidered down the edges of the split.

One of the best portrayals of everyday Jewish dress was found on the Sennacherib sculpture which depicted the Assyrian king's defeat of Lachish. The surrendering people

Even more spectacular clothes, worn here by Tutankhamun and his wife, depicted on the Golden Throne (about 1340 BC).

stand or kneel before him, and they wear ankle-length tunics. The women in the group also wear a long cape which covers their heads and reaches to their ankles. None seem to wear girdles or sandals.

There are references, however, to girdles in the Bible, and men and women must have needed a belt to tuck their tunics in or to prevent the tunics from billowing when they were working, or walking in rough, open countryside. Short skirt-like tunics presumably needed some waist support in days long before elastic was invented. Elijah had a leather girdle round his hair-cloth garment, for example, and Jonathan gave David a belt which may have held some kind of scabbard for his sword.

There is little further information

◁ 2 Kings 1: 8

◁ 1 Samuel 18: 4

The Sennacherib sculpture (about 700 BC), showing typical Jewish dress of the time.

7

The Israelite tribute-bearers as described on page 102, showing also their sandals and pointed caps worn for travel.

about dress in Bible lands until the coming of the Greeks. They had fewer inhibitions about nakedness than the Jews, and this led to conflict between the two races. When Jason, a high priest, co-operated with the occupying Greek forces in building a gymnasium near Jerusalem, he was called 'that ungodly wretch'. There, Greek games could be played by Jewish boys who wore, like all Greek athletes, little or nothing. Even some priests were known to join in the activities of the gymnasium.

Jewish boys were also required there to wear the broad-brimmed Greek hat called a *petasus*. It was associated with figures of Mercury, the presiding god of gymnasia in the Greek pantheon, and pious Jews regarded it as an idolatrous symbol. Resistance to such compromise in dress and other aspects of life was widespread, and eventually led to the Maccabean revolt.

2 Maccabees 4: ▷
12-13
(Apocrypha)

Luke 3: 11▷▷

Luke 9: 3▷▷

John 19: 23-24 ▷▷

Acts 9: 39 ▷▷

Numbers 15: 37ff. ▷▷

CLOTHING IN NEW TESTAMENT TIMES

Both men and women in first-century Palestine wore a close-fitting tunic or coat next to their skin, reaching to their ankles. When John the Baptist told people who had two tunics to give one to a person who had none, he was referring to this garment. When Jesus sent out the twelve apostles they were to take only one tunic with them. And when he was crucified, the tunic taken from him was seamless, woven from head to foot, and the soldiers threw dice to see who could have it. Dorcas, the seamstress whom Peter raised from the dead, specialized in making tunics.

Over the tunic people wore a cloak which, according to the law of Moses, had tassels (borders or fringes) attached to its four corners. When the woman who suffered from continuous bleeding came to Jesus in a crowd, it was this fringe which she touched in her desire to be healed.

Clearly the cloak was not worn all the time, but only in cooler weather, because in his advice about the 'last days' Jesus tells people working in the fields not to return home to collect their cloaks before fleeing for their lives. When Stephen, the first Christian martyr, was stoned to death, his executioners laid down their cloaks to free them for their task.

Jesus told those involved in lawsuits to surrender their cloak as well as their tunic, and implied that robbers rather naturally took the outer garment first but were not to be resisted if they wanted the tunic also. He was emphasizing that those who followed him were to have no trace of self-concern, even over the very basic elements of clothing.

Another robe-like garment, the *stole*, was a long flowing garment for special occasions, and which the scribes wore as a matter of course. It would not have been worn while doing manual tasks. This was what the father put on his returning son who had been lost, and which inhabitants of heaven wear. In both cases, the robe becomes a symbol of the new life or righteousness which the Bible says God gives to those who return to him and believe in Jesus.

People also seem to have worn belts. John the Baptist had one made of leather. They were used not only for keeping robes tidy but also as purses for money: when Jesus sent out the twelve he told them to take 'no money in your belts'.

The Pharisees were distinguishable in a crowd by their clothes. They wore the finest white linen, which was often embroidered, and the hem or edge of their garments was enlarged and often

dyed blue. They then attached long tassels to the hems to draw attention to themselves.

Hardly an item of clothing, but a religious article, was the phylactery, a leather box worn by Pharisees. Four paragraphs from the Old Testament law (Exodus 13: 1-10, 11-16;

◁Matthew 23: 5

◁◁Luke 8: 44

Roman consul wearing a tunic and toga.

◁◁Matthew 24: 18

◁◁Acts 7: 58

7

◁◁Matthew 5: 40

◁◁Luke 6: 29

◁◁Mark 12: 38

◁◁Luke 15: 22
◁◁Revelation 7: 14;
22: 14

◁◁Matthew 3: 4

◁◁Mark 6: 8

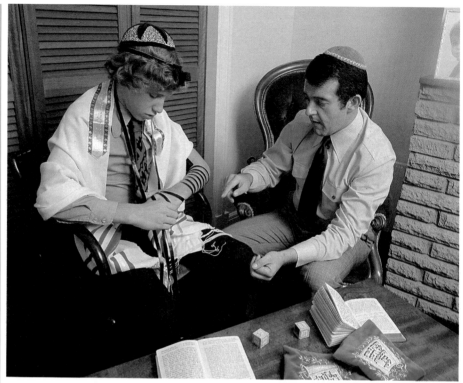

Deuteronomy 6: 4-9; 11: 13-21) were written on one piece of parchment, then again on four separate parchments. The four pieces were put into a special leather box with four

Jewish boy learning to put on the phylactery before his Bar Mitzvah. The four paragraphs from the law are fastened to his head and the single parchment is being attached by the 'tephillin' wound seven times round his left arm as described on this page.

HATS AND SHOES

There is little evidence of hats in the Bible until the time of the exile except for the formal head-dress of the priests. By then, Ezekiel is told not to remove his turban as a normal sign of mourning, so it was presumably a normal item of dress. Women also wore this type of head-dress, according to Isaiah. Sometimes it was made from linen.

The Israelites depicted on the Black Obelisk of Shalmaneser III (859-825 BC) appear to be wearing cloth caps. The men on Sennacherib's bas-relief at Lachish in 701 BC were bare-headed, although the women had a cape which covered their heads.

In New Testament times a sort of handkerchief twisted into a turban seems to have been the normal head covering, and there were hats made of light material or felt. It was considered disrespectful to walk past people if one's head was bared; slaves covered their heads in the presence of their masters, and of course all Jews covered their heads to pray.

There are many references to shoes in both Testaments, but unfortunately for us they are generally descriptions of what was done with them rather than what they looked like. It seems probable that throughout the period open leather sandals were worn by both men and women, consisting of a leather (or occasionally wooden) sole strapped to each foot.

Moses had to take his shoes off at the burning bush because the ground was 'holy', as did Joshua when he met the angelic commander near Jericho. The relative of Ruth's husband refused to marry her and removed his shoe, which was a customary sign of confirming a transaction in those days. Isaiah walked barefoot as a symbolic act visualizing God's impending judgment.

Exodus 28: 4, 37-39▷▷

Ezekiel 24: 17 ▷

Isaiah 3: 20 ▷
Ezekiel 44: 18 ▷

Exodus 3: 5 ▷▷

Joshua 5: 15 ▷▷

Ruth 4: 7 ▷▷

Isaiah 20: 2ff.▷▷

compartments, and this was tied to the forehead by a band round the head and fastened at the nape of the neck by a knot in the shape of the Hebrew letter D (*daleth*). The single parchment was put into another box. This was strapped to the biceps of the left arm, fastened with a knot in the shape of the letter Y (*yod*), with the rest of the strap wound seven times round the arm, three times round the middle finger, and the rest wound round the palm, forming the letter SH (*shin*). The three letters made the name for God, SH-D-Y = *Shaddai*.

These were supposed to be worn (and still are) by all Jewish men aged thirteen and over when they pray. The Law was to be bound as a sign upon their hands and as 'frontlets' between their eyes, said Moses. But the Pharisees wore them all day long. It was yet another example of ostentation, an attempt to project an image of holiness and goodness to the world. Jesus called such people 'whitewashed tombs', painted on the outside but inwardly rotten. They should have known better; their own Scriptures reminded them that '"man looks at the outward appearance, but the LORD looks at the heart"'.

◁ Deuteronomy 6: 8; 11: 18

◁ Matthew 23: 27

7

◁ 1 Samuel 16: 7

FOR FURTHER READING

Bellinger, L., 'Cloth', *IDB*, 1 (New York, Abingdon, 1962), pp.650–655.

Crowfoot, G.M., 'Linen Textiles from the Cave of Ain Feshkha in the Jordan', *PEQ* (1951), pp.5–31.

Edersheim, A., *Life and Times of Jesus the Messiah* (1901) Vol. I, pp.620–627; Vol. II, pp.278f. (New ed. Pickering & Inglis, 1959).

Mare, W.G., 'Dress', *ZPEB*, 2 (Grand Rapids, Zondervan, 1975), pp.164–170.

Miller, M.S. and J.L., *Encyclopedia of Bible Life* (A. and C. Black, 1979), pp.48–55.

Myers, J.M., 'Dress and Ornaments', *IDB*, 1 (New York, Abingdon, 1962), pp.869–871.

Paul, S.M. and Dever, W.G., *Biblical Archaeology* (Jerusalem, Keter, 1973), pp.224–229.

Pritchard, James B., 'Syrians as pictured in the paintings of the Theban Tombs', *BASOR*, 122, Apr. 1951, pp.36–41.

Wit, C. de., 'Dress', *IBD*, 1 (IVP, 1980), pp.394–398.

Women drawing water from a very deep well.

SECTION III:
Food and drink

Water-supply 8

Water is taken for granted in most western countries. At the turn of a tap, fresh water gushes out, sufficient for bathing or watering the garden, pure enough to drink without first boiling it. Yet two-thirds or more of the world's population still does not have access to an adequate water-supply. Some people have to draw water by hand from muddy or polluted streams, others depend on wells or wadis (water-courses which dry up at certain times of the year). The African drought and famine during the late 1970s and 1980s revealed to the developed world just how dependent people are on regular rainfall, and how disastrous it can be when the seasonal rains fail to come.

The contrast between developed and under-developed countries – and hence between today's western world and the world of Bible times – is great. The total consumption of water in Great Britain is about 450 litres (100 gallons) per person per day. That includes industrial usage, but the consumption per household is about 180 litres (40 gallons) per day. Much of that water goes down the drain, of course, from the flushing lavatory, the washing machine and the bath or shower.

Imagine having to carry all that water home each day, like shopping, from a well or stream. Water is very heavy! Or think about the rainwater butt which some people have in their gardens to collect rain running off an outhouse roof, and imagine that is your only source of water, when rain is infrequent.

In those circumstances, most people would be very careful about how much water they used. Lavatories would be flushed less often, baths would be a luxury, and clothes would be washed in a small bowl or a nearby river. If you wanted a drink, you might be somewhat deterred by the colour and smell of the water which had been standing for some while in a rainwater butt, or by the thought that the bubbling brook was also used by sheep and cattle. And always in the back of your mind would be the knowledge that during the hot summer months from May to September – just the time when you needed most water – not a drop of rain was likely to fall from the sky.

It is small wonder, then, that water became a powerful symbol of God's blessing in Bible times. A shower of rain could transform a desert, causing little plants and flowers to spring up; an oasis was a lush green island in a dusty, brown land; a river was a source of life.

'The desert and the parched land will be glad; the wilderness will rejoice and blossom', wrote Isaiah, looking forward to the day when Israel would be saved from exile. 'Like the crocus, it will burst into bloom. ... The burning sand will become a pool, the thirsty ground bubbling springs. In the haunts where jackals once lay, grass and reeds and papyrus will grow.' A delightful prospect.

The psalmist likens his deep desire for God to the thirst of a panting animal: 'As the deer pants for streams

◁ Isaiah 35: 1,7

A dried-up wadi in the foothills near the Dead Sea. Rain transforms the watercourse into a fast-flowing river in a very short time and plants and flowers appear.

of water, so my soul pants for you, O God. My soul thirsts for God, for the living God. When can I go and meet with God?' When God does draw near and bless those who seek him, then it is as if 'he makes me lie down in green pastures, he leads me beside quiet waters, he restores my soul'.

Psalm 42: 1-2 ▷

Psalm 23: 2 ▷

In the New Testament, during the Jewish Feast of Tabernacles which at the time included a ritual libation (or 'pouring out') of water in the temple, Jesus stood up and proclaimed, '"If a man is thirsty, let him come to me and drink. Whoever believes in me, as the Scripture has said, streams of living water will flow from within him.'"' John's Gospel records an encounter between Jesus and a Samaritan woman who came to draw water from a well. To her he said, '"Everyone who drinks this water will be thirsty again, but whoever drinks the water I give him will never thirst. Indeed, the water I give him will become in him a spring of water welling up to eternal life."'

Revelation 7: 17 ▷▷

John 7: 37f. ▷

Revelation 22: 1f. ▷▷

John 4: 13-14 ▷

The fresh spiritual dynamic which he offered, he was saying, was like a perennial (constant) stream, never drying up, satisfying like a long cool drink on a hot day, and itself the source of 'eternal life'. The idea is completed in the book of Revelation, where God in heaven is seen leading his people 'to springs of living water' flowing through the new, heavenly Jerusalem. 'The river of the water of life, as clear as crystal' is seen 'flowing from the throne of God and of the Lamb', and watering the 'tree of life'.

WELLS TO TAP GROUND WATER

A family which owned a well was fortunate for two reasons. There was a ready supply of water outside the door,

8

This well at Beer-sheba, built about 12th-11th century BC, continued in use for nearly 1000 years. Curved stone slabs form the upper part, the lower being a circular shaft cut in the rock just outside the city gate. Depth 35-40 m (114 to 140 ft), diameter 2 m (6½ ft).

Woman and child with donkeys laden with water containers, travelling home from the well in early morning (Judaean desert).

Genesis 21: 25-31 ▷▷

Genesis 26: 12-22 ▷▷

Genesis 29: 2, 9 ▷▷

Exodus 2: 15 ▷▷

John 4: 12 ▷▷
Genesis 16: 7, 14 ▷

2 Peter 2: 17 ▷▷

and it was likely to be less polluted than water in a stream or storage cistern. 'Ground water', which is rainfall percolating through the rocks, tends to collect below ground. It is closest to the surface beneath wadis (intermittent streams) and in flat, low-lying areas.

No one knows for certain when people first began to dig wells, but it is interesting to notice that many late Neolithic settlements in the Near East dating from 8000 to 7000 BC seem to correspond with areas where wells have been or still are common sources of water.

The first references to wells in the Bible are in the patriarchal narratives. When Abraham's servant girl, Hagar, fled, an angel found her beside a spring in the desert. The place was called Beer Lahai Roi, 'well of the One who sees me'. The Hebrew word *beer* means 'well'; in this case it is unclear whether the water was a well dug by the

nomads of the area, or a natural spring.

Abraham clashed with Abimelech, king of Gerar, over a well the patriarch had dug at Beer-sheba but which Abimelech's servants had captured. Abraham gave the king seven ewes to seal a covenant that the well did indeed belong to him. Another dispute arose when Philistines began filling in wells Abraham had dug. Isaac, his son, camped in the valley of Gerar and re-opened them – and discovered fresh sources of water at the same time, which the Philistines promptly laid claim to.

The communal well seems to have been a natural meeting-point for people. Jacob met his future bride Rachel at one where sheep were being watered, and Moses sat down at one in Midian until the local priest invited him to join his household. Once dug, a well probably lasted for centuries; Jesus met a Samaritan woman beside a well allegedly dug by the patriarch Jacob. It could, of course, dry up, in which case it was totally useless, a fact which 2 Peter uses as a graphic description of false teachers, 'springs without water'.

CISTERNS TO STORE RAINWATER

A cistern, in biblical and archaeological terms, is a small reservoir dug in the ground to collect and store rainwater. Most cisterns were bulb-shaped with a neck wide enough for the man digging them to climb through, but obviously as narrow as possible to reduce the risk of both evaporation and contamination. Beneath the surface they were enlarged usually to a rounded bulbous shape, although they could also be quite irregular. Water was channelled into the cistern by drains from roofs, courtyards, streets and even, in some places, open areas of land. Normally, the entrance had a stone or wooden cover, partly to stop people and animals falling in.

The practice of storing water to ensure a year-round supply and to supplement the naturally-occurring surface and ground water supplies probably began before 3000 BC. In the patriarchal period (Middle Bronze Age, 1800-1550 BC) archaeologists have evidence of underground cisterns in Palestine which were waterproofed with plaster and had a capacity of 20 cu m (706 cu ft).

Most homes probably had their own cistern; although using the term metaphorically, the book of Proverbs encourages young men to 'drink water from your own cistern, running water from your own well'. King Mesha of Moab, a mid-ninth century BC contemporary of the Israelite king Ahab, recorded on the famous Moabite Stone, 'There was no cistern inside the town at Qarhoh, so I said to all the people, "Let each of you make a cistern for himself in his own house."'

Ancient cisterns are often the source of important historical information. Women who came to draw water sometimes dropped their containers into the cistern, and broken pottery

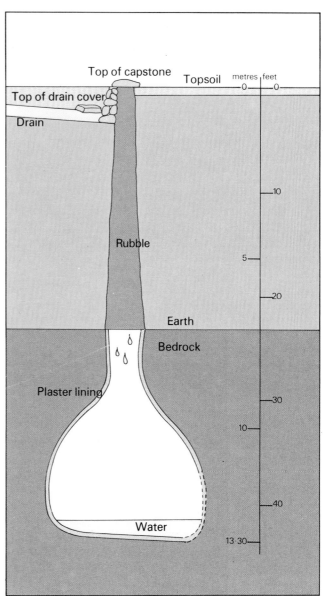

Sectional drawing of a cistern, fed by an underground drain, excavated at Tell Ta'annek. Water would be drawn, using a bucket. Rubble has since filled the neck of the cistern.

◁◁ Proverbs 5: 15

gives an idea of both the time at which the cistern was dug and the period during which it remained in use.

Numerous cisterns date from the Iron I period, the early days of Israelite settlement, especially in the highlands where there were no streams or rivers and few springs. The early Israelite settlers seem to have dug many

8

cisterns, a life-saving device in the early days of their fight for a foothold in Palestine. Cisterns were in general use in western Asia by 1500 BC and have remained in use to the present day.

There is one biblical example of a cistern being used as a dungeon. The prophet Jeremiah, forever incurring the wrath of the Jerusalem officials who accused him of 'discouraging the soldiers … as well as all the people', was thrown into a cistern in the guards' courtyard. He was lowered down on ropes – and eventually rescued in a similar way – and fortunately for him there was no water in it, only thick mud into which he sank uncomfortably.

Earlier in his life Jeremiah had spoken of the folly of people who dug cisterns which developed cracks and leaked, rather than drawing on springs of flowing water – a picture of Israel's devotion to idols rather than the living God. For once, though, he must have been glad that the guards' cistern had leaked! Joseph, centuries before, had a similar experience when his jealous brothers threw him into a dry cistern, only to pull him out again and sell him as a slave to a passing posse of Ishmaelite traders on their way to Egypt.

In addition to private cisterns, many Near Eastern towns also had communal underground reservoirs. Saul, in his search for David, 'went to the great cistern at Secu'. There were forty or so such reservoirs at Qumran near the Dead Sea, and at least one of them dated from the eighth century BC. Another was found to have been damaged during an earthquake in 31 BC.

From a much earlier period comes a hollow inside the city of Arad, which could have stored up to 2,000 cu m

Jeremiah 38: 4-13 ▷

Jeremiah 2: 13 ▷

Genesis 37: 20-28 ▷

1 Samuel 19: 22 ▷

Stairway around the shaft leading down to the pool of Gibeon, described on page 118.

(70,600 cu ft) of rainwater even in a drought year. At Ai during the period from 2700 to 2550 BC there was a reservoir in a corner of the walls to collect rainwater run-off. The pool was 3 m (almost 10 ft) deep and could hold about 1,700 cu m (60,540 cu ft) of water. The pool was walled on three sides and was paved with slabs of stone sealed with clay to reduce water loss due to seepage.

TUNNELS AND CHANNELS TO REACH DISTANT WATER

If a settlement, especially one on a hill, had no natural water-supply, and little likelihood of sufficient rainfall to keep its inhabitants and their animals alive and flourishing, water had to be channelled into it from an outside source. Some remarkable engineering projects, involving tunnels and shafts cut through the rock beneath towns, enabled some places to enjoy a good supply of fresh water usually undetected by invading or encircling attackers who hoped to force their inhabitants into premature submission through hunger and thirst.

In Megiddo in the ninth century BC, for example, a vertical shaft was sunk 34 m (115 ft) deep. The upper part cut through the accumulated debris of centuries of occupation, and was lined with masonry so that it would not collapse. The lower part cut through solid rock and ended in a sloping stairway. From the foot of this shaft a horizontal gallery ran for 60 m (200 ft) to a spring which lay in a valley outside the city wall. A wall prevented people from damming the spring outside. The alignment of the gallery is remarkably accurate and reveals considerable surveying skill. The enormous task of digging the shaft and gallery by hand with primitive hammers and axes, and then hauling all the rubble to the

8

surface in baskets hanging from ropes, must have taken large gangs of workers a long time to complete.

A century before, King Solomon had built a passage through the town's casemate wall and continued it to a point above the spring, where stairs led down to the water. He covered this outside pathway and stairs with a timber and earth roof, giving some protection to the people of Megiddo as they clambered down each day for their water.

The inhabitants of Hazor in the patriarchal age were already using large underground cisterns waterproofed with lime plaster, and during the period from 1600 to 1400 BC they built a large underground reservoir with a capacity of 110 cu m (4,000 cu ft). During the ninth century they began a much more ambitious project to tap the water-table below the mound of the lower city which was by then disused.

First, they sank a shaft 29 m (95 ft) below the surface, encircled by five flights of steps. From its foot a sloping tunnel led a further 19 m (65 ft) down to the water-table, ending up 37 m (125 ft) below street level. Even today excavators find themselves waist-deep in water at the bottom of the tunnel. The lower steps had been cut in very hard basalt.

2 Samuel 2: 13-17▷ At Gibeon, in David's time, there was a well-known pool where his twelve young champions met in contest with those of Ishbosheth, Saul's son. During the last century, visitors to the site noticed a large depression in the ground, 18 m (60 ft) across and 2 m (8 ft) deep, which caught the overflow from a nearby spring. This proved to be a reservoir dating from Roman times, but a more important discovery was made by J.B. Pritchard during the 1950s, who also found jar handles inscribed with the name 'Gibeon', confirming the identity of the site.

He discovered that the city had two separate water systems, both of which constituted major engineering achievements. The first was a deep cylindrical reservoir 11 m (37 ft) in diameter and almost as deep with near-vertical sides. Over 3,000 tonnes of limestone rock would have been carved out by hand to make this reservoir in the tenth century BC, and it is reckoned to be the actual pool of Gibeon known to David.
It filled with rainwater during the wet season, and people reached it by going down a spiral staircase guarded by a low balustrade and cut into the rock.

Another section was added at a later time by burrowing a narrow slanting tunnel for 14 m (45 ft) into the hillside to reach the water-table some 24 m (80 ft) below street level. At the foot of this tunnel was a kidney-shaped chamber 7 m x 3.5 m (22 ft x 11 ft), with daylight coming in through two vertical shafts.

This first system clearly proved inadequate for the expanding population of Gibeon, and a second one was built only 3 m (10 ft) away, probably during the ninth century BC. It had a long (43m/146 ft) stepped tunnel cut beneath the wall from inside the city to a water-chamber outside. This cave-like chamber also had an entrance from the hillside, which was presumably blocked if the city came under siege. From the chamber there was a horizontal zig-zag tunnel following the natural cleavages in the bedrock and leading to the actual spring which was almost directly beneath the city wall.

These are not the only water systems which have been discovered in Palestine. There was an important one in Beer-sheba (described in chapter 3),

The slanting tunnel, described on this page. It had ninety-three steps.

8

WATER FOR JERUSALEM

The problem for townspeople in Bible times was that if they wanted to be secure, they had to build their town on a hill. But if they wanted a regular water-supply, they usually needed to build in a valley. Security was a high priority for Jerusalem, so water had to be brought into it.

When the Assyrian king, Sennacherib, surrounded Jerusalem during Hezekiah's reign (715-687 BC) he offered peace in return for submission, and said that then "'every one of you will ... drink water from his own cistern'". That may well imply that many homes in the city had their own cistern for storing rainwater.

Isaiah 36: 16 ▷

However, during Hezekiah's reign a 630 m (1,750 ft) tunnel was dug under the walls to connect the city to a spring outside it. The tunnel sloped slightly so that the water flowed gently along it in a simple gravity-feed system before it emerged at a pool in the city.

2 Kings 20: 20 ▷

It was built by tunnelling from both ends, and the famous Siloam Inscription tells of the day when the two workgangs met:

> While there were still three cubits to be cut through, [there was heard] the voice of a man calling to his fellow, for there was an overlap [or crack] in the rock on the right [and on the left]. And when the tunnel was driven through, the quarrymen hewed [the rock], each man toward his fellow, axe against axe; and the water flowed from the spring toward the reservoir for 1200 cubits, and the height of the rock above the heads of the quarrymen was 100 cubits.

2 Samuel 5: 6-8 ▷

This tunnel followed, for part of its course, an older tunnel discovered by Charles Warren in 1867. The Gihon spring threw its plenteous water-supply into the Kidron valley, so the 'pre-Israelite' or 'Jebusite' inhabitants cut a tunnel 15 m (50 ft) into the hillside to divert the water into the city. At the end of the tunnel was an underground reservoir, and a shaft about 15 m (50 ft) high rose from it. When people wanted to draw water they went down steps to another tunnel beneath the streets which connected with this vertical shaft,

down which they lowered their water jars on a rope. When David captured Jerusalem he sent his men up a water shaft to get into the city, and it may have been this one, although others are known to have existed.

By the time of the Romans Jerusalem's water-supply was overground as well as underground. A series of aqueducts was built in the time between the return of the Jews from exile in the sixth century BC and the first century AD. They brought water, again by gravity feed, from southern sources in Wadi Arrub, Wadi Biyar and 'Solomon's Pools' to the Temple Mount which lay below these. The meandering courses of these aqueducts can now be

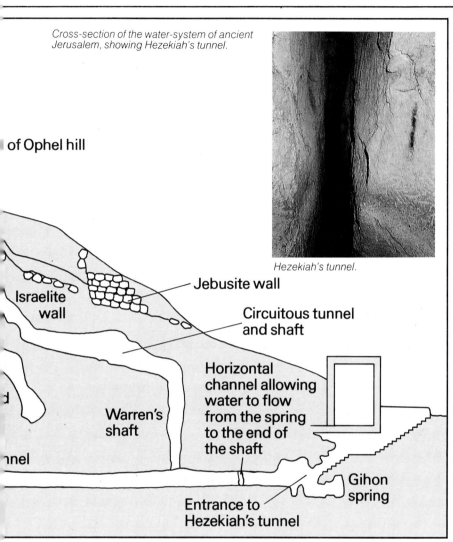

Cross-section of the water-system of ancient Jerusalem, showing Hezekiah's tunnel.

of Ophel hill

Hezekiah's tunnel.

Jebusite wall

Israelite wall

Circuitous tunnel and shaft

Horizontal channel allowing water to flow from the spring to the end of the shaft

Warren's shaft

Gihon spring

Entrance to Hezekiah's tunnel

8

traced with some accuracy, and along them archaeologists have discovered tunnels, barrel vaulting, open channels and even plastered ducts where the limestone was soft and porous.

More recent excavations in Jerusalem have revealed that the water brought by these aqueducts was stored in either open pools (*birkets*) or large underground cisterns. At least thirty-seven large cisterns have been found under the temple mount, and one huge rock-hewn cavern 13 m (43 ft) deep had a capacity of some nine million litres (two million gallons).

John's Gospel refers to the colonnaded pool of Bethesda (or Bethzatha) where Jesus healed an invalid. Excavations in the grounds of the Church of St Anne to the north-east of the temple area in 1871 revealed an ancient reservoir beneath the debris of the centuries. Subsequent excavations have revealed two rock-hewn pools standing side by side and roughly rectangular in shape. The northern one was approximately 50 m x 39 m (165 ft x 131 ft) and the southern one about 60 m x 48 m (200 ft x 160 ft). Fragments of columns, capitals and bases in the area indicate that the pools had colonnades along the four major sides and a fifth dividing the two pools. It is possible, though not beyond doubt, that these are the pools mentioned by John in his Gospel.

◁◁ John 5: 2

Two views of the Roman aqueduct at Caesarea.

d stepped tunnels at Ibleam to the
orth of modern Jenin, at Gezer, and at
ell es-Sa'idiyeh east of the Jordan and
idway between the Sea of Galilee and
e Dead Sea. It would seem likely that
ost towns of any size would have
ome kind of underground water
stem.

But there were also some
verground systems using conduits or
queducts. Isaiah writes of the 'gently
owing waters of Shiloah' which
robably refers to the quiet Jerusalem
ater-supply flowing in a conduit
om the Virgin's Fountain (the Gibeon
pring).

One of the best-known aqueducts,
hich still remains largely intact, is the
npressive high-level arched structure
Caesarea, dating from Roman times.
carried water for 9 km (over 5 miles)
om springs on the southern slopes of
Mount Carmel. The town also
ceived water from a dam across the

river Zerqa along a 5-km (3-mile)
low-level aqueduct. It is believed that
the high-level aqueduct carried
drinking and domestic water while the
other supplied irrigation water for
gardens and farms near the town.

Throughout biblical times the
remarkable ingenuity of the people of
Israel enabled them to exploit and
conserve many sources of water for
personal use, for their animals and their
crops. Even on such a waterless crag as
the rock of Masada, which stands 390 m
(1,300 ft) above the Dead Sea, King
Herod was able to excavate enormous
cisterns in the rock to preserve the
water that fell in torrential rainstorms.
Two of these had a capacity of about
2,950 cu m (140,000 cu ft) but the total
capacity of all the cisterns was ten
times as much.

◁◁ Isaiah 8: 6

8

*Vast cistern under the summit of the rock of
Masada dating from the time of Herod the
Great, 1st century* BC.

FOR FURTHER READING

Cole, D., 'How Water Tunnels Worked', *BAR*, VI (2), (1980), pp.8–29.
Mazar, A., 'The Aqueducts of Jerusalem' in Y. Yadin (ed.) *Jerusalem Revealed. Archaeology in the Holy City* (Jerusalem, Israel Exploration Society, 1975), pp.78–89.
Pritchard, J.B., *Gibeon where the Sun Stood Still* (Princeton, 1962).
Paul, S.M. and Dever, W.G., *Biblical Archaeology* (Jerusalem, Keter, 1973), pp.127–143.
Whitcomb, J.C., 'Cistern', *IBD*, 1 (IVP, 1980), pp.289–290.
Wilkinson, J., 'Ancient Jerusalem. Its Water Supply and Population', *PEQ* (1974), pp.33–51.
Wiseman, D.J., 'Siloam', *IBD*, 3 (IVP, 1980), pp.1452–1454.

Note: details of individual water systems are to be found in the separate excavation reports.

Agriculture 9

The majority of people in the west today live in urban communities. They experience the sights, sounds and smells of the countryside only rarely, perhaps on holidays or during weekend trips. In biblical times, many people who lived in towns also worked in the fields beyond the wall, and they stabled their own animals in the courtyard or rooms of their house (see page 59). Without the convenience of large stores stocking the frozen, canned and preserved produce of many lands, they were more consciously dependent upon the harvest of the soil their own lands had worked.

The land they lived in, despite its southern desert and barren central highlands, was known as 'a land flowing with milk and honey', that is, one which was rich and fertile, able to feed many people. As early as the twentieth century BC, a political refugee from Egypt named Sinuhe fled to Canaan and settled for some while with an Amorite clan. He wrote about his adoptive land: 'It was a good land, named Yaa. Figs were in it, and grapes. It had more wine than water. Plentiful was its honey; abundant its olives. Every [kind of] fruit was on its trees. Barley was there and emmer. There was no limit to any [kind of] cattle.'

Sinuhe's description is almost exactly paralleled in the biblical book of Deuteronomy. It was 'a good land… with wheat and barley, vines and fig trees, pomegranates, olive oil and honey; a land where bread will not be scarce and you will lack nothing'.

◁◁ Numbers 14: 8

◁ Deuteronomy 8: 7–9

Pomegranates.

PLOUGHS AND HOES

Ploughing with an ass, south of Jerusalem.

Modern agriculture is highly mechanized. Tractors plough several furrows at at time and sow seeds quickly. Combine harvesters cut broad swaths of corn and can reap crops in huge fields in a few hours. Throughout Bible times, however, tools were primitive and work was slow; the only 'mechanization' was a pair of oxen pulling a single-furrow plough, and they worked at walking pace.

Luke 9: 62 ▷▷

The farmer had a small range of implements. During Saul's time there seem to have been four chief ones: 'Israel went down to the Philistines to have their ploughshares, mattocks, axes and sickles sharpened.' The same passage also mentions forks, and goads (pointed implements to urge oxen to move, as cowboys use spurs on horses). Different Bible versions, however, translate the word differently, and the RSV adds the necessary footnote: 'The Hebrew of this verse is obscure.' We depend on archaeology to find ancient tools and identify them with the words used in the Bible.

1 Samuel 13: 20 ▷

The plough, the farmer's basic tool for turning the soil over and breaking up fallow ground to prepare it for sowing, had a single point and could turn only one furrow at a time. When Jesus said, '"No-one who puts his hand to the plough and looks back is fit for service in the kingdom of God"', his hearers would have realized it was a vivid and challenging word picture.

If the field was to be properly prepared each furrow had to be straight, and exactly parallel to the next one. The ploughman would have to concentrate hard and physically hold the plough straight when it hit a clump of grass or stone and so threatened to deviate from the line. One glance over his shoulder, at someone shouting in the next field, perhaps, and he would wander off course. The Christian life, Jesus was saying, demands a person's undiverted attention.

The early Israelite plough was little more than a forked stick. Usually the stem of the stick was attached to the centre of the yoke which was fixed to the shoulders of the oxen. Between the two forks there was a slanting piece of wood, reaching from the ploughman's hand to the earth. At the top of this

Stone boundary markers south of Hebron.

Senedjem and his wife harvesting grain and reeds. This Egyptian tomb painting of about 1200 BC shows clearly the sickle of the period and the method of reaping described on this page and the next.

was a cross-piece handle, and at the bottom was the plough point which cut down into the soil and turned it over. Furrows were by no means as deep as those ploughed today. Sometimes a cruder version was used, with the plough piece being tied to the shaft from the yoke. Plough points were made from stone, bronze or hardwood until about the tenth century BC when iron became common.

Isaiah 7: 25 ▷▷

Ploughs could be drawn by a single ox or mule, two oxen or two mules, and even an ox and a mule yoked together – a practice forbidden, however, in the Mosaic law. When Elijah the prophet found his successor Elisha, the latter 'was ploughing with twelve yoke of oxen, and he himself was driving the twelfth pair'. This would seem to indicate that a large field was being worked by a team of a

Deuteronomy 22: 10 ▷

1 Kings 19: 19 ▷

dozen men, just as several tractors today will work in the same field to get the job done more quickly. The oxen and plough were obviously Elisha's own, whether or not the field was, because after his call he killed the animals for a feast and roasted them on a fire made from his ploughing equipment.

To cultivate the ground further by breaking up hard lumps of soil and removing weeds between rows of plants, farmers used a hoe or mattock. Probably the hoe was broader and lighter than the mattock. Isaiah records that hoes were used to clear hillsides or to work the soil in terraces where oxen might not be able to plough.

In New Testament times the Roman mattock had two prongs behind the heavy blade. Farmers also used a combined pick and hoe, which had a rounded hoe blade and a pick projecting behind it.

Finally, the sickle was the tool with which crops were cut down. Sickles were hand held, and in early times were made from sharp flints set into a

Winnowing. This illustration is from a wall painting in the tomb of Menna at Thebes, 15th century BC.

9

haft. From the tenth century BC onwards they were normally made from iron, and the remains which have been discovered reveal that the crescent shape was similar to that of modern sickles, although the ancient tools were usually smaller than their modern western equivalents.

WHEAT AND BARLEY

Wheat and barley were grown extensively in Palestine, providing the population with bread. Wheat was the more popular and was grown on the well-drained lower areas while barley did better in drier places. Sometimes barley was grown on the poorer soil in areas where wheat was more usual; both crops were growing near Bethlehem in the time of Ruth. Barley was probably the 'standing corn' of the Philistines which Samson set alight. Spelt, an inferior kind of wheat, was also planted around the borders of wheat and barley fields.

Before the farmer could sow grain, he had to clear the ground of stones.

Even the best soil contained many stones, and these had to be picked out by hand and heaped up around the boundaries of the field. A larger pile might serve as a special landmark and the law made interfering with a landmark a serious offence. Then the ground was broken up with a plough, and the seed sown.

The seed was sown 'broadcast' from mid-November to mid-January. The farmer walked up and down the field carrying a bag of seed and scattering handfuls over the ground. Then he ploughed the field so that the seed would be covered up. Otherwise the sower followed the plough and threw the seed into the furrows. Then the oxen were driven back over the field to trample the seed into the earth.

Inevitably the sowing was uneven and some of the seed was wasted. Jesus' famous parable of the sower illustrates this. Some seed fell on the

◁ Deuteronomy 19: 14
Deuteronomy 27: 17

◁◁ Ruth 2: 23

◁◁ Judges 15: 5

◁ Matthew 13: 3–9

2 Samuel 6: 6f ▷▷

2 Samuel 24: ▷▷
18–25

Deuteronomy 25: 4 ▷▷

Isaiah 41: 15 ▷▷

Isaiah 28: 27 ▷▷

Deuteronomy 24: ▷
19–22

path beside the field to be eaten by birds; some fell on stony, unploughed patches where the roots could not feed properly; and some fell in the undergrowth or was choked by weeds which grew in the field.

The Assyrians and Babylonians developed a prototype seed-drill which was fixed on to the plough. It had a seedbox on top of a hollow tube, and seeds would drop down the tube into the furrow behind the plough point. There is no evidence that the Israelite farmers copied the idea.

Once the crop began to grow it had to be protected from birds which enjoyed eating the young shoots; no doubt the children of the family were employed as living scarecrows. The ground between rows of growing corn was cultivated with hoes to keep the soil loose and free from weeds.

By mid-April or early May the barley was ready for harvest and the wheat was cut about a month later. The whole family would stop everything else and help with the harvest, a long and tiresome process; larger landowners might hire outside labourers.

The reaper held several stalks in one hand and cut them close to the ears of corn with a sickle. The cut stalks were laid on the ground, and other people tied them in small bundles with a straw, then gathered the bundles into sheaves. The law required some corn (indeed some of all crops) to be left in the fields for the widows, orphans and strangers who had no land to harvest. The fruit of the earth was to be shared fairly. Once the cut corn had fully dried in the sun (rain at harvest time was a major disaster) it was taken to the threshing-floor where the grain kernels could be separated from the stalks and husks.

The threshing-floor was a flat area of land or a large rocky surface, chosen because it would catch the breeze.

Threshing-floors are often mentioned as well-known places in the Bible; for example, when David recaptured the ark of the covenant from the Philistines, the oxen pulling the cart stumbled at 'the threshing-floor of Nacon'. A man called Uzzah tried to steady the rocking ark and he died as a result. Each farmer had an area of the floor, or, if he was rich, he might have one all to himself. David bought one from Araunah.

Small quantities of grain (and more delicate crops such as dill or cummin) were beaten with rods cut from a tree. Larger quantities were threshed by allowing animals to trample over them, although oxen were not allowed to be muzzled so that they too could share in the harvest and eat while they worked. As an alternative method of threshing a bumper harvest, some farmers used a threshing-sledge, a flat board which curved upwards at the front. Sharp stones or metal fragments were set into the bottom of the board, and it was pulled round by a beast tethered to a vertical central pole. To give it extra weight, the farmer usually stood on the sledge.

The book of Isaiah has two passages which illustrate the threshing process. In one the prophet describes 'a threshing-sledge, new and sharp, with many teeth'. In the other he points out how different crops required different treatment: 'Caraway is not threshed with a sledge, nor is a cartwheel rolled over cummin; caraway is beaten out with a rod, and cummin with a stick.'

The threshing process got the grains off the stalks, but of course they were still mixed up on the floor. In the morning or evening, when there was a breeze, the farmer took a wooden fork with broad prongs, picked up a pile of chaff and grain and tossed it into the air, an operation called winnowing. The heavy grains fell into a pile and the lighter chaff was blown away to fall

9

into a separate pile on one side of the floor. The grains were then collected and stored, later to be turned into flour for baking.

Once the local people had gathered in the harvest, they usually had a party to celebrate: 'people rejoice at the harvest'. It was a momentous time: food was stored up for the months ahead and a period of back-breaking work was over. The Feast of Weeks (later known as Pentecost) celebrated the wheat harvest. The contemporary 'harvest festival' in churches has its origin in the same emotions of relief and gratitude felt by Europeans who, before the industrial revolution, lived as close to the land as did the Israelites.

A fork is used to winnow grain by fanning it into the wind from a threshing floor on a high place.

That may help to explain why Jesus and the apostles saw the climactic end to history as a harvest; once again a deeply significant event in their lives was turned into a powerful symbol of God's purposes. Jesus spoke of the kingdom of God being like a man who sowed seed, watched it grow, and then 'puts the sickle to it'. In the book of Revelation, John sees someone '"like a son of man" with a crown of gold on his head and a sharp sickle in his hand.' A voice called out, '"Take your sickle and reap, because the time to reap has come, for the harvest of the earth is ripe."'

◁◁ Isaiah 9: 3

◁ Mark 4: 26–29

◁ Revelation 14: 14–16

AGRICULTURE THROUGH THE CENTURIES

1 Kings 4: 25 ▷▷

The Bible spans a broad period of history, and over the centuries farming methods and knowledge slowly developed and changed. Agriculture was practised in Palestine long before the Israelites arrived there, and there is evidence that the inhabitants had passed from the hunting stage of human development to the cultivating stage by the Mesolithic Period which began about 10,000 BC.

1 Kings 21: 1–16 ▷▷

1 Chronicles 27: ▷▷
26–31

The twin pillars on which farming is built – cultivating crops and caring for animals – were distinguished early in the biblical narratives. Adam's son Abel 'kept flocks', while Cain 'worked the soil'. Abraham seems to have been more of a herdsman than a cultivator, although he must have obtained grain and fruit from somewhere. As a nomad, he moved round the edges of settlements with his sheep, cattle, donkeys and camels, looking for fresh pasture. Isaac his son 'planted crops in that land', however, and his grandson Joseph got himself into trouble dreaming about sheaves of wheat, with which he must have been familiar.

Genesis 4: 2 ▷

Genesis 12: 16 ▷

Genesis 26: 12 ▷

Genesis 37: 5–7 ▷

Crops and flocks must have been equally important in the emerging nation of Israel as it settled into Canaan during the time of the Judges. The Midianites regularly raided Israelite settlements 'and ruined the crops all the way to Gaza and did not spare a living thing for Israel, neither sheep nor cattle nor donkeys'. Gideon, who was to defeat Midian, had cattle, sheep, vineyards and wheat fields. Vineyards and olive groves had been taken over from the Canaanites by the invading Israelites under Joshua.

2 Chronicles 26: 10▷▷

Judges 6: 4 ▷

Judges 6: 11, 25, ▷
37;
Judges 8: 2

Under David and Solomon peace was slowly established and the people 'ate, they drank and they were happy'. New political pressures caused Solomon to impose heavy taxes, but their size indicates that agriculture was prospering. The king's daily requirements included 6.6 kilolitres (185 bushels) of fine flour and twice as much meal; ten stall-fed cattle, twenty pasture-fed cattle and a hundred sheep and goats, 'as well as deer, gazelles, roebucks and choice fowl'.

1 Kings 4: 20 ▷

Jeremiah 39: 10▷▷
Jeremiah 40: 10 ▷▷
Jeremiah 41: 8 ▷▷

1 Kings 4: 22f ▷

However, this also meant the rise of the landlord. Under Solomon each man 'lived in safety under his own vine and fig tree', but his successors began buying out smallholders and the seizure of Naboth's vineyard by the petulant King Ahab was only one example among many of compulsory purchase or outright theft of agricultural lands by unscrupulous leaders. Even in David's time there appear to have been royal estates including grain fields, vineyards, olive and sycamore groves, and pastureland. The prophets denounced landowners who swallowed up people's livelihoods and demanded huge consignments of grain to pay off mortgage debts.

Large government storehouses have been excavated in Megiddo, Hazor, Beer-sheba and Beth-shemesh, where grain, wine and olive oil were kept. This was either collected as taxes, or was surplus from royal or other large estates. Documents written on broken pottery (ostraca) found in the palace at Samaria refer to collections of wine and oil and probably date from the reign of Jeroboam II (c. 786–746 BC).

Tools improved from the time of the Kings, and iron ploughs, sickles and hoes replaced older implements made from bronze. People moved to the fringes of arable land and brought new areas under the plough. King Uzziah, who 'loved the soil', 'built towers in the desert and dug many cisterns, because he had much livestock in the foothills, and in the plain'. Fortresses with associated farming settlements have been found in the central Negeb dating from the ninth to the seventh centuries BC, and the later (second and third centuries BC) Nabataeans dammed and distributed water along otherwise waterless hill slopes.

After the fall of Jerusalem and the deportation of 587 BC, the ruling Babylonians gave vineyards and fields to 'some of the poor people, who owned nothing'. Their crops yielded wine, summer fruit and oil, and they built up stores of wheat, barley, oil and honey. In later centuries Persian and Greek armies traversed the land; since they needed large and local food supplies, agriculture in Palestine was presumably flourishing again by then.

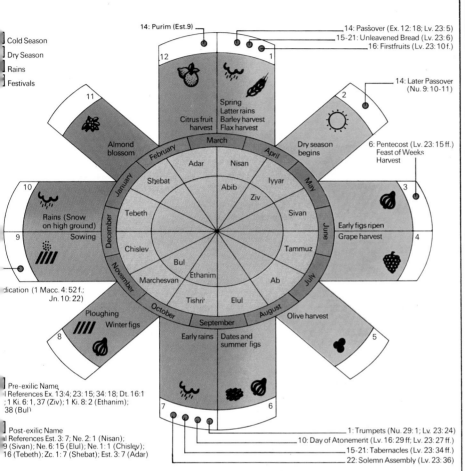

14: Purim (Est. 9)
14: Passover (Ex. 12: 18; Lv. 23: 5)
15-21: Unleavened Bread (Lv. 23: 6)
16: Firstfruits (Lv. 23: 10 f.)
14: Later Passover (Nu. 9: 10-11)
6: Pentecost (Lv. 23: 15 ff.) Feast of Weeks Harvest

Cold Season
Dry Season
Rains
Festivals

Spring
Latter rains
Citrus fruit
harvest
Barley harvest
Flax harvest

Dry season
begins

Almond
blossom

Adar   Nisan
Shebat   Iyyar
Abib
Ziv
Tebeth   Sivan
Early figs ripen
Grape harvest

Rains (Snow
on high ground)
Sowing

Chislev   Tammuz
Bul
Marchesvan   Ethanim
Ab

...dication (1 Macc. 4: 52 f.; Jn. 10: 22)

Tishri   Elul

Ploughing
Winter figs

Early rains   Dates and
summer figs

Olive harvest

Pre-exilic Name
References Ex. 13:4; 23: 15; 34: 18; Dt. 16:1
; 1 Ki. 6: 1, 37 (Ziv); 1 Ki. 8: 2 (Ethanim);
38 (Bul)

Post-exilic Name
References Est. 3: 7; Ne. 2: 1 (Nisan);
9 (Sivan); Ne. 6: 15 (Elul); Ne. 1: 1 (Chislev);
16 (Tebeth); Zc. 1: 7 (Shebat); Est. 3: 7 (Adar)

1: Trumpets (Nu. 29: 1; Lv. 23: 24)
10: Day of Atonement (Lv. 16: 29 ff; Lv. 23: 27 ff.)
15-21: Tabernacles (Lv. 23: 34 ff.)
22: Solemn Assembly (Lv. 23: 36)

The Hebrew calendar, based on the agricultural and religious year, showing seasons and festivals with their modern equivalents.

In the New Testament period, rice began to be grown in wet areas such as the Plains of Esdraelon. Chickens had made an appearance, too, according to Jesus, and his reference to Peter's denial 'before the cock crows' suggests they were common. The few Old Testament references to eggs seem to be those of non-domestic birds which were found, rather than farmed, but there are two stamp seals from *c.* 600 BC which depict cocks, both bearing Hebrew names.

Landowning seems to have continued on a large scale. Jesus told stories about a rich fool with huge barns, landowners with tenant farmers, and labourers who worked a day at a time for farmers who needed them. A bigger change came through the expansion of trade. It had not been lacking in Old Testament times, but the new Roman roads opened up western Asia, Anatolia and Europe to each other. Roman aqueducts also opened up new agricultural areas.

Both improved trade and water–supplies encouraged the development of huge wheat fields in northern Palestine, lower Galilee, Bashan east of Jordan, and in Lebanon, to feed the demands of the expanding Roman Empire. The area east of Galilee, the Hauran of southern Syria (including the ancient Bashan) became one of the great granaries of the Empire. It is not surprising, then, that in his parable of the debtors Jesus depicted one man owing 35 kilolitres (1,000 bushels) of wheat.

◁◁ Matthew 23: 37

◁◁ Matthew 26: 34

◁◁ *E.g.* Deuteronomy 22: 6; Isaiah 10: 14

◁◁ Luke 12: 6–21;

◁◁ Matthew 21: 33–41;

◁◁ Matthew 20: 1–7

◁ Luke 16: 7

9

GRAPES AND OLIVES

After the grain harvest, the weeks between mid–June and mid–August were used for tending the vineyards. Grape-vines grow easily throughout Palestine, especially on the sunny hillsides. Once planted they need minimal care except for soil cultivation and branch pruning in spring, after the plant has blossomed and again after harvest.

Isaiah described it thus: 'Before the harvest, when the blossom is gone and the flower becomes a ripening grape, he will cut off the shoots with pruning knives, and cut down and take away the spreading branches.' The intention was to channel all the plant's energy into producing fruit rather than wood, an idea which Jesus used vividly when describing God's habit of 'pruning' his followers so that they will be more useful to him. The pruning hook used by Israelite farmers had a small, sharp, curved blade; it could quite easily be beaten into a spear – and, therefore, a spear could become a pruning hook, as in Isaiah's vision of peace.

The grapes ripened towards the end of July and were harvested in August and September. Thieves, birds and animals all liked a plump ripe grape, and farmers had to build 'watchtowers' – small shelters – in their vineyards where they lived and slept like guards during the harvest period. (They did the same in vegetable gardens, too, and the practice continues to this day in the Near East.)

The farmer usually harvested his own grapes, although large landowners would sub-let their vineyards to tenants for a 'rent' of a share in the harvest, as one of Jesus' parables revealed. The gathered grapes were eaten fresh, dried into raisins, or turned into wine.

Vineyard on a hillside near Hebron.

Olive trees were often grown on the higher slopes above the vineyards in the western part of Palestine. Olives grow in shallow soil and are able to withstand long periods of drought, but they do not thrive in the long cold periods which can occur in southern Judah. They require very little attention except for hoeing the soil.

The olive harvest was the last major event of the agricultural year. It could be done in a more leisurely way than the grain or grape harvest because the fruit ripened slowly, and it often lasted from mid–September until after the start of the rains in late October. Most olives were picked by hand although those on the higher branches would be shaken or beaten down. Although they are slow to mature, olive trees can live for hundreds of years, and today old gnarled trees are sometimes uprooted and planted in new groves. A good tree can produce 45 to 68 litres (10 to 15 gallons) of oil each year.

◁◁ Isaiah 18: 5

9

◁◁ John 15: 1f

FRUIT, FLAX AND VEGETABLES

◁◁ Isaiah 2: 4

A number of fruits associated with the Near East today do not seem to have been known there even in New Testament times. Apricots were introduced to the west from China no earlier than the first century BC, and citrus fruit (oranges, lemons and grapefruit), which now thrive in Israel, together with apples, tomatoes and squash, arrived after the apostolic age, probably with the Arabs who moved into the region.

◁◁ Isaiah 1: 8; Isaiah 5: 2

While wheat, grapes and olives seem to have been the chief crops in Bible times (they are often named together), there were other fruits and some vegetables to give variety to people's diets. Figs provided fruit in the early summer, and as they were seen as a sign that summer was coming, Jesus

◁◁ Matthew 21: 33–46

used them as a symbol of the approach of God's judgment. The shady fig tree was seen as a symbol of security, too: 'every man will sit under his own vine and under his own fig-tree, and no-one will make them afraid.'

Related to the fig was the sycamore★, a sturdy tree reaching between 9 and 12 m (30 and 40 ft) in height. It grows in the lowlands of Palestine and also in Egypt, and its fruit, with yellow and black spots, grows directly on the trunk and branches of the tree. The prophet Amos 'took care of sycamore fig-trees', which means he cut the top off each fig to make sure the ripening fruit was clean and free from insects. It was this kind of tree which Zacchaeus, the diminutive tax collector, climbed in order to see Jesus.

Another harbinger of summer was the almond tree, which burst into pink and white blossoms while all other trees were bare. That is why the book of Jeremiah opens with a play on words. The prophet sees an almond tree (*shāqēd*), and God says, 'I am watching' (*shôqēd*) ('I am early on the watch', NEB), meaning he is getting ready to act.

Pomegranates were gathered, too. Their shape was carved in the temple decorations, and the Song of Solomon mentions a wine made from their juice. Their large numbers of separate seeds made them symbolic of fertility.

There are many biblical references to the palm tree, suggesting that dates grew in some parts of Palestine, although there are no references to dates as such. The palm grew well in the Jordan valley north of the Dead Sea and was mentioned in Jewish writings

★ The correct spelling is sycomore, although most Bible versions have an *a* instead of an *o*, which may cause confusion with the leafy and rapid growing European sycamore tree which does not produce edible fruit.

Olive grove in the Hinnom valley, Jerusalem.

like the Mishna and Talmud, and referred to by the Roman writer Pliny and the Jewish historian Josephus. The palm often gave its name *tāmār* to the place where it grew, *e.g.* Tamar and Hazezon Tamar. Jericho was also known as 'the city of palms'.

Flax, although not a food crop, was cultivated and was important because it was used to make linen cloth and rope. It was harvested a month before barley. It was cut off with a hoe at ground level, then laid out to dry in the sun. Joshua's spies hid from guards under stalks of flax laid out to dry on the flat roof of Rahab's house in Jericho.

There are a number of vegetables mentioned in passing in the Bible. These include beans, chick peas and lentils, all important sources of protein. For flavouring, the people grew onions, leeks, garlic and cucumber, and spices such as dill, cummin and mint.

SHEEP AND SHEPHERDS

From the arrival in Egypt of Joseph's family, whom he described as shepherds, to the angelic announcement of the birth of Jesus to the men watching their flocks outside Bethlehem, raising and caring for sheep was a vital part of Israelite economy.

The sheep were a fat-tailed variety and provided milk as well as meat and wool. They were hardy and could live outdoors all the year round. Although they required water every day, they could live off sparse grass if necessary. There were in fact good pasture lands in the central highlands and on the Transjordan plateaux.

In the early days of Israel, almost every family owned a few sheep and therefore someone in the family was a shepherd. Jacob's future wife, Rachel,

◁◁ Mark 13: 28f

◁◁ Micah 4: 4
◁◁ Ezekiel 47: 18–19
    Genesis 14: 7
  ◁ 2 Chronicles 28: 15

◁◁ Amos 7: 14

◁ Joshua 2: 6

◁◁ Luke 19: 4

9

◁◁ 1 Kings 7: 18

◁◁ Song 8: 2

◁ Genesis 29: 6–10

Above: shepherd on a donkey leading his flock of sheep in Syria. This clearly illustrates the ancient custom of going before, rather than driving the sheep.

Right: Arab woman watching over her goats between Bethlehem and Hebron.

had the job of watering the sheep, and the future king, David, the youngest of eight brothers, had the task of watching the sheep. Each animal represented part of a person's wealth in the days before riches were measured in terms of figures on a bank statement. A lost sheep meant lost wool and milk and meat; a lost ewe meant fewer lambs next year. When Jesus told a parable about a lost sheep, meaning a person who had wandered from God, he was talking about a disaster, not a mishap.

The shepherd (or in the case of large flocks, the head-shepherd) had to find adequate pasture and water for the flock, and this often involved seasonal migrations. He also needed to know the location of caves, where he could shelter from storms, cold nights and wild animals, and of wadis and rocks where he could find shade on hot days. He carried a sling and a wooden club to fend off lions, bears, wolves, jackals and hyenas which would attack the flock; and a staff to prod the sheep as they moved on or rescue them from crevasses.

When the flock was far from home the shepherd set up a camp near a water source. A fire provided warmth and

1 Samuel 16: 11 ▷

Luke 15: 3–7 ▷

9

WHERE FARMING TOOK PLACE

Not all areas of Palestine were equally suited to all crops and livestock. Wheat flourished best on the well-drained areas of the valley of Jezreel, in lower Samaria and Galilee, and in much of Transjordan. Barley grew in the drier areas of the south and east, and in the Philistine territory in the south-west.

Olives require the warm Mediterranean climate to survive, and they grew abundantly in the fertile valleys of Ephraim, on the western slopes of Gilead, and in parts of Judah. Vines are more hardy, and grew in Judah and Galilee.

discouraged wild animals. A simple pen or 'sheepfold' built from stones lying around would have kept the animals together at night. People who owned only a couple of sheep would send their animals out each morning under the care of a village shepherd, who led them to pasture beyond the cultivated fields and returned them at night to their owners' houses.

John 10: 25–33 ▷▷

The shepherd developed a close relationship with his sheep, and had a distinctive call which the sheep could recognize. At a watering place several flocks might mingle together, but each shepherd could extract his own sheep from the rest simply by calling them. Unlike most modern shepherds, he would lead the sheep from in front rather than drive them from behind.

Matthew 25: 32f ▷▷

Jesus took up this everyday image and applied it to himself. He was the good shepherd, he said, who knew all his people by name, so that when he called, they followed. He protected them from attack, and was prepared to die so that they could live. It was a familiar symbol to the Jew, who already knew that:

John 10: 1–18 ▷

E.g. Ezekiel 34: 17 ▷▷

The LORD is my shepherd,
   I shall lack nothing.
He makes me lie down
   in green pastures,
he leads me beside
   quiet waters,
   he restores my soul. ...
I will fear no evil,
   for you are with me;
your rod and staff,
   they comfort me.

Proverbs 27: 23, 27 ▷▷

Psalm 23: 1–4 ▷

In applying the image to himself, Jesus was virtually claiming equality with God, something he stated explicitly shortly afterwards in John's narrative, as he returned again to the shepherd picture.

GOATS AND OXEN

Goats played a more important role in the Palestinian economy than cattle. They often mingled with, and sometimes had to be separated from, the sheep (giving Jesus a natural picture of the division of mankind at the day of judgment). Goats and sheep were more mobile and able to live on poorer grass than cattle.

Palestinian goats had long ears and long curved horns. They could be black, black and white or brown and white. When they were kept with sheep they tended to be the dominant animals of the group, which may explain why the Old Testament sometimes describes political leaders as goats.

Goats provided milk, meat, hair and skins for their owners. The book of Proverbs urges its readers to 'give careful attention to your herds' so that 'you will have plenty of goats' milk to feed you and your family and to nourish your servant girls'. A good nanny-goat would yield 3.5 litres (6 pints) of milk a day. Goats' hair was coarse and used for making rough cloth and for stuffing pillows. When a goat's skin was scraped, cleaned and had its hair removed, it could be used as a container for water, milk or wine.

THE FARMER'S YEAR

A calendar of the farmer's year was found at Gezer in 1908. It is inscribed in old Hebrew script on a rectangular block of soft limestone small enough to be held in the hand, and is generally reckoned to be a schoolboy's writing exercise from the tenth century BC. It was probably a well-known verse like the English 'Thirty days hath September ...'

Months of vintage and oil harvest;
Months of sowing;
Months of spring pasture;
Month of flax pulling;
Month of barley harvest;
Month of wheat harvest and measuring;
Months of pruning;
Month of summer fruit.

Some translators take the word 'months' here to be 'two months' which, since it occurs four times, accounts for eight months. The other four make up the twelve months. This calendar follows the civil year although the true agricultural year began with the planting or sowing season (second on the list).

The winter rains came in late October, lasting until mid-January. That was the time for ploughing and sowing. Wheat and barley were planted in late October or early November and other grains (sesame, millet and lentils) were sown, along with vegetables like cucumbers, chick peas, onions, leeks and garlic, from mid-January to mid-March.

Flax was harvested in March-April, barley in April-May and wheat in May-June. Then came the pruning season for vines until mid-August. Grapes were gathered in August and September, followed by olives until mid-November. The hot dry summer lasted, theoretically, from June to August.

9

The Gezer calendar, listing the agricultural tasks for the year. It measures 11 cm (just over 4 in) high.

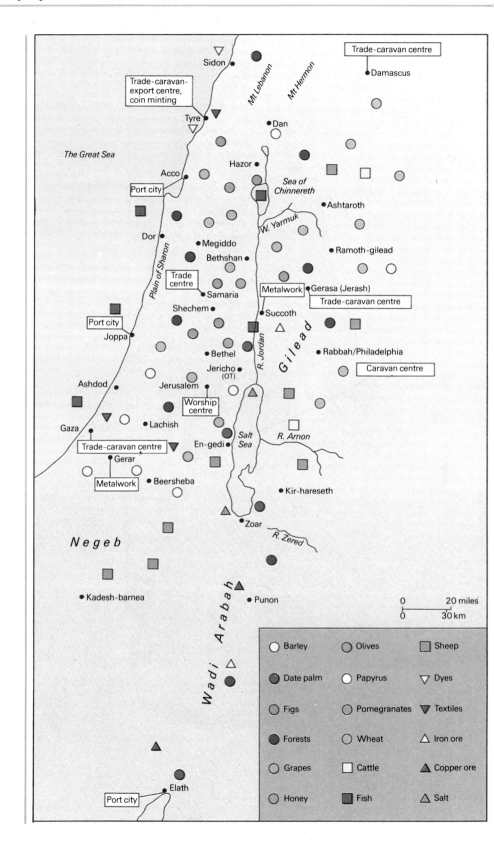

The Great Sea

Trade-caravan centre — Damascus

Trade-caravan-export centre, coin minting — Tyre

Sidon

Mt Lebanon Mt Hermon

Dan

Hazor Sea of Chinnereth

Ashtaroth

Acco
Port city

Dor

W. Yarmuk

Megiddo
Bethshan

Ramoth-gilead

Trade centre
Samaria

Metalwork — Gerasa (Jerash)
Trade-caravan centre

Shechem Succoth

Gilead

Port city
Joppa

R. Jordan

Bethel

Rabbah/Philadelphia

Jericho (OT)

Caravan centre

Ashdod

Jerusalem

Worship centre

Gaza Lachish

En-gedi Salt Sea R. Arnon

Trade-caravan centre
Gerar

Metalwork Beersheba

Kir-hareseth

Negeb

Zoar R. Zered

Kadesh-barnea Punon

0   20 miles
0   30 km

Wadi Arabah

Elath
Port city

○ Barley	◐ Olives	▢ Sheep
● Date palm	○ Papyrus	▽ Dyes
○ Figs	○ Pomegranates	▼ Textiles
● Forests	○ Wheat	△ Iron ore
○ Grapes	□ Cattle	▲ Copper ore
○ Honey	▨ Fish	△ Salt

Some goat herds were quite large: Jacob had at least 220 animals and Nabal 1,000. Goats are destructive animals, however, and have been largely responsible for the deforestation of parts of Palestine and the Levant area, destroying even the young cedars of Lebanon by nibbling the shoots.

Oxen also provided milk and meat, but they were more work animals than sources of food. They pulled ploughs and carts even as early as the exodus, when they helped transport Israel through the desert. Their need of good pasture and water made them generally unsuitable for nomadic groups, however, although Abraham had herds of cattle, as he stayed in some places for long periods. Job is said to have had 500 yoke (pairs) of oxen before calamity struck him, and 1,000 pairs afterwards. They are unlikely to have been nearly so numerous as the more versatile goats.

DROUGHTS AND DISASTERS

The land 'flowing with milk and honey' was not a perfect place, a new Eden where everything in the garden was lovely. Farmers in Palestine, like those the world over, faced their share of pests and natural disasters which hindered their work and threatened their livelihood.

The book of Genesis suggests that the universal battle against nature arose ultimately because people turned their backs on God:

Cursed is the ground because of you; through painful toil you will eat of it all the days of your life. It will produce thorns and thistles for you,

and you will eat the plants of the field. By the sweat of your brow you will eat your food until you return to the ground, since from it you were taken...

Paul in the New Testament takes up the theme and writes that

the creation was subjected to frustration ... in hope that the creation itself will be liberated from its bondage to decay and brought into the glorious freedom of the children of God.

The Palestinian farmer fought the elements on three fronts: the weather, disease and pests. The weather was a constant problem. There was a drought every year from June to August (sometimes even from May to September), but this was a seasonal pattern the farmer learned to live with. More problems arose when the first winter rains came early, followed by another period of drought. The rain caused seeds in the ground to germinate, but the drought killed off the young shoots.

Almost as bad was the delay of the winter rains until early December. In the steppe lands of the Negeb and parts of the southern Jordan valley the top soil had been baked dry for months and all the vegetation had been burned off by the sun. The later the rains came, the more soil erosion took place; there were no plant roots to hold the earth together.

Long-term droughts are recorded in the Bible. One predicted by Elijah the prophet lasted for three years. Such droughts were often regarded as signs of God's judgment on the people; God said through Amos,

'I also withheld rain from you when the harvest was still three months away.

◁◁ Genesis 32: 14;

◁◁ 1 Samuel 25: 2

◁ Romans 8: 20f

◁◁ Numbers 7: 3, 6–8

◁◁ Job 1: 3; Job 42: 12

◁ 1 Kings 17: 1

◁◁ Genesis 3: 17–19

◁ Amos 4: 7f

9

The economy of ancient Palestine.

I sent rain on one town,
　　but withheld it from another.
…
People staggered from town to town
　　for water
　　　but did not get enough to
　　　drink,
　　yet you have not returned to
　　me,'
　　　　　declares the Lord.

Jeremiah records a pathetic poem, in the form of a lament, during a drought. He writes of people who

Joel 2: 25 ▷▷

'… return with their jars unfilled;
　　dismayed and despairing,
　　they cover their heads. …
Even the doe in the field
　　deserts her newborn fawn
　　because there is no grass.
Wild donkeys stand on the
　　barren heights
　　and pant like jackals;
their eyesight fails
　　for lack of pasture.'

Jeremiah 14: 3–6 ▷

Other weather problems included the hot sirocco or khamsin winds which desiccated (or blighted) vegetation in the spring and autumn, bringing the highest temperatures of the year. Hailstorms could destroy crops and animals. 'He destroyed their vines with hail', recalls the psalmist, 'and their sycamore-figs with sleet. He gave over their cattle to the hail, their livestock to bolts of lightning.' Floods could wash out the crops, too.

Psalm 78: 47f ▷

Joel 2: 1–11 ▷▷

One of the Israelite farmer's worst enemies was the locust. There are two groups, the 'runners' (*cursuria*) which the Israelites regarded as unclean, and the 'leapers' (*saltatoria*) which the Levitical law described as winged creatures with 'jointed legs for hopping on the ground' and thus declared 'clean' and edible; locusts and grasshoppers are still regarded as a delicacy in the East.

Amos 4: 9 ▷▷

Leviticus 11: 21 ▷

Matthew 3: 4 ▷

Locusts are migratory creatures largely wind-driven from the Arabian desert, but their migrations do not occur at fixed seasons or regular intervals; they can arrive at any time. The female lays her eggs in holes in the ground, and the wingless larvae that hatch out devour all the vegetation in their path. After a series of moults they develop wings and fly in great dark clouds, and they are equally voracious at every stage.

The Old Testament uses a variety of Hebrew names for them. The prophet Joel lists several: 'the great locust and the young locust, the other locusts and the locust swarm'. This attention to different varieties of locusts and different stages of their growth shows how much they occupied the Israelite mind. Indeed, Joel pictures the coming Day of the Lord as like a locust swarm.

Before them the land is like the
　　garden of Eden,
　　behind them, a desert waste –
　　nothing escapes them. …
They all march in line,
　　not swerving from their course.
　　　…
They climb into the houses;
　　like thieves they enter
　　　through the windows.
Before them the earth shakes,
　　the sky trembles,
the sun and moon are darkened,
　　and the stars no longer
　　shine.

Some plant diseases are recorded in the Bible, although their exact nature is uncertain. Mildew is mentioned by Amos (along with blight, the effect of the hot wind) and this was probably a fungoid disease. Some scholars identify it as *puccinia graminis*. Isaiah may have referred to the fly and maggot which trouble modern sheep when he wrote 'the worm will devour them like wool'.

The final hazard faced by farmers in Bible times was human. Raiders from neighbouring countries or conquerors from further afield would have had little respect for crops and livestock. Rural life was far from idyllic. It was hard and insecure. People lived from month to month, often not knowing whether there would be sufficient food available for everyone.

FOR FURTHER READING

Hepper, F.N., *Bible Plants at Kew* (HMSO, 1981).
Hepper, F.N., 'Trees', *IBD*, 3 (IVP, 1980), pp.1585–1593.
Jennings, G.J., 'Agriculture', *ZPEB*, 1 (Grand Rapids, Zondervan 1975), pp.71–78.
Kelso, J.L. and Hepper, F.N., 'Agriculture', *IBD*, 1 (IVP, 1980), pp.20–22.
Madeline, S. and Miller, J. Lane, *Encyclopedia of Bible Life*, rev.edn (A. and C. Black, 1979), pp.121–188.
Patch, J.A. and Armerding, C.E., 'Agriculture', *ISBE*, 1 (Grand Rapids, Eerdmans, 1979), pp.72–75.
Paul, S.M. and Dever, W.G., *Biblical Archaeology* (Jerusalem, Keter, 1973), pp.147-162.
Richardson, H.N., 'Agriculture', *IDB*, 1 (New York, Abingdon, 1962), pp.56–60.
Walker, W., *All the Plants of the Bible* (New York, Harper, 1957).
Zohary, M., *Plants of the Bible* (Cambridge UP, 1982).

9

An Assyrian fishing in a pond with a line. His catch is in a basket on his back. This relief from Sennacherib's palace at Nineveh dates from 704-681 BC.

Food and its preparation

10

During the whole period of Bible history the main meal of a typical family would have been in the evening. Preparing meals took a long time; so while the men worked in the fields or workshops, the women would spend at least part of the day preparing food – and that might well include milking goats and sheep as well as cleaning vegetables and baking bread.

Almost all the food eaten was prepared at home, bread included, and cooked over a wood fire. There were no convenience foods in freezers or cans, no ready-cooked products that needed only heating up. There were no microwave ovens or pressure cookers for speedy cooking, no take-away restaurants for those evenings when even opening a can seems too much effort. The choice of food was much narrower than it is today. Preservation was difficult in a hot country before the age of refrigeration or canning, so exotic foods were rarely imported from other countries, and the daily meal reflected the seasonal availability of fruit and vegetables.

The average daily meal probably consisted of a variety of vegetables, boiled with herbs to give them more flavour, and bread. Meat was probably a luxury and not eaten every day; when the prodigal son came home his father killed the fatted calf for a feast. Fish, at least in the northern part of Palestine around Galilee, was a relatively common source of protein, if the feeding of the five thousand and Jesus' resurrection appearance in Galilee are anything to go by. Fish could be dried and salted for keeping.

Evening meals were probably leisurely affairs. After a hard day's work people relaxed over their food. As the night drew in and the lamps in the alcoves of the main living room were lit, there was nothing else to do except eat, talk and tell stories, sing and eventually sleep. It was too dark to read, there was no radio or television, and the local town did not boast a community centre, cinema, pub or social club where you could while away the hours.

But from the Gospel records it does seem as if people went out to meals with each other. Jesus was often invited to supper parties – he invited himself to the house of Zacchaeus the tax collector – and he ate with his friends. He told a story about a great banquet. And the reaction of one of his closest friends, Martha, when he was in her house, revealed that the bustle and tension in the kitchen when visitors come has not changed through the centuries. 'Martha was distracted by all the preparations that had to be made'; the sight of her sister Mary sitting with the men as they talked was too much for her, and she asked Jesus to tell Mary to get back to the kitchen. He seemed to think the meal could

◁◁ John 6: 9; 21: 9

◁ John 12: 2

◁ Luke 19: 5
◁ Luke 22: 14f.

◁ Luke 14: 16-24

◁ Luke 10: 38-42

◁◁ Luke 15: 23

Roman banquet scene from Pompeii. The supper parties of Mary and Martha and even of Zacchaeus would have been much more homely. Pagan customs in matters of food and drink caused problems for the early church (see page 156).

wait; "'Martha, Martha, ... you are worried and upset about many things. ... Mary has chosen what is better.'"

THE STAFF OF LIFE

Bread was clearly a vital and staple part of everyone's diet. During a famine, it was just about the last thing that the widow of Zarephath, Elijah's hostess, had left. It was the main content of the travelling picnic carried by a lad following Jesus which became the source of a meal for over 5,000 other people. But it was not stored for long. When Abraham and Sarah had unexpected visitors, Sarah took meal (flour) and oil to bake bread while they waited. (They must have waited some time for their dinner, as Abraham's servant also selected a calf from the herd, slaughtered, butchered and cooked it, so that they could have meat with their bread! This was in fact normal practice. Eating came last, after talk. The Last Supper shows this same pattern.)

Bread was so common and necessary that only nine of the thirty-nine Old Testament books do not refer to it (Esther, Song of Songs, Joel, Jonah, Micah, Nahum, Habakkuk, Zephaniah and Zechariah). It is frequently mentioned in the Gospels and the Acts of the Apostles, the historical narratives of the New Testament.

Bread was made from either wheat or barley, the latter being more commonly used by poorer people. The relative value of the two cereals is shown in the book of Revelation,

1 Kings 17: 12 ▷
John 6: 9-13 ▷

Genesis 18: 6 ▷

A Bedouin woman making unleavened bread.

10

Breadmaking in Egypt. One servant is kneading dough while the other tends the fire. This model is from Asyut and dates from about 1900 BC.

Revelation 6: 6▷

where in John's vision a day's wages bought l litre (2 pints) of wheat and 3 litres (6 pints) of barley. There are occasional references to people roasting and eating grains of wheat without making bread. David took roasted corn and bread to his brothers at the 1 Samuel 17: 17▷ battlefront, for example.

Loaves were probably round and fairly flat, much as they still are in the Near East. The dough is spread on the hot oven floor and turned over, rather than being put in a baking tin to rise into a rectangular shape as in western bakeries. The flour was usually mixed with olive oil and some form of yeast to make it rise, although at certain religious festivals including the Passover 'unleavened bread', that is, bread without yeast, was eaten.

In early Israel turning the grain into flour was, like harvesting the corn, a household activity. It probably remained so among the poorer people of New Testament times, although by then commercial mills and even bakeries were in existence. There are no references to professional millers as such in the Old Testament, but archaeological finds point to their existence.

For example, in Middle Bronze Age Jericho (during the time of the patriarchs) two-storied buildings have been found where the downstairs part was used for small industry. In one area fifty-two saddle-querns for grinding grain were found, far more than a normal household would require. Large jars were also found full of grain, probably for sale.

The saddle-quern was used for grinding by hand. It had a rectangular, slightly concave stone, usually a little thicker at one end, varying from 45 cm (18 in) to 75 cm (30 in) long and 25 cm (10 in) to 38 cm (15 in) wide which rested on the ground. The upper stone was flat on one side and elliptical on the other, and much smaller in size. It was just wide enough to be grasped by the hands. This upper stone was pushed backwards and forwards on the lower one, with the grain in between.

This kind of domestic mill was used in Palestine from Neolithic to Hellenistic times. The stone thrown by a woman from the wall of Thebez which killed king Abimelech would have been the upper stone of a saddle-quern.

A rotary quern came into use during the time of the Kings. It had two circular flat slabs each about 45 cm to 50 cm (18 to 20 in) across. The top one was pierced with a funnel-shaped hole and it rotated on a pivot fixed in the lower stone which stayed still. Grain was fed through the hole in the top stone, and the flour spilled out of the sides on to the ground.

The Israelite depended on the hand mill for his daily bread, and so the ancient law said it could not be taken as a pledge against a debt. The sound of grinding must have been familiar and regular in Israelite settlements, and its cessation was a sign of desolation and death: 'I will banish from them the sounds of joy and gladness, the voices of bride and bridegroom, the sound of millstone and the light of the lamp.'

Grinding corn was normally women's work. Jesus spoke of two women grinding when he returned to earth, one being taken to heaven and the other left. But the Bible also occasionally refers to men grinding at the mill. Samson was forced as a punishment to grind in a prison mill. This may have produced flour for the inmates, but probably also produced it for people outside; perhaps as it was a hard and boring task, the community used forced labour to do it whenever possible.

Some people would have used a mortar and pestle rather than a little mill. The mortar was a hollowed-out stone into which grain was placed. The grain was ground by the pestle, a cylindrical stone rod with a rounded end. For grinding flour very fine, for spices and cosmetics, both mortar and pestle might be made from wood. Occasionally there were de-luxe versions; the stone mortar was

◁ Jeremiah 25: 10

◁ Matthew 24: 41

◁◁ Judges 9: 52f.

◁ Judges 16: 21

◁◁ Deuteronomy 24: 6 **10**

This Egyptian tomb model shows a woman using a saddle-quern as described on the facing page.

supported on three legs and elaborately decorated.

In Hellenistic times huge circular millstones were rolled over large flat stones to grind grain. They were operated by animals or even water-power, and must have belonged to large community mills. Jesus spoke of the large millstone: 'If anyone causes one of these little ones who believe in me to sin, it would be better for him to be thrown into the sea with a large millstone tied around his neck.' The fact that the stone was too large to tie round a person's neck, and probably too heavy for one person to lift, underlines the seriousness of the point he was making about leading others astray.

Genesis 8: 11▷▷

Mark 9: 42 ▷

This was one of several methods of grinding grain between hard, sharp basalt or quartz stones which remained rough, however often they were used. Another, again used for large scale milling, was to set a round stone a metre or more in diameter (4 or 5 ft) on its edge and roll it round a large flat base stone. A vertical pole in the centre of the base stone was fixed to a horizontal pole through the rolling stone so that it could be pushed round and round without falling over.

So central was bread to the life of every Jew that Jesus called himself 'the bread of life' – the divine power that no human being could do without. His 'bread', he said, was more wonderful than the manna, the supernatural bread which fed the Israelites in the desert as they fled from Egypt; it was the source of eternal life.

John 6: 32-51 ▷

OIL FROM THE TREES

Olive oil was one of the vital ingredients for meals in Bible times. Food was cooked with it and in it, and it was used as a garnish. It also provided fuel for lights in and around the house. Although some olives were pickled in brine and eaten with meals, the bulk of the crop was crushed to extract the valuable oil.

The olive makes an early appearance in the Bible narrative when the dove released from Noah's boat returned with a fresh olive leaf, a sign that the floods had subsided from the hillsides. It is mentioned almost incidentally from then on, both in the Bible and in other contemporary records. Receipts inscribed on pottery found in Samaria from the days of Jeroboam II (about 786-746 BC) refer to jars of fine oil, and military documents from Arad dating from the last days of the kingdom of Judah record olive oil requisitions from the local HQ (commisary).

The production of olive oil had two stages. First, the barely-ripe olives were bruised or partially crushed – in the early days of Bible history usually by being trodden on or pounded in a shallow rock-cut basin. Care was taken not to crush the kernel but only bruise the flesh. Then the crushed pulp was pressed or squeezed to obtain the oil. The best oil, and probably the cleanest, was obtained by beating or pounding the olives in a stone or rock-cut mortar with a pestle. The oil collected in the basin and was separated from the pulp by pressing it out. An olive press of this kind was found at Gibeon.

Sometimes the pulp was put into a wicker basket and gently shaken. The basket acted as a strainer and the oil and other juices (mostly water) were drained into another container, where they settled. The oil floated to the top and the water beneath was drained off through a spout in the bottom of the basin.

In New Testament times there were more sophisticated methods for extracting oil. The usual method was to use a circular stone pushed round a circular trough by a long handle through the stone. This both crushed and squeezed the fruit, and the crude

An olive press made from basalt in Capernaum. The long handle is missing from the rotating stone.

10

oil flowed from an opening at the bottom. It was allowed to settle in jars so that the pure oil would rise to the top.

The archaeologist W.F. Albright claimed to have found such a press, dating from the time of the Kings, at Tell Beit Mirsim. He found a room 7 m x 5 m (23 ft x 16 ft) in which were two shallow stone vats over a metre in diameter. In the wall were openings through which shafts could have been inserted and on the floor were large perforated stones and large jars.

In Roman times the olive crusher was a stone-cut basin with a circular trough. In the centre of the trough was a T-shaped column. Two wheel–shaped millstones were fixed to the ends of the crosspiece and rotated round the trough. Washers and wedges prevented the stones from actually crushing the kernels by keeping the stones away from the sides and slightly above the bottom.

The crushed pulp was then put in a basket or net over a shallow basin covered with wooden blocks. A weighted lever pressed down on the pulp, and the oil ran down a channel into a vat. When the bulk of the oil had been squeezed out, heavier weights could be added to the lever to get more oil, but of poorer quality, from the olive pulp.

HOW GRAIN WAS STORED

Everyone needed grain, and most people probably grew their own. It is likely that it was stored as grain, and ground into flour when needed, rather than keeping large quantities of flour in the house.

At home, grain was stored in large pottery jars or in stone-lined granaries (often called silos) sunk in the floor or in the ground outside the house. The jars were usually made from thick pottery and had two or four substantial handles — so they were very heavy even before they were filled with grain. Their shape varied with the centuries but the most usual design had a rounded or pointed base which would be less easily broken when the jar was moved. Such jars were probably leant against a wall or sunk into the floor, and their shape made them more suitable for slinging in baskets on donkeys for transport. (Jars with flat bases and sharp corners would crack easily if knocked.)

In Jericho rows of jars were found which had carbonized grain in them. They belonged to the town which had been destroyed by fire during patriarchal times (Middle Bronze Age). It is possible that some of the places where they were found were shops.

Stone-lined silos have been found from all times during the biblical period. They were particularly common in the early stages of the Iron Age, apparently when Israel was occupying the land. At one small site now called Izbet Sartah, there were dozens of circular silos dug into the bedrock beside two or three houses. Old silos were used as rubbish pits, and often contain broken pottery.

There is also evidence that grain was stored in very large quantities. Silos have been found which were too large even for several mills to use, and this has caused scholars to speculate whether there were government programmes for distributing grain to either the civilian population or the armed forces. The story of Joseph in Egypt shows that central storage and distribution of grain was not unknown in the ancient world. 'Joseph stored up huge quantities of corn, like the sand of the sea; it was so much that he stopped keeping records because it was beyond measure.'

Genesis 41: 49 ▷

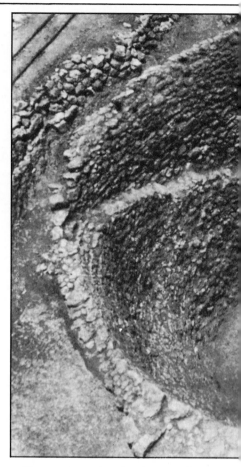

The most spectacular storage pit was found in Palestine at Megiddo. During the Israelite period a large silo was dug down through previous levels of occupation. It was about 7 m (23 ft) deep and measured almost 11 m (36 ft) across the top and 8 m (26 ft) across the bottom. It was built of uncoursed rubble and it had never been plastered. Two stone staircases ran down against the sides. It could have been in use during the prosperous days of Jeroboam II (about 784-748 BC), and later.

Another large stone-lined silo was dug at Beth-Shemesh around 900 BC, slightly smaller than that at Megiddo (5.5 m/19 ft deep by 7 m/23 ft diameter at the top). It too had been dug through the debris of former cities and was situated within the precincts of the governor's house.

Large store houses seem to have been used for government holdings of flour, oil and wine as well as grain.

10

These were of two kinds. One had long parallel rooms, such as that at Beth-Shemesh. The walls of the rooms were over a metre thick, and the floor was raised above the foundations, which helped to keep the grain from spoiling. At Beth-Shemesh they may have been part of the governor's residence; at Lachish a similar structure was close to a citadel or palace dating from David's time.

The second kind of structure was built to allow the animals carrying the grain to walk right into the store. On either side of the walkway were store rooms, and the grain was offloaded directly into them. Stone troughs suggest that the animals were fed and watered while their loads were being removed. Such stores have been found at Hazor, Beer-sheba and Megiddo. Those at Megiddo were once believed to have been stables for horses, but they are now considered more likely to have been

Storage-pit at Megiddo (about 780-650 BC) showing the winding stairs leading to the bottom of the pit which is 7 m (about 23 ft) deep. It has a capacity of 12,800 bushels (about 46.5 kilolitres).

stores. Bowls, cooking pots, storage jars, jugs and flasks found at Beer-sheba suggest that people came in to have goods measured out and then distributed them to the local populace or military personnel.

At the fortress of Masada, built by Herod the Great, there were two groups of stores in the palace area. The walls were built of double rows of stone slabs each weighing 180 to 226 kg (400 to 500 pounds) and standing over 3 m (11 ft) high. Wine, grain and oil were stored here, and the Jewish historian Josephus records that there was enough food in Masada to withstand a long siege. It is easy for us to forget how capable were the people of those days.

Fragment of a wooden dish found in a Jericho tomb, still bearing the remains of a joint of meat.

MEAT DISHES

Mark 7: 18-20 ▷▷

Meat seems to have been a regular, if not always frequent, part of the Israelite's diet. The range of animals available to him was wide although not unrestricted. Genesis records that when God first allowed mankind to eat flesh, after the flood, he told Noah, "'Everything that lives and moves will

Acts 10: 9-15 ▷▷

be food for you. Just as I gave you the green plants, I now give you everything. But you must not eat meat

Genesis 9: 3f.▷

that has its lifeblood still in it.'" This 'kosher' rule – that meat must be killed in a certain way so that the blood

Acts 15: 20▷▷

drains away before it can be eaten – is still strictly observed by Jews today. It gave significance to the sacrificial

Leviticus 17: 11▷

system: 'the life of a creature is in the blood, and I have given it to you to make atonement for yourselves on the altar.' The blood was too precious and symbolic to eat. The New Testament

views Jesus' death as a blood-sacrifice for sins.

The prohibition on pork, a notorious disease-bearer in hot countries, is also still observed by Jews. However, pigs were not the only forbidden animals. The law spelled out the qualifications for edible (or 'clean') flesh: 'any animal that has a split hoof divided in two and that chews the cud'. That included deer, gazelle, roe deer, wild goat, ibex, antelope and mountain sheep as well as the domestic ox, sheep and goat. It excluded all animals which had only one of the two characteristics: that covered camels, rabbits and rock badgers which only chewed the cud, and pigs which had cloven hooves but did not chew the cud (Deuteronomy 14: 6).

Incidentally, these dietary laws were to create problems for non-Jewish Christians in the early church. Jesus had already paved the way for the abolition of the laws by declaring that it was not what food a person ate which made him or her 'unclean' in God's sight, but what words and deeds came out of the heart. Shortly before Peter was asked to go to a Gentile house to preach the gospel, he had a vision in which a great net full of clean and unclean animals was let down in front of him. Commanded to eat, he refused, until he heard God say to him, "'Do not call anything impure that God has made clean.'"

The church council, meeting in Jerusalem to discuss the matter, decided it could not impose Jewish regulations on non-Jewish Christians, and asked them to abstain only from strangled meat and from eating blood, which would be too offensive to their Jewish brothers and, perhaps, insensitive to the fact that Christ had shed his blood for them. Both Gentile and Jewish Christians had other problems in the meat markets. Some meat on sale had been slaughtered in

Fishermen by the Sea of Galilee in the early morning, a scene that has changed little since biblical times.

10

pagan religious ceremonies. Paul told the Corinthian Christians that 'an idol is nothing' and that 'we are no worse if we do not eat, and no better if we do'. Other people's consciences might be sensitive, he added, and for that reason discretion might on occasions be the better part of valour.

Some meat, especially in the early history of Israel, would have been hunted. The ageing Isaac sent his son Esau out to hunt wild game with his bow and arrow, and then to 'prepare me the kind of tasty food I like'. Probably most meat came from domestic animals. The rich in Amos' day enjoyed veal and lamb, an extravagance because the animals never matured to give their full weight of meat and were lost to longer-term milk and wool production.

Birds also provided meat dishes sometimes. The Israelites fed off a flock of migrating quails which were grounded in the desert. David referred to men hunting partridge in the mountains, and doves and chickens might also have been on the menu at times (see page 133). The food laws banned a number of unclean, mostly carnivorous or scavenging birds, including eagles, vultures, ravens and hawks, ostriches, pelicans, storks and herons. Eggs, presumably from chickens, are mentioned by Jesus as a natural food given to children.

If you were very hungry or sat at regal tables, grasshoppers and locusts might provide a mouthful or a delicacy; John the Baptist seems to have lived on them in the desert. Fish was an important part of the diet in Jesus' time; his disciples Peter and Andrew, James and John, Thomas and Nathaniel, and probably Philip, were all either professional fishermen on the sea of Galilee, or familiar enough with the art to go out in the boats. Tourists in Galilee today are often encouraged

◁1 Samuel 26: 20

◁◁1 Corinthians 8: 1-13

◁ Luke 11: 12
◁◁Genesis 27: 3f.

◁◁Amos 6: 4
◁ Matthew 3: 4

◁◁Exodus 16: 13
◁John 21: 2f.

Nehemiah 3: 3 ▷

Nehemiah 13: 16 ▷

Genesis 43: 11 ▷▷

Deuteronomy 16: 7 ▷

Deuteronomy 14: 21 ▷

2 Kings 20: 7 ▷▷

to eat 'Peter's fish', which can be bought fresh by the lakeside.

Jerusalem had a 'fish gate' in the city wall at the time of Nehemiah after the exile, which suggests that there was a regular fish market there, and men from Tyre up on the Mediterranean coast brought fish to Jerusalem.

Meat – whether animal, bird or fish – was always cooked and never eaten raw. Boiling seems to have been the usual method, although roasting over an open fire is also mentioned in the Bible. The Passover lamb was always roasted. As a reminder that even in killing and cooking animals people should not be cruel towards that part of God's creation, the Israelites were expressly forbidden to boil a goat kid in its mother's milk.

Sixth-century mosaic showing loaves and fishes, from Tabgha, Galilee.

FRUIT, VEGETABLES AND SEASONING

Meals in Palestine would normally have had plenty of fruit and vegetables to accompany the bread and meat. Lentils, beans, cucumbers, melons, leeks, onions and garlic all grow well in the land and were eaten either raw or cooked. Almonds, pistachio nuts and other nuts were also included in vegetable stews or eaten raw; Jacob sent his son Joseph, by then virtually the ruler of Egypt, a gift of almonds and pistachios (or 'terebinth seeds'), together with spices, as a rich present for a great man.

Probably the most common fruit to be eaten was the fig. It was sometimes pressed into cakes, as it still is for export today. Figs were used medicinally as well as being a regular part of the diet; Hezekiah had a

poultice of pressed figs applied to a boil, and it healed. Pomegranates were also widely eaten, as were grapes, although these were primarily grown for wine-making. The modern citrus fruits began to appear in Palestine only after the New Testament era.

To add flavour to their food, the people of Palestine used salt. "'Is tasteless food eaten without salt?'" asked Job. The Persian king Cyrus recognized that along with animals, grain and oil the Jews returning to Jerusalem also needed salt. Jesus said that Christians who did not apply their faith in the wider world around them were like salt which had lost its ability to flavour food, and is thrown away. He may also have been thinking about the preservative powers of salt. Almost the only means open to ancient people of keeping meat and vegetables for any length of time was to pack them in salt. The Christian function in a world which disowns God is to prevent it from going completely bad.

Herbs were also used to add flavour to meals. Among those mentioned in the New Testament, which the Pharisees diligently tithed along with the rest of their agricultural produce, were mint, dill, cummin and rue. Mustard was also grown and therefore presumably used as a food additive. With herbs, mustard, garlic and onions, dishes in Bible times were probably hot and tasty, even if there was little variety in the main ingredients.

For those with a sweet tooth, honey was collected from rocks and trees, although there is no evidence that the Israelites practised bee-keeping, even though the neighbouring Egyptians did. Samson found honey in a wild bees' nest and this inspired one of his famous riddles. Saul's starving army found honey on the ground in the woods. When Jonathan, Saul's son, ate some, 'his eyes brightened'. Isaiah reckoned that curds and honey were food fit for the Messiah. Sugar extracted from beet or cane was not known during Bible times in Palestine.

◁ Isaiah 7: 15

THE COMMON DRINK

Water was drunk in Bible times, but there was always the attendant danger of pollution. Gideon's men drank water from a spring; David longed to drink from a well in Bethlehem; but Paul advised Timothy to avoid water in favour of wine 'because of your stomach and your frequent illnesses'.

◁ Judges 7: 1, 4
◁◁ Job 6. 6
◁ 1 Chronicles 11: 17

◁◁ Ezra 6: 9
◁ 1 Timothy 5: 23

Wine in its various forms was the most common drink for people in Palestine. It was praised by the psalmist, along with bread and oil, as God's good provision to 'gladden the heart of man'. It was less likely than water or even milk to be contaminated as its alcohol content killed germs. Several names are given in the Old Testament to describe its various forms; sweet grape juice, sweet or new wine, half-fermented must or new wine, and fully fermented wine. Wine which had turned into acid vinegar was diluted with water and used as a cheap drink to refresh field workers. Boaz offered Ruth bread dipped in wine vinegar, and a sponge soaked in it was also offered to Jesus on the cross.

◁◁ Matthew 5: 13

◁ Psalm 104: 15

◁◁ Matthew 23: 23;
◁◁ Luke 11: 42
◁ Ruth 2: 14;
◁ John 19: 29f.

The juice was generally squeezed from the grapes by people treading over them in a large shallow rock basin. The process was used in the book of Isaiah to picture the wrath of God trampling his enemies, his garments stained crimson with blood just as those of the wine-treaders would be stained by the grape juice. But it was usually a joyful time; as people trampled the pulp they shouted and sang.

◁ Isaiah 63: 3

◁ Jeremiah 48: 33

As the grapes were trodden the liquid flowed down into a vat cut in the rock where the sediment, pips and skin could settle, and the juice drained out

◁◁ Judges 14: 8

◁◁ 1 Samuel 14: 25-27

10

HOW FOOD WAS COOKED

Exodus 8: 3 ▷

Bread and some meals were cooked in ovens. Israel's ancestors in Egypt saw their overlords using them and presumably copied the practice. Later in the Old Testament period the bakers of Hosea's time used them: he described the people as 'adulterers, burning like an oven whose fire the baker need not stir from the kneading of the dough till it rises. ... All of them are hot as an oven; they devour their rulers.'

Hosea 7: 4, 7 ▷
Matthew 6: 30 (RSV) ▷

In New Testament times Jesus spoke of grass cut in the field and thrown into an oven, presumably as kindling for the fire.

Most homes had an oven which stood in the open courtyard. It would have been round, or a hemisphere, less than a metre in diameter (2-3 ft). It was made from rough pottery or mud or mud bricks coated in mud plaster, with air holes in the side to allow hot gases to escape; bread ovens were not always completely covered. There were holes in the base too; a fire was kindled on pebbles underneath it, and the heat rose up through the holes.

Once the oven was hot enough, the flat cakes of dough were stuck to the sides, or placed on the pebbles after the ash from the fire had been scraped away.

Home ovens were fired by dry grass and the thorn-bushes which grew in abundance. Dried animal dung mixed with straw may also have been used as fuel, as it is in the Near East today.

Ezekiel 4: 12-15 ▷

Ezekiel saw this practice as unclean, especially where human excrement was used.

The other main method of cooking was in pots on an open fire. A large oval hearth 2 m (over 6 ft) across dating from the eighth century BC has been found at Shechem. It was filled with stones, and several cooking pots could have bubbled away at the same time on this ancient version of a family-size stove.

Most cooking pots were wide-necked with a rounded base, and some had two handles and ribbing round the neck.

Exodus 27: 3; ▷▷
Jeremiah 52: 18f. ▷▷

The usual size was no larger than 304 mm (12 in) across and 177 mm (7 in) deep. In patriarchal times a cylindrical pot with a flat base was used. It had a row of holes round the rim, and must

therefore have had a lid on top – the holes let the steam out. Cooking pots were generally made from pottery, but bronze ones were used in the tabernacle and the temple. A medium sized bowl about 253 mm (10 in) wide and 70 mm (3 in) deep was probably

10

used for kneading dough prior to baking bread.

If the diet in Bible times was unvaried, for most people, there is no need to suppose that it was tasteless or badly cooked. The variety of utensils makes this clear.

A plastered bread oven. This modern equivalent of the ancient examples described on the opposite page shows flat loaves on the top of the oven.

Egyptians harvesting and treading grapes for wine-making. Copy of a wall-painting in the tomb of Nakht, Thebes (original about 1420 BC).

of the upper part of it into the collecting vat. The new wine could then be scooped out and poured into jars or bottles of skin for fermentation, a process that had begun during the few hours the wine was in the vat.

The containers had a small opening to allow the gases to escape and prevent the skin bursting or the jar breaking. Elihu, the fourth man who came with advice for the suffering Job, described himself as 'full of words ... inside I am like bottled-up wine, like new wineskins ready to burst'. Fresh wine was put into new skins (usually goat hides tied at the legs and the neck) because it could split old ones which had already stretched. Jesus mentioned this practice to illustrate the fact that the 'new wine' of his truth could not be contained by the 'old wineskins' of Jewish tradition.

Job 32: 18f. ▷

Luke 5: 37f. ▷

The wine jars or skins were then stored in cool cellars to mature. Such cellars have been found by excavators in many places, but one of the largest and most elaborate was found by J. B. Pritchard at Gibeon. Cellars were cut into the limestone hillsides, and smaller areas in the vicinity were quarried out for pressing the grapes and separating the wine from the pulp. The pottery found there showed that this winery was in use during the last days of the kingdom of Judah, the Iron II period, and was at the peak of its production around the late seventh and early sixth centuries BC. Coins of Pontius Pilate and Antonius Felix, Roman procurators of New Testament times, were found there, as well as some later Byzantine coins, so the place was in use for many centuries, although not as a winery. The cellars were used in the later period as tombs, or storage or refuse pits.

The cellars were built so that the wine could be stored at an even temperature. They were bell-shaped, and hewn to an average depth of 2 m (7 ft). The narrow entrances (61 cm/2 ft) could be closed with a stone slab. The bulbous sides of the cellar were generally unplastered, as they did not need to be waterproofed. Sixty-three of these cellars have survived, and as each had a volume of about 6,800 litres

(1,500 gallons), the total capacity would have been over 454,000 litres (100,000 gallons). As the wine was in containers the actual quantity stored would have been considerably less – probably around 114,000 litres (25,000 gallons). But this was still much more than a village the size of Gibeon would have required, so presumably the plant provided wine for sale to other places as well.

MILK AND MILK PRODUCTS

Milk from sheep and goats (although not often from cattle) was part of the staple diet. 'Curds and milk from herd and flock' were part of God's gift to his people in Canaan. The Jews later looked forward to the restoration of Israel after the Day of the Lord when 'the hills will flow with milk'. They will also 'drip new wine', and wine and milk probably satisfied most people's thirst at home.

Milk was not only drunk but also used to make other things. 'Churning milk produces butter', says the book of Proverbs, adding to that the obvious fact that just as inevitably 'stirring up anger produces strife'. Whether this was butter as it is known today is uncertain; it is probably more likely to have been curds or *leben*, a form of yoghurt which had remained a local product in the Levant area to the present day. It was *leben* that Jael served to Sisera; 'in a bowl fit for nobles she brought him curdled milk', before driving a tent-peg through his temple and ridding Israel of one of its enemies.

King David, like many other people, enjoyed cheese, and in one reference this is explicitly said to have been made from cows' milk, and was presumably rarer than the more rank cheese made from goats' milk. Job, reflecting on his birth, says to God, '"Did you not pour me out like milk and curdle me like cheese"', an unusual metaphor to describe the development and maturing of a human being, but one which implies that the cheese-making process was familiar at the time.

◁ Proverbs 30: 33

◁ Judges 5: 25

◁◁ Deuteronomy 32: 14
◁ 2 Samuel 17: 29

◁ Job 10: 10

◁◁ Joel 3: 18

10

FOR FURTHER READING

Douglas, J.D., 'Fruit, Fruits', *IBD*, 1 (IVP, 1980), pp.528–529.
Douglas, J.D., 'Meat Market', *IBD*, 2 (IVP, 1980), p.969.
Fitzsimmons, F.S., 'Wine and Strong Drink', *IBD*, 3 (IVP, 1980), pp.1647–1650.
Harrison, R.K. and Hepper, F.N., 'Olive', *IBD*, 2 (IVP, 1980), pp.1112–1114.
Harrison, R.K., 'Meals', *IBD*, 2 (IVP, 1980), pp.965–969.
Kitchen, K.A. and Martin, R.P., 'Food', *IBD*, 1 (IVP, 1980), pp.513–518.
Lewis, J.P., 'Food', *ZPEB*, 2 (Grand Rapids, Zondervan, 1975), pp.581–587.
Martin, W.J., 'Bread', *IBD*, 1 (IVP, 1980), pp.205–206.
Madeline, S. and Miller, J. Lane, *Encyclopedia of Bible Life* (A. and C. Black, 1979), pp.40–48.
Rainey, A.F., 'Wine from Royal Vineyards', *BASOR* 245 (1982), pp.57–62.
Ross, J.F., 'Food', *IDB*, 2 (New York, Abingdon, 1962), pp.304–308.
Selms, A. Van, 'Food' *ISBE*, II (Grand Rapids, Eerdmans, 1982), pp.327–331.

Oxen and log-cart in northern Turkey.

SECTION IV:
Industry and commerce

Weights and measures

11

A person buying or selling goods needs to have a standard by which to value them, scales for dry goods and measuring containers for liquids, a means of calculating lengths and areas; and money to give in exchange for them. The Bible reader is confronted by weights, measures and money which are totally foreign to the modern world of kilograms and kilometres, of ounces and inches, of pounds, dollars and credit cards.

There are three reasons why many Bible versions do not print modern equivalents. One is that modern equivalents can be only approximate; some ancient measures themselves varied from place to place and time to time. Another is that monetary values are out of date as soon as Bibles are printed, and it is almost impossible to compare purchasing power across the centuries. And the third is that Bible translations often serve countries such as England and Australia which have different systems. In this chapter we have set out in tabular form the main biblical terms with their approximate modern equivalents, followed by a brief explanation of how and when some of the measures were used.

It is emphasized that these tables do not claim to be accurate.

Scene in Beersheva market. Buying and selling has always demanded methods of measuring and weighing goods.

WEIGHTS

In the days of the Old Testament, before coins were in use, people bought either by exchanging goods or by paying an agreed weight of silver or gold. So Abraham paid 400 shekels of silver (a weight, not a unit of currency) for his field at Machpelah. Jeremiah paid seventeen shekels of silver for his ancestral land at Anathoth. That some people cheated by having wrongly balanced scales or light weights is evident from the injunctions in the Bible: 'The Lord abhors dishonest scales, but accurate weights are his delight', according to the book of Proverbs. The law commanded '"Do not use dishonest standards when measuring length, weight or quantity."'

Genesis 23: 16 ▷
1 Kings 10: 14 ▷▷
2 Kings 18: 14 ▷▷
Jeremiah 32: 9 ▷

Proverbs 11:1▷

Leviticus 19: 35f.▷

Ezekiel 45: 12 ▷▷

Weights which were used in such deals were made of stone and often carved into attractive shapes with a flat base. Some were barrel-shaped, others oval; some bronze weights discovered at Nimrud in Assyria were shaped like lions. The value of the weight was sometimes inscribed on it. Weights were carried in a pouch or wallet, and were checked against each other when a deal was made. Weighing balances are known to have existed, but so far none have been discovered although Assyrian bas-reliefs picture hand-held scales.

The *talent* was used for weighing gold, silver and bronze. In one year Solomon's income included 666 talents of gold, and on one occasion Hezekiah paid thirty talents of gold to the Assyrian king Sennacherib, a transaction which appears both in the Bible and in Assyrian annals. The Babylonians appear to have had a heavy or double-standard talent which weighed about 60 kg (132 lb).

The *mina* was used to weigh gold, silver and other commodities. It was widely used in the second millennium BC, and the round figures, all multiples of fifty, recorded in biblical and other texts suggest that the 50-shekel mina was a common unit of exchange. In later days Ezekiel suggested a revaluation of the mina to sixty shekels.

The *shekel* was the basic unit in all Semitic weight systems, although it varied considerably according to place and date. The royal shekel was standardized by the kings, but the

WEIGHTS

Biblical term	Biblical equivalent	Approximate modern equivalents	
Old Testament			
Talent (light)	3,000 shekels	30 kg	66 lb
Mina	1/60 talent; 50 shekels	0.5 kg	1.6 lb
Shekel (royal)		13 g	0.5 oz
Shekel (common)		11.5 g	0.4 oz
Shekel (temple)	1/2 or 1/3 shekel	5 g	0.2 oz
Pim		7.5 g	0.25 oz
Beka	1/2 shekel	6 g	0.25 oz
Gerah	1/20 shekel	0.5 g	0.02 oz
New Testament			
Pound (*litra*)	(Latin *libra*)	327 g	7.5 lb
Talent	125 libra	40 kg	88 lb

Selection of 'duck-weights' from Iraq.

common shekel was the standard weight for commodities. An interesting parallel to the current British practice of using dual systems was noticed on inscriptions on common shekel weights found in Palestine and dating from Hezekiah's time. They followed the usual Israelite decimal notation – 5, 10, 20, *etc.*, but the actual weights of the stones did not correspond to the numbers which went up in units of eight.

The numerals were in the Egyptian hieratic script which was often used for this purpose by Hebrew scribes who had no numerical signs of their own. The basic unit in Egypt was the *deben* which has the weight of eight shekels. Presumably traders coped with the dual system just as British people cope with pounds and kilos.

Several weights marked *pim* have been found. They showed the correct interpretation of 1 Samuel 13: 21, which had defeated translators until the twentieth century. It was the price, ⅔ shekel, which had to be paid for renovating iron agricultural implements. Other weights marked *beqa'* weighed half a shekel. This was the amount the Law required Israelites to pay as a poll-tax during a census.

◁Exodus 38: 26

Other weights that have been found, but which are not mentioned in the Bible, are the *neseph* weighing ten gm (⅓ oz), which was probably ⅚ shekel, and a turtle-shaped bronze weight found at Samaria inscribed *ḥmš*, 'one fifth', and weighing 2.5 gm. Another subdivision of a shekel, the *peres* (plural *parsin*), is mentioned in the story of Belshazzar's feast. The writing on the

Bronze 'lion-weights' from Nimrud, Assyria (8th century BC).

Daniel 5: 26-28 ▷

wall, 'MENE, MENE, TEKEL, PARSIN', from which Daniel deduced that the high-living godless king was 'weighed on the scales and found wanting', was literally three weights, mina, shekel and fraction, the words also carrying the meanings of numbered, weighed and divided.

Only two weights are mentioned in the New Testament. The costly ointment used by Mary to anoint Jesus weighed a pound. The metaphorical hailstones dropping to the earth in the book of Revelation weighed a *talent* (NIV renders it 'about a hundred pounds'); they would have been the size of large meteorites.

Below: 1, 2, 4, 8 and 40 shekel weights.

Facing page: figure holding scales and a bag of weights from Marash, 8th century BC.

11

DRY MEASURES

Dry commodities such as flour, wheat and barley were measured out in large pottery (and in later times metal) containers of a standard size. Both the container and its capacity were referred to by the same name.

The largest Old Testament measure, the *homer*, meant 'a donkey load', and was used throughout the Near East for cereals. When the quails fell out of the sky each Israelite refugee family collected ten homers of them – a very considerable quantity. They seem to have paid for their gluttony with a form of food poisoning which proved fatal to some people. Under famine conditions Isaiah predicted that a homer of seed would yield only an ephah (one-tenth of a homer) of grain.

The *cor*, equal to the homer, was used for measuring fine flour and meal as well as wheat and barley, and was also a liquid measure. Solomon paid Hiram king of Tyre 20,000 cors of wheat and a similar quantity of oil for the timber used in building the temple. The *ephah* was in use from the time of the exodus onwards, and was the same as the liquid measure *bath*. The prophet

Zechariah 5: 5-11 ▷▷

Numbers 11: 31-34 ▷
Exodus 16: 18 ▷▷
2 Kings 6: 25 ▷▷

Isaiah 5: 10 ▷

2 Chronicles 2: 10 ▷

From left to right, beqa', pim and nesef stone weights. The nesef or 'part' may have been the same as the 'temple shekel' mentioned in Exodus 30: 13 and Leviticus 5: 15. The weights pictured here are from the 7th century BC and weigh approximately 6, 8 and 10 g respectively (⅕, ½ and ⅓ ounce).

Zechariah had a vision of a woman in a large measuring basket, the Hebrew for which was *ephah*.

The *seah* was used for flour and cereals, but the *omer* is referred to only in connection with the manna in the desert. The *cab* also has only one reference when, during the siege of Samaria a quarter of a cab of carob pods (often used as animal feed) were sold for five shekels of silver.

The four common Greek and Roman measures of the first century AD are all mentioned in the New Testament. Herodotus said that the *quart* was the daily ration of grain to each soldier in Xerxes' invasion army. The *saton* was the Old Testament *seah* and in some versions of the Bible is simply referred to as 'a large measure'. Jesus' little parable about the kingdom of God being like yeast in rising dough refers to 'a large amount' (*saton*) of flour.

DRY MEASURES (VOLUME)

Biblical term	Biblical equivalent	Approximate modern equivalents	
Old Testament			
Homer		220 litres	48.5 gallons
Cor	Equal to homer	220 litres	48.5 gallons
Ephah	⅒ homer	22 litres	38.5 pints
Seah		7.3 litres	13 pints
Omer	⅒ ephah	2 litres	3.5 pints
Cab	¼ seah	2 litres	3.5 pints
New Testament			
Koros		525 litres	114 gallons
Saton (*sata*)		12.3 litres	21 pints
Bushel (*modios*)	8 quarts	8.5 litres	15 pints
Quart (*choinix*)		1 litre	1.7 pints

LIQUID MEASURES

The *bath* was used to measure water, oil and wine and was the base measurement from which all others were derived. Despite its English-sounding name, the container would have been pot-shaped rather than bath-shaped, and fragments of large jars marked *bath* have been found at Lachish and Tell Beit Mirsim. In Hellenistic times the *bath* was reduced slightly to 21.5 litres. The *log* is mentioned only in Leviticus as a measure of oil in the religious ceremony of cleansing a leper. The GNB has 'a third of a litre'.

There are few references to liquid measurements in the New Testament, and most are translated with appropriate modern equivalents. The stone water pots used by Jesus at the Cana wedding reception held two to three *metrētēs* each.

◁ Leviticus 14: 10

11

LIQUID MEASURES

Biblical term	Biblical equivalent	Approximate modern equivalents	
Old Testament			
Bath	Ephah (dry measure)	22 litres	38.5 pints
Hin	⅙ bath	3.6 litres	6 pints
Log		0.3 litre	0.5 pint
New Testament			
Measure (*batos*)		39.5 litres	9 gallons
Firkin (*metrētēs*)		39.5 litres	9 gallons
Pot (*xestes*)		500 cc	1 pint

Roman road at Ephesus, originally linking the
city with its harbour.

Insert left: Roman milestone at Dan.

MEASUREMENTS OF LENGTH AND AREA

While people in Bible times had no need of the micro-millimetre accuracy which modern engineering requires, they did need some degree of exactness for building construction and furniture making. Their units of measurement were derived from the human body – the length of the forearm and the width of the span from thumb to little finger. Isaiah used that fact to compare God's greatness with man's smallness: 'Who had measured the waters in the hollow of his hand, or with the breadth of his hand marked off the heavens?'

In Old Testament times the basic unit of length was the *cubit*, the distance from the elbow to the finger-tip. Clearly, as people varied in size, so did the cubit. The Siloam tunnel, 533 m (1,749 ft) long was recorded as 1,200 cubits, making each cubit 44.42 cm (17.49 in). The Egyptian cubit was longer, at 44.7 cm (17.6 in). There was also a royal cubit which was a palm longer than the normal cubit, measuring 51.8 cm (20.4 in). Cubits were used to measure everything from heights of people and depths of water to distances between places.

The *span* was the length of the outstretched hand from thumb to little finger, and the palm was the width of the hand at the base of the four fingers. Relatively small objects were measured in these units, although the psalmist uses them metaphorically to describe the comparative brevity of human life: 'You have made my days a mere handbreadth; the span of my years is as nothing before you.' The *digit* or finger was the smallest subdivision of the cubit and was used in Egypt and Mesopotamia. Long-distance journeys were measured vaguely, usually in terms of time ('three days' journey') or the length of a bow shot.

In the times recorded in the books of Maccabees, Greek measurements were common, but by New Testament times the Roman system was in use. There were two *cubit* lengths, the

◁ Psalm 39: 5

◁◁ Isaiah 40: 12

1

MEASUREMENT OF LENGTH

Biblical term	Biblical equivalent	Approximate modern equivalents	
Old Testament			
Cubit		44.45 cm	17.5 in
Span	½ cubit	23 cm	9 in
Palm		7.37 cm	3 in
Digit	¼ palm	1.85 cm	0.75 in
Gomed	⅔ cubit	29.6 cm	11.75 in
Reed	6 cubits	266.7 cm	8 ft 9 in
Hellenistic times			
Schoinos		184.9 cm	196.5 yd
Stadion		6.1 km	3.75 miles
New Testament			
Cubit		44.4 cm/52.5 cm	17.5 in/21 in
Fathom (*orgyia*)		1.8 m	6 ft
Furlong (*stadium*)	100 fathoms	185 m	202 yd
Mile (*milion*)	8 furlongs	1478 m	1,618 yd

Matthew 5: 41▷

Numbers 35: 4-5▷

longer one being used in Egypt and Palestine. The *fathom* was the length of the outstretched arms. The racecourse at Olympia was exactly a *stadion* long. The Roman *milia*, not much different from the modern British mile, was reckoned to be a thousand paces, the enforced march which Jesus in the Sermon on the Mount suggests should be doubled voluntarily. The Jews of Jesus' day talked in terms of a sabbath day's journey. This was fixed by the rabbis as 2,000 cubits.

The measurement of area was much less precise than the measurement of length in Old Testament times. There are several accounts in the Bible of people from Abraham to Jeremiah buying land, but no indication is given as to how the plots were measured. Usually area was determined by how much a pair of oxen could plough in a day, and this they called an acre. In New Testament times this was expressed in Latin as a *jugum* or *jugerum*, about five-eighths of a British acre. Another method of calculating area was according to the amount of seed which could be sown in it. Cities were sometimes measured by length and breadth; the Levitical cities, for example, were to be 2,000 cubits square.

FOR FURTHER READING

Barrois, G.A., 'Chronology, Metrology, *etc.*', *IDB*, 1 (New York, Abingdon, 1962), pp.142–164.

Bratcher, R.G., 'Weights, Money, Measures and Time', *The Bible Translator*, 10 (4), (1959), pp.165ff.

Scott, R.B.Y., 'Weights and Measures of the Bible', *BA*, 22 (1951), pp.22–40.

Vaux, R. de, 'Weights and Measures', chapter 13 in *Ancient Israel: its Life and Institutions* (Darton, Longman and Todd, 1962. US ed. New York, McGraw-Hill, 1961), pp.195–209. (New UK ed. 1973).

Wiseman, D.J. and Wheaton, D.H., 'Weights and Measures', *IBD*, 3 (1980), pp.1634–1639.

Industry

During the eighteenth-century Industrial Revolution there was a major shift in life-style as a result of a change in methods of production. Instead of manufacturing being based on the home or the small-town workshop it became concentrated in big-city factories. Cotton mills thrived in Britain's Lancashire, for example; Detroit was to become the home of America's motor trade; the Ruhr valley was to produce iron and steel for the rest of Germany. That trend began to reverse in the second half of the twentieth century. Heavy industry sagged, world trade became more competitive, and new lighter industries based on plastics and microtechnology appeared, often revitalizing small-town industrial estates far from the smoke-covered cities.

So perhaps massive centralization is already becoming a feature of the past. To people in Bible times it was an undreamed-of thing of the future. Even when people began pooling their energies and resources in local workshops, they were still generally meeting the demand of the local town or group of villages; travel was slow and trade was slack further afield. There were no large container terminals, no articulated trucks or multi-wagon trains to carry bulky goods from long distances. As a result there was less standardization; pottery, for example, often revealed local characteristics in much the same way as antique Dresden or Staffordshire china is stamped with the unique design features of master craftsmen from an earlier century.

The habit of specializing in the same trade or working in allied trades grouped together in part of a town is ancient, however. Jeremiah implies that in the sixth century BC the potters and the bakers of Jerusalem had their own quarters of the city. Nehemiah's record of when he apportioned out the repair work for the city wall, implies that goldsmiths and perfume-makers worked closely together in their trades, because he names 'one of the goldsmiths' and 'one of the perfume-makers'. He also refers to 'the Valley of the Craftsmen'. The lists of clans in the Old Testament speak of 'the clans of the linen workers at Beth Ashbea', and of royal potters who lived and worked near fine clay deposits at Netaim and Gederah.

No doubt in smaller towns and villages 'cottage industry' continued to be a dominant feature of ordinary people's lives. If they wanted a house, the family built it themselves. They grew and processed their own food, wine and oil. They raised their own sheep and made their own clothes from the wool. From the remains of early industrial 'plants' and from the artefacts found in ordinary homes, we can sketch a picture of how people made things in Bible times.

THE CLOTHING TRADE

Most clothes were made from wool. It was more readily available than linen which was made from flax grown mainly around the Jericho area or

◁ Jeremiah 19: 1-2; 37: 21

◁ Nehemiah 3: 8

◁ Nehemiah 11: 35

◁ 1 Chronicles 4: 21-23

Lady spinning, shown on a stone relief from Susa, Iran (early 1st millennium BC).

imported from Egypt. When the sheep or goat was sheared, the wool went to the 'fuller' or 'washerman' who washed, bleached, shrank and beat it. The fibres contain natural oils which had to be removed before the wool could be dyed, spun and woven.

Isaiah 7: 3; ▷
36: 2

There was a fuller's or washerman's field on the east side of Jerusalem, away from the residential areas. The same foul smells were given off by the process then as are still given off in modern wool-scouring plants. Malachi refers to 'launderer's soap'; solutions of naturally occurring alkalis such as saltpetre (nitre, or potassium nitrate), or potash from burned plants, were used for cleaning and bleaching.

Malachi 3: 2 ▷

A similar process was used for flax, which after harvest, was dried in the sun. Then it was soaked in water for several days to loosen the fibres, drawn over the edge of a stone or board to separate them, then beaten with a wooden mallet and finally combed.

Next, the fibres may have been dyed, although linen was usually kept white. The Bible never refers to the dyeing process, although it does refer to coloured cloth. Dyeing was an ancient art, and the highly valued purple or scarlet dye extracted from the murex shellfish found along the Phoenician coast may have given Canaan its name; it literally means 'Land of the Purple'.

Solomon asked Hiram king of Tyre (a town on the coast) to send him a

Weaving: two girls in Cappadocia, Turkey using a vertical loom.

12

man '"skilled to work ... in purple, crimson and blue yarn"' to help decorate the temple; these seem to have been the basic colours for fine clothes and curtains in Bible times.

The wool or linen was spun by feeding the threads on to a wooden spindle which was turned in order to twist the threads into yarn. Sometimes the spindle was rotated in one hand and the thread fed to it from the mass of wool or flax with the other. But the spindle could also hang loose, leaving the spinner's hands free to draw out the threads and wind them on to the spindle.

Cloth was made from the yarn on wooden-framed looms, which move together vertical threads (the warp) fixed to the frame by threading horizontal threads (the woof) under and over the warp by a shuttle. Looms could be laid horizontally or stood vertically on the ground. The loom beams may have been supported on the upright stone pillars which have been found in the courtyards of some Israelite houses. Most clothes would be woven in two or three pieces before being sewn together by hand, although some robes were seamless.

◁◁ 2 Chronicles 2: 7

THE POTTERIES

'Craftsmen', says the book of Ecclesiasticus in the Apocrypha, dating from the early second century BC, concentrate 'on making an exact representation, and sit up late to finish their task'. Take the potter, for example:

Ecclesiasticus 38: ▷
29-30 (NEB)
(Apocrypha)

> So it is with the potter, sitting at his
>   work,
> turning the wheel with his feet,
> always engrossed in the task
> of making up his tally;
> he moulds the clay with his arm,
> crouching forward to apply his
>   strength.
> He concentrates on finishing the
>   glazing,
> and stays awake to clean out the
>   furnace.

Without such people, the writer continues,

Ecclesiasticus 38: ▷
32-34 (NEB)
(Apocrypha)

> ... a city would have no inhabitants;
> no settlers or travellers would come
>   to it.
> ... they maintain the fabric of this
>   world,
> and their prayers are about their
>   daily work.

They are not destined to become wise, however, because they have no leisure to meditate and study.

That passage gives a unique insight into the workaday lives of ordinary people in Bible times (it also refers to the farmer and the blacksmith). Theirs was a dawn-till-dusk occupation, with only religious festivals to provide a welcome break from the necessary routine of making and selling. The passage also gives a comprehensive description of the potter's art.

The potter was a key person in Israelite society. He had become a specialist craftsman by the time of Saul and David (around 1000 BC). Jeremiah visited a pottery shop in Jerusalem to buy a decanter, and he smashed it (as a sign of what God was going to do to

Jeremiah 18: 1-2; ▷
19: 1-2

Egyptian potter working by the roadside near Asyut. He is turning the wheel with his feet just as his predecessors did in biblical times.

12

Israel) near the Potsherd Gate along the Hinnom valley, where the potters probably dumped their broken products. The potters may generally have worked on the south side of the city near the valley. An entire potters' quarter has been found at the Phoenician city of Sarafend (the biblical Zarephath), in use from the fifteenth to the seventh centuries BC.

Potters then, as now, 'threw' their bowls and jars on a 'wheel'. There were two types. The slow wheel was a simple wooden or stone turntable rotated by hand or foot. The flat turntable slotted on to a conical pin projecting from the lower stone. The potter put the clay on the turntable, shaping the object with his hands as it rotated.

This type of wheel would not allow the potter to make high-class products which needed to be perfectly symmetrical. The fast wheel gave him more versatility and a faster rate of production. The throwing table was connected by an axle to a stone or wooden flywheel which the potter kicked with his foot, producing greater speed and leaving both his hands free to work the clay.

Once the vessel was correctly shaped, it was put out on the ground to dry, then dipped in a thin clay solution ('slip') to seal the pores. Any decorating was done at this stage, by scratching, burnishing (rubbing the surface with a smooth hard stone), or painting, though in the days of the kings of Israel and Judah decoration was rare.

Then it was baked, usually with a batch of other pots, in an oven or kiln. Firing took several days because the temperature of the kiln was raised and lowered slowly. Bowls and jars would crack if there was a sudden change of temperature. Three kilns have been found at Tell en-Nasbeh, north of Jerusalem. Only the lower part remained, the dome covering the firing area and the flues which took the hot air into the ovens having disappeared. The kilns were U-shaped in plan and the fire was built in the centre. The hot air flowed through flues into the side chambers stacked with pottery. U-shaped kilns have also been found at Megiddo, dating from the period of the Kings. Temperatures in them could rise to 1000°C.

A circular kiln was found at Tell el-Ajjul in south-western Palestine. A series of brick vaults supported a baking table about 1.5 m (5 ft) in diameter. Vertical flues piercing the table took the hot air from the fire beneath to the pots stacked on top.

A POTTER'S SHOP

A potter's workshop was cut like a cave into the limestone at Lachish shortly before Israel emerged as a nation in the Late Bronze Age. The cave would create an even temperature for drying, and being outside the town walls reduced the fire risk from the kiln, which was located deep in the cave.

There was a space for preparing the clay, another for storing both clay and fuel for the kiln, a drying area and a storage area for pots which needed a second treatment.

Among the tools discovered was a stone mortar for grinding the pigments used in painting the products. There were pottery templates used to smooth the surface of the object on the wheel, a bone point for cutting surplus clay from the rim, pebbles used for burnishing, and stone bases for a slow wheel. Several people would have worked together in this pottery.

METAL WORKING

Metal was at a premium in the ancient Near East. Without the benefits of modern technology, metal was difficult to obtain and the melting process hard to control. Until iron-working was mastered, by about 1000 BC, metal tools were always expensive. The booty lists of Assyrians and others list metal objects prominently as spoils of war; skilled craftsmen were prized, too, and were deported from Jerusalem to Babylon by Nebuchadnezzar's forces.

The land Israel occupied has no extensive metal deposits, although there was copper in the Arabah valley south of the Dead Sea, especially at Timna. Mining went on there under the Egyptians in the Ramesside Period (thirteenth to mid-twelfth centuries BC), perhaps during the eighth century BC, and under the Romans.

Israel had to import metals and ores. Ships from Tarshish, perhaps Tarsus in southern Turkey, or maybe Tartessus in Spain, brought silver, iron, tin and lead. Copper was probably imported from Cyprus because the ore deposits in the Wadi Arabah were insufficient. The large amounts of copper and iron used by Solomon in the temple may have been obtained by trade or captured in war from the Aramaeans. David is said to have taken much bronze from the cities of Hadadezer from which Solomon made the bronze Sea, the pillars and the bronze vessels for the temple (1 Chronicles 18: 3).

The people of Israel were aware of the mining process, however. There is a graphic description of it in the book of Job, which mentions mines for gold, silver, precious stones, iron and copper.

Man puts an end to the darkness;
    he searches the farthest recesses
    for ore in the blackest darkness.
Far from where people dwell he cuts
    a shaft …
    far from men he dangles and
        sways. …
He tunnels through the rock;
    his eyes see all its treasures.

◁ Job 28: 3-11

◁◁ 2 Kings 25: 13-17

A number of biblical passages show knowledge of the metal-working processes. Jeremiah compares the smelting of silver ore to God's method of purifying his people of their wickedness.

◁◁ 2 Kings 24: 14

'The bellows blow fiercely
    to burn away the lead with fire,
but the refining goes on in vain;
    the wicked are not purged out.
They are called rejected silver,
    because the LORD has rejected
        them.'

◁ Jeremiah 6: 29-30

When lead was put in the crucible with silver ore and heated to a high temperature, the lead oxidized and acted as a flux to collect impurities. All that should remain is pure silver, but in Jeremiah's picture there is none, just worthless slag.

◁◁ Ezekiel 27: 12

The bellows he refers to may well have been 'pot bellows'. A cylindrical

12

Bellows similar to those described on page 184 excavated at Tell edh-Dhibai, Iraq (about 1750 BC). Diameter 44 cm (about 18 in), height 18 cm (about 7½ in).

The New Testament makes no reference to metal working, but this marble relief of a coppersmith's workshop from Pompeii shows several of the processes involved.

In the centre the smith steadies on the anvil a lump of hot metal which is about to be struck by an assistant with a heavy hammer. Above them are the double doors of the furnace. On the left the smith weighs out small items and on the right he engraves or embosses a large circular dish. Completed wares decorate the walls. A child (left) and a watch-dog (right) complete the scene which appears to be an example of home-based industry.

1 Samuel 13: 19-21▷▷

1 Kings 7: 13–45▷

Isaiah 54: 16;▷
cf. 44: 12

earthenware vessel was covered with an animal skin. When the skin was trodden on, the air below it was compressed and forced through a tube into the furnace causing it to burn more fiercely.

Metal ingots needed further purifying before they could be used for making weapons or tools, and the Israelites seem to have acquired the skill from people like Huram of Tyre. The later chapters of Isaiah referring to the exilic period, speak of 'the blacksmith who fans the coals into flame and forges a weapon fit for its work'. The raw ingot was reheated in a crucible, covered with charcoal, or placed over a charcoal fire and blown with bellows in order to remove impurities. It was then poured into a stone or clay mould, or on to a flat surface and hammered into shape.

In the days of Saul 'not a blacksmith could be found in the whole land of Israel'. The people were dependent on the Philistines for tools and were unable to make weapons with which to rebel against their oppressors. Once Saul and David broke the power of the Philistines iron came into common use in Israel and iron tools dating from about 1100 BC have been found in excavations. It is possible that the Kenites (their name literally means 'smith') and Midianite travelling smiths introduced metal working into Israel before the period of the Judges.

The Canaanites who lived in Palestine long before Israel appeared on the scene had produced bronze or copper implements and weapons. During the Middle Bronze Age (the patriarchal period) moulds for molten metal were cut out of limestone blocks. Limestone moulds, crucibles and an ingot of copper were found together at Tell Beit Mirsim.

In later periods in Israel skilled metal workers, like the goldsmiths and silversmiths, banded together in guilds called 'families'. They could beat swords into ploughshares (or vice versa as required), and their line of business was making axes, adzes, mattocks, forks, sickles, plough-points, ox-goads, knives, pins, arrowheads, spearheads, javelins and swords. The variety of products indicates that the metal industry was flourishing and found a ready market.

It presumably continued to flourish in New Testament times, although the apostles make no reference to metal-working. In pre-Christian times the high priest John Hyrcanus (134-104 BC) had to stop the iron and bronze workers working in Jerusalem on certain feast days because they made too much noise.

Josephus the Jewish historian, writing at the end of the first century AD, refers to a smith's bazaar in Jerusalem's New City. No doubt bronze and iron goods were forged in the workshops behind the shop fronts and sold from the shops in much the same way as they still are in the east today. Josephus also says that at times of war the Jerusalem smiths were busy making arms and armour.

◁◁ Isaiah 2: 4

THE BUILDING TRADES
THE STONE-MASON
Many ordinary houses in Bible times would have been built from roughly-cut stones, but big administrative buildings, the temples, aqueducts, and the houses of the rich were built with 'ashlar' masonry, and that required the skills of the stone-mason.

Ashlar masonry is the name given to large rectangular blocks of limestone. They are carefully cut so that they fit

Reconstructed copper-smelting furnace from Timnah (about 1250 BC). Bellows force air into the fire. A plug is removed to allow the slag to run off, leaving copper ore in the bottom of the furnace.

12

exactly on top of each other without needing mortar to bind them, usually in a stretcher (lengthways) and header (widthways) pattern to give stability to the wall. Sometimes the whole face of the completed wall would be rubbed down to a smooth surface. Ashlar was sometimes used for foundations or for corners to increase the strength of the walls, with the rest of the building being completed with rougher stones.

One of the best remaining examples of this work can be seen at the 'Wailing Wall' in Jerusalem, which once formed part of the temple area built by King Herod shortly before the birth of Christ. The largest building block so far found in Jerusalem measured almost 5 m (16 ft) long and 4 m (13 ft) wide; it must have required a huge gang of builders to manoeuvre it into

position. The temple area has revealed to researchers just how well developed the stone-mason's art was in Herodian times; arches, monumental stairways, columns and ornamental stonework have all been found. In Samaria, the ashlar foundation stones, remains of the citadel dating from the time of Kings Omri and Ahab, still bear the marks of the chisels and adzes used by the masons.

The stones were quarried throughout the hill country, and for most projects builders would have used local limestone to avoid the expensive and difficult task of transporting it for long distances. Long disused quarries have been found near Jerusalem, Megiddo, Samaria, Ramat Rahel (near Bethlehem), Hazor, Taanach and Gezer. Solomon conscripted tens of thousands of men as stonecutters in the hills to provide building blocks for his temple, and his

2 Chronicles 2:2 ▷▷

The largest building block so far found in the base of Herod's temple wall.

Part of the wall of Ahab's citadel at Samaria, showing 'header and stretcher' masonry bearing the marks made by the masons.

father David had already set the aliens living in Jerusalem the task of preparing 'dressed stone' for it. They apparently had suitable saws with which to cut it cleanly, and did not simply hack it with hammers and chisels.

One quarry was found within Jerusalem itself. When the modern Lutheran church planned to extend its building in the Muristan area south of the Church of the Holy Sepulchre, they called in Dr Kathleen Kenyon to check it out archaeologically. She found no building remains before the Roman period, but only a deep pit filled with debris from the seventh century BC and the first century AD. At the bottom she found a series of steps and ledges, typical of a quarry. It had been filled in after the Romans turned Jerusalem into a pagan town in AD 135. The site lay outside the city wall of New Testament times.

THE BRICKMAKER

Two kinds of bricks were used in Bible times. There were baked clay bricks, which were probably used in building the tower of Babel in Mesopotamia but became common in Palestine only in New Testament times. (The fiery furnace into which Daniel's friends were thrown may well have been a brick-kiln.) There were also unbaked mud bricks which were widely used in Egypt and which the Israelite slaves were probably making before their liberation. The usual Hebrew word for brick, *lebena*, is derived from the word 'white', which gives some indication of the common brick colour. Mineral deposits in the clay could affect the colour, however, and a light red brick was also common.

The earliest mud bricks were shaped by hand and were oval in shape. But the use of a rectangular wooden frame to mould (or 'strike') the bricks led to a more standardized shape. The mud and some clay were mixed with sand and chopped straw to act as binding agents,

◁ Genesis 11: 3
◁◁ 1 Chronicles 22: 2

◁◁ 1 Kings 7: 9
◁ Daniel 3

◁ Exodus 1: 14

12

Above: Egyptian workman casting mud bricks
in moulds, using Nile mud and straw.

Below: loading kiln-baked bricks from the
furnace on to a cart. Egypt.

to make the clay more workable and to prevent it cracking. As the straw rotted, it released an acid substance which gave the clay greater plasticity. The brickmaker usually mixed the ingredients with his feet before he put the mixture in moulds. Once the bricks were set, the moulds were removed and the bricks allowed to dry thoroughly in the sun.

The sun-dried brick was used in Egypt for all except the most important buildings which were constructed in stone. The use of straw in brickmaking there is confirmed by official reports dating from the thirteenth and twelfth centuries BC; one official complained that he had neither straw nor people to complete his quota.

In Palestine the unbaked or partially baked brick was sometimes used for the upper courses of buildings. In Lachish a section of wall dating from the seventh century BC had a foundation of river stones on which bricks were laid and bonded together with mud mortar (see page 61).

By New Testament times kiln-baked bricks had become common, the use of them having spread east from Rome itself, although they had long been used in Mesopotamia.

THE WOODWORKER

Jesus was known as 'the carpenter', following, as the eldest child, the family tradition of Joseph. The work was varied. Many houses had wooden doors and roof beams, and larger homes had wooden floors and wall panels. The carpenter would have been a jobbing builder, but also, if he was sufficiently skilled, a furniture-maker as well. There was a tradition of fine furniture-making in Canaan which went back to patriarchal times. Farmers and merchants needed carts and wagons, and the construction of these would also have come within the province of the woodworker.

Israel had its own supplies of wood. Some cypress and cedar grew in the north, sycamore (not the European variety but a fig tree) in the foothills region, olive everywhere; there may have been acacia (*shittim* in some Bible versions), oak and ash in the area too. Few of these trees yielded long timbers, however, so for the prestige project of the temple Solomon imported cypress, cedar and almug wood from Lebanon and Ophir.

Isaiah portrays the carpenter selecting the wood for a job. 'He cut down cedars, or perhaps took a cypress or oak. He let it grow among the trees of the forest, or planted a pine, and the rain made it grow'. He also describes the woodworking process. 'The carpenter measures with a line and makes an outline with a marker; he roughs it out with chisels and marks it with compasses'. Among the tools found by archaeologists are a marking tool, compass or dividers, an adze, a chopper, an iron saw, files, a bow drill, a mallet, a hammer, and various chisels and awls. By New Testament times Joseph and Jesus also would have had wood planes and spoke shaves in their workshop.

◁ Isaiah 44: 14

◁ Isaiah 44: 13

12

◁◁ Mark 6: 3
Matthew 13: 55

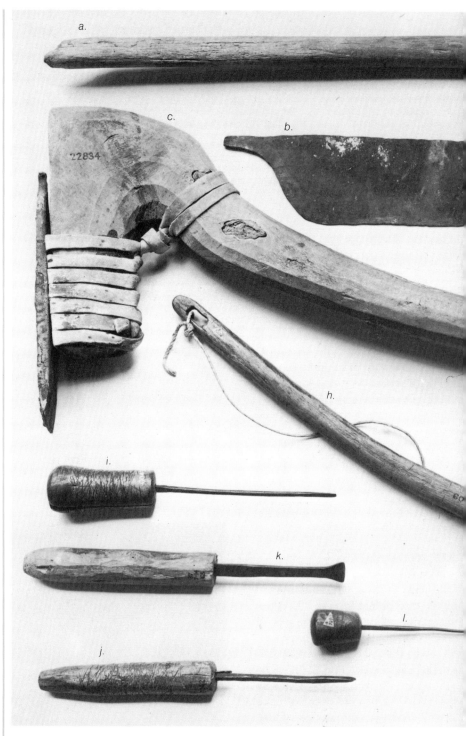

Egyptian carpenter's tools, from Thebes.

a. Bronze-headed axe.

b. Bronze saw blade.

c. Large adze, with bronze blade held in place by leather thongs.

d. Small handsaw with bronze blade.

[30245]

6046

d.

e.

g.

6061

f.

12

e. Horn fitted with a lip for pouring, used as an oil-flask.

f. Green slate hone for sharpening tools.

g. Model bronze-bladed adze.

h, i, j. Wooden bow-drill with two metal tools possibly used as drilling bits.

k. Bronze chisel with wooden handle.

l. Bronze bradawl.

First century BC mosaic from Praeneste, showing various types of ships being built on the Nile Delta.

Revelation 21: 1 ▷▷

BOAT BUILDING IN PALESTINE

1 Kings 9: 26-27 ▷▷

Jesus sometimes taught from a boat or travelled in one, and some of his disciples were fishermen. There is no evidence that the people of Israel built large ships at any time in their history, although the fishing boats on the inland Sea of Galilee must have been made locally. Indeed, the Israelites seem to

Ezekiel 27: 5-9 ▷▷

have had little interest in the sea, even to the extent of having a fear of it, which perhaps stemmed from the ancient Semitic habit of personifying the deep sea as the power of evil which fought against God. In John's vision of the new heaven and the new earth, the first thing he noticed about it was that the sea no longer existed.

When Solomon had a fleet of ships to trade in the Red Sea area, he used Phoenicians to build and crew them. The Phoenicians were renowned for their fine ships which sailed long distances. In a lament for Tyre, the prophet Ezekiel describes what ships were made of. They had pine timbers from Senir, cedar masts from Lebanon, oak oars from Bashan, cypress decks

from Cyprus, embroidered linen from Egypt for sails and flags, blue and purple cloth from the Phoenician coast for deck awnings. He says veteran craftsmen from Gebel (Byblos modern Jebeil) were the shipwrights who caulked the seams with flax and bitumen. The oarsmen came from Sidon and Arvad.

The commercial (or 'round') ships had a rounded hull and raised prow and stern, and were used for trade along the coast. The 'long' ships were much larger, with a pointed ram at the prow and a high curved stern. Two banks of oars projected from the sides and two steering oars from the stern. They had a central mast and a high upper deck from which the warriors' shields hung. These may have been the ships of Tarshish which are frequently mentioned in the Old Testament.

The sea provided Bible writers with useful metaphors. Job spoke of his days skimming past 'like boats of papyrus'. The psalmist sang about the fear of those who stagger like drunks on a reeling deck, and about their gratitude to God when a storm died down and they reached port safely. It was in such a situation on the Sea of Galilee that Jesus demonstrated God's power over nature by commanding a sudden squall to be still.

◁ Job 9: 26
◁ Psalm 107: 23-32

◁ Matthew 8: 23-27

Jewellers in their workshop. From the tomb of Sebek-hotep, Thebes, about 1420 BC.

Ezekiel 16: 11-13 ▷▷

THE LUXURY INDUSTRIES

From what has been said so far, you might begin to think that life in Bible times was a rather drab routine concerned only with growing or making the necessities of life. That may have been true for poor people, although as we shall see later they played games and they took time off for religious festivals which were more like contemporary Christian ones than the puritanical Sunday. But like people in every age, the Israelites liked to have ornaments and trinkets around them whenever they could afford them. That desire sponsored the luxury industries dealing in gold, silver, precious stones and ivory.

In an allegory about the unfaithful people of Jerusalem, Ezekiel indicates the kinds of luxury goods available in his time. He likens the city to a beautiful woman rescued from poverty. God, her rescuer, says,

I adorned you with jewellery: I put bracelets on your arms and a necklace around your neck, and I put a ring on your nose, ear-rings on your ears and a beautiful crown on your head. So you are adorned with gold and silver ....

There is some difficulty in knowing precisely which precious stones are meant by the Hebrew and Greek words of the Bible, and translations vary. For example, Proverbs 3: 15 states 'She is more precious than *peninim*', which is rendered 'jewels' in the RSV and GNB, 'red coral' in the NEB, 'pearls' in the JB and 'rubies' in the NIV. However, most versions include rubies, sapphires, topaz, emeralds, jasper and amethyst among the Old Testament stones. 'Diamonds' are mentioned in many versions but there is no evidence that diamonds were known in Old Testament times. The NIV avoids the word. Jasper, sapphire,

Jewellery of the Egyptian 12th Dynasty (about 1850 BC). The decoration of the girdle includes electrum cowrie shells and silver fish pendants. The flying scarab beetle and the fish amulet are both inlaid.

12

emerald, beryl, topaz and amethyst are included among the New Testament stones.

Precious stones were set then, as now, in gold or silver, and some samples have been discovered buried under floors and in graves. Jewellery would have been a prime target for plunderers when towns were attacked, and so the quantities which remain to the present day are small.

There were goldsmiths in Nehemiah's time. They were people who probably were rich enough to buy the raw materials and well connected with the wealthy people who would be their clients. There was a guild of silversmiths in Ephesus in New Testament times, making silver images for worshippers at the temple of Diana.

The raw materials were sometimes brought to Israel as plunder or diplomatic gifts. Phoenician merchants traded in precious stones, gold and silver, according to Ezekiel; Jeremiah says silver came from Tarshish and gold from Uphaz. An ostracon, a document written on a fragment of pottery found at Tell Qasile north of Jaffa and dating from the eighth century BC, refers to 'gold of Ophir, to Beth Horon, thirty shekels'.

The smiths refined their gold and silver on charcoal braziers – usually pottery bowls on stands. The metal was melted in a small crucible which stood on the hot charcoal, and when the smith blew on the liquid through a blowpipe the impurities oxidized out into slag. Molten gold was sometimes poured into a mould cut from a fine-grained stone to form an ornament. Silver was harder to purify because it occurs in the same ore as lead; the

◁ *E.g.* 2 Samuel 8: 9-12

◁ Ezekiel 27: 12-22
◁ Jeremiah 10: 9

◁◁ Nehemiah 3: 8, 31-32

◁◁ Acts 19: 24ff.

IVORY CARVING

Carved ivory has always been a luxury, and it was used to decorate thrones and furniture and even, it seems, to adorn the walls of rooms; King Ahab built a palace 'inlaid with ivory' (though the reference may be to ivory furniture). It was widely used to decorate boxes, gaming boards, cosmetic spoons, jars, figurines, amulets, combs and jewellery, often inlaid with precious stones and overlaid with gold foil.

1 Kings 22: 39 ▷

A hoard of 383 pieces of carved ivory was recovered from excavations at Megiddo, dating from 1350 to 1150 BC, about the time when the Israelites were establishing themselves in Palestine. The hoard was Canaanite, not Israelite, and it included a fine single comb with an ibex and a dog carved in relief, a double comb decorated with a lion and trees in relief, a spoon with female figurines carved on the handle, and a box depicting lions and cherubs.

The finest Israelite collection comes from what may have been Ahab's house of ivory in Samaria. Most of the fragments are plaques in low relief or in open fretwork. Some carvings were enriched with gold foil and glass and paste insets. They were probably made by Phoenician craftsmen who copied Egyptian styles, even carving Egyptian gods on them, and Egyptian hieroglyphs. Phoenician letters, scratched on the backs or edges, guided the cabinet-makers in fitting the pieces on to the furniture.

Much of the ivory came from Syrian (or Asiatic) elephants which roamed the upper Euphrates area until they were hunted to extinction a few centuries before Christ. Some was imported by merchants from India and Africa. Ivory has a homogenous texture, so that intricate and delicate designs can be cut into it. One of the most beautiful pieces to come from biblical times was found at Nimrud in Assyria. It portrayed a lion attacking a man among the papyrus and lotus plants. The trousers and hair of the man were decorated in gold leaf, and the plants were inlaid with carnelian and lapis lazuli. Nothing so exquisite has been found among Israelite remains.

Egyptian bow-drill as described on this page. See also the bow-drill and drilling bits on pages 190–191.

Ivory from 9th-century BC Samaria. This furniture decoration shows a lion grappling with a bull. Height 4.2 cm (about 1½ in), length 11.4 cm (about 4½ in).

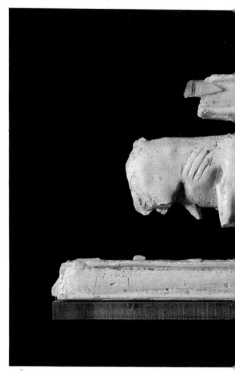

Above: the lion ivory from Nimrud (9th century BC), probably the work of a Phoenician craftsman using Egyptian motifs. It may have formed part of the decoration of a throne, as one of a pair.

Psalm 12: 6 ▷

psalmist refers to 'silver refined in a furnace of clay, purified seven times'.

Jewellers who worked in precious and semi-precious stones used abrasive stones for filing, fine quartz sand for smoothing and wool or fibre pads for polishing. They probably used bronze or iron chisels, and perhaps engraving tools for cutting patterns in the stones. Jeremiah 17: 1 ▷ Jeremiah speaks of an iron tool with a flint (or hard stone) point turned for engraving. Jewellers drilled holes in beads by using a bow drill (see illustration). The taut 'bowstring' imparted high speed to the drill, whose point turned on abrasive sand.

Some Jewish writings from the first century AD show that the jeweller's techniques remained much the same as they had been in Old Testament times. In prohibiting sabbath work, Mishna Shabbat refers to bellow's-hole or mouthpiece of the goldsmith's crucible, Mishna Kelim to the goldsmith's anvil, hammer and balances.

Of course, many people could not afford real jewellery, and they had to be content with substitute ornaments made from baked clay, bone, limestone, wood and leather. Beads, for example, were commonly made from bone, clay or inexpensive stones, and were probably fashioned by the wearer's family at home, instead of by a professional artisan.

FOR FURTHER READING

Amiran, R., *Ancient Pottery of the Holy Land* (Jerusalem, Masada Press, 1969. US ed. Rutgers UP, 1970).

Barnett, R.D., *Ancient Ivories in the Middle East* (Jerusalem, Israel Exploration Society, 1982).

Crowfoot, J.W. and G.M., *Early Ivories from Samaria* (Palestine Exploration Fund, 1938).

Emmerson, G.I., 'Spinning and Weaving', *IBD*, 3 (IVP, 1980), pp.1477f.

Guillaume, A., 'Metallurgy in the Old Testament', *PEQ* (1962), pp.128–132.

Harrison, R.K., 'Oil', *IBD*, 2 (IVP, 1980), pp.1112–1114.

Kitchen, K.A., 'Brick', *IBD*, 1 (IVP, 1980), p.208f.

Loud, G., *The Megiddo Ivories* (Chicago, Oriental Institute Publication, 1939).

Marshall, I.H., 'Jewels and Precious Stones', *IBD*, 2 (IVP, 1980), pp.781–787.

Maxwell-Hyslop, K.R., *Western Asiatic Jewellery c.3000–612 BC (Methuen, 1971)*.

Millard, A.R., 'Potter, Pottery', *IBD*, 3 (IVP, 1980), pp.1248–1254.

Paul, S.M. and Dever, W.G., *Biblical Archaeology* (Jerusalem, Keter, 1975).

Pritchard, J.B., *Wineries, Defense and Soundings at Gibeon* (Pennsylvania, University Museum, 1964).

Stuart, A. and Ruffle, J., 'Mining and Metals', *IBD* 2 (IVP, 1980), pp.1002–1006.

Wiseman, D.J., 'Arts and Crafts', *IBD*, 1 (IVP, 1980), pp.123–128.

Wiseman, D.J., 'Ivory', *IBD*, 2 (IVP, 1980), pp.722–724.

Trade and travel **13**

Abraham was unusual in many respects, not least because he moved his home from Haran to Bethel, some 800 km (500 miles) away. Group migrations happened throughout Bible times, of course, and merchants sailed the seas and trekked across land, but individual travel beyond the next town or village was rare.

By New Testament times travel had been improved by the Roman road system. The apostle Paul joined the many merchants and government officials who tramped round the Empire, and on his three missionary journeys covered over 9,600 km (6,000 miles), mostly on foot or in small merchant sailing ships. Even so, the majority of people did not venture far from home. There were no scheduled public transport services, hotels *en route* were often of dubious character, and even short journeys such as that from Jerusalem to Jericho could be hazardous, as the lone traveller in Jesus' story found to his cost when he was left for dead by muggers until he was rescued and cared for by a kindly Samaritan.

THE ROAD NETWORK

In Old Testament times the roads were always bad and sometimes impassable. Conquering kings used to send slaves ahead of them to 'prepare the way', to 'make straight in the wilderness a highway', an image Isaiah applied to the people of God as they awaited God's triumphal entry into Jerusalem. Such road building or repairing consisted largely of removing boulders and bushes, of partially levelling some steep gradients, and above all of treading down the soil to compact the surface and prevent it breaking up under heavy traffic. No roads outside city walls were paved until the Romans began their monumental trans-European roadways with the Appian Way in 312 BC. Roman roads were paved with stone blocks set on a hardcore and gravel base, and were usually cambered to allow rainwater to drain off the sides.

There were inter-city tracks in Old Testament times, however, trodden down by generations of soldiers, merchants, pilgrims and animals. An international route ran up the Euphrates from Babylon then due west to the Mediterranean Sea, with a branch then turning south through Syria and Palestine to Egypt. That was the road invaders from Assyria and Babylonia took to Israel, for it was rare to travel directly across the desert of north Arabia.

There were three international roads running from north to south through Israel. The most important followed the coast down the narrow strip of fertile land between the sea and desert. It began at Damascus, then cut south-west through Hazor, Megiddo, and then down the coast through Gaza, and on into Egypt. Also leading to Egypt was the Sinai road, cutting inland from the coastal towns of Sidon, Tyre and Acco to Shechem, Bethel, Jerusalem, Hebron and Beer-sheba. From there it went through the Negeb to Egypt.

◁◁Luke 10: 30-37

◁◁Isaiah 40: 3

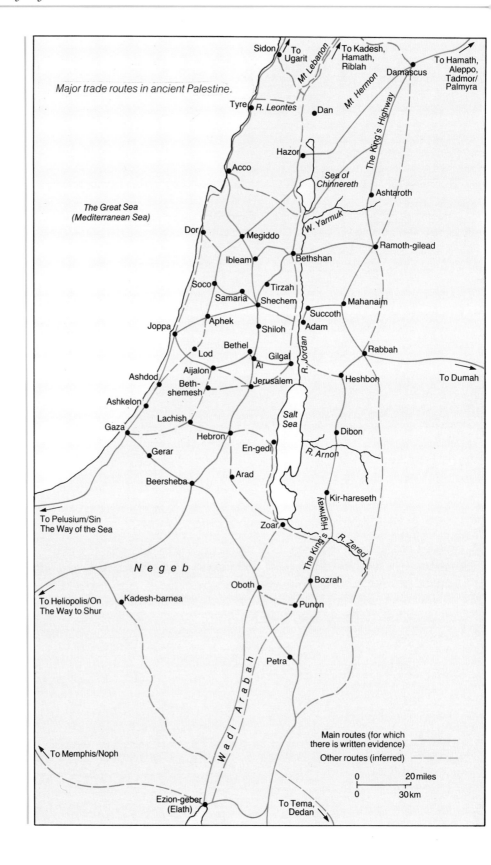

Major trade routes in ancient Palestine.

The third route, the Red Sea road, was also known as the King's Highway to the travelling Israelites who wished to use it to pass through Amorite territory. It ran from Damascus to the ports of Elath and Ezion-Geber on the Gulf of Aqabah, via the mountain region of Transjordan. A branch of this road ran south overland to the incense-producing areas of southern Arabia, modern Yemen.

Another coastal road was developed in Roman times when the port of Caesarea was built. This ran from Acco to Joppa via Dor and Caesarea, encountering problems in the marshlands of the Plain of Sharon.

Among the east–west roads was one from Arabia to Gaza via Beer-sheba, with a fork to Petra. Another linked with the northern Arabah route at En Gedi on the Dead Sea and led across country through Hebron and Gath to Ashkelon on the Mediterranean Sea. The port of Joppa was served by a road from beyond the Jordan via Jericho and Bethel, and by one from Gilead in Transjordan via Shechem. Roads from Galilee to the east and Ibleam to the south-east ran to the port of Acco, later known as Ptolemais.

◁◁Numbers 20: 17; 21: 22

Part of the Appian Way in Rome. The camber on the road and wheel-ruts are clearly visible.

13

TRANSPORT AND TRAVEL

Apart from Paul's journeys across Asia Minor and into Greece and eventually Italy, other travels are recorded in the Gospels and Acts. Joseph and Mary took the baby Jesus into Egypt to escape from the infanticide law of Herod, having already travelled from Galilee to Judaea for the census during which Jesus was born. They also visited Jerusalem each year for the Passover, and on one such occasion the twelve-year-old Jesus lingered in the temple while the travellers made for home. During his ministry Jesus travelled all round Palestine; he visited Jericho in the south-east, Tyre and Sidon in the north-west; he visited Samaria at least twice and almost commuted between Jerusalem and Galilee.

◁Matthew 2: 13-18

◁Luke 2: 1-4

◁Luke 2: 41-50

As in earlier times, these journeys were largely for business or religious observance, and not simply for pleasure. The Old Testament also records similar travels, as when David was on the run from Saul. Almost all these journeys would have been made on foot, covering a maximum of perhaps 24 to 32 km (15 to 20 miles) a day. But throughout biblical times animals were used for travel, often to carry goods as well as people.

13

Donkeys (called asses in some Bible versions) were common beasts of burden. Abraham used one when he went to sacrifice in the desert, for example, and Saul was looking for some which had escaped when Samuel first anointed him king. Kings commonly rode on donkeys (and also on mules) in Old Testament times; Solomon rode on his father David's mule when he went to his coronation. Jesus' triumphal entry into Jerusalem on a donkey was a clear demonstration of his kingship, which angered his

◁Genesis 22: 3

◁1 Samuel 9:3

◁1 Kings 1: 33

◁Matthew 21: 2-7

Horses drew Tutankhamun's war chariot as depicted on his wooden chest, about 1340 BC.

Assyrian ox-cart, relief from the palace of Ashurbanipal about 640 BC.

opponents even though he claimed that his kingship was different from that of earthly rulers. Such animals were clearly valuable and therefore cared for; on one occasion Jesus rebuked the religious leaders for their inconsistency in objecting to his healing a woman on the sabbath when they would water or rescue an ass on that day.

Luke 13: 15; ▷
14: 5

Horses do not seem to have been used much for everyday transport, except perhaps by the Romans; in Bible times they were essentially animals of war. The horse may have been introduced into the ancient Near East from the Russian steppe as early as 2300 BC, and it is regularly attested from the nineteenth century BC onwards. Its domestication led to the development of the light war chariot, which was used infrequently in Israel because of the generally hilly terrain.

It is interesting to note in passing that the first reference to horses in the Bible is during Joseph's stay in Egypt. They are not mentioned among the livestock of Abraham and the other patriarchs, which implies that the stories reflect those times accurately.

Horses could cover about 40 km (25 miles) a day, although some Roman couriers are known to have galloped 160 km (100 miles) with frequent changes of horse.

Camels became regular features of life in the biblical world from the twelfth century BC. They were known before that time, but their origin and

This scene from Turkey illustrates dramatically some of the problems of travel in remote areas of the Near East.

13

Model of a merchant ship from Solomon's fleet, 10th century BC.

Genesis 24: 10 ▷
Genesis 37: 25 ▷
1 Kings 10: 2 ▷
Joshua 9: 9-13 ▷▷
Ezra 2: 67 ▷
Nehemiah 7: 69 ▷
Matthew 19: 24 ▷
Matthew 3: 4 ▷
Exodus 4: 24 ▷▷
Song of Solomon 3: 9 ▷

the date of their domestication is obscure. Abraham's servant used camel transport when he went to Mesopotamia to find a wife for Isaac, and Joseph's brothers sold the young dreamer to a band of Ishmaelites driving a camel-train of goods down to Egypt. The Queen of Sheba brought camel-loads of presents for Solomon, and the Jews who returned to Jerusalem from exile in Babylon brought back 435 camels. Jesus made a humorous comment about a camel, and his cousin John wore a camel's hair cloak, so the animal was a familiar part of the first-century landscape.

The ox was also used for transport, to pull wooden carts. The Lachish reliefs include an illustration of Judaeans riding in carts. They probably resembled those of the Assyrians and other neighbouring people, which generally had two large spoked wheels. The Song of Solomon refers to a palanquin, or covered litter, made from Lebanese wood and decorated with silver and gold, a carriage fit for a king.

Very little is recorded in the Bible about stopping-places for travellers. The men of Gibeon who pretended to have come a long way to see Joshua brought provisions with them, and this presumably was the custom of travellers; they camped where they could and fended for themselves. The Old Testament also has some obscure references to 'lodging places'; Moses was at one when the mysterious attempt was made on his life. There were inns in New Testament times, to judge from the narratives of Jesus' birth and the story of the good Samaritan. Many inns may have been little more than brothels, but proper provision was made for Roman officials to rest or change horses every

25 Roman miles along main roads.

Sea travel was clearly hazardous; Paul recalls three shipwrecks, during one of which he spent a day and a night in the sea. Indeed, the same passage lists many travelling hazards, some of them vague but clearly real; rivers (presumably waded through), bandits, cold weather and hunger are among the problems he encountered in having 'been constantly on the move'. Most ships stayed in port from mid-November to mid-March. Paul's journey to Rome was extremely dangerous because it was out of season; the shipwreck off Malta was not unexpected.

So travel was hard, hazardous and very slow. That is why wanderlust affected very few people; there was no guarantee of a safe arrival. Letters took months to be delivered, and perishable goods well and truly perished on long journeys, so were rarely transported any distance.

Nevertheless ships sailed from Tyre to Cyprus, Rhodes and Tarshish and provided Israel with an indirect link with countries otherwise beyond their reach.

◁ Acts 27: 9-15
◁◁ 2 Corinthians 11: 25

Trade routes in Solomon's time

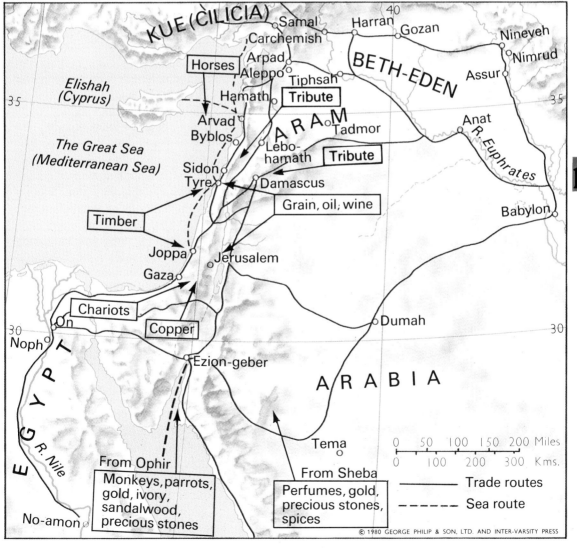

13

© 1980 GEORGE PHILIP & SON, LTD. AND INTER-VARSITY PRESS

Part of the caravan party depicted on the tomb walls of Khnum-hotep.

THE GOODS TRADE

Genesis 37: 25-28 ▷▷

Palestine was the only land-bridge between Egypt and Africa in the south and Anatolia, Assyria, Babylonia and Persia in the north. Although a poor area with few natural resources, it was constantly enriched by the traders who passed through it. Ezekiel lists the goods which traders dealt in: silver, iron, tin, lead; slaves and bronze wares; horses and mules; ivory and ebony; turquoise, purple fabric, fine linen, coral and rubies; wheat, honey, oil and balm; wine and wool, cassia and calamus; saddle blankets; lambs, rams and goats; spices, precious stones and gold; beautiful garments, blue fabric, embroidered work and multi-coloured rugs.

Judges 5: 6 (NEB) ▷▷

Ezekiel 27: 12-24 ▷

It was quite a selection! And the main traders were not usually lone tinkers and tailors, the forerunners of door-to-door salesmen carrying suitcases full of household goods; merchants usually travelled in 'caravans' — groups of people and pack animals. From about 2000 BC to 1750 BC there was considerable caravan traffic between Anatolia and Assyria, between Mari and west Asian states, and between western Asia and Egypt. The caravans could number up to 500 donkeys. From 1900 BC onwards the stronger mule replaced the donkey as the main beast of burden, and camels generally replaced mules by the eleventh century BC.

1 Kings 5: 9-11 ▷▷

A caravan party of 37 Asiatics, probably travelling metal workers, was depicted on the tomb walls of Khnum-hotep at Beni-Hasan around 1900 BC. Joseph was sold as a slave to a caravan of merchants taking spices, balm and myrrh to Egypt. Caravan traders are mentioned in Deborah's song of victory: 'In the days of Jael, caravans plied no longer; men who had followed the high roads went round by devious paths'.

As Deborah makes clear, merchants usually used the main routes across the country, described earlier in this chapter. But the avoidance of such routes because of political unrest, to which she refers, had an interesting parallel a few centuries later. When Assyria was fighting wars in northern Mesopotamia during the eighth century BC, the important trade from Arabia was diverted through Palestine. Israel (the northern kingdom) and Judah imposed import duties and transit taxes on the traders, and also bought some of the goods originally destined for Assyria. The growth in prosperity of the two kingdoms at this time was partly due to this unexpected windfall.

The trade was not all one-way, however, and the people of Israel also exported some of their own produce. Solomon paid for building materials for the temple by exporting grain, wine and oil to Tyre, a largely manufacturing and trading area which did not have sufficient local agricultural resources to feed its people. The desert peoples to the east of the Jordan became more numerous at this time, too, and they bought some of Israel's farm produce. The spoils of war were sometimes resold; David's conquests in Syria brought him much booty, particularly in metals, which were thus available for home use and for export to countries like Egypt and Phoenicia. Evidence is lacking, but the idea is feasible. Israel's neighbour Moab was a major wool producer, and although Israel had substantial flocks of its own, it took large quantities of Moabite wool in the days of King Omri as tax and probably exported some of it.

Israel was short of timber, however, which it had to import from Lebanon. Other imports included minerals and luxury goods. Nehemiah complained that men of Tyre were bringing fish 'and all kinds of merchandise' to Jerusalem and were selling it on the sabbath.

During the fourth and fifth centuries BC the Greeks set up trading posts along the Mediterranean coast. They colonized the towns and used them as distribution centres for their commodities. By New Testament times Herod the Great had followed their example and attempted to improve the poor natural harbours on the coast by building an artificial harbour at Caesarea. Elaborate stone breakwaters turned the city into a celebrated maritime trading centre. It was used by Paul when he escaped to Tarsus, on his return from his second and third missionary journeys, and for his departure to Rome.

◁◁2 Samuel

◁◁2 Kings 3: 4

Throughout the New Testament period trade was firmly in the hands of the Romans. The state interference in free trade, which was to plague the later Imperial Rome, was already in evidence in the first century. The laws which required licensed traders to be marked on the forehead or right hand had already been enacted. John foresaw them being extended at the end time. Some of the early Christians also had to face problems familiar to trade

◁◁Nehemiah 13: 16

◁Revelation 13: 16-17

COMMERCIAL DOCUMENTS

A great deal of business in Bible times would have had no written documentation, not even the ancient equivalent of a till receipt. Larger transactions were documented, however, and the sale of land to Jeremiah was one such example. The account of Abraham buying a field at Machpelah contains a detailed description of the extent and contents of the land, which may well have been documented.

The pottery fragments (*ostraca*, see page 236) used as 'scrap paper' from eighth century BC Samaria list a variety of commodities delivered to the palace, names of people who brought them, and the date of the transaction. Aramaic documents from the fifth century BC found at the Jewish settlement at Elephantine in Egypt include contracts for supplying corn to the garrison, statements of building rights, contracts for loans, settlements of claims and some conveyancing documents. Clearly that society was closely controlled through legal paperwork.

Documents from Arad, dating from the sixth century BC, show how military outposts requisitioned supplies. A great many Aramaic documents from the same site record the distribution of rations to horsemen, donkey drivers and their animals in the period after the return from exile. Excavations have recovered many personal seals at sites all over Palestine. People fixed their seals to documents, packages and handles of jars filled with food to authenticate their ownership.

Legal proceedings often took place at the city gate, where people would be constantly passing by and could be called on to become witnesses to documents. It was there that Boaz settled the issue of his proposed marriage to Ruth, before the elders of the town and other casual witnesses.

◁◁Jeremiah 32: 9-14

◁◁Genesis 23: 3-18

◁ Ruth 4: 1, 11

THE COINS OF BIBLE TIMES

Nehemiah 5: 15; ▷▷
10: 32

1 Kings 10: 29▷

1 Maccabees 15: 6▷▷
(Apocrypha)

Coins were first introduced into Asia Minor in the middle of the sixth century BC. Before that, people either exchanged commodities or paid for goods in silver by its weight in shekels. Silver was in fact so common that the word is often omitted in the Hebrew text; for example, it says that Solomon purchased chariots 'at 600' (shekels). The same passage says silver was as common as stones in Jerusalem at the time.

The first known coins were struck in electrum (an alloy of gold and silver) in Lydia; Herodotus attributes the introduction of coins to Croesus, king of Lydia (561-546 BC). Darius I (521-486 BC) introduced the idea into Persia, and his name was used for the thick gold coin, a *daric*, which pictured him half-length or kneeling, with a bow and arrow; the daric weighed 130 g (4.5 oz).

The spread of coins into Judah was slow, possibly because they carried images of people, which the Jews believed were banned by the ten commandments. It is therefore more likely that the silver shekels referred to by Nehemiah were weights rather than coins. The Phoenicians were minting coins in the fifth century BC at Byblos, Tyre and Sidon, and these began to circulate in Palestine along with Syrian, Egyptian and Greek coins. Some Jewish coins bearing the name Judah were made around 400 BC by permission of the ruling Persians.

When the independent Jewish state was established in the days of the Maccabean rulers, Simon Maccabaeus was given authority to strike coins, but no examples have yet been found. His successor John Hyrcanus I (134-104 BC) struck bronze coins inscribed on one side with 'Johanan High Priest and the Community of the Jews' and with a picture of cornucopias and a pomegranate on the reverse.

From then on the Jews used a variety of coins. Those of the Ptolemies and

Gold/silver stater from Lydia, the first state to use coined money. This coin is 15 mm (about ²/₃ in) in diameter and dates from about 600 BC.

Coin of John Hyrcanus, 134-104 BC, diameter about 13 mm (¹/₂ in).

Seleucids have been found. The standard coin was the silver drachma, and bronze coins were used for local trade. Once the Romans arrived, it must have been a money-changer's haven, with many adjustments of values and the chance of a quick profit in the process, which provoked Jesus into turning the money-changers out of the temple.

The basic Roman coin was the *as*, made from bronze; fractions and multiples of it were also minted in bronze, silver and gold. The silver *denarius* was worth 16 *asses* and the gold *aureus* was worth 25 denarii. The Romans also permitted Herod and his family to mint small bronze coins.

In the New Testament, the word often translated penny (as in 'are not five sparrows sold for two pennies?') is the Roman *as*. The little copper coins put in the collecting box by a poor widow were the Jewish *lepta*, one of which was worth an eighth of an *as*.

In his parables Jesus referred to the Roman denarius, which was the daily wage of a labourer. It cost the good Samaritan two denarii for the wounded traveller's lodging. It was the *denarius* which was also used in the trick question 'is it right to pay taxes to Caesar?', as it carried an image of the Emperor Tiberius on it. Jesus' reference to that image, which belonged to Caesar, was paralleled with an oblique reference to God's image in man, which 'belongs to God'.

The *stater*, referred to as payment for the temple tax, which Peter found in the mouth of a fish, was a Greek coin widely used in parts of the Roman Empire. One *stater* was roughly equal in value to four *drachmas*. It may also have been the coin with which Judas was paid for revealing the whereabouts of Jesus.

The *drachma*, roughly equal in value to a *denarius*, is mentioned only in the parable of the lost silver coin, which the woman rejoiced to find.

◁ Matthew 20: 1-16

◁ Luke 10: 5

◁ Matthew 22: 17
◁◁ John 2: 15

◁ Matthew 17: 27

◁ Luke 12: 6
◁◁ Matthew 26: 15
◁◁ Mark 12: 42
◁ Luke 15: 8-10

Bronze as *of Tiberius, AD 22-23, diameter 30 mm (about 1¼ in).*

Gold daric of Darius II, king of Persia. The king holds a sceptre and bow. Coin is 15 mm (about ²/₃in) in diameter. Late 5th century BC.

Acts 19: 23-27 ▷
Amos 8: 5 ▷

Acts 16: 14 ▷

Revelation 3: 18▷

Jeremiah 32: 1-15▷

Leviticus 25 ▷▷

unionists today; some trade guilds were opposed to Christianity, the silver-trade guild of Ephesus being the most obvious.

Ephesus was not the only place Paul visited which was a centre of specialist industry and trade. At Thyatira, Lydia became a Christian; she was 'a dealer in purple cloth'. Thyatira was a centre of trade and commerce, and archaeological evidence has revealed that wood and leather workers, tanners, potters, bronze-smiths and even slave-traders were active there, as well as linen workers and dyers. The dyers got their purple from the madder root, which was cheaper than the murex shell used for the famous purple dye of Tyre. The warning to the Laodicean church in the book of Revelation urged them to obtain 'white clothes'; Laodicea was a renowned trading centre for black woollen garments.

BUYING AND SELLING

Fixed prices are a relatively modern phenomenon; in the east even today much buying and selling is preceded by bargaining until a price is reached which is agreeable to both vendor and purchaser. The Bible is full of references to deals, but in only a few cases are the details recorded.

Jeremiah, for example, bought a field at Anathoth. The agreed price was seventeen shekels of silver, which he weighed out. Two copies of the deed of purchase were signed and one was sealed in the presence of witnesses, and both copies were placed in an earthenware jar for safe keeping; being relatively airtight the documents would 'last a long time'. It was an acted parable for Jeremiah, pointing to the hope that after the Babylonian troubles the people of Jerusalem would once again buy homes and fields in their own country.

There was more room for cheating when food or other goods were bought and sold. Amos records the fact that traders gave short measures of grain, and that their weights for weighing out the silver were too heavy; they sold less grain for more silver than they should.

By New Testament times the Jews had developed strict regulations to discourage false deals. The traditional law written down about AD 200 gives numerous instructions (the Mishnah, tract Baba Bathra). Wholesale dealers had to clean their measures once a month, their weights once a week, and their scales every time they were used. The seller had to give slightly more than the stated amount for deals over 4.5 kg (10 lb) of goods. A contract was not complete until both parties had received their goods, although it was considered dishonourable for a buyer to draw back after he had parted with his money.

If a purchaser discovered he had been overcharged he could return the product or reclaim the balance in money provided he applied for it after he had shown the product to another merchant or to a relative. Merchants were not obliged to name the lowest price if the questioner had no intention of buying the product, nor might they be induced to drop their prices by being reminded of having overcharged on previous deals. Money changers were allowed to charge a fixed discount, but currency speculation was regarded as a sin like usury (charging interest). Merchants were entitled to proper commission and compensation for their time and trouble, but high profits were considered improper.

Another, much earlier, sign that consideration and modesty rather than selfishness and greed should characterize trade, was enshrined in the jubilee laws. In this kind of 'leasehold' system, prices were determined by the number of years before the next jubilee (held every fifty years). No land could be sold outright (although of course the crops could), so the price fixed for a field was the value of the crops to the next jubilee, when the land would automatically revert to the original owner without further payment. If the land was redeemed by the original owner or a member of his family, he had to pay the tenant the balance of the value of crops until the next jubilee.

Scholars are unsure whether the jubilee principle was ever applied on a wide scale. Some contemporary commentators have seen in it God's concern that social structures should not allow some families to be poor and landless for more than a generation, and that there should be some curb on those denounced by the prophets for joining field to field and thus becoming huge landowners.

◁Isaiah 5: 8

The concept of buying and selling is lifted on to quite a different plane in the New Testament where it is used metaphorically of Christians. Twice Paul tells the Corinthians, 'You were bought at a price'. Being received into God's kingdom was not a matter of personal merit or achievement, but of being bought like a slave from one owner in order to serve another in perfect freedom. The redemption price was the death of Jesus Christ on the cross.

◁1 Corinthians 6: 20; 7: 23

FOR FURTHER READING

Archer, G.L., 'Coins', *ZPEB*, 1 (Grand Rapids, Zondervan, 1975), pp.902–911.
Baly, D., *The Geography of the Bible* (Lutterworth, 1964), pp.109–112.
Banks, F.A., *Coins of Bible Days* (New York, Macmillan, 1955).
Barrois, A., 'Trade and Commerce', *IDB*, 4 (New York, Abingdon, 1962), pp.677–683.
Blaiklock, E.M., 'Trade and Commerce. II. In the New Testament', *IBD*, 3 (IVP, 1980), pp.1578–1580.
Bulliet, R.W., *The Camel and the Wheel* (Cambridge, Mass., 1975), pp.28–56.
Free, J.P., 'Abraham's Camels', *JNES*, III, 1944, pp.187–193.
Kanael, S., 'Ancient Jewish Coins and their historical importance', *BA*, 26 (2), (1963), pp.38–62.
Kelso, J.L., 'Trade and Commerce. I. In the Old Testament', *IBD*, 3 (IVP,1980), pp.1577–1578.
McCasland, S.V., 'Trade and Commerce in the New Testament', *IDB*, 4 (New York, Abingdon, 1962), pp.690–693.
Mendelsohn, I., 'Travel and communication in the New Testament', *IDB*, 4 (New York, Abingdon, 1962), pp.688–690.
Meshorer, Y., *Ancient Jewish Coinage*, I and II (New York, Amphora Books, 1982).
Wheaton, D.H., 'Money. II. In the New Testament', *IBD*, 2 (IVP, 1980), pp.1021–1023.
Wilkinson, J., 'The Way from Jerusalem to Jericho', *BA*, 38 (1), (1975), pp.10–24.
Wiseman, D.J., 'Money.I. In the Old Testament', *IBD*, 2 (IVP, 1980), pp.1018–1021.

13

The flail and crook were insignia of royalty in ancient Egypt. This painting is from the tomb of Senedjem at Thebes.

Civil government 14

From its earliest days, the nation of Israel was self-consciously distinct from other peoples. The Israelites saw themselves as 'people of promise', who had entered into a covenant with God in which he promised, 'I will walk among you and be your God, and you will be my people.'

That promise, first made to Abraham even before the nation existed, was renewed several times through Israel's long and chequered history. As the prophet Jeremiah looked forward to better things to come while the leading people were in Babylon, he heard God saying,

> "'I will give them a heart to know me, that I am the LORD. They will be my people, and I will be their God, for they will return to me with all their heart.'"

Ezekiel used similar words, as he perceived God's promise of 'an undivided heart' and 'a new spirit'.

After the first renewal of the original covenant with Abraham, made by Moses and the people in the desert after their flight from Egypt, Israel was intended to be a nation which owned God as its head and which accepted his commands for its social ethics. For that reason, the detailed laws of the Old Testament concentrate not only on social structures but on both religious and social duties; those who 'walk in all the way that the LORD your God has commanded' will 'live and prosper and prolong your days in the land that you will possess'. In theory, they did not need central government because they had a unifying faith and purpose, and local issues could be settled by the priests. But the ideal of the 'theocracy', of being governed by God, slowly degenerated over the centuries. The nation became more centralized, then collapsed under foreign invaders, never fully to enjoy again the status it had achieved under Joshua and the wealth it had gained under Solomon. Through the biblical period there were four distinct phases of social organization.

◁◁Leviticus 26: 12

THE FAMILY PHASE: THE PATRIARCHS

Patriarchal society was semi-nomadic and pastoral, a tribal society based on family units. Inter-family relationships were largely governed by blood ties; Isaac and Jacob sought wives from their ancestral land. The head of the family directed its civil life.

◁◁Jeremiah 24: 7

There were some matters of law and order, security and justice, which were written not so much in laws as in the deep-rooted tradition of the family. They included blood-vengeance to provide personal security and integrity; the practice of hospitality; levirate (brother-in-law) marriage to preserve the male line of the family and so conserve family property; and the rule of family solidarity which required one member to help and protect another.

◁◁Ezekiel 11: 19f.

THE TRIBAL PHASE: THE JUDGES

Once Israel was settled in Palestine, it lacked any real political cohesion.

◁◁Deuteronomy 5: 33

Judges 7: 24 ▷▷

There was no capital city, no central government, no standing army, no taxation and no extensive international trade. If that sounds idyllic to modern ears used to the clamour of huge bureaucracies seeking political allegiance, demanding taxes and enforcing all kinds of legislation, it had the grave disadvantage of not possessing any sense of group identity; 'everyone did as he saw fit'.

Judges 21: 25 ▷

Most Israelites lived in small villages and worked their small farms. Nearby were larger towns which became administrative and trading centres, markets and perhaps cities of refuge in times of family feuds or tribal wars. With the gradual dispersal of the tribes and the gentile influence of the Canaanite customs and institutions which had remained in the land after the Israelite conquest, the authority of the tribal patriarch declined. The twelve tribes remained in a loose confederation, sometimes but rather simplistically called an 'amphictyony', a term used to describe the much later federations of Greek states.

Certainly it was possible to call on other tribes for help in times of emergency. Deborah summoned the men of Naphtali and Zebulun to fight

Judges 4 ▷

the Canaanites, and Gideon called on men in the hill country of Ephraim to beat back nomadic invaders. But for the most part people lived independently, and local disputes seem to have been the province of two kinds of leader: elders and judges.

The role of elders dates back to the time of Moses; then, elders were heads of families who ruled a clan. In Gideon's day, however, the elders of Succoth were apparently not the same people as the chiefs. In the story of Ruth the elders supervised the legal procedures which cleared the way for Boaz to marry Ruth. When eventually, after the time of the judges, Israel petitioned Samuel for a king, it was the elders who were the spokesmen. The elders too, it seems, appointed the judges.

Judges were individuals with authority to make decisions on many aspects of public life. They were military leaders when Israel was attacked or oppressed; they were arbiters in personal disputes and judges

'We shall be like all the other nations.' Darius I (521-486 BC) King of Persia and Babylon, receives homage from an ambassador. Six centuries earlier the people of Israel had longed to have such a king for themselves.

of criminal cases; they were administrators rather than dynastic rulers, and their authority was generally limited to a few of Israel's twelve tribes; some of the judges referred to in the Bible may well have been contemporaries. The legal side of the judge continued long after the wider leadership role was taken by the king; King Jehoshaphat for example appointed judges 'in each of the fortified cities of Judah'.

THE NATIONAL PHASE: THE KINGS

Israel did not change from a federation to a monarchy overnight. After Saul had been acclaimed king he 'went to his home in Gibeah, accompanied by valiant men whose hearts God had touched.' There was no palace for him to inherit, no established civil service to ensure that his commands were obeyed throughout the land. Tribal and clan traditions persisted, and it was only the threat from other nations (mainly the Philistines but also the Moabites, Edomites and Ammonites) which compelled the nation of Israel to unite.

But from the beginning, the people had what they wanted in theory if not in fact, a king so that 'we shall be like all the other nations'. It was a hard request for Samuel, the last of the great judges and also a prophet, to concede; he did so only when he realized that it was not him the people were rejecting, but God as their rightful king.

It was David who finally drew the nation into such a cohesive unit that it became possible for the familiar institutions of centralized government to develop. He established Jerusalem as the royal capital and transferred the ark of the covenant there so that it became both the religious and the political centre of Israel. He appointed royal cabinet officials over the standing army, the priests, the secretariat, the record keepers, and the forced-labour battalions. His standing army, made up of Israelite soldiers and foreign mercenaries, gave him an authority and power that no-one had enjoyed before.

David's son Solomon consolidated his position by developing trading contacts with, and marrying into, neighbouring states. He strengthened the administration and appointed more officers (including an officer in charge of the officers), and organized the nation into twelve administrative districts. He put his relatives in charge of some districts. Each district had to provide the food, wine and oil the royal household needed for one month in the year, an early form of tax. This and his conscription of forced labour for building projects fostered discontent among the people and at his death the northern tribes rebelled against his dynasty and the nation was effectively split in two, with separate kings ruling each part.

Samuel's prophecy came true: the price of unity was loss of freedom, a growing rift between rich and poor, and corruption.

> 'This is what the king who will reign over you will do: He will take your sons and make them serve with his chariots and horses. ... He will take your daughters to be perfumers and cooks and bakers. He will take the best of your fields and vineyards and olive groves, and give them to his attendants. ... He will take a tenth of your flocks, and you yourselves will become his slaves. When that day comes, you will cry out for relief from the king you have chosen, and the LORD will not answer you in that day.'

Although the kings exerted considerable power, they could not become complete dictators because the

◁◁2 Chronicles 19: 5

◁◁ 1 Samuel 10: 26

◁◁1 Samuel 8: 19

◁1 Samuel 8: 10-18

14

elders in Israel acted as some kind of restraining influence. It was the elders who had once appointed judges who now asked Samuel for a king. Saul had to ask Samuel to 'honour me before the elders' when he disobeyed God after the defeat of the Amalekites. David and Abner negotiated with the elders of the northern tribes after Saul's death, and they eventually went to

1 Samuel 8: 4f. ▷
1 Samuel 15: 30 ▷

Hebron to accept David as king over them.

After Solomon's death, the northern tribes were again in revolt. Jeroboam

Right: one of Solomon's building projects: Hazor. The Solomonic gate is in the foreground. The later (8th century BC) storehouse can be seen in the background.

Below: Solomon's administrative districts as described in 1 Kings 4: 7-19.

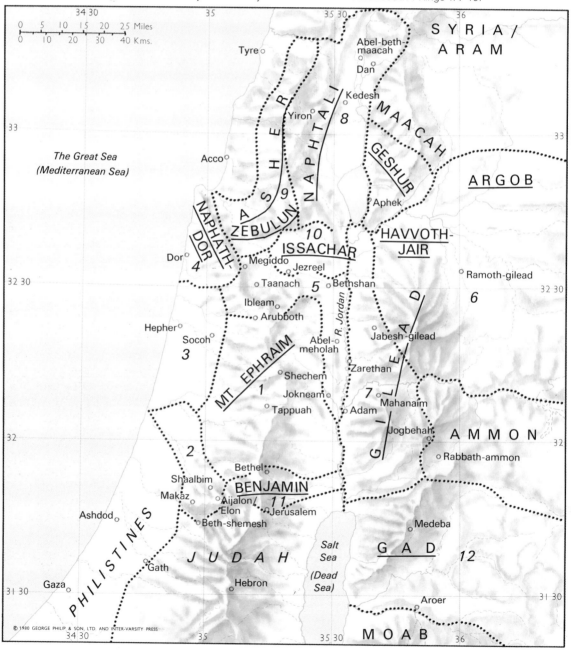

© 1980 GEORGE PHILIP & SON, LTD. AND INTER-VARSITY PRESS

14

1 Kings 12: 1-11 ▷

'and the whole assembly of Israel' negotiated a settlement with the harsh ruler of southern Judah, Rehoboam, Solomon's son. This assembly, made up of representatives of the tribes, had been the supreme authoritative body in the days before the monarchy, and clearly acted as a kind of parliament in

THE KING AND HIS COURT

1 Kings 4: 6 ▷▷

2 Kings 15: 5 ▷▷

1 Kings 4: 7-28 ▷

Isaiah 22: 15-25; ▷▷
36: 3

1 Kings 21: 1-16▷

The kings in Israel exercised supreme authority, and had under their control an increasingly complex bureaucracy to manage the economy. The king appointed his own cabinet and district administrators, and was the supreme judge and court of final appeal. He owned royal estates to produce meat, grain, wine and oil, which were sometimes expanded by conquest and sometimes by outright commandeering, as when Ahab took over Naboth's vineyard.

The kings increased their wealth by developing trade links with other nations, and by taking goods as tribute or taxes from conquered lands. Their huge wealth, and that of the large landowners who flourished under their patronage, drew the anger of the socially conscious prophets such as Isaiah and Amos.

2 Kings 18: 17-37 ▷▷

The kings also built on a vast scale. Solomon is famed for his temple and palace, but he also built massive city walls to fortify such towns as Hazor, Megiddo and Gezer. Omri and his son Ahab in Israel (the northern kingdom) built their capital and palace in Samaria, where evidence of their wealth remains in the superb masonry and the large collection of carved ivories found in the palace ruins.

Amos 6: 1-7; 8: 4-6 ▷▷

In military matters the king worked through field commanders but could intervene in top-level decisions. David himself directed operations against the Syrians and Ammonites, and Ahab led his forces into battle against the Syrians. He even had supreme authority in religion; Solomon dismissed the high priest and banished him to Anathoth.

1 Kings 2: 26-27 ▷

The king controlled the temple treasury and one like Josiah could carry through profound religious reforms.

The king was surrounded by personal attendants and officials. His wife (or wives) and the Queen Mother often exerted considerable influence. He had an armour-bearer, or military aide, and a contingent of personal bodyguards.

The highest official was the Royal Steward, 'in charge of the palace' and probably overseer of the king's estates with a similar role to that once exercised by Joseph as the Vizier of Egypt. Jotham had this title and governed the people when King Uzziah fell sick, although he was also the prince regent. A man called Shebna, during the reign of Hezekiah, although dismissed and replaced by Eliakim, later became Royal Secretary, and a tomb found on the east side of the Kidron valley might have been his.

The Royal Secretary was the second highest official and responsible for correspondence and for the royal archives and annals. The Old Testament has several references to royal annals which recorded battles, building projects and conspiracies. The Secretary also supervised the collection of money to restore the temple in Jehoash's and Josiah's day, and acted as negotiator between King Hezekiah and the Assyrian Sennacherib. The Royal Herald probably worked closely with him, communicating the king's decisions to the people.

Solomon and Ahab had district governors to supervise tax collection, and over them was a general superintendent. The king had officers in charge of forced labour too, and the bureaucracy must have been both extensive and oppressive. In later times the administrators, judges, officials and even priests made the most of their opportunities to grow rich. They were often lazy, and generally made the life of the ordinary citizen more miserable than it needed to be.

This early Hebrew inscription (7th century BC) formed the lintel of the tomb at Siloam, Jerusalem described on this page. The inscription reads '[ ]-yahu, a royal steward, "he who is over the house"'. If this is the tomb of Shebna it lends weight to the accusation of Isaiah (Isaiah 22: 15-16) ... 'Go, say to this steward, to Shebna ... who gave you permission to cut out a grave for yourself here, hewing your grave on the height and chiselling your resting place in the rock?'

the absence of a recognized king. During the discussions, Rehoboam consulted the elders as well as a group of young princes in his court. The heir to the throne rejected the elders' advice; he thus lost control of the northern tribes, but the split signalled the decline in the elders' own power.

David's authority in religious matters was not unusual for monarchs of the period. Here an Assyrian king carries a libation cup. From a glazed brick at Calah (Nimrud) early 9th century BC.

14

UNDER OCCUPATION: THE FOREIGN INVADERS

Nehemiah 2: 5f.; ▷▷
5: 14

From the moment Nebuchadrezzar of Babylon destroyed Jerusalem in 587 BC, Israel ceased to be an independent nation. From then until the Christian era it was ruled by a succession of foreign powers – Babylonians, Persians, Hellenists and finally Romans. There was no longer an Israelite king, no Israelite army and no Israelite government administration, but some of the local institutions which did not carry political power survived.

The elders became middlemen between the authorities and the exiles in Babylonian labour camps, and the Persians used the elders to administer some civil and religious affairs. The occupying powers installed their own local governors; Nehemiah, having been a trusted servant of the Persian king, was sent back to the province of Judah as governor of Jerusalem.

Life for the Israelite villagers and townspeople was controlled by both local and foreign dignitaries, court officials and governors. The occupiers set up military camps at strategic centres so that they could maintain control. The Jews were still not essentially a political people but a theocratic community; the high priest and the Sanhedrin exercised considerable influence and foreign rulers often referred civil matters to them. But always there would have

been the sight and sound of foreign soldiers and military equipment moving about the land. Foreign currencies were introduced, and taxes had to be paid to the current occupiers who were themselves liable to change now and again as they were overpowered by a new dynasty. Then a new regime, with new customs and new demands, imposed itself on the strategically important bridgehead of Palestine.

During the Persian period Palestine and Syria were part of the 'fifth satrapy' called 'Beyond the River'.

This was a large province sub-divided into smaller provinces (such as Judah) and ruled by governors who were responsible to the satrap based at Damascus. The Bible refers to Sheshbazzar and Zerubbabel, and later Nehemiah, as governors; the Elephantine documents mention one Bagoas, and sealings found in Judah name Yehoezer, Ahzai and Elnathan. Taxes were paid in the form of 'taxes, tribute or duty', although temple personnel (priests, Levites and so on) were exempt from payment at least in the reign of Artaxerxes I (465–425 BC). Nehemiah waived his right to levy a tax for his own upkeep, presumably a rare gesture of solidarity with his people and a rare example of someone

◁ Ezra 5: 14;
  Haggai 1: 1

◁ Ezra 4: 13

◁ Ezra 7: 24

◁ Nehemiah 5: 14f.

Six city officials ('politarchs') from Thessalonica are named on this Greek inscription (2nd century AD) found on a Roman arch at Thessalonica. White marble.

14

The Roman Empire.

not profiteering from the gift of power bestowed on him by a foreign and distant king.

Under Hellenistic rule the high priests had authority to deal with matters of Jewish religious law, although the Seleucid kings retained the right to appoint the high priest – usually on the basis of how much tribute money he could promise them. On one occasion the pious and conscientious priest Onias was removed from office and Jason took over because he promised to make rich gifts to Seleucus IV and to promote

2 Maccabees ▷
4: 7-10
(Apocrypha)

vigorously a Hellenization policy in Jerusalem. He in turn was replaced by Menelaus who offered still more cash to the Greek king.

When Jesus was still a boy in Nazareth, the Romans deposed Herod Archelaus in AD 6 and installed a procurator or regional governor in Judaea. The procurator came under the direct supervision of the Roman legate in Syria, was based at Caesarea, and as supreme authority was responsible for the financial administration and military control of the province. Pontius Pilate (AD 26–36) is the most

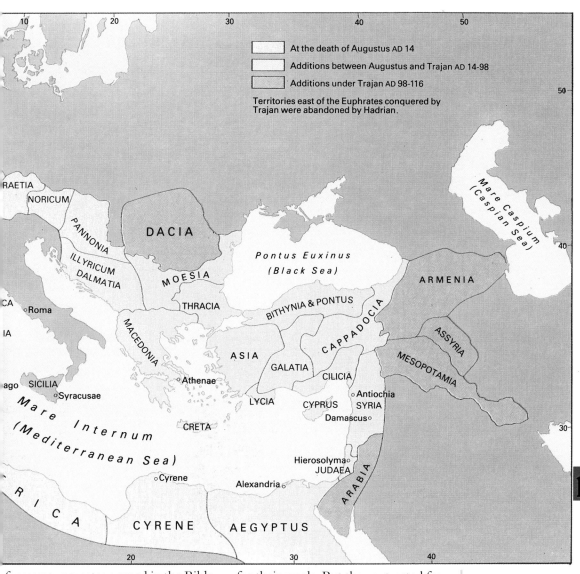

At the death of Augustus AD 14

Additions between Augustus and Trajan AD 14-98

Additions under Trajan AD 98-116

Territories east of the Euphrates conquered by
Trajan were abandoned by Hadrian.

14

famous procurator named in the Bible, being in charge when Jesus was crucified. Antonius Felix (*c.* AD 52–58) and Porcius Festus (*c.* AD 58–62) are mentioned in the Acts of the Apostles and were associated with Paul's arrest and imprisonment.

Taxation was heavy for the people of Judaea at the time, which explains why tax collectors were among the most despised of people, not least because they were Jews working for the hated Romans. Tax collectors paid a fee to the authorities which covered the tax and allowed them an adequate reward

for their work. But they extracted far more than was reasonable from the people and made a handsome profit. Zacchaeus is described as a chief tax collector and a rich man, whose conversion led him to a very generous restitution of property and money he had gained by extortion. Jesus chose a tax collector or customs official, Matthew, to be one of his closest disciples. Among the taxes people had to pay were land tax, poll tax (based on censuses such as the one which took Joseph and Mary to Bethlehem), property tax, and customs dues on

◁Luke 19: 2-8

exports and imports. Jerusalem residents also paid a house tax and everyone had to pay the temple tax on top of all the civil demands.

Jewish authorities had some freedom to enforce their own law. They could not execute criminals, however, and had to obtain permission from Pilate to crucify Jesus, although the arrest and trial were entirely under their

Acts 4 ▷ direction. Peter and John were charged with teaching false doctrine and Paul

Acts 22 - 24 ▷ with breaking the Mosaic law. But the procurator could intervene quite independently of any Jewish court, as he did when he rescued Paul from an assassination plot.

An inscription from Caesarea, naming Pontius Pilate ('PILATVS'), found on a building erected by him in honour of the Emperor Tiberius. Pilate was the fifth prefect of Judaea (AD 26-36).

FOR FURTHER READING

Banwell, B.O., 'King, Kingship', *IBD*, 2 (IVP, 1980), pp.851–853.
Judge, E.A., 'Government in the New Testament', *IBD*, 2 (IVP, 1980), pp.586f.
Manley, G.T. and Wiseman, D.J., 'Judges', *IBD*, 2 (IVP, 1980)], pp.832f.
Thompson, J.A., 'Sanhedrin', *IBD*, 3 (IVP, 1980), pp.1390–1391.
Vaux, R. de, *Ancient Israel: its Life and Institutions* (Darton, Longman and Todd, 1962. US ed. New York, McGraw-Hill, 1961), pp.65–209. (New ed. 1973).
Young, E.J. and Bruce, F.F., 'Government in the Old Testament', *IBD*, 2 (IVP, 1980), pp.585f.

SECTION V:
Culture and health

Writing and literature

15

Imagine what your life would be like if you lived in the days before telephones and computers, and you could not read or write. You would not be able to scan this page and thereby increase your knowledge of times past! You would not be able to read the Bible, so would depend on others to read it aloud to you and on your memory alone to retain its teaching. You would have no access to the collective store of knowledge recorded in libraries. You would not be able to communicate with friends or relatives far away, unless you dictated letters or messages to a professional scribe. You would have no idea about what was happening in the world, until you heard, by word of mouth.

Yet that has been the experience of people in every age before modern times, and still is the experience of millions of people in some Third World countries. Without the benefit of literacy we cannot store large amounts of information, nor can we communicate easily with people beyond those we meet personally. Those who can read and write in such a society are naturally very influential. Throughout Bible times writing was practised – and read – by relatively few.

Papyrus plants, used for making the ancient equivalent of paper (see page 231).

PENS AND PAPER

2 John 12 ▷

The apostle John was able to read and write, although he told 'the chosen lady' that he would rather not 'use paper and ink. Instead, I hope to visit you and talk with you face to face.' By 'paper' he meant papyrus. Paper as we know it was not made until the Middle Ages.

Papyrus was manufactured from the

Aramaic writing on papyrus from Elephantine, 416 BC. A slave, Yedoniah, is handed over by Zakkur to Uriah for adoption in this formal deed.

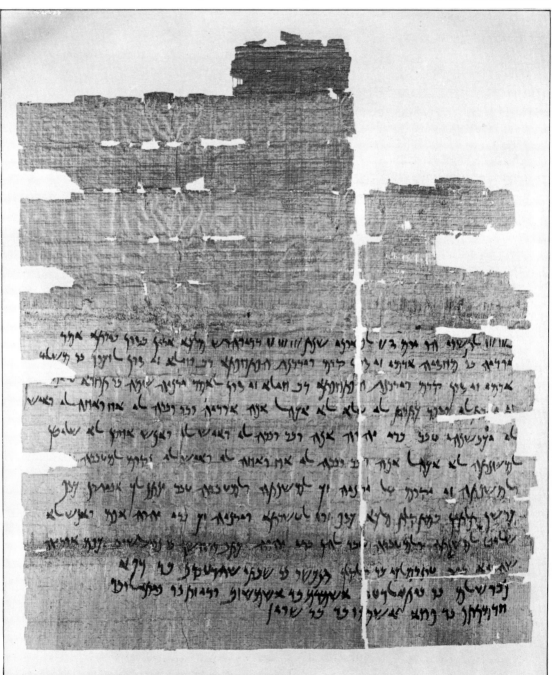

Part of the Qumran 'Temple Scroll'.

pithy stem of the papyrus reed. Strips were laid side by side vertically, then others across them horizontally. The sheet was pressed and dried in the sun, then rubbed smooth with pumice and beaten hard. The result was a flexible sheet of creamy white writing-paper. For copying lengthy documents and books, the sheets would be pasted side by side to make a scroll. Papyrus was almost indestructible if it was kept dry. Because there is little moisture in Egypt outside the Nile valley, enormous numbers of ancient papyrus documents have survived there. Buried in the warm sand, they have turned brown and brittle and are often recovered in pieces.

Papyrus came into use in Egypt soon after 3000 BC and was the normal writing material. Scribes sat cross-legged with the papyrus resting on their taut kilts. Palestine was partly under Egyptian control during the period 1450–1150 BC, and there can be no doubt that government scribes working there wrote on papyrus. Probably it was imported into the country in earlier centuries too. After Egypt's power declined, papyrus was still in demand in Syria and Palestine. A report of an Egyptian sent to obtain cedar wood from Byblos in Lebanon about 1075 BC includes '500 rolls of finished papyrus' as part of the price. As Israel settled in Canaan she took over much of the culture of the Canaanites, including writing with ink on papyrus. The documents have disappeared because the soil of Palestine is too damp for buried papyri to last long. (One scrap from the seventh century BC was found in a very dry cave near the Dead Sea.) Proof that papyrus documents did exist is given by scores of tiny lumps of clay found in the ruins of Israelite towns. These were once pressed over folded papyri to seal them. On the backs they have the imprints of the papyrus fibres and the cords that tied the folded documents. On the fronts they bear the impressions of the seals of the parties involved, often with their names (see below).

In addition to papyrus, the Egyptians wrote on leather scrolls. Often what they wrote on them were accounts and other everyday matters which, once out of date, could be erased by washing away the ink, so that the leather could be reused. There is no evidence for the use of leather scrolls elsewhere until the sixth and fifth centuries BC. At that time leather sheets and rolls became common in

15

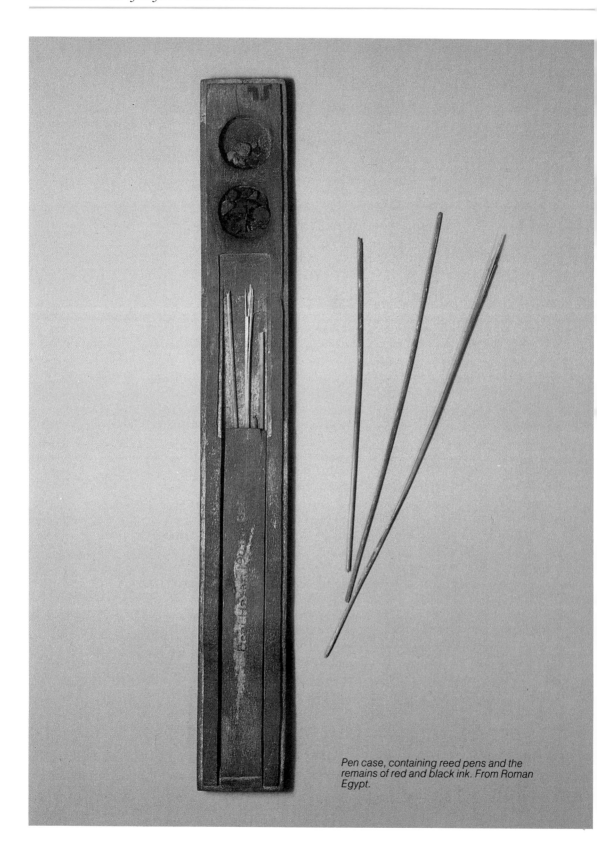

Pen case, containing reed pens and the remains of red and black ink. From Roman Egypt.

Babylonia and Persia, where Aramaic writing was normal, probably because papyrus was difficult to obtain. From this time onwards, the time of the exile, it is likely the Jews wrote their books on leather scrolls as well as on papyrus. The oldest surviving examples are those found in the caves near Qumran, the Dead Sea Scrolls. They show the form of Scriptures current in Palestine in the time of the gospel story. They allow us to picture Jesus in the synagogue at Capernaum reading from a leather scroll of Isaiah like the famous one from a Dead Sea cave.

For writing on papyrus and leather scribes made pens from reeds and rushes sharpened with a knife. Two or three would be kept in a pen-case with cakes of ink. Black carbon from charcoal was mixed with oil or gum and dried to make the ink. The writer moistened the tip of the pen in water then dipped it on the cake, thus mixing his ink as he wrote.

Egyptian papyrus (early 11th century BC). It is covered with pitch.

OTHER WRITING MATERIALS

But papyrus and leather were not constantly available or reusable. An alternative writing material, easily re-used, was the wooden tablet coated on one side with wax. Such tablets are depicted on sculptures of the early first millennium BC from north Syria, and were perhaps inscribed by the Hittites rather earlier. Examples made from ivory, for an Assyrian king, were found in a palace well at Nimrud. Wooden ones from Egypt bear notes and school-exercises in Greek. Some boards were hinged to make two or more leaves. When the dumb Zechariah took a writing tablet to tell his relatives that his baby son would be called John (the Baptist), he probably wrote on a waxed board.

◁ Luke 1: 63

Cheaper than anything else were the pieces of broken pottery that were strewn in the streets and houses of ancient times. These, and flakes of stone, were ready-made surfaces for anyone who wanted to write a message in ink or scratch it with a sharp point.

15

The Greeks often did this, and the term now given to such inscribed potsherds is *ostracon* (plural *ostraca*) the Greek word for a potsherd.

Even in Egypt, the home of papyrus, potsherds often served as scrap-paper. People would scribble on them short messages or notes which had no long-term importance. Where both papyri and ostraca survive, as in the partly Jewish garrison town at Elephantine, flourishing during the fifth century BC, it is clear that any permanent or important records were written on papyrus.

Realizing this makes it easier to understand the situation revealed by archaeological discoveries in Israel. Between 150 and 200 ostraca have been unearthed there, bearing short texts in the ancient Hebrew script and language. These were only notes of little value; the seal impressions and the fuller evidence from Egypt leave no doubt that most writing in ancient Israel was done on papyrus.

In Babylonia another common substance used as writing material, was clay. With a reed stylus scribes would impress the wedge-shaped strokes of the cuneiform script on to the soft

Part of an ivory writing-board, linked with hinges. There are traces of wax overlay. Assyrian scribes used such boards as an alternative to clay tablets. This example is from the reign of Sargon II, 721-705 BC.

15

An ostracon (pottery fragment) from Lachish at the time of Jeremiah, about 590-587 BC. It is a good example of cursive Hebrew writing and lists nine Hebrew names, seven of which are compounded with Yhwh.

Proto–Sinaitic c. 1500 BC	Canaanite c. 1400 – 1100 BC	Represents	S. Arabian c. 300 BC	Phoenician c. 1000 BC	Early Hebrew		Aram. Eleph. c. 45
					Siloam c. 700 BC	Lachish c. 586 BC	
		ox					
		house					
		throw-stick					
		fish					
		man with raised arms					
		prop					
		weapon?					
		fence?					
		palm of hand					
		staff					
		water					
		snake					
		fish					
		eye					
		mouth					
		plant?					
		monkey?					
		head					
		bow?					
		cross-mark					

Chart showing the development of the alphabet in various scripts in use in ancient Palestine.

Hebrew 1st cent. AD	Hebrew name	Phonetic value	Early Greek 8th cent. BC	Classical Greek: Athens 5th cent. BC	Greek name	Roman
ℵ	ʾalep̄		A	A	alpha	A
ב	bêṯ	b	B	B	bēta	B
ג	gīmel	g	Γ, ⟨	Γ	gamma	G
ד	dāleṯ	d	Δ	Δ	delta	D
ה	hē	h	⅀	E	epsilon	E
ו	waw	w	F	Y	(digamma) upsilon	F Y
ז	zayin	z	I	Z	zēta	Z
ח	ḥêṯ	ḥ	⊟	H	ēta	H
ט	ṭêṯ	ṭ	⊕	⊙	thēta	
י	yôḏ	y	⟨, ∫	I	iota	I
כ	kap̄	k	K	K	kappa	K
ל	lāmeḏ	l	⌐, Γ	L	lambda	L
מ	mēm	m	M	M	mu	M
נ	nûn	n	N	N	nu	N
ס	sāmeḵ	s	Ξ	Ξ	xi	
ע	ʾayin	ʿ	O	O	omicron	O
פ	pêʾ	p	Γ	Γ	pi	P
צ	ṣaḏê	ṣ	M		(san)	
ק	qôp̄	q	ϙ		(koppa)	Q
ר	rêš	r	P, R	P	rhō	R
ש	šin	š	⟨, ⟨	⟨	sigma	S
ת	taw	t	T	T	tau	T

15

Left: cuneiform clay tablet (about 650 BC) recording the Babylonian account of the flood. Tablet XI of the Assyrian version of the Epic of Gilgamesh.

surface of slabs of clay small enough to be held in the hand. After drying in the sun and baking in an oven these tablets became hard and durable. This Babylonian practice spread all over the Near East, and some scribes in Canaanite cities wrote in cuneiform, although there is no suggestion that the Israelites did so.

Kings everywhere would have their deeds carved on stone monuments and on the walls of buildings. Other people sometimes had inscriptions engraved on stone, usually for tombs. Especially after the alphabet had become widely used, many people would scratch their names or short notes on all sorts of stone and metal objects including pots and pans.

WRITTEN RECORDS FROM ANCIENT CANAAN AND ISRAEL

Egyptian and Babylonian scripts were current in Canaan before Israel invaded. Stimulated by them and by other writing systems, a scribe invented a new script, the alphabet. Examples of the alphabet in its early stages date from about 1500 BC, and the invention can be dated a little before. Whereas Egyptian and Babylonian had several hundred signs standing for syllables and words, the alphabet worked with only twenty to thirty signs. Instead of standing for the word for 'water', *maim*, or for the sound *maim*, a picture of water, ∿∿ , simply marked the sound *m*. This made writing a much simpler and easier affair, and the alphabet spread through Canaan and Syria. At Ugarit on the coast of Syria local scribes trained to write in the Babylonian fashion saw the advantages of the

alphabet and made their own imitation with twenty-nine cuneiform signs. The stories, lists of gods, letters and legal deeds, which they wrote with this script on clay tablets, give invaluable information about the life and culture of a city similar to the Canannite cities at the time of Moses. By the year 1000 BC the letters of the alphabet had reached a standard form and had replaced all other scripts that had been in use in Palestine.

The oldest inscription from the days of Israel's kings is the Gezer Calendar. Late in the tenth century BC someone, perhaps a schoolboy, wrote the farmer's tasks for each month of the year on a small stone tablet (see page 141).

No Israelite royal inscriptions have yet been found, but there is a famous one set up by a neighbour. This is the Moabite Stone written in a language very close to Hebrew and in a form of the alphabet which shows some development. The inscription is on a stone slab which Mesha, king of Moab, set up to celebrate the victories which he believed his god Chemosh had enabled him to win over Omri, king of Israel, and his successor. It also refers to the God of Israel by name, Yahweh, the oldest document outside the Bible to do so.

People who could afford large tombs sometimes had short notices engraved on the doorways. One found in Silwan, looking across the valley to Jerusalem, may mark the tomb of the Royal Steward whom Isaiah denounced for making his burial place so ostentatious (see the illustration of the inscription on the lintel of this tomb on page 221).

The best-known example of ancient Hebrew writing illustrates the readiness of some Israelites to write. Two gangs of workmen were digging a tunnel to carry water from one part of Jerusalem to another (from the

15

◁ Isaiah 22: 15-19

Virgin's Fountain to the Pool of Siloam), in the time of King Hezekiah, about 705 BC. They tunnelled from each end, met deep underground, and the water flowed through. This was such a success that a record of it was engraved on the rock wall inside the tunnel. Since its discovery in 1880, it has been called the Siloam Inscription (see page 120).

Hebrew ostraca are known from three major collections and many scattered examples. They are mostly written in a flowing script, the work of trained clerks. A few show stilted letters and strange forms which suggest they were not written by professional scribes. At Samaria over 100 ostraca were found in the ruins of the Israelite palace. They date from the mid–eighth century BC, and survived because they had been used as rubble to make up a floor. They are mostly receipts for oil and wine, probably brought in as taxes, from estates around Samaria. From Lachish come more ostraca, including several letters. The captain of a military outpost wrote to his commander as the soldiers of Nebuchadrezzar were overrunning the country in 587 BC: 'we can no longer see the signals of Azekah'. Letters and accounts also written on ostraca lay in the fortress of Arad, destroyed at the same time. One of them mentions 'the house of Yahweh', which could be the temple in Jerusalem or, possibly, a local shrine.

As well as all these examples of formal writing, the names of individuals scratched on pots and various other examples of writing, show that the skill was widely known in ancient Israel.

The first recorded alphabet from Ugarit. There were thirty characters on a clay tablet. This may have been a school exercise. 14th century BC.

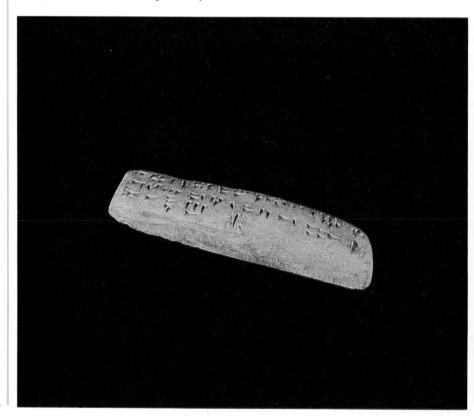

LANGUAGES AND WRITING IN NEW TESTAMENT TIMES

By the time of the Babylonian conquest Hebrew's sister language, Aramaic, had become the international language of the Near East. In exile the Jews spoke it, and those who went back to their land used it there. Some Jewish seals and coins from the time of the Persian Empire illustrate that. Books of the Old Testament, although in Hebrew, were now copied in the Aramaic form of the alphabet, which developed into the 'square script' still used for printing Hebrew. The old Hebrew style of the letters became uncommon, except when it was used on Jewish coins to assert the nation's identity.

Evidence that people commonly spoke Aramaic in the New Testament period comes from Jewish burials where the names of the dead are often written in Aramaic. It was in Aramaic too that Jesus spoke to Jairus' daughter when he told her to get up. With many Jews speaking Aramaic, it became necessary to translate the Bible as the lessons were read in the synagogues. Eventually these translations were written down and are known as Targums. The oldest available is one on the book of Job found among the Dead Sea Scrolls.

Hebrew was still spoken by some Jews, especially in Jerusalem, and was normal in religious circles. It had changed during the centuries after the exile, becoming what scholars describe as Mishnaic or Rabbinic Hebrew. A few specimens survive in letters of the first and second centuries AD found in caves near the Dead Sea. The rabbis gave their opinions in Hebrew about how the law applied to daily life, and a collection of them was made by Rabbi Judah the Prince, who was born in AD 135. This is the Mishnah. It has six

Old Hebrew script on the silver 'shekel of Israel' minted at the time of the first Jewish revolt, AD *66-70.*

major divisions or orders, each divided into chapters (tractates), dealing with offerings, feasts, oaths, the place of women, ritual cleanness and many other religious topics, including a description of Herod's temple in Jerusalem.

By New Testament times Greek was widespread in Palestine. This was *koine* Greek, a development from the classical language which grew up after Alexander the Great had opened the Near East to Greek culture. There are inscriptions in Greek from towns and cities of Palestine, and some of the notices in Herod's temple were engraved in Greek to warn non-Jews not to enter the sacred courtyard. *Koine* Greek is now very well-known through thousands of papyrus documents which have been recovered from the dried-out rubbish-heaps of Egyptian towns. They cover the centuries following Alexander's conquests to the rise of Islam (roughly 300 BC to AD 650), and deal with every aspect of life.

Until the papyri were found, several Greek words were known only from the New Testament, and their meanings were not always quite clear. When such words came to light in the

◁◁Mark 5: 41

15

Facing page: the 'Moabite stone'.

everyday speech of the papyri, their meanings could be better defined. For example, Paul says that the Holy Spirit is a 'guarantee' (RSV), 'pledge' (NEB) or 'deposit' (NIV), using the Greek word *arrabōn*. In the commercial world an advance payment was often given to secure an item or service and to guarantee that the full payment would be made. Commercial documents referring to such down-payments have helped the modern understanding of the Holy Spirit as God's guarantee or advance on earth of something greater to come in heaven.

When goods were bought, a receipt was often issued. In the papyri this receipt was sometimes called an *apoche*, and indicated that the seller had been paid in full. Jesus used the related verb in the Sermon on the Mount which is translated 'have' in 'the hypocrites have received their reward in full'. The verb is compound in form, consisting of a verb and a preposition, and seems a complicated word to use for what seems a simple need (there was a simpler Greek word), but it aptly captures Jesus' meaning. The people who do religious acts simply to be seen by men, rather than to serve God, have had their full receipt – the praise of men. There is no further reward for their actions.

The papyri also show that the form of Paul's letters was the usual one of the time. Letters in the collection began with the writer's name, followed by the person addressed, and ended with parting greetings. Some also contained a prayer and thanksgiving similar to those found in Paul's letters.

Paul's letters were written in Greek and the whole of the New Testament was available in Greek before the end of the first century. By then Greek was the normal language for writing and speech for the majority of Christians who were Gentiles from outside Palestine. Some scholars have argued that Aramaic manuscripts lie behind the Greek Gospels, but none has so far been found.

When Jesus was crucified on the authority of Pontius Pilate, the Roman governor, an inscription was put on his cross in Hebrew, Greek and Latin. Palestine was ruled by the Romans, and while Greek remained the international language, Latin inscriptions and documents have turned up in Palestine. In Italy every educated Roman was bilingual in Greek and Latin.

◁◁ 2 Corinthians 1: 22; 5: 5

One inscription of special interest to Bible readers comes from the theatre area at Caesarea. It says that Pontius Pilate had erected a building called the Tiberium in honour of the Emperor (see page 356).

◁◁ Matthew 6: 2, 5, 16

READERS AND WRITERS

There were enough literate people in ancient Israel to produce and use all kinds of written documents, from business receipts to the annals of kings. But how many people other than the professional scribes (see feature) could read and write is unclear. A young prisoner of war caught by Gideon was able to write down the names of seventy-seven elders in the town of Succoth in about the twelfth century BC. In the eighth century Isaiah foretold a time when 'the remaining trees of the forests will be so few that a child could write them down'. This implies that children were taught to write. In a later, obscure passage, Isaiah may also be referring to children learning their letters. He describes the drunken revellers who mocked him; their slurred speech may have sounded like children reciting the alphabet.

◁ Judges 8: 14

◁ Isaiah 10: 19

◁ Isaiah 28: 7-10

Letters of the alphabet written in order on potsherds and seal-stones seem to be the work of people learning

15

THE SCRIBES

Ezra 7: 6, 10 ▷▷

Jeremiah 36: 4 ▷

1 Chronicles 2: 55 ▷

Jeremiah 36: 10, 12 ▷

Ezekiel 9: 2f. ▷

Professional scribes came into existence as the nation developed a centralized administration. The king's scribes were government officials who were counsellors, secretaries of state and tax officials, as well as writers of documents. Jeremiah dictated his prophecies to the scribe Baruch, probably just as other employers used their scribes.

There were professional guilds of scribes, just as there were of other specialized workers, and they had special quarters in the temple or palace. From the description given by Ezekiel, it seems they carried a writing case attached to their girdle – just like the scribes in Egypt and Mesopotamia. As in some Third World countries today, scribes probably sat in some public place to read or write documents for the illiterate majority of the population. The scribe therefore had both prestige and power in society.

After the exile, the role of the scribe changed. He still fulfilled his basic writing functions, but increasingly he became a recorder and interpreter of the law. Scribal decisions about legal matters were collected into a corpus of oral tradition which the Pharisees considered to have equal authority with the written law of God.

The profession was open to anyone who completed the training, and was not hereditary. By the first century AD the scribes were a powerful group of Jewish leaders, who, with the Pharisees, were sometimes the target of Jesus' sharpest words.

Scribes recording booty taken on the military campaigns of Tiglath-Pileser III (744-727 BC). One uses a clay tablet, the other papyrus. From Nimrud.

The tomb slab of Uzziah. It is written in Aramaic and reads, 'Hither were brought the bones of Uzziah king of Judah. Not to be opened.' It is probably to be dated in the 1st century AD when the king's bones were reburied.

to write or engrave their letters. The number who learnt to read and write in ancient Israel was never very large, but the simplicity of the alphabet meant that anyone who wanted to make the effort could learn it more quickly, and much more easily than Babylonian or Egyptian scripts. From the wide distribution of inscribed objects in Israel and Judah, especially from about 750 BC onwards, it appears that no one would have had difficulty in finding someone who could read and write, even if he was not a professional scribe. Teaching was probably done in very small groups in private houses, not in school classes.

By New Testament times probably more children received a basic education in a school attached to the synagogue, although attendance was not compulsory and the schools were probably still patronized by the sons of wealthier people who did not need the extra manpower all the time.

The Dead Sea Scrolls show the products of Jewish scribes in the last century BC and the first century AD. In the ruins of the building at Qumran, where the probable owners of the Scrolls lived, there were found ink-wells, benches on which, it is thought, scribes sat, and a potsherd with the letters of the alphabet written on it as an exercise.

In a collection of Rabbinic sayings known as *Pirqe Aboth* (Chapters of the Fathers) there is a reference to education:

At five years old one is fit for the Scriptures, at ten years for the Mishna, at thirteen for the fulfilling of the commandments, at fifteen for the Talmud ...

Page from a Greek codex (Acts 17: 9-17), written in 'rustic capitals', 3rd century AD.

Young men were to marry at eighteen. Education for their specific profession followed.

While the primary reference here is to reading, the companion art of writing is to be presumed as part of Jewish education. Fathers may also have taught their sons the elements of reading and writing. By 75 BC Rabbi Ben Shetach decreed that children, that is boys, should attend elementary schools. This may have been a response to Greek influences which were already strong in Palestine. Education was an important aspect of Greek life and demanded vigorous intellectual activity until a person was aged at least eighteen.

The ordinary Jewish boy was skilled in reading and writing Hebrew and perhaps Aramaic as well. Literacy in Greek was not nearly so widespread. The Jewish historian Josephus remarked (for the benefit of his Greek readers) that he had been at great pains to obtain Greek learning because his nation did not encourage children to learn the languages of other nations.

FOR FURTHER READING

Carmon, E. and Grafman, R., *Inscriptions Reveal, Documents from the time of the Bible, the Mishna and the Talmud* (Jerusalem, Israel Museum, 1973).

Diringer, D., *The Alphabet*, 3rd ed. (Hutchinson, 1968).

Feinberg, C.L., 'Scribes', *IBD*, 3 (IVP, 1980), pp.1403–1404.

Harris, B.F., 'Papyri and Ostraca', *IBD*, 2 (IVP, 1980), pp.1142–1150.

McCown, C.C., 'The Earliest Christian Books', *BA*, 6 (2), (1943), pp.21–31.

Millard, A.R., 'The Practice of Writing in Ancient Israel', *BA*, 35 (4), (1972), pp.98–111.

Milligan, G., *Here and there among the Papyri* (1923).

Pritchard, J.B., *Ancient Near East texts relating to the Old Testament*, 3rd ed. (Princeton UP, 1969).

Thomas, D.W. (ed.), *Documents from Old Testament Times* (Harper & Row, 1965).

White, W. Jr., 'Writing', *ZPEB*, 5 (Grand Rapids, Zondervan, 1975), pp.995–1015.

Williams, R.J., 'Writing and Writing Materials', *IDB*, 5 (New York, Abingdon, 1962), pp.909–921.

Wiseman, D.J., Kitchen, K.A. and Millard, A.R., 'Writing', *IBD*, 3 (IVP, 1980), pp.1657–1671.

15

Music and games 16

Walk down any western city street and you will almost certainly hear music blaring from shops and see people wearing earphones plugged into their own private, portable music centres. On holiday beaches from Bondi to the Bahamas, and in kitchens from Alabama to Zeebrugge, radios and cassette-players pump out an incessant stream of music to accompany the leisure-seekers and the home-makers in their play and their work. And when the sun has set, the electric world of concert and dance halls beats with the varied rhythms of classical opera and new-wave pop, which are wafted through the air, made available to anyone who can afford a receiver.

There are few people who do not at some time or another like to hear or listen to music. So imagine a world where there are no records, no cassettes, no radios or televisions; where professional touring orchestras or dance bands are not thought of; where the only music you could hear would be live, and, except in the temple or the royal court, made almost entirely by your friends, relatives – and yourself.

Quiet? Dull? They were hardly the sentiments of the Israelite psalmist whose description of musical worship had all the marks of a stirring celebration which seems far removed from the caricatured sobriety of some western church services.

Facing page: bronze figure of an Etruscan dancing girl, about 460 BC.

Praise him with the sounding of the trumpet,
  praise him with the harp and lyre,
praise him with tambourine and dancing,
  praise him with the strings and flute,
praise him with the clash of cymbals,
  praise him with resounding cymbals.

Let everything that has breath praise the LORD.

Praise the LORD.

◁ Psalm 150: 3-6

And if the song of birds and bleat of sheep was not enough to deaden the sound of silence while you worked in the fields, there was usually someone around with a shepherd's pipe to blow or a stringed lyre to pluck. And there were plenty of songs with simple, catchy tunes to sing as you worked by day and relaxed over the dimly-lit meal table at night. Music in ancient Israel was live, lively and probably made by almost everyone.

MUSICAL OCCASIONS

Perhaps because they were not saturated with music at all hours of the day and night, the people of Bible times seem to have made almost every unusual occasion an excuse for music and singing. When Jacob left his father-in-law Laban without warning, the old man caught up with him and said,

Exodus 15: 20f. ▷▷
Genesis 31: 27 ▷

'"Why didn't you tell me, so I could send you away with joy and singing to the music of tambourines and harps?"' Even saying goodbye was a time for festivities.

People sang and danced when they celebrated military victories. Miriam 'took a tambourine in her hand, and all

A shepherd boy playing a pipe at Palmyra, Syria.

the women followed her, with tambourines and dancing. Miriam sang to them …' when Pharaoh's horsemen had drowned in the Red Sea as they attempted to recapture the fleeing Israelites. The men of Judah and Jerusalem 'returned joyfully' with King Jehoshaphat after victory over Ammon and Moab, and 'went to the temple of the LORD with harps and lutes and trumpets'.

Feasts and festivals seem always to have had a music group to entertain the guests and enliven the proceedings. Isaiah once described the merrymaking: 'They have harps and lyres at their banquets, tambourines and flutes and wine'. Isaiah implies that there were once ancient equivalents of bawdy drinking songs, quoting the words of revellers: '"Let us eat and drink … for tomorrow we die!"' and '"Let me get wine! Let us drink our fill of beer! And tomorrow will be like today, or even far better."'

The prophets sometimes speak of the joy of the winepress or the harvest. Working-songs were no doubt used by labourers to encourage one another in the fields and on building-sites. Psalm 67 among others was probably used as a celebratory song as people worked or relaxed at the end of the day. Isaiah records a love song – which has elements of lament, too – about Israel, and the Song of Songs is one of the most beautiful of wedding songs known to the world. As both music and love could be corrupted then as now, prostitutes walked the streets singing in order to make themselves more seductive.

Shepherds such as David out in the fields sang or played to themselves and their flocks, and young men gathered to play and listen to music, not at street corners, but at the communal meeting places at the city gates. David 'danced before the LORD with all his might' when the ark of the covenant was brought home to Jerusalem; another biblical example of the full-blooded and almost extravagant worship Israelites sometimes enjoyed.

There was sad music too, of course. A mournful dirge was sung at times of bereavement or distress. David lamented the deaths of Saul and Jonathan with a dirge, and the book of Lamentations is a series of such songs as the poet contemplated the destruction of Jerusalem by its enemies.

◁◁ 2 Chronicles 20: 27f.

◁ 2 Samuel 1: 17-27

In early times there were probably no professional musicians, and it seems that women tended to be the main music-makers. Groups of women sang for the young warrior David, for example. Choruses of singing and dancing women are known in Egypt from an early date. When David became king he sponsored professional musicians, and their names are recorded in the first book of Chronicles. They were primarily associated with the temple, but they also had special functions within the palace and at times of war. Amos may be contrasting the professionals and amateurs when he complains of the idle rich, 'You sing idle songs to the sound of the harp, and fancy yourselves to be as great musicians as King David was.'

◁◁ Isaiah 5: 12

◁ 1 Samuel 18: 6-7

◁◁ Isaiah 22: 13

◁ 1 Chronicles 6: 31-47

◁◁ Isaiah 56: 12

◁ Amos 6: 5 (LB)

By New Testament times music was clearly a common part of daily life, and Jesus and the apostles used musical allusions on the assumption that they would be readily understood. The Christian is not to 'sound a trumpet' when he gives away money, for example. Jesus told about contrary children who called out, 'we played the flute for you, and you did not dance; we sang a dirge, and you did not cry.' And Paul likened Christians without love to 'a resounding gong or a clanging cymbal' – in other words they were people whose lives, as it were, made a rather empty, hollow sound, and who were not genuine.

16

◁◁ Isaiah 5: 1

◁◁ Isaiah 23: 16

◁ Matthew 6: 2

◁ Luke 7: 32

◁ 1 Corinthians 13: 1

Musicians playing double pipes, accompany girls dancing at a banquet. From a wall painting in the tomb of Nebamun, Egypt, about 1400 BC.

Paul, already familiar as a Jew with psalms, hymns and spiritual songs, encouraged the young churches to 'sing and make music in your heart to the Lord'. The people in heaven are said to have a new song to sing, but they had been given it on earth for their command and delight was to 'rejoice in

Ephesians 5: 19 ▷

Revelation 5: 9-10 ▷

Philippians 4: 4 ▷

the Lord always'. Music played a vital part in Jewish and early Christian worship, and we will examine that in more detail in the final chapters of this book.

MUSICAL INSTRUMENTS

Music in Bible times was relatively simple because the instruments available to the people were simple and

STRINGED INSTRUMENTS

The first instrument mentioned in the Bible is the *kinnor*, pioneered it seems by Jubal, 'the father of all who play the *kinnor* and flute'. It is translated as lyre in the RSV, and as harp in the AV and NIV, and is mentioned some forty times in the Old Testament. It may have had Syrian origins. It could have been used in the farewell celebrations of Laban the Syrian if his son-in-law Jacob had given him the opportunity. It was an instrument small enough to be carried by the prophets whom Saul met, and to be hung up on trees by the exiled Israelites in Babylon who were in no mood to be happy and to sing songs.

◁ Genesis 4: 21

◁ Genesis 31: 27

◁ 1 Samuel 10: 5

◁ Psalm 137: 2

The *kinnor* was made of wood, and the Beni–Hasan wall paintings, dating from about 1900 BC, depict a Semitic nomad playing an eight-stringed instrument with a wooden frame. Assyrian reliefs show stringed instruments of many different kinds. An Egyptian painting from about the fifteenth century BC depicts a stringed instrument, and Jewish coins of the second century AD depict the later *kinnor* of Palestine. In all the illustrations the strings were stretched between the frame and a sounding box. The Jewish Mishna says that the entrails of birds were used to make strings for the *kinnor*.

The *nebel* is mentioned twenty-seven times in the Old Testament and is generally translated harp although also as lyre in some places in the NIV and as psaltery or viol in the AV. Made of cypress wood and later of almug, it was used alongside the lyre and therefore was different from it (see illustration). The AV translation 'psaltery' comes from the Greek Old Testament which uses the word *psallo* to translate the Hebrew. *Psallo* means 'to pluck', which confirms that the instrument was a harp.

The *nebel* was probably larger than the lyre, perhaps providing the bass

limited in range. But from biblical references and archaeological discoveries (especially in Egypt and Assyria) we know that there was a variety of stringed, wind and percussion instruments. Bible versions vary in the way they translate some Hebrew words, and where there is doubt we have given the alternative names and used a transliterated form of the Hebrew to avoid confusion.

16

A Sumerian musician playing an eleven-stringed lyre which is decorated with a bull's head. This is part of the 'Ur Standard' from about 2500 BC.

notes, and it seems to have had more and larger strings. According to the Jewish Talmud its strings were made from the large intestines of a sheep so that it could make a louder and deeper sound than the lyre.

Some other stringed instruments are occasionally mentioned in the Bible. The Psalms, for example, mention a ten-stringed lyre.

WIND INSTRUMENTS

There are three Hebrew words variously translated as 'flute' or 'pipe', and even, in the AV, 'organ'. Descriptions of the instrument and

their usage in the Bible are insufficient to identify their exact nature. The Hebrew word *khalil* (usually flute in RSV and NIV, pipe in AV), occurs only six times in the Old Testament. The Hebrew word derives from a root meaning 'to bore' and 'to pierce', and its Greek equivalent *aulos* derives from a root meaning 'to blow'. However, this could cover reed instruments such as the oboe and clarinet, and instruments like the flute which are played by blowing across or through a hole.

It was used in festivals ('when people go up with flutes to the mountain of the LORD') and in children's games ('we played the flute for you, and you did not dance'). It was also used at funerals, and was being played before Jesus raised Jairus' daughter from the

Daniel 3: 5 ▷

E.g. Psalm 33: 2 ▷

Isaiah 30: 29 ▷▷

Matthew 11: 17 ▷▷

Matthew 9: 23 ▷▷

dead. Jeremiah implies that it could produce a plaintive note ('my heart laments for Moab like a flute'), and Paul says that it could produce indistinct notes. It is generally reckoned to be like a simple clarinet or oboe, and some Assyrian sources suggest a double oboe.

The second Hebrew word rendered flute is *ugab* (organ in AV), and occurs only four times in the Old Testament . It cannot easily be identified and may have been a generic term for all wind instruments. The third word is Aramaic, *mashroqita*, related to a verb meaning to whistle or hiss. Most pipes or whistles make a hissing sound when they are played, and so it is usually translated flute in its four occurrences in the book of Daniel. The simple flute or pipe is still used today by shepherds in the Near East, and the player blows across an open end.

There are also several words which are translated as trumpet or horn. The *qeren* was made of horn, wood or metal, and was used more to sound signals than to make music. The *shofar*

◁◁ Jeremiah 48: 36

◁◁ Daniel 3: 5, 7, 10, 15

A small bronze figure (6 cm, just over 2 in high) of a trumpet player from Caria in Turkey, about 800 BC.

Orthodox Jew sounding the shofar *at the Western Wall, Jerusalem.*

is a ram's horn, and is still used in synagogues today. Heated in steam to make it soft, the wide end was bent to form a right angle. The trumpeter blew into the smaller end and could produce a variety of tones. It was used mostly to give war signals, to sound an alarm, proclaim the year of jubilee and the new and full moons, and to announce a king's coronation.

The *hatsotsera* was a metal trumpet; Moses ordered two to be made from silver to summon the people, to break camp, and to sound the alarm.

◁ Numbers 10: 2

Trumpets are depicted on the first-century Arch of Titus in Rome, erected in memory of that emperor's subjugation of the Jews, and also on second-century Jewish coins.

PERCUSSION INSTRUMENTS
Cymbals were used for religious music in Old Testament times, and appear to

16

have been played by men only. Assyrian bas-reliefs depict two sorts which probably correspond to the two Hebrew words usually translated 'cymbals'. One sort consisted of a shallow metal cup held in each hand and struck together. The other also had two pieces but one was held stationary while the other was struck sharply against it. A pair of bronze cymbals was found at Beth-shemesh dating from about the fourteenth or thirteenth century BC.

The tambourine (timbrel or tabret in AV) seems to have been used largely by women and was a popular instrument in processions, dances and feasts. It was held in one hand and struck with the other. It may have had two membranes with pieces of bronze inserted in the frame which rattled

Below: bronze cymbals from Luristan (Iran), 9th-7th centuries BC.

Right: an Egyptian sistrum, later than 850 BC.

when the sides were struck or shaken. Remains of such instruments have been found in Mesopotamia.

Another instrument which was shaken was the sistrum. It is referred to rarely in the Bible but it was well known in the Near East. It usually had an oval loop with cross-pieces in it; the cross-pieces held loose rings which jangled together when the sistrum was shaken. There are no biblical references to drums at all, but a big drum was used in Lower Mesopotamia and a small hand-drum was common in Assyria. As its neighbours used drums, it is likely that Israel also used them.

INDOOR GAMES

Feasting, singing and dancing were among the most popular forms of

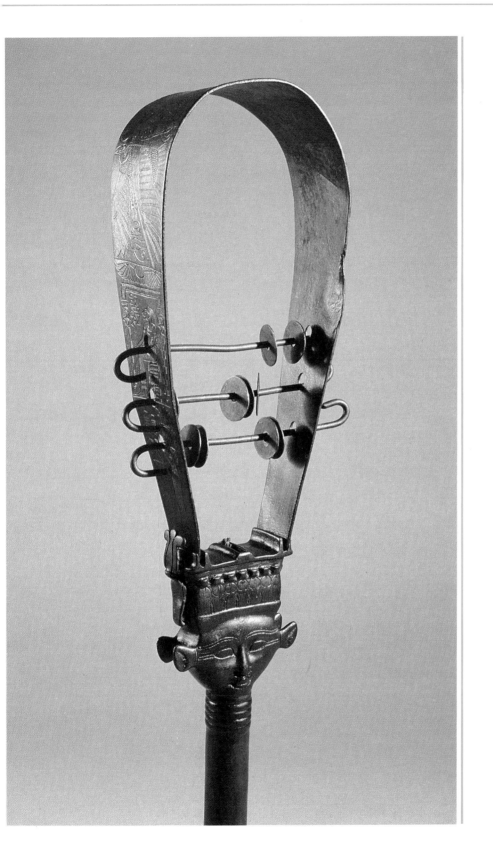

16

recreation in the ancient biblical world. It was a sign of national calamity when these things ceased. Story-telling and propounding riddles were also popular pastimes; Samson told riddles and the prophets at least used allegories and parables. But people played games, too. Life was by no means lacking in such pastimes.

Judges 14: 12; ▷

Ezekiel 17: 2 ▷

Gaming-boards have been discovered in Palestine and elsewhere in the Near East. One found at Megiddo dating between 1350 and 1150 BC had fifty-eight holes bored in it. One found at Gezer was made of stone (dating from about 1200 BC) while others were made from wood or clay. Some were shaped like a violin or

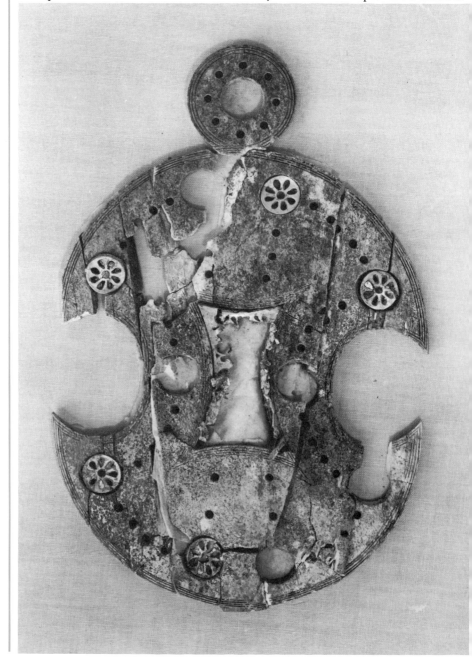

Board used for the game of senet *from Tutankhamun's tomb. Moves were decided by throwing knuckle-bones or dice.*

a stylized human being and pierced with peg holes. How the games were played on them is unknown.

Draught boards were widely known in western Asia. They had twenty or thirty squares and were made from stone, clay, ebony or ivory. Some were hollowed at the back to store the pieces. Moves were determined by throwing dice. Sets of playing pieces have been found in Egypt, Mesopotamia and Palestine. An ivory die dating to the seventeenth century BC was found at Tell Beit Mirsim, together with a set of ten movable pieces, five of which were cone-shaped and five were tetrahedrons. Knuckle-bones and small tops or discs which could be spun with the fingers were sometimes used instead of dice. A pyramid-shaped ivory die or teetotum,

pierced on four sides with varying numbers of holes from one to four, was also found there.

Some of the boards from Mesopotamia and Egypt are remarkably ornate and set with beautiful inlay work. A fine board divided into thirty squares was found in the tomb of Tutankhamun dating from about 1360 BC. A game was evidently played on it with conical and spool-shaped pieces. Another board of ivory and veneer came from the tomb of Renseneb at Thebes dating from the twelfth dynasty (about 1990–1780 BC).

One remarkably well preserved board game was discovered in Jerusalem during excavations at the convent of the Sisters of Zion. The area has sometimes been identified with the pavement where Pilate judged Jesus, and is thought to have belonged originally to the Tower of Antonia. Patterns scratched into the stones of the

Facing page: the gaming-board from Megiddo mentioned on this page. It is nearly 27 cm (about 11 in) high and made from ivory with gold leaf and paste inlays. Presumably pegs were inserted in the holes. Gold studs found nearby may have been parts of the pegs.

16

John 19: 13 ▷

pavement in several places seem to represent the play board for a popular game played by the soldiers of the Roman garrison.

OUTDOOR SPORTS

Genesis 32: 24-26 ▷▷

The Egyptians, Mesopotamians, Greeks and Romans all enjoyed running, throwing, wrestling and shooting. References to such activities are rare in the Bible but it would have been strange if the people of Israel had

2 Samuel 2: 14-16 ▷▷

not enjoyed them too.

The patriarch Jacob had a night-encounter in which he wrestled with a stranger. This was a life-changing event for Jacob and could in no way be described as organized sport, but it is interesting to note that belt-wrestling was well known throughout the ancient Near East. One of the rules forbade holds below the waist. Jacob's divine assailant touched the hollow of his thigh and dislocated his hip, signifying an end to the 'contest'.

The servants of Joab and those of David decided to settle a dispute by arranging a boxing or wrestling match, which ended in bloodshed.

Jonathan, David's friend and son of

The so-called 'King's Game' scratched on the pavement in the courtyard of the Antonia fortress.

CHILDREN'S GAMES

Above: this delightful toy hedgehog on wheels comes from Susa and dates from 13th-12th centuries BC.

One of the features of the restoration of Israel to Jerusalem would be that '"the city streets will be filled with boys and girls playing there"'.

Egyptian reliefs show girls dancing or playing a singing game, and boys playing tug-of-war. The book of Job refers to children dancing and singing. And a marble statue from Athens, dating from about 500 BC, depicts youths hitting a ball with sticks similar to those used centuries later for hockey.

Archaeologists have discovered small baked clay figurines which may have been dolls. Whistles, rattles, model animals and chariots have also been found and were probably children's toys.

The Bible narrative never refers specifically to toys. But since play is a universal part of growing up, the Israelite children must have used toys such as those discovered, and played all kinds of games together in the fields and streets.

◁◁ Zechariah 8: 5

This marble statue-base from Athens, about 500 BC, shows what appears to be the 'bully-off' in a game very like hockey.

16

1 Samuel 20: 20 ▷

King Saul, signalled the king's intentions towards David in a pre-arranged archery practice. Assyrian bas-reliefs indicate that archery was practised among Israel's neighbours, and it was well known too in Egypt. Pharaoh Tuthmosis III and his son, Amenophis II, both boasted of their skill with the bow, shooting arrows through bronze targets. Archery may therefore have been a game of skill as well as a means of hunting and waging war.

Greek athletic games were introduced into Palestine at the time of the Seleucids and they caused the Jews of the day grave concern, for two reasons. One was that the games were associated with pagan religious festivals, the other was that contestants were often naked.

On the Greek peninsular the Olympic Games at Olympia, the Pythian Games at Delphi, the Nemean Games at Argos and the Isthmian Games at Corinth were held regularly and were governed by strict rules of training over a long period. The games

themselves were strictly organized too, and included running and chariot races, boxing, wrestling, and discus and javelin throwing. Winners won only a crown of olive, pine, laurel or parsley leaves, but they were held in high honour by their fellow citizens.

Paul drew lessons from these games for the young churches. He urged the Christians at Corinth, familiar with the games, to emulate the athlete's strict training by living a disciplined, self–controlled life. Runners and boxers, he said, had to race and fight purposefully

◁◁ 1 Corinthians 9: 24-27

Roman glass bell found at Ephesus.

and not aimlessly beat the air; so Christians should not drift aimlessly but live faithfully in order to gain the unfading crown of God's approval which was waiting to be claimed in heaven. The writer to the Hebrews used a similar picture when he urged his readers to live the Christian life as if it were a race in front of a great crowd of spectators, former heroes who were urging them on. They should discard every hindrance to their speed and victory, just as a runner discarded every unnecessary article of clothing.

◁ Hebrews 12: 1-2

Some commentators have suggested that Paul describes a chariot race in his letter to the Christians at Philippi, a Roman colony which would have been familiar with such scenes. He says he is 'forgetting what is behind and straining towards what is ahead'. It seems like a picture of a chariot driver bent over the curved rail against which he presses his knees; the reins are round his body and stretching over the horse's back, and he leans his whole weight against them. A glance back would be fatal. So, says Paul, the Christian is to press on towards the end of the race of life, where a prize awaits him in heaven.

◁ Philippians 3: 13-14

16

The excitement of the Roman chariot race is captured in this plaque. The team of four horses is about to turn round the pillars or turning-posts at the end of the straight. Naufragia ('shipwrecks') often occurred at this point in the race. The charioteer needed intense concentration.

FOR FURTHER READING

Blaiklock, E.M., 'Games in the New Testament', *IBD*, 1 (IVP, 1980), pp.541–542.

Cartledge, S.A., 'Games, New Testament', *IDB*, 2 (New York, Abingdon, 1962), pp.353–354.

Rimmer, J., *Ancient Musical Instruments of Western Asia* (British Museum, 1969).

Rothmuller, A.M., *The Music of the Jews* (Valentine Mitchell, 1953).

Schnell, R.F., 'Games in the Old Testament', *IBD*, 2 (New York, Abingdon, 1962), pp.352–353.

Sellers, O.R., 'Musical Instruments of Israel', *BA*, 4 (3), (1941), pp.33–47.

Stradling, D.G. and Kitchen, K.A., 'Music and Musical Instruments', *IBD*, 2 (IVP, 1980), pp. 1031–1040.

Werner, W., 'Musical Instruments', *IDB*, 3 (New York, Abingdon, 1962), pp.469–476.

Wiseman, D.J., 'Games in the Old Testament', *IBD*, 1 (IVP, 1980), p.540.

Health and healing 17

The story of Jesus' birth brings home to people in the modern world the stark contrast between the sterile maternity units of western hospitals and the insanitary conditions of an eastern dwelling in the ancient world. When Jesus was born there was no running hot water in which to wash the new baby, no gas and air to help the labouring mother to relax her muscles.

There were, for Jesus, no teams of skilled doctors and midwives to monitor and ease his apparently undignified entrance into the world he had long before seen spun into orbit by the creative hand of his Father. There were just the ordinary smells and sounds of Palestinian domestic life, where humans shared quarters with animals.

During her pregnancy Mary would not have had the benefit of ultra-sound scans, regular check-ups at the clinic and vitamin supplements to ensure the healthy growth of her unborn child.

Roman medical instruments from the 1st century BC. These include, from the top, a rectal speculum, bleeding cup, box for drugs, probes, scalpel, spatula, hook, spoon and forceps.

Nor, if then or at any other time of her life she had fallen sick with anything from a cold to cancer, would she have been able to obtain fast-acting pain-relieving drugs, medicines to ease the symptoms of disease if not to cure it, or general anaesthetic if she required surgery.

Medical practice in biblical times was crude, and often mixed with superstition, magic and sorcery. Indeed, until Greek times it had generally been the task of the priest, not a trained expert, to diagnose and prescribe remedies for disease. The Egyptians had a god of healing, Imhotep, who had been a minister of Pharaoh Djoser (*c.* 2850 BC) and was deified a thousand years after his death because of his outstanding skills as a scribe, sage and probably a physician. Apis of Memphis, and Isis, were also gods of healing, and the Edwin Smith Papyrus, dating from about 1710-1550 BC but based on a document composed 1,000 years before, gives a lot of practical information about how diseases were treated.

In Mesopotamia several gods were believed to be involved in healing, including Ea, the patron deity, Ishtar, the goddess of fertility, Gula, the patroness of physicians and Shamash, the sun god. Castor oil, herbs and vegetables were used as medicines to assist recovery once the spirit which caused the illness had been identified and exorcized.

DOCTORS IN ISRAEL

The medical principles of the Israelites were enshrined in the law of Moses, the Pentateuch. They had advanced from the views of the tribes around them in that they rejected magic and

Magical rites. This cylinder seal from Assyria (about 1100 BC) shows a sick man and some of the rites used in an attempt to cure him. It was probably used as an amulet or charm.

CHILDBIRTH IN BIBLE TIMES

The first commandment in the Bible is to 'be fruitful and increase in number', and the pain associated with childbirth is attributed to the disobedience of Adam and Eve in Eden. In Bible times childbirth, while a joyous event, was also a dangerous one, and the death of mothers as they gave birth was not as exceptional as it is today. Jacob's wife Rachel died as she gave birth to Benjamin, a boy she called 'son of my trouble' (Ben-Oni) as she breathed her last.

A midwife usually assisted at the birth, although there is no indication that Mary the mother of Jesus had this help. In Egypt and in Babylon it seems the mother often sat on a birthstool, probably a pair of stones set one under each thigh. The Egyptian midwives told Pharoah that the Israelite women gave birth quickly. This was probably a ploy to excuse themselves from carrying out his command to kill the children, rather than a statement of physiological fact.

As soon as the baby was born the umbilical cord was cut and the child washed. It was then rubbed with salt, which was probably recognized as a disinfectant, and then wrapped in long bandages from the navel to the feet. It was believed that the leg movements of a newborn infant would harm its soft bones.

Because of the urgency of childbirth the work performed by both midwife and mother was never seen as a violation of the sabbath if it happened on that day. The father was never present during the delivery but informed of the event afterwards. Occasionally a child was born onto the knees of an adoptive mother, an act which seems to have sealed her legal right to the child.

◁Exodus 1: 19

◁◁Genesis 1: 28
◁ Ezekiel 16: 4
◁◁Genesis 3: 16

Genesis 35: 17

◁◁Exodus 1: 16

◁Genesis 30: 3

considered disease empirically or spiritually, as a thing in itself or a symptom of a person's relationship with God. 'The LORD's hand was heavy upon the [Philistine] people of Ashdod and its vicinity; he brought devastation upon them and afflicted them with tumours.'

They clearly believed that there was a causal relationship between good health and a life lived in obedience to God, which is why Job's so-called comforters could offer him no comfort; they believed he had brought his suffering on himself by his sin. The psalmist moaned, 'Because of your wrath there is no health in my body; my bones have no soundness because of my sin,' and his reaction was, 'I confess my iniquity; I am troubled by my sin. ... Come quickly to help me, O Lord my Saviour.'

The New Testament, written at a time when the medical profession was at least respectable enough for Luke, the companion of Paul and other apostles, to belong to it, also recognizes a relationship between body and spirit which some medical experts now themselves acknowledge. Guilt can cause stress which may be expressed by physical symptoms. The sick, says James, should confess their sins when the church meets to pray for them.

The medical responsibilities of priests were part of their religious duties. The book of Leviticus describes both religious and medical 'purification', including cleansing after childbirth (chapter 12), leprosy (chapter 13), venereal disease and menstruation (chapter 15). The prophets had a medical diagnostic role as well as their more familiar task of spiritual analysis and prescription. This is to be expected in a society which did not distinguish between the sacred and the secular. Elisha, for example, purified the water of Jericho, neutralized poisonous herbs, and assisted in the medical care of Naaman the Syrian and the son of the Shunammite woman.

◁James 5: 13-16

◁◁1 Samuel 5: 6

◁◁*E.g.* Job 4: 8

17

◁◁Psalm 38: 3, 18, 22
◁2 Kings 2: 19-22;
◁2 Kings 4: 39-41;
◁2 Kings 5: 3;

◁2 Kings 4: 32-35

A major hindrance to the growth of medical knowledge was the Israelite attitude to the human body. The corpse was an object of revulsion. This was especially so in a climate which caused rapid decomposition and consequent risk of infection. If the body was touched it was reckoned to cause a ritual uncleanness which had to be removed by religious ceremonies. There was therefore little opportunity to learn about the body's functions and diseases by autopsy or post-mortem examination. The origins of life were also wrapped in mystery and were not investigated; 'My frame was not hidden from you [God] when I was made in the secret place.' It was left to the Greeks, late in the Old Testament period, to explore the facts of human health and disease.

Psalm 139: 15 ▷

SICKNESS IN THE BIBLE

Such descriptions as exist in the Bible are mostly of ailments which could be observed externally, such as ulcers, swellings and haemorrhages; or what could be experienced by the patient, such as fever, dysentery or paralysis. Diseases of a microbiological nature were not understood. The term 'plague' refers to a variety of epidemics and is not the infection now given that name.

However, it is possible to identify some of the diseases which people suffered in Palestine in Bible times. They included malaria, typhoid fever, dysentery, enteric fevers (caused by

The muddy waters of the river Jordan, seen here in flood, repelled Naaman, the Syrian general, when he was told to bathe in them.

diseases in the alimentary canal and by parasitic worms), leprosy, boils, tuberculosis, pneumonia, smallpox, bubonic plague, scurvy, conjunctivitis, epilepsy, gout and polio.

As we do today people used general words to cover illnesses of many kinds. When Jacob was in Egypt, nearing the end of his life, his son Joseph was told, "'Your father is ill'"; some versions render the word 'weak', meaning 'ailing'. The same Hebrew word is used throughout the Old Testament to denote both physical injury and unspecified illness.

Often biblical words give little idea of the kind of illness which a person was suffering. For example, among the promised punishments given by God to an errant Israel is 'fever'. It could refer to the fever associated with malaria (as may have been suffered by Assyrian soldiers moving from the steamy coastal regions to the cooler climate of Jerusalem in the days of King Hezekiah), or it may have been sunstroke such as that which afflicted a boy whom Elisha later raised from the dead. Peter's mother-in-law once had a 'high fever' which Matthew and Mark, lacking Luke's specialist knowledge, merely called 'fever', but even Luke had no other name for what might have been anything from malaria to sunstroke.

Bubonic plague, the later 'plague of London' which scourged England in the seventeenth century, spread rapidly among the Philistines on one occasion. When the ark of the covenant was returned to Israel following the outbreak, the Philistines also sent with it five golden tumours and five golden mice. We can assume that there had been a plague of mice or rats at the same time, rodents which are traditional carriers of the disease.

Elsewhere in the Bible the term plague is a general one. An unspecified epidemic followed King David's unwise census, and when his son Solomon dedicated the temple he asked God to hear the people's prayer for deliverance from epidemics. Some experts have concluded from the apparently rapid spread of such 'plagues' that they may have been cholera epidemics which can be transmitted quickly through untreated drinking water.

◁1 Kings 8: 37, 39

◁◁Genesis 48: 1

Dysentery was – and still is – a common ailment in the Near East. It can appear in some people in sporadic attacks of diarrhoea; in more severe cases it can result in a prolapse of the lower part of the colon. This may well have been the affliction of Jehoram, who had 'a lingering disease of the bowels'. Eventually 'his bowels came out because of the disease, and he died in great pain.' This may have been chronic dysentery which resulted in intestinal obstruction.

◁2 Chronicles 21: 15, 18-19
◁◁Leviticus 26: 16
◁◁2 Kings 19: 35

SKIN DISEASES

The Bible reader is likely to be surprised at the number of recorded incidents of skin diseases, due no doubt to the fact that such afflictions were obvious to all and a source of some dread.

◁◁2 Kings 4: 18-20

◁◁Luke 4: 38

Boils are first met in the sixth plague in Egypt. The boils broke out on people and animals, and the Hebrew term could suggest abscesses, blisters and ulcers. Some commentators have suggested it was Nile scab, a persistent skin irritation which occurred when the waters of the Nile were rising. It may also have been a form of 'prickly heat', an eruptive skin rash common in all tropical countries. Hezekiah had a 'boil' which was treated by a poultice of figs, but this and the 'painful sores' which broke out on Job could have been any number of conditions.

◁Exodus 9: 9-11

17

◁◁1 Samuel 5: 6
◁2 Kings 20: 7
◁Job 2: 7

Four Hebrew terms are used to describe dry, crusty patches on the skin, and none of them is sufficiently

◁◁2 Samuel 24: 13

A blind harpist from Egypt, about 1350 BC.

clear to identify the exact disease. Some versions refer to them as sores or spots.

The greatest confusion of all is caused by the biblical use of 'leprosy' for conditions which are not leprosy as it is understood today, a disease caused by bacteria. In the book of Leviticus the diagnosis of 'leprosy' included pale or depigmented patches on the skin; the same word was used for discoloured patches on walls or clothes. Some of the features described in Leviticus 13–14 do not occur in true leprosy and suggest conditions like erysipelas next to a boil, ringworm and dermatitis.

The same is true in the New Testament. Lepers came for healing to Jesus; on one occasion a group of ten came to him and while all ten were 'cleansed' only one was 'made well', the one who returned to give thanks. There is no clue as to whether this was true leprosy, although it is certain that it existed in the world of the New Testament.

PHYSICAL DISABILITY

Eye diseases caused by climatic factors, infection, venereal disease, and the effects of heredity or senility were common in Bible times. Total blindness occurred in newborn infants (Jesus healed a man blind from birth), and this may have been a severe conjunctivitis which results from venereal infection. (If so, that would have given a double edge to the Pharisees' rejection of the man as 'steeped in sin at birth'.)

Trachoma was a common form of blindness and is still rampant in the Third World. Caused by a virus, it produces bleary, itching or painful eyes. Without the total cure available

from modern antibiotics, sufferers in the ancient world faced a life of pain and inconvenience. The Old Testament records a temporary blindness which afflicted the whole Syrian army, but this may have been a supernatural rather than physical blindness. Although Egyptian documents like the Ebers Papyrus (*c.*1500 BC) refer to a variety of eye washes, the Old Testament laws do not provide any instructions for eye care.

◁2 Kings 6: 18

Jesus restored the sight of some blind people, and one of the more unusual cases was the two-stage healing of a man in Bethsaida. He was first able to see shapes and light without clear definition; the people he saw looked like walking trees. The second stage of the healing gave him clear sight. A similar confusion is sometimes experienced by people who are given a corneal graft or who undergo cataract surgery.

◁Mark 8: 22-25

Deafness was also common in ancient times, although the causes are unknown. The people of Israel were told to be kind to the deaf, and the opening of deaf ears (along with the opening of blind eyes) was often seen as a characteristic of the days of the Messiah.

◁◁Luke 17: 11-19

◁Leviticus 19: 14

◁Isaiah 29: 18

People who were deaf and dumb seem to have been relatively common in Jesus' time. Several came to him for healing; after one man was able to hear and speak clearly, the people commented of Jesus, '"He has done everything well. He even makes the deaf hear and the dumb speak."'

◁◁John 9: 1-41

◁ *E.g.* Mark 7: 32-37

Paralysis also seems to have been common, and the paralysed man, possibly a paraplegic, lowered through the roof in Capernaum by his friends so that Jesus could heal him, is one of several victims of the condition mentioned in the Gospels. Some cases of paralysis may well have been caused by polio. The centurion's servant who

◁ Mark 2: 3-12

17

This carving on an Egyptian stele (standing stone) shows a Syrian settler whose leg has been deformed, probably by infantile paralysis.

1 Kings 13: 4 ▷▷

Matthew 8: 6 ▷

lay "'at home paralysed in terrible suffering'" suggests a frightening respiratory paralysis which sometimes occurs in polio. People with withered hands presented themselves to Jesus, and they may have been the victims of an infantile polio attack.

There is one recorded incident in the Old Testament which suggests the paralysis which follows a stroke. King Jeroboam stretched out his arm towards a prophet in anger, and he could not pull it back again; he was paralysed down one side.

MENTAL DISORDER

The New Testament describes some physical disorders which if they occurred today would probably be seen as the result of an emotional or psychological disturbance. The dumbness of Zechariah, father of John the Baptist, was a sign from God but could also be seen in terms of emotional shock. Paul's temporary blindness on the road to Damascus resulted from a meeting with the risen Christ. At the same time it was the result of severe emotional and spiritual conflict.

There are references to madness or mindlessness in Paul's writings, and although they are metaphorical, not literal, the apostle is clearly drawing on common experience of the mentally disordered people who would have roamed the streets of the Roman Empire in days long before hospital psychiatric units and even mediaeval-type 'mad houses'. He said of himself on one occasion that he was talking like a madman.

Many cases of demon possession are recorded in the Gospels, one of the most notable being the bizarre figure of a naked man running wild among the tombs of a Gadarene burial ground, exerting superhuman strength and raging incoherently. Some modern scholars dismiss all such accounts as examples of acute psychiatric disorder. Even today, however, such people sometimes seem to be taken over by personalities quite unlike their normal selves. The diagnosis of Jesus cannot be relegated to the realms of magic and superstition. Demon possession among some tribal peoples is commonly reported by missionaries, too. Jesus took the existence of evil forces seriously, and saw them attacking people at all areas of their lives, including their minds.

Two cases of apparent madness are noteworthy in the Old Testament. David pretended to be mad in order to get away from Achish, king of Gath. He scratched on the doors and foamed at the mouth. Saul, the man from whom he was fleeing, went through bouts of frenzy and depression which sound like a form of paranoid schizophrenia. The ailment is described mysteriously as 'an evil spirit from the LORD'.

◁◁ Luke 1: 11-25, 57-64

◁ 1 Samuel 16: 14-23

◁◁ Acts 9: 8

MEDICAL TREATMENT

There is no doubt that doctors existed in the New Testament times. Luke is called 'our dear friend, the doctor' by Paul, and Jesus quotes a proverb, 'Physician, heal yourself!' The woman with a haemorrhage had spent all her money on doctors and was no better. In Old Testament times Jeremiah laments the absence of a doctor in Gilead, although generally it is the Lord God who is regarded as the healer: '"I am the LORD who heals you."'

◁ Colossians 4: 14

◁ Luke 4: 23
◁ Luke 8: 43

◁ Jeremiah 8: 22

◁◁ 2 Corinthians 11: 23
◁ Exodus 15: 26

In the Roman Empire the profession of doctor was well known, and there were even women doctors. At first they had learned their art by being apprenticed to experienced doctors, but by New Testament times there were medical schools which taught the elements of anatomy and medical care. A fine collection of surgical instruments was discovered in the ruins of Pompeii, dating from the first century AD.

◁◁ Mark 5: 1-20

The only surgical operation actually mentioned in the Bible is the relatively minor matter of circumcision. It was performed, usually with flint knives, on eight-day old boys and on household slaves brought into Israel as prisoners of war. It was seen primarily as a religious symbol of God's covenant with Israel and was probably not regarded as a hygienic or prophylactic measure.

◁ Leviticus 12: 3

17

Also of a religious and social significance was the practice of affixing a slave to the master's doorpost by boring a hole in the slave's ear with an awl: a sign that the slave had covenanted to serve the master for ever.

◁◁ 1 Samuel 21: 12-15
◁ Exodus 21: 6

People must have broken their limbs, but there is little evidence that splints were used to mend them. Ezekiel alone mentions the practice:

Luke 10: 34 ▷▷

'I have broken the arm of Pharaoh king of Egypt. It had not been bound up for healing or put in a splint so as to become strong enough to hold a sword.'

Ezekiel 30: 21 ▷

Excavations in Palestine have revealed that trepanning, the removal of bone from the skull, was sometimes practised either to relieve 'pressure' in the brain or to allow evil spirits to escape. Three examples were found in Lachish, dating from the time Nebuchadrezzar destroyed the city. In two cases a square of bone had been removed by saw-cuts; the surgery was crude and the patients did not survive. In the third case a hole had been scraped in the bone, and the patient had lived long enough for the bone to heal. The practice was also known in Egypt.

In many respects the role of the apothecary – the ancient equivalent of pharmacist – was more important than that of the doctor. He prepared the oils, ointments and potions which were given to the sick, the spices for embalming the dead, fragrant incense and sacred anointing oils for the temple, and a range of cosmetics for everyday use. Evidently a problem they faced in the hot climate was the attraction their perfumes had for insects. The flies that got stuck in the ointment gave it 'a bad smell', just as 'a little folly outweighs wisdom and honour'.

Ecclesiastes 10: 1▷

One of the main ingredients of the apothecary's remedies was olive oil. Not only was it used domestically for cooking and lighting, religiously for anointing kings and priests, and even for preparing a warrior's shield for battle (shields were covered with leather which cracked if allowed to

Mark 15: 23 ▷▷

become too dry); it was also used as an emollient to soften dried-out skin, and as a remedy for wounds, abrasions and burns. The good Samaritan poured oil and wine on the wounds of the injured man as he bandaged them up. Honey was sometimes mixed with oil and applied to a wound, kept in place by a lint.

Palestine must have been a smelly place; the odours of disease and unclean bodies, smoke, drainage, cooking, refuse and animal droppings would have been familiar in the streets of the towns. A variety of resins, gums and balsams from the trees and shrubs were mixed with spices to produce a wide range of pleasant perfumes, and some of these had medical uses as well.

Frankincense and myrrh, two of the gifts offered to the infant Jesus by the Persian astrologers, were made by taking the gum resin from beneath the bark of certain shrubs. Frankincense flows as a milky fluid when the bark of the shrub is split, but later darkens; myrrh is red-brown in colour. The fluids harden and can be ground into powder.

While used primarily for religious and cosmetic purposes, the substances were also used to make remedies to stop bleeding, to clean and heal wounds, to attempt the mending of cracked skulls, to cure abscesses and ulcers, to reduce haemorrhoids and to cure a variety of internal pains. Egyptian, Greek and Roman medical manuals which have survived the centuries refer to the medicinal value of frankincense and myrrh. Myrrh, for example, is now known to inhibit the growth of some bacteria, a fact observed but never understood as such by ancient healers.

Some potions were mixed to ease pain. Sour wine mixed with gall and myrrh was given to people being crucified, although the effect was minimal as myrrh had only a slight sedative effect. Sometimes opium was also added, and that stronger narcotic content may have been the reason Jesus refused the drink; he wanted to keep his head clear, despite the pain, for his dying hours.

Superstition was clearly mixed with some remedies; Rachel and Leah used mandrakes (assumed to be aphrodisiacs) to increase their husbands' sexual desire during a time of infertility. But the wise teacher also knew, far in advance of the discoveries of psychosomatic medicine, that 'a cheerful heart is good medicine, but a crushed spirit dries up the bones'.

HYGIENE AND SANITATION

From the earliest times the homes of wealthy people were connected to drains. An underground sewer was found in Jericho, and in Bethel in the immediate pre-Israelite period (Late Bronze Age) a well-built drainage system took rain water and sewage out of the city. In the days of the kings there were drains running through Megiddo, Gezer and Beer-sheba, and these may have served private houses. As a rule, however, human excrement was disposed of in the soil of a convenient patch of waste ground.

Mud, refuse, sewage, animal manure and general debris probably littered the streets of many towns and created an unsuspected but very real health hazard. Dirt and dust were everywhere, and evil-smelling gases rose from decomposing piles of sewage and garbage, creating a natural breeding ground for rats, flies, cockroaches and an infinite variety of micro-organisms.

Roman cities in New Testament times may have been healthier. In Pompeii most houses had a lavatory, and some of these had a stream of running water beneath them to carry

Terracotta drainpipes at a Roman villa in Ephesus.

the waste away. Otherwise, cesspits were regularly emptied by carts during the night. Whether these refinements reached Palestine is doubtful, however.

Even the art of cooking, designed to kill micro-organisms, attracted infection. The smells drew insects, and dirt collected inside ovens, on hearths, and in pottery cooking vessels and water storage cisterns. Many homes were crowded, and this increased the risk of spreading infection. There was a high rate of maternal and infant mortality throughout the biblical period.

The laws of the Pentateuch point to a concern for health and hygiene although there was never any guarantee that people heeded the advice. Water supplies were to be kept clean, and it was recognized that a polluted source of water could lead to disease and even death. Elisha took steps to clean up a spring that was believed to be causing an epidemic of miscarriages and death in Jericho.

◁◁Genesis 30: 14-16

◁◁Proverbs 17: 22

◁2 Kings 2: 19-22

17

Leviticus 11: 29-36 ▷

Leviticus 12: 1-5, ▷▷

Leviticus 15 ▷

Leviticus 11: 39f; ▷▷

Jeremiah 2: 22 ▷▷

Large pools and running streams were reckoned safe unless they were polluted by dead or ceremonially unclean animals. Contagious diseases, especially those producing discharges, were subject to stringent regulations, as were some animals known to be carriers of disease (see page 269).

Little is known about ancient Jewish attitudes to personal cleanliness. The law prescribed ritual washings after menstruation, childbirth and contact with dead bodies, but how much this was out of concern for personal hygiene is uncertain. Perfumes and scented oils helped to counteract body odours, and some cleansing agents are known to have existed. '"Although you wash yourself with soda and use an abundance of soap, the stain of your guilt is still before me,"' was God's

Latrines in Philippi, an example of Roman hygiene.

Murals decorating the walls of the steam bath in a Roman villa in 2nd-century AD Ephesus.

word to Judah through Jeremiah.

Mephibosheth's failure to wash his clothes for the whole of David's absence from Jerusalem was regarded as unusual. Joseph washed his face to remove the sign of tears when he faced his brothers. It was customary to wash a visitor's feet when he came into your house; Simon the Pharisee's failure to do this for Jesus was an insult. The Jews of Jesus' time also punctiliously washed their hands before meals, for both ceremonial and hygienic reasons.

The Romans, of course, had some excellent public baths which acted almost as social centres or clubs. The wealthy citizens had bathrooms in their own homes; some of the houses excavated on the hill to the west of Jerusalem's temple area were equipped with elaborate bathrooms. Herod's

◁ Matthew 15: 1f.

◁◁ 2 Samuel 19: 24

◁◁ Genesis 43: 31

◁◁ Luke 7: 44

THE USE OF COSMETICS

The rather unhygienic life-style of people in ancient Palestine made cosmetics – in the form of perfumes – more of a necessity than a luxury. The apothecary mixed cosmetics as well as medicines, and besides body and clothing perfumes he made eye-paint, rouge, powder and hair dye.

The eye-paint was made of a thin galena (lead sulphide) powder which was black (kohl), or of malachite (a copper compound) which was green. Excavations have unearthed little kohl pots and decorated stone palettes used for grinding and mixing the paint ingredients. The paste was applied with an ivory, bone or wood 'kohl stick'. A typical palette was a round shallow basin about 10 cm (4 in) across. In some biblical passages eye-paint is associated with prostitutes.

A toilet-set for a woman who could afford such a luxury would have included a polished bronze mirror, eye-paint ingredients, a curling rod, an ivory comb and assorted hair pins of ivory, bone or metal, tweezers and spoons. The cosmetics were contained in little jars with lids. Henna oil was used to dye nails and to darken hair.

Below: wooden toilet box from Thebes (about 1400 BC). It is decorated with veneers of ebony and inlays of ivory and blue glazed composition.

Facing page: Egyptian ivory kohl tube and cosmetic dish from Qau.

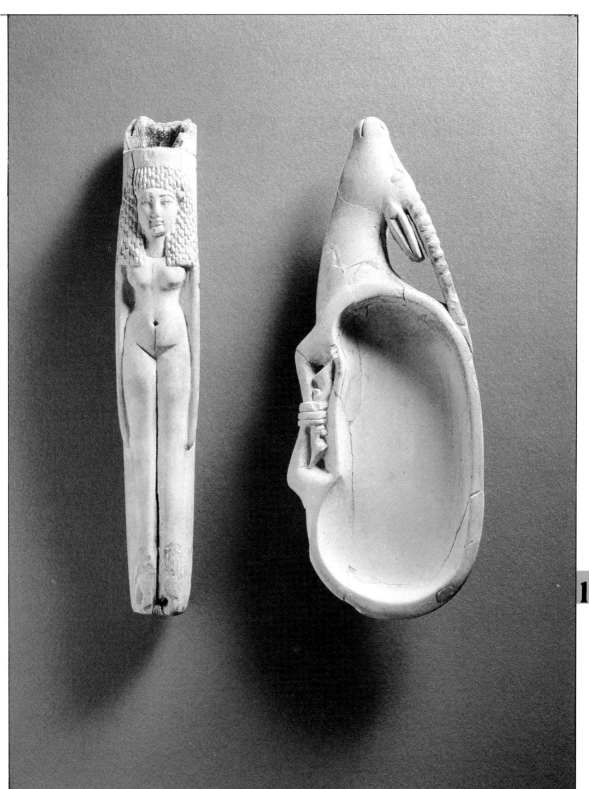

17

palaces had hot rooms, warm rooms, cold rooms and dressing rooms in what almost sounds like the forerunner to the sauna bath.

Throughout the Bible, washing the body is taken as a symbol or illustration for the spiritual cleansing from sin which every person is said to require. David, reflecting on his affair with Bathsheba and subsequent murder of her husband, says to God, 'Cleanse me with hyssop, and I shall be clean; wash me, and I shall be whiter than snow.' Jesus when he donned the servant's towel and performed the host's task of washing his disciples' feet, seems to have used the physical act as an illustration of the spiritual forgiveness he offered: '"Unless I wash you, you have no part with me."' He then pointed out that the humility he had shown in doing such a menial and unpleasant task was to be an example for them to follow in their service for him and for each other.

John 13: 8 ▷▷

Psalm 51: 7 ▷

FOR FURTHER READING

Adolph, P.E., 'Healing, Health', *ZPEB*, 3 (Grand Rapids, Zondervan, 1975), pp.54–57.

Blaiklock, D.A., 'Medicine', *ZPEB*, 2 (Grand Rapids, Zondervan, 1975), pp.159–163.

Bousma, R.H., 'Diseases of the Bible', *ZPEB*, 2 (Grand Rapids, Zondervan, 1975), pp.132–142.

Brown, S.G., *'Leprosy' in the Bible* (Christian Medical Fellowship, 1970).

Harrison, R.K., 'Disease', *IDB*, 1 (New York, Abingdon, 1962), pp.847–854.

Trapnell, D.H., 'Health, Disease and Healing', *IDB*, 2 (New York, Abingdon, 1962), pp.616–625.

Yadin, Y., *Masada* (Weidenfeld and Nicholson, 1966), pp.75–85.

SECTION VI:
Warfare

The rise of national conflict 18

There has never been a period in human history in which nations or tribes have not been fighting each other somewhere in the world. The reader of the New Testament soon becomes aware that the Jews of Palestine lived in subjection to Roman invaders; there was an uneasy tension in the land which provoked occasional uprisings and constant resentment. '"Should we pay taxes to Caesar?"' was no academic question but one of burning importance; the Pharisees who asked it no doubt hoped to trap Jesus into betraying his Jewishness or advocating rebellion against the occupying power.

The Old Testament is only four chapters old and the writer is still peering back through the centuries when Abel is killed in anger by his brother Cain. It is the first story of murder in the Bible. Conflict between nations is from then on a recurring theme in almost all its thirty-nine books. Many of its great heroes were warriors as well as spiritual leaders: Moses, Joshua, David. Even prophets like Elijah acted as advisors on strategy to the kings. Both prophets and historians record a saga of battles and treaties, of victories and defeats, as the fortunes of the nations rose and fell on waves of spilled blood.

Looking forward to the end times, Jesus gave his followers no hope that the tide of history, with its wars and rumours of wars, would be turned,

and that spears would be beaten into ploughshares, until after the final conflict between good and evil which the book of Revelation prefigures. Paul even took up the familiar image of the armed Roman soldier, who patrolled the city streets and inter-city roads across the Empire, and applied it to the spiritual conflict which besets every follower of Jesus Christ.

◁Ephesians 6: 10-17

◁◁Mark 12: 13-17

PATRIARCHAL WARRIORS

War was clearly a fact of life long before Abraham and his descendants appeared on the stage of world history. Jericho in the pre-pottery Neolithic period about 8000 BC had huge walls and towers for its protection. The moat around the walls was some 8.5 m (28 ft) wide and 3 m (10 ft) deep. A tapering defensive tower 13 m (43 ft) in diameter at the base and 10 m (33 ft) at the top rose 10 m above the ground. Clearly the inhabitants expected to be attacked.

◁◁Genesis 4: 8

The patriarchal narratives of the Old Testament open with Abraham (Abram as he was then) being involved in tribal disputes. His nephew Lot was captured, so 'he called out the 318 trained men born in his household and went in pursuit'. The band of guerrilla raiders accomplished their mission and returned people and property to their rightful homes.

◁Genesis 14: 8-16

During the period from 2200 to

◁◁Matthew 24: 6-7

Abraham's trained men may well have looked like these 'Asiatic' soldiers as described on this page.

2 Samuel 2: 23 ▷▷

1750 BC there were mass tribal movements across the Near East, and conflicts followed in their wake. As tribe fought tribe, the skills and weapons of battle were refined. Battering rams were invented to beat down the stout wooden doors and stone walls of fortified cities. And men with spears and bows began riding on horses for greater speed and mobility in attack.

From the wall-paintings of Khnum-hotep III at Beni Hasan in Egypt, dating from about 1900 BC, we can picture what Abraham's trained men looked like and how they fought. The paintings show Semitic tribesmen from Shutu in Sinai armed with spears, bows, axes and throwing sticks. The axe had a 'duck bill' blade (seen carried on the shoulder of the first soldier in the illustration). By the eighteenth century BC this axe had given way,to one with a long thin blade designed for better piercing of armour; graves in Palestine dating from patriarchal times have contained these weapons.

Swords were in use too. Originally they were like sickles, used for slashing at opponents rather than for thrusting at them. There were short dagger-like swords, too, used for close combat. The first spears and javelins had their bronze heads embedded in, and then bound to, the wooden haft, but later versions had a socket joint. Some had a sharp metal point at the other end, and this was used for sticking the spear into the ground. Abner killed his pursuer Asahel with this end of the spear.

Long-range fire power came from bows and arrows. The bow was at first a simple double-convex shape, but the Hyksos warriors probably introduced the composite bow in the Middle Bronze Age (see box). Large shields made of wood and covered with leather were used for personal protection.

Middle Bronze Age towns were very well fortified, as we know from artistic representations and, more importantly, from archaeological excavations. They had high walls with battlements and balconies so that bowmen could fire at the attackers. The lower part of the walls was protected by a sloping bank or glacis which was hard to climb and offered

BOWS AND ARROWS

Bows and arrows are among the earliest known weapons. The first bows were made from a single convex arc of wood, but were limited in their effectiveness. The arrow could be fired with greater power when the bow was shaped into a double convex or double span.

It was the composite bow which gave the weapon its greatest battle potential, however. This was built up from sections of wood and animal horn, from animal tendons and sinews, all glued together. The bow was first shaped from thin pieces of strong wood which varied in pliability to suit the different tension requirements throughout the bow. Then strips and bands of sinew were glued to the parts furthest from the core. Animal horn was glued to the inner surface of the bow, making the completed weapon

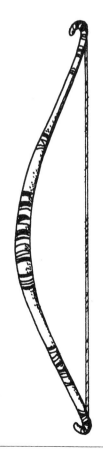

Composite bows (made from a variety of materials glued together) were either triangular in shape or 'recurved'. Both are depicted in wall paintings in Egypt from the time of the captivity.

bend the wrong way until the string was attached.

The archer needed to be very strong in order to pull the arms of the bow back to attach the string. The completed weapon was thus in great tension, and the tension increased as the string was drawn back for firing an arrow. It could have a range of 275 to 365 m (300 to 400 yd).

Arrows had hard pointed heads and feathered tails. Their design changed often during the centuries covered by the Bible. Archers were the most technically skilled of all ancient warriors.

18

attackers no cover from defenders' arrows. This glacis was faced with smooth stones or plaster, and usually had a deep moat at its foot. Huge earth ramparts, often between 6 and 12 m (20 and 40 ft) high were thrown up as the moat was dug. The ramparts were made stable by layers of stone, clay and soil.

One of the finest of such fortified towns was Hazor. The area enclosed by the rampart 15 m (50 ft) high was 700 m (2296 ft) long by 90 m (295 ft) broad. The moat was 15 m (50 ft) deep and 80 m wide (262 ft) at the surface, and half as wide at the bottom. Attackers approached the city gate up a gentle slope from the right, thus exposing their right sides to defensive arrows; shields were normally carried in the left hand.

Although the horse-drawn four-wheeled chariot had been used for

This drawing shows how town walls were constructed and strengthened against attack in Middle Bronze Age times in Palestine.

some centuries, lighter chariots with two wheels were introduced by the Hyksos, and the Egyptians they conquered, from the end of the eighteenth century BC. From the same period a wooden model of soldiers found in an Egyptian tomb at Assuit shows the army drawn up into disciplined units.

A cuneiform document from Mari on the Middle Euphrates, dating from about 1750 BC, refers to assault units of 300 men, companies of 100 men and section units of ten men each.

THE CONQUEST OF CANAAN

It was the chariot which made the most outstanding advance in military tactics during the period from about 1550 to 1200 BC, in the centuries up to the Israelites' arrival in Canaan. From the sixteenth century BC onwards, chariots were generally light, with two wheels each having four spokes. The wooden frame was covered with leather and the

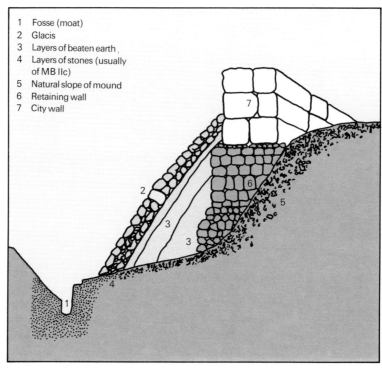

1 Fosse (moat)
2 Glacis
3 Layers of beaten earth
4 Layers of stones (usually of MB IIc)
5 Natural slope of mound
6 Retaining wall
7 City wall

chariot was pulled by two horses. The body of the vehicle was narrow, no more than 1 m (40 in) across, room enough for one man to stand in. The axle may have been as wide as 1.5 m (5 ft), to make the chariot stable when cornering at speed. Egyptian chariots tended to be heavier than those of other nations, and they had eight-spoked wheels in the fourteenth century BC. The Israelites themselves did not use chariots at this time.

The Egyptians – Israel's taskmasters in the first centuries of this period – used the Hyksos type axes to oust their inventors from the Nile region. The blade became shorter with a narrow edge. Sword blades became larger during this period, but many were still curved. A straight sword with a half-metre (two-foot) blade bearing the name of Pharaoh Merenptah (*c.*1236–1223 BC) was found as far north as Ugarit.

A light-weight Egyptian war chariot, depicted in limestone on the outside wall of the temple of Seth at Abydos.

In a battle, the units carrying spears and shields, sword-bearers and axe-bearers, formed the main attacking force. Defenders and charioteers also used spears, but the decisive weapon in all big armies became the composite bow. It was used by infantry, charioteers and defenders. The arrows were carried in a quiver (a cylindrical leather container) over the bowman's shoulder. They were made from strong, easily shaped reeds, with bronze heads rather thick in the middle.

This arrowhead was designed to penetrate the coats of mail which soldiers were beginning to use; the thickening of the head prevented it from being pushed back into the reed shaft and splitting it when it hit a

18

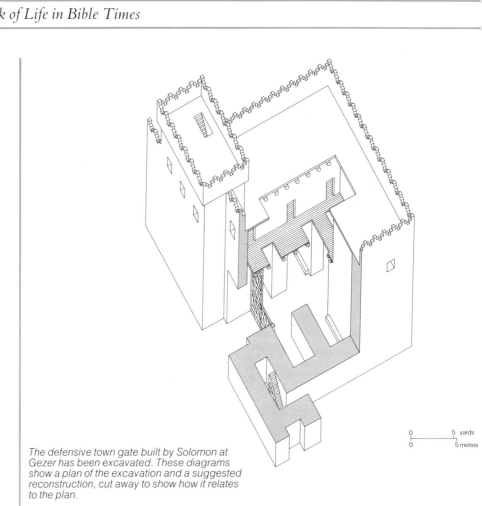

The defensive town gate built by Solomon at
Gezer has been excavated. These diagrams
show a plan of the excavation and a suggested
reconstruction, cut away to show how it relates
to the plan.

| 0 | 5 yards |
| 0 | 5 metres |

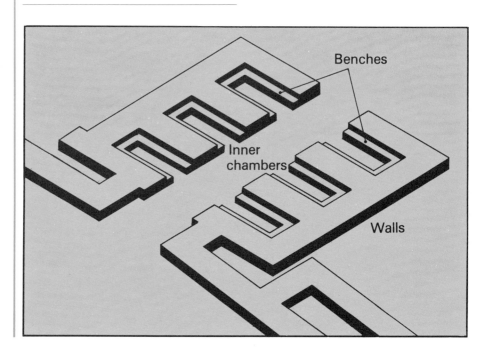

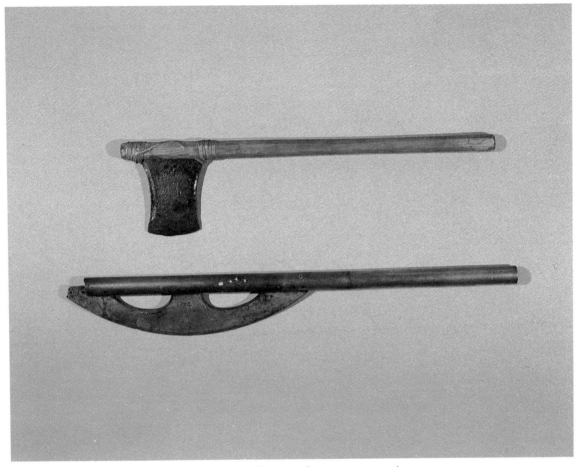

Egyptian weapons. The head of this copper battle-axe (below) is secured to the handle by copper rivets. It may have been gilded. It dates from about 1800 BC.
The bronze hand-axe (above) still has its original haft. The head is lashed on to the handle with leather thongs. It is inscribed with the name Thutmosis III (1475 BC).

target. Thothmes III (1479-1425 BC) recorded that in the battle of Megiddo in 1467 BC he captured over 200 coats of mail. They were made of bronze scales sewn with strong thread on to leather or cloth garments, but they were heavy to wear and complicated to make. Wall-paintings from the period show that soldiers often wore helmets, too. The Asiatics engaged in battle by Thothmes IV (1396-1386 BC) had slightly pointed helmets which covered their ears and forehead down to their eyebrows.

The use of armour meant that soldiers could carry smaller shields. Each nation had its own distinctive shield. The Sea Peoples used round shields, and these were adopted later in Palestine. The Egyptian shields were rectangular with a rounded top, no larger than 60 cm x 30 cm (2 ft x 1 ft) although Tutankhamun's was 72 cm x 51 cm (2 ft 6 in x 1 ft 8 in). They were made of plaited reeds or wood covered with leather and studded with small metal discs.

Throughout Asia there were many well-fortified towns, some of them built on the ruins of former settlements and utilizing what remained of their defences. Roads and water supplies were sometimes guarded with 'migdols' or towers.

The early Israelites had their own

18

equivalent of the Geneva Convention for rules of war, although these were not observed by other nations and may not have been followed by all Israelite armies either. The whole of Deuteronomy chapter 20 is devoted to the law of war. It includes religious encouragement from the priest;

Judges 4: 8-16 ▷▷

humanitarian rules to exempt from battle newly married men and those who had just begun a farm or built a home; a harsh decree that all people of defeated cities which worshipped other gods should be put to death lest they should corrupt the faith of Israel; and one which outlawed 'blitzkrieg' warfare: 'When you lay siege to a city

Deuteronomy 20: 19 ▷

... do not destroy its trees by putting an axe to them, because you can eat their fruit. Do not cut them down. Are the trees of the field men, that you should besiege them?'

The book of Joshua is almost a war history, and it reveals some of the tactics used by the emerging nation.

Judges 7: 1-25 ▷▷

Jericho was defeated without a battle

Joshua 6 ▷

after only a week's ritual 'siege', and the walls were breached after the steady marching of troops round them day by day. Ambushes, and tempting city dwellers out of their gates by

E.g. Joshua 8: 1-29 ▷

pretending to withdraw, were all part of Joshua's military repertoire.

THE RISE OF THE STANDING ARMY

1 Samuel 13: 2 ▷▷

Once Israel was settled in Canaan, the tribes tended to keep to themselves, isolated in their own area. Only in times of emergency, when one tribe was being hard pressed by an enemy,

1 Samuel 17 ▷▷

did men from the other tribes leave their homes and farms and band together to wage war.

Several incidents in the book of Judges are worth noting. The story of Ehud contains a reference to a weapon which some versions translate as 'a

Judges 3: 16 ▷

double-edged sword'. The Hebrew

literally means 'a sword with two mouths', which may refer to the habit of making the hilt of a sword in the shape of an animal's head – or even two heads – with the blade coming out of its mouth, though the usual meaning of 'double-edged sword' is at least as likely.

In the campaign of Deborah and Barak and the northern and central tribes against Sisera the Canaanite who controlled the valley of Jezreel, the Israelites faced a superior enemy which had 'iron chariots' – persumably chariots with iron fittings. So the part-time soldiers of Israel took up their lines on hilly ground to take their enemy by surprise while the river Kishon was in flood. The chariots stuck in the mud and the Canaanites were ignominiously defeated.

Under God's instruction Gideon used his knowledge of the terrain and of the character of his enemy to defeat raiders. He selected a tiny army of 300 out of the 32,000 who volunteered, and by little more than play-acting a surprise attack scared the Midianites into panic and unintentional civil war as they hacked each other down in the dark.

Civil war was prevalent during the reign of Saul, but it was Saul's jealousy of David which provoked it. He may have collected a small standing army; there is one reference to him choosing 3,000 men who may have made up a more permanent body than the temporary militia raised by the earlier judges to meet specific threats.

Most of Saul's battles were against the Philistines and the most famous involved the giant Goliath, who was eventually slain by a well-aimed stone from the young David's sling. The duel between two representatives of opposing armies, rather than a full-scale pitched battle, was a style of warfare practised in Egypt and elsewhere in the Near East. David's men 'fought' Saul's in a contest between twelve champions from each army; the fight was to the death.

Once David became king he embarked on many military campaigns. Many of the biblical records of his battles provide insufficient detail for us to discover his precise tactics. It is clear, however, that he had a small regular army which was based in Jerusalem, the city he had captured by sending his men up a water shaft which ran under the city wall.

The regular army was composed of men of Israel under the leadership of Joab, and a group of foreign mercenaries commanded by Benaiah. David also turned the temporary militia into a highly efficient and well-organized fighting force. There were twelve formations of 24,000 men each. The tribes sent a quota of men according to their size, and each formation served for a month at a time. The system gave David great flexibility. He could call up the entire army or one formation; in peacetime he could dispense with the monthly conscription. For emergencies in specific areas he could call on the regional commander or tribal or town chief to mobilize local units quickly. It was his need to organize the militia which may have led David to plan the census which earned him a soldier's rebuke and God's punishment.

David may have begun to build a chariot force, the first Israelite leader to do so. As most of the population lived in the highlands, chariots were of little use there, but David's son Absalom had chariots and horses as a bodyguard and show of strength, and David took chariots and horses from the Syrians as plunder. It is open to conjecture that he met the Syrian (Aramaean) forces on their own terms with chariot-riding fighters.

But there is no doubt that his

◁◁ 2 Samuel 2: 12-17

successor to the throne, Solomon, built up a considerable force of chariots, and he had trained horsemen and even special chariot towns. He concentrated them in places like Megiddo, which guarded the Plain of Esdraelon – an ideal place for the chariot divisions of the army to operate. Solomon bought his horses from Egypt in the south and Kue in Asia Minor.

◁ 1 Kings 10: 26

◁ 1 Kings 10: 28

Both David and Solomon continued to strengthen the fortifications of Israelite towns and built up a series of fortified posts to guard the southern borders in the Negeb. These square, rectangular or oval fortresses were occupied for a relatively brief period during the tenth century BC. Notable in Solomon's time were the distinctive city gateways flanked by square towers. The towers contained guardrooms, and casemate walls surrounded the whole settlement. (See also chapter 3.)

◁◁ 2 Samuel 5: 8

◁◁ 2 Samuel 20: 23

◁◁ 1 Chronicles 27

BATTLES WITH THE ASSYRIANS

The Assyrian war-machine was the most advanced and efficient of its time. Under great rulers such as Ashurnasirpal II (883-859 BC), Tiglath-Pileser III (745-727 BC) and Sennacherib (704-681 BC), Assyria subdued large areas of western Asia – including the kingdoms of Israel and Judah. When she conquered a territory, she often drafted the vanquished soldiers into her own forces. Thus after the defeat of Carchemish, Sargon II (721-705 BC) wrote: 'I formed from among them a contingent of 50 chariots, 200 men on horseback and 3000 foot soldiers, and added it to my royal corps.' Such contingents can sometimes be seen on Assyrian reliefs, distinguished from the native forces by differences in dress.

The awe which the efficiency of the Assyrian war-machine inspired can be

◁◁ 2 Samuel 24: 1-17

18

◁◁ 2 Samuel 15: 1

◁◁ 2 Samuel 8: 3-4

HOW A CITY WAS ATTACKED

When an ancient army arrived outside a fortified city it intended to capture, its commanders had several options open to them. The most obvious was to climb over the walls. Archers and soldiers using stone-throwing machines could concentrate their fire on the section of wall to be scaled in order to keep the defenders away while ladders were raised and troops scrambled up them.

If the defence was too good, or the walls too difficult to scale, the next obvious thing was to try to demolish them. Some attackers might use hand-held hammers and axes to dislodge masonry, but more usually a battering ram was wheeled up to the walls so that the head of the ram could be inserted in the wall between the stones. By moving this head-piece from side to side stones could be prised apart. The ram itself was suspended from a rope and could be readily moved to and fro. There was a protective tower built over the ram to shield its operators from defenders' stones and arrows. Because the machine was often very heavy it was pulled into place by animals.

City walls were usually thicker at the base where a stout buttress provided extra strength. Attackers sometimes built a gently sloping ramp against the wall so that the battering ram could operate at the higher, thinner part of the wall which was very often made of mud bricks and could therefore be more readily dislodged. Ramps were built of stones, logs and trodden-down earth.

The Assyrian King Sennacherib (704-681 BC) recorded in his annals how he attacked towns in Judah in 701 BC. 'I conquered them by means of well-stamped earth ramps and battering rams brought near to the walls, combined with the attack by foot soldiers using mines (tunnels), breaches as well as sapper work'.

Patience was a virtue for attackers, because very few fortified cities would be self-sufficient for long periods. Agricultural land usually lay outside the walls, and it was only a matter of time before the besieged defenders would run out of food stocks. Water cisterns inside cities were usually inadequate for long sieges, although some places had tunnels giving access to streams outside (see page 120). Sieges could last for years, however; Samaria was besieged by Assyria for three years, Jerusalem by the Babylonians for eighteen months, and Masada, the Jewish fortress near the Dead Sea, for several years during the first Jewish revolt (AD 66-73). While they waited, attackers built themselves fortified camps to protect themselves from forays by the city's soldiers or from counter-attack by the city's allies.

◁ 2 Kings 17: 5
◁ Jeremiah 52: 4f.

Below left: a reconstruction of the siege of Lachish by Sennacherib's Assyrian army in 701 BC. This painting shows the double walls, city gate, siege-ramp and battering-rams as well as the offensive and defensive weapons employed. Judaean refugees leave the city.

Below: this relief from the S.W. palace at Nineveh shows the siege of Lachish in progress. A siege engine is battering the walls. Israelites are emerging from the gateway.

18

understood from reading Isaiah 5: 26-30.

Assyrian forces were divided into three branches: infantry, cavalry and chariots. The infantry was further divided into spearmen, archers and slingmen. The spearmen carried swords as well as spears, the swords being held in a sheath over the left thigh suspended from a belt and shoulder strap. They wore helmets (often crested) and coats of mail. The shields they carried varied in shape. Those of Ashurnasirpal in the ninth century BC were rectangular and medium-sized. But the troops of most later rulers used small round shields, except those of Ashurbanipal who used large curved shields with rounded tops to protect the whole body. The shields were made from plaited reeds, or from leather stretched over a frame.

The main power of the army came from the archers. They had the advanced composite bow and wore long coats of mail. They were often accompanied by shield-bearers who wore armour and carried small round shields. For siege warfare after the days of Tiglath-Pileser III (747-727 BC) the Assyrians employed shield-bearers with huge heavy shields made from plaited reeds, with tops which curved over to protect the archers from arrows fired in retaliation from city walls above them.

Sling-throwers appear late in the Assyrian records. By the eighth century BC they operated in pairs behind archers. They were useful in attacks on walled cities because they could direct high-angled fire up steep slopes.

Mounted cavalry was used only in open warfare, not in attacks on cities. The riders used either spears or bows. Mounted archers could not defend themselves easily because they needed both hands to hold the bow, and so they often rode alongside a mounted

Assyrian slingers, working in pairs and wearing copper helmets and coats of mail. From Nineveh about 690 BC.

shield-bearer who also held the reins of both horses.

The principal Assyrian forces in open battle were the charioteers. Ashurnasirpal's chariots used three horses, but as there was only one pole between two of the horses and attached to the chariot, the third horse was probably a reserve and did not actually pull the vehicle. Each chariot had a crew of a driver and an archer. The king rode with a driver and a shield-bearer, and over the centuries the three-man chariot became common, but the number of horses was reduced to two. By the time of Ashurbanipal (668-630 BC) the crew was increased to four: a driver, an archer and two shield-bearers. The chariot driver usually had the use of a long spear which was carried at the rear of the chariot. Two quivers for arrows were fixed to the chariot body, as was a flag to identify the army to which it belonged. The earlier Assyrian chariot wheels had six spokes, but these were increased to eight when the three-man crew became common by the time of Sargon (721-705 BC).

According to the Assyrian king Shalmaneser III (858-824 BC), King Ahab of Israel sent 2,000 chariots as well as foot soldiers to the battle of Karkar in 853 BC. If this is true, Israel had clearly built up a considerable chariot force, although as this was in a period when Israel and Judah were on good terms, Judah may also have contributed to the force. Jehoshaphat of Judah told Ahab, and later Ahab's son Joram, "'I am as you are, my people as your people, my horses as your horses.'"

Israel and Judah were, however, no match for the superior Assyrian army. Tiglath-Pileser invaded Israel in the eighth century, during the time of King Pekah, and shortly afterwards Ahaz king of Judah became a vassal of Assyria. Israel's capital Samaria was captured by Shalmaneser V in 722 BC, and under his successor Sargon II the district of Samaria was reorganized as an Assyrian province. This marked the end of the northern kingdom. Under Sennacherib, Assyrian forces appeared in Judah in 701 BC, destroying many towns and besieging Jerusalem.

◁ 2 Kings 18: 13 – 19: 37

For over a century (*c.* 732-612 BC) Israel and Judah were subject to the Assyrians, whose army was able to adapt to all kinds of terrain. In wooded areas they used spearmen, who sometimes protected columns of cavalry. In swamps, they operated from boats. They crossed rivers and streams on small boats, inflated skins, or pontoon bridges.

◁◁ 1 Kings 22: 4; 2 Kings 3: 7

They were also skilled at breaching the walls of cities. They improved the efficiency of the battering ram. Ashurnasirpal used a heavy machine on six wheels, built on a wooden frame

◁◁ 2 Kings 15: 29

◁◁ 2 Kings 16: 7f.

Sennacherib's soldiers (about 700 BC) showing their large round shields.

18

PHILISTINE RAIDERS

The Israelites encountered Philistine raiders on their land during the days of Samuel and Saul. The Philistines were part of a migration of 'Sea Peoples' from the Mediterranean islands and from Asia Minor. As early as the time of the exodus, when Pharaoh Rameses II (1279-1213 BC) was ruling Egypt, one group of Sea Peoples, the Sherdan, were serving as mercenaries in his army. By the time of Rameses III (1185-1154 BC) they were pressing into Egyptian-held areas and had to be warded off.

Judges 3: 3 ▷

Philistines were numbered with the Canaanites whom Israel had to drive out. Errant Israelites were defeated by them as a punishment for their sins, and Samson had several colourful encounters with them. They invaded Israel as far as Shiloh in the days of Samuel, and captured the ark of the covenant. Saul and Jonathan died in battle against them at Mt Gilboa. David finally broke their power and confined them to an area south-west of Judah.

Judges 10: 6f. ▷
1 Samuel 4 ▷

In land battles, as Egyptian sculptures show, the Philistine soldiers used a round shield and carried two spears and a long straight sword. They wore feather-capped helmets which had long chin straps, and some wore armour on the upper part of the body, made from strips of metal and leather laid in a V-shape. They used three-man chariots with six-spoked wheels pulled by two horses; charioteers were armed with spears for close fighting after an initial charge.

Reliefs from the reign of Rameses III (1185-1154 BC) depict sea battles between Philistine and Egyptian ships close to the shore and supported by archers based on the coast. The Egyptian ships were crescent-shaped and driven by oars and sails; they had a single mast and were steered by a large paddle. The prow carried the head of a lioness. The Sea Peoples' vessels carried no oars but were driven by sails. They had a crow's nest, a high stern and a prow which ended in a duck-head with a bill used as a battering ram. The sailors of both nations were armed with swords and spears, and the Egyptians also had long-range bows and arrows and slings. The Egyptians therefore had the advantage in sea battles as they could damage their opponents at long range.

Philistine prisoners of war in Egypt captured by Rameses III (1185-1154 BC).

The Assyrian attack on Gaza in about 721 BC when Sargon II set up his royal image there. Drawings of a relief from the king's palace at Khorsabad.

and covered with leather and wicker. It had a turret 3 m (10 ft) high housing archers, and a rope to suspend the ram itself. Its head was shaped like an axe blade, so that it could be forced between stones or bricks, then moved from side to side to lever them apart. Later machines were lighter, with four wheels and two rams each.

Mobile towers moved alongside the ram to protect supporting soldiers. Then attackers built sloping ramps large enough to carry several rams. In addition soldiers sometimes tried to tunnel under the walls. They were protected in this hazardous activity by a constant stream of arrows directed against the wall from behind large shields. Some rams had built-in fire-fighting equipment to douse the burning torches hurled at them by defenders: a large ladle poured water on the ram.

By 612 BC the Assyrian capital Nineveh had fallen and the nation was finally overthrown by the Chaldeans (Babylonians) in 609 BC. Four years later Judah became part of this, the next great empire to take the Near Eastern limelight, the Babylonian. There are few records of their war tactics and troops, however, although the prophet Habakkuk has left a description of them which includes phrases like, 'they are a law to themselves', 'their horses are swifter than leopards', 'they fly like a vulture swooping to devour; they all come bent on violence', they 'gather prisoners like sand' and 'deride kings'. Clearly they were a fearsome foe.

◁Habakkuk 1: 6-11

For centuries Judah, and formerly Israel, had been fighting other enemies besides the Assyrians, the Aramaeans (Syrians) among them. But with the coming of the Babylonians their history changed completely. Only for a brief period under the Maccabean leaders (152–37 BC) were they to have any semblance of independence. Even then it was very precarious because they were under the nominal rule of

18

the Seleucid rulers from Syria. But after the fall of Jerusalem to the Babylonians in 587 BC the scene was set for successive empires to rule the region until Jesus was born into a puppet state governed by the Romans.

FOR FURTHER READING

Cohen, R., 'The Iron Age Fortresses in the Central Negeb', *BASOR*, 236 (1979), pp.61–79.
Gordon, R.P., 'War', *IBD*, 3 (IVP, 1980), pp.1628–1631.
Gordon, R.P., 'Army', *IBD*, 1 (IVP, 1980), pp.116–117.
Paul, S.M. and Dever, W.G., *Biblical Archaeology* (Jerusalem, Keter, 1973), pp.84–117.
Vaux, R. de, *Ancient Israel: its Life and Institutions*. (Darton, Longman and Todd, 1962. US ed. New York, McGraw-Hill, 1961), pp.213–267 (New UK ed. 1973).
Yadin, Y., *The Art of Warfare in Biblical Lands in the Light of Archaeological Discovery* (Weidenfeld & Nicolson Ltd., 1963).

Israel under subjection

19

During the period from the exile to the apostolic church, which is covered by the books of the post-exilic prophets, some of the Apocryphal books, and the whole of the New Testament, the nation of Israel was a subject state, ruled by successive alien empires. Therefore, apart from occasional organized or spontaneous rebellions against occupying forces, Israel did not go to war during this period in the same way that it had done in earlier times. But the sight of troops in the streets was common, and their battle methods were well known. The New Testament often refers to the presence and even the armour of Roman soldiers, and its writers draw analogies from the familiar sight to illustrate spiritual truths.

PERSIAN LIBERATORS

When the Babylonian Empire fell in 539 BC Persia, ruled by King Cyrus, replaced it as the dominant Near Eastern power. The Persians liberated many long-standing prisoners of war in Babylon, including the Jews, allowing them to return to their own country and to worship their own gods if they wished.

At the heart of the army was an élite corps, ten thousand strong, who guarded the king; called the Immortals, it is said, because a recruit was always ready to replace a man who fell. As the empire grew, contingents from many nationalities were added, Medes and Elamites first, then others. They wore distinctive national dress and carried their own weapons, the Persians themselves being known for the bow and short sword.

In the provinces of the empire the satraps, or governors, had charge of their own bodyguards and of local troops, but the garrisons of the Persian army came under the direct control of the central palace. Groups of mercenary soldiers were used as garrisons, and one is especially well-known. This was on the island of Elephantine, near Aswan in southern Egypt. Some of the houses of the soldiers and their families have been excavated, and in them were papyri and ostraca (see page 234), written in Aramaic, dealing with their family and communal affairs. Some of the soldiers were Jewish, and these documents give a fascinating glimpse of their beliefs and the opposition they faced from local Egyptian priests.

The Persians also had a navy, using their own vessels supplemented by some from Egypt and Phoenicia. With these forces they could land troops in Europe and invade Greek territories. The Jews of Israel would have known little of the sea-going ventures, but they would have seen troops marching through their land between Persia and Egypt going to, or returning from,

◁◁ Ezra 1:1–4

security duties in riot-torn Egypt. The armies were usually large, and the Immortals and the higher officials took their own food, servants and even concubines on long route marches. Most of the soldiers, however, would demand provisions from the lands they marched across.

FROM ALEXANDER TO ANTIOCHUS

Persian control of Palestine came to an end once Alexander the Great had defeated the Persian forces of Darius III (336–331 BC) at the Battle of Issus near the north-east corner of the Mediterranean in 333 BC. The following year Alexander pressed south into Palestine and Egypt and began the long Greek domination of the region. The Ptolemies in Egypt and the Seleucids in Syria then fought for the control of Palestine, the Seleucids eventually prevailing.

Relationships between Jews and Greeks were generally peaceful, and the invaders' rule was, like that of the Persians, benign. A large colony of Jews flourished in Alexandria where the Greek version of the Hebrew Bible, the Septuagint, was produced. Some peaceful attempts were made to combine the Jewish way of life with the prevailing Greek culture.

Those attempts became more sinister and forceful when Antiochus IV came to the Syrian throne in 175 BC. He called himself 'Epiphanes', God-manifest. He was a Seleucid, and his dynasty, which had suffered heavy defeat by the Romans in 189 BC, was also warring against the Ptolemies. The Romans exacted heavy financial tribute from Antiochus, and he began to covet the wealth of the Jews. In order to acquire some of it, and to buttress himself against the Romans, he attempted to force Egypt into subjection and to Hellenize the whole region.

In 169 BC he bullied the Jews and ransacked the temple treasury. The next year he looted Jerusalem, killing several hundred Jews and demolishing part of the city wall. Then he built a

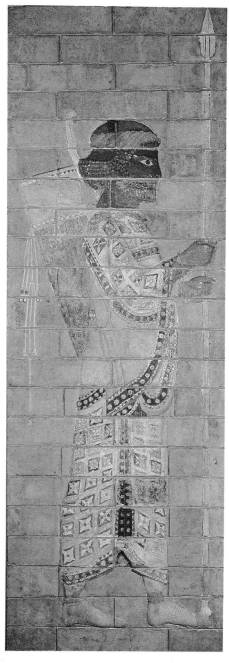

Persian guard in the palace of Darius I, Susa, about 500 BC.

Alexander the Great. From the Issus mosaic, about 100 BC.

citadel called the Acra and put in a garrison which remained there for twenty-five years. He banned the sabbath, circumcision and temple sacrifices, and destroyed all the scrolls of the Law which he could find. He built an altar to the Greek god Zeus in the temple and sacrificed a pig there. Altars to Greek gods were erected across the land and Jews were forced by armed soldiers to sacrifice at them.

The signal for a Jewish revolt was given by the Jew, Mattathias. At Modein on the Jerusalem to Jaffa road he refused to comply with the order to sacrifice. He killed the fellow Jew who through fear had offered the sacrifice for him, and the Greek official supervising the ritual. He and his sons fled to the hills and called the Jews to arms. In 165 BC Mattathias died and his third son, Judas, nicknamed Maccabaeus ('the Hammer') became leader of the revolt. His guerilla army achieved wonders with small resources. In the summer of 165 BC he met a Seleucid army of 5,000 infantry and 1,000 picked cavalry, and his poorly-equipped force of only 3,000 men routed them. In the autumn Antiochus IV's viceroy, Lysias, himself led 60,000 infantry and 5,000 cavalry against the Jewish rebels, and Judas defeated him with a guerilla army of 10,000. After this disaster, Antiochus IV resorted to diplomacy to end the conflict, which was draining his resources. In 164 BC a Roman embassy threw its weight behind the Jewish cause, and an agreement was reached in which the ban on religious practices was withdrawn. The Jerusalem temple was cleansed of all defilements and rededicated, an event still celebrated by the Jewish festival of Hanukkah, commonly known as the 'Feast of Lights'.

Although the struggle for religious freedom was won, however, the struggle for political independence was only just beginning. This was carried on by Judas, his brothers and their descendants (often referred to collectively as 'the Maccabees' from Judas' own nickname) with limited success until 128 BC. One notable development during this period was the popular bestowal of the high-priesthood on Simon (a brother of Judas) in 140 BC. This hereditary office thereafter remained with Simon's descendants.

In 128 BC the Seleucid emperor Antiochus VII died in battle against the Parthians. After this the power of the Seleucids was so weak that Judaea was able to achieve full independence under John Hyrcanus, Simon's son and successor. This independence, however, was relatively short-lived. Another power was rising in the west.

THE RISE OF ROME

The liberation of Judaea did not mean the end of Maccabean ambitions. Judaea's rulers now became hungry for more power and territory. John Hyrcanus (134–104 BC) and his brother Alexander Jannaeus (103–76 BC) assumed the title and powers of kings while at the same time holding in their blood-stained hands the position of high priest. With the aid of mercenaries John Hyrcanus occupied areas of Transjordan, Idumaea and coastal areas, eventually destroying Samaria and the temple on Mt Gerizim, thus

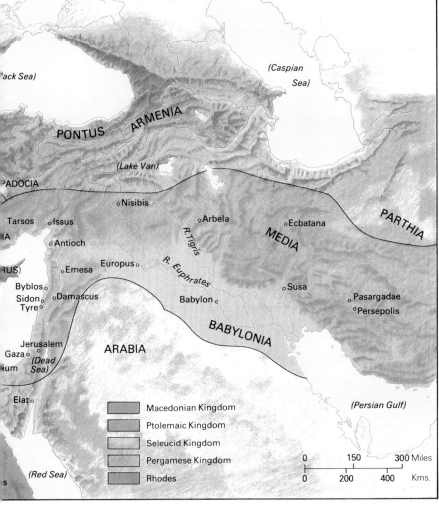

The Hellenistic kingdoms during Maccabean times (after 188 BC).

further aggravating Jewish-Samaritan tensions. (Idumaea was the southern part of Judah, occupied by descendants of the Edomites.)

The two sons of Alexander Jannaeus, Hyrcanus II and Aristobulus, became enmeshed in civil war. Both appealed to Pompey, the Roman governor in the east, who was only too glad to intervene and thus strengthen the Empire's eastern borders. He entered Jerusalem, breaking down the north wall of the temple with catapults as he flushed out defenders. He entered the temple itself and even the Holy of Holies, which infuriated the Jews.

From 63 BC onwards Judaea came fully under Roman control. Hyrcanus II continued as high priest, but Aristobulus was taken off to Rome as a prisoner. Judaea was split into provinces governed by people appointed from Rome, and ten Greek cities (the Decapolis), built by settlers in Transjordan after Alexander's conquests, were formed into a federation under Rome.

When descendants of the Jewish rebels began to exert their strength

19

again, the Romans appointed Herod, whom they trusted, as their 'client king' in 37 BC. Julius Caesar, who had been helped by Herod's father Antipater, granted the Jews exemption from military service, and Herod was given a contingent of Roman soldiers to help him consolidate his political power. Thereafter he built up his own army of professional soldiers, mostly Idumaeans and Greek-Syrian mercenaries, who were loyal to him alone. Herod did not trust the Jews whose main function, in his view, was to pay taxes and provide conscript labour for his building projects. Jesus Christ was thus born into a time and place which was peaceful and well organized.

When Herod died in 4 BC the Roman army returned in strength to enforce law and order in a more efficient manner than the puppet king had achieved. Neither war nor military

Palestine under the Romans, administered by the 'tetrarchs'.

service interrupted the lives of the ordinary people. But they were always conscious of the Roman military presence.

War was therefore a fact of daily life for Israel during the century before Christ, although the majority of people remained apathetic towards the ambitions of the rulers and annoyed by the taxes, conscription and forced labour which fell on them.

MILITARY ALLUSIONS IN THE NEW TESTAMENT

Paul was more aware of it than most when he encountered the military at close quarters on several occasions. He was once protected from the Jews by a

Model of the Antonia fortress, Jerusalem.

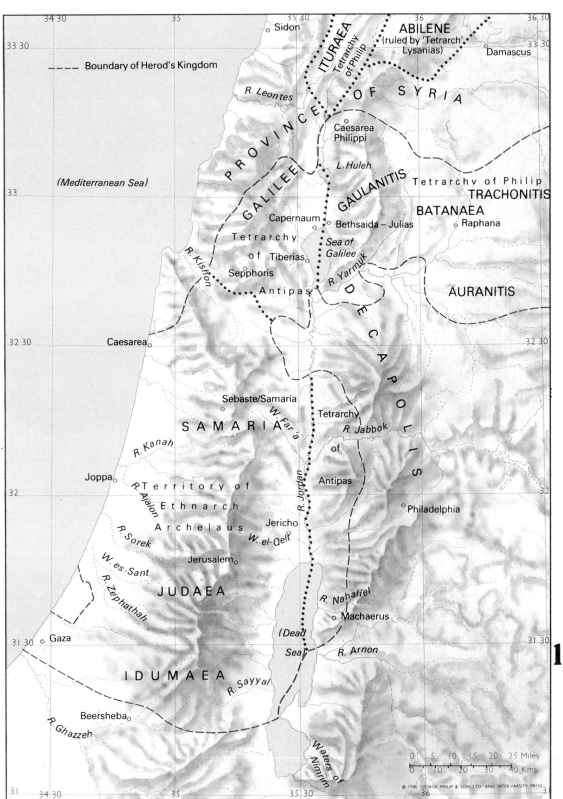

- - - Boundary of Herod's Kingdom

(Mediterranean Sea)

Sidon

ABILENE
(ruled by 'Tetrarch'
Lysanias)

Damascus

ITURAEA
Tetrarchy
of Philip

PROVINCE OF SYRIA

R. Leontes

Caesarea
Philippi

L. Huleh

GALILEE

GAULANITIS

Tetrarchy of Philip

TRACHONITIS

BATANAEA

Capernaum

Bethsaida – Julias

Raphana

Tetrarchy

of Tiberias

Sea of
Galilee

R. Kishon

Sepphoris

Antipas

R. Yarmuk

DECAPOLIS

AURANITIS

Caesarea

Sebaste/Samaria

W. Far'a

Tetrarchy

R. Jabbok

of

Antipas

SAMARIA

R. Kanah

Joppa

R. Ajalon

Territory of
Ethnarch

Archelaus

Philadelphia

Jericho

W. el-Qelt

R. Sorek

W. es-Sant

Jerusalem

R. Jordan

R. Zephathah

JUDAEA

R. Nahaliel

Machaerus

Gaza

(Dead
Sea)

R. Arnon

IDUMAEA

R. Sayyal

Beersheba

R. Ghazzeh

Waters of
Nimrim

0 5 10 15 20 25 Miles
0   10   20   30   40 Kms.

© 1980 GEORGE PHILIP & SON, LTD AND INTER-VARSITY PRESS

19

Herodium, one of Herod the Great's fortresses, viewed from the north-west.

19

Acts 23:10 ▷

commander (*chiliarchos*) who ordered his troops (*strateuma*) to imprison Paul in their barracks (*parembolê*). The commander would have had between 600 and 1,000 infantry under him; the barracks may have been the Tower of Antonia sited at the north-western corner of the temple enclosure. A pavement discovered in that area had a gaming board scratched on it where

THE ROMAN ARMY

By the first century AD the highly efficient Roman army had overrun large areas of Europe, North Africa and the Near East. It had originally been a citizen's militia but had grown into a professional and highly trained force.

The old battle order seems to have been the phalanx, a formation of infantry several files deep, organized into 'centuries' (hundreds) and legions of about 3,000 men. There were more mobile infantry and cavalry units too. Later, the phalanx gave way to an organization of units of 120–200 men (a maniple), thirty of which made up a legion. In battle, maniples were separated by a space which was covered by a second line of javelin throwers using weapons 2 m (6.5 ft) long.

Under General Scipio Africanus in the third century BC the army was organized into cohorts numbering between 500 and 1,000 men, some of whom were mounted. There were ten units to a legion commanded by a legate and assisted by a prefect, legionary tribunes and other officers. A legion generally consisted of about 5,500 men. In the first century twenty-five legions, each with its own name, patrolled the frontiers of the Roman Empire. The tenth legion was called Fretensis, commemorating a battle near the straits between Italy and Sicily in 36 BC (from Latin *fretum*, sea), and it was this legion which destroyed Jerusalem in AD 70 under General Titus.

The army was a heavy infantry force supported by wings of 500 cavalrymen. Specialist groups or auxiliaries – slingers and archers – were added when needed. Other specialists included messengers and secretaries, interrogators, torturers and executioners. Engineers were trained to use battering rams and huge catapults; sappers learned the art of building ramps and tunnelling under walls.

Among the weapons used were javelins 2 m long. The leading half was made from iron attached by rivets to a wooden shaft. The head was a 15-cm (6-in) hardened spike so barbed that it

A bronze statuette of a Roman legionary (2nd century BC), wearing the armour described on this page.

off-duty soldiers used to while away the hours (see p.260).

Peter had his contacts with the military, too. A centurion from the Italian cohort, the tenth part of a Roman legion comprising 600 men, sent a soldier to Peter at Joppa to ask him to explain the Christian faith. Shortly afterwards Peter found himself on the wrong side of the military when Herod Agrippa ordered four squads of four men each to guard the apostle in jail. No wonder 'there was a great commotion among the soldiers' the next morning when it was discovered that despite their close attention the preacher had nonetheless been rescued in the night. ◁Acts 12:18

John the Baptist told the soldiers who came to him at the river Jordan that their repentance should be evidenced by their refusal to join in the deadly pranks of conscienceless bullies who extorted money at sword-point or accused innocent citizens of crimes as a show of power. A centurion came to Jesus and asked him to heal his dying servant, which Jesus did. Jesus marvelled at the man's faith in his powers because he had spontaneously likened the Roman army chain of command to the spiritual authority he saw wielded by Jesus: '"I myself am a man under authority, with soldiers under me. I tell this one, 'Go,' and he goes."' Therefore, he told Jesus, '"just say the word, and my servant will be healed."' ◁Luke 3:14 ◁Matthew 8:8f.

War has no glamour in the New Testament. It is recognized as something unpleasant and for that very reason is used symbolically to describe the spiritual battle between good and evil. Judgment will fall on people at the end of the age and will be accompanied by war, Jesus said. It would be so bad that 'there will be great distress, unequalled from the beginning of the world till now'. ◁Matthew 24:21

Paul told Timothy to 'fight the good fight of the faith', and in his letter to the Ephesians drew on the familiar figure of the patrolling Roman soldier to instruct the Christians about their spiritual defences (see description and ◁1 Timothy 6:12 ◁Ephesians 6:10–18

could stick to a shield and force the opponent to drop his guard.

The sword was double-edged and about 60 cm (2 ft) long. It was used like a bayonet for thrusting at close range, and was carried in a scabbard suspended on the right-hand side from a girdle round the waist and supported by a shoulder strap. Being on the right, it did not interfere with the shield carried in the left hand. A dagger was carried on the left side of the belt and was used for cutting as well as for self-defence. Cavalry carried darts (usually seven of them) which were just over a metre long (4 ft).

Soldiers were protected by an oval shield made from thin sheets of wood glued together with the wood grain of one layer running in the opposite direction to the next. The edges were bound with bronze or iron, and the outer side covered with leather. Bronze helmets with an iron skull plate inside were worn, projecting over the neck and forehead. Cheek guards protected the jaw, and coloured plumes enabled soldiers in battle to be identified with their cohort. A sleeveless jacket of hardened leather covered with strips of metal protected the upper body. Some soldiers wore leg guards and some had armour vests.

Catapults were used in battle. The *scorpion* could hurl several small burning javelins at once. The *wild ass* (it had a hard kick when fired) slung huge stones. The *ballista* hurled smaller stones up to 23 kg (55 lb) in weight, a distance of up to 400 m (440 yd), according to Josephus; it was used effectively in the siege of Jerusalem in AD 70. The four ton machine was made of a heavy wooden frame with a movable arm. The power to hurl the stone from the arm was created by twisting heavy skeins of rope on a windlass. A trigger released the windlass and the arm shot forward and hurled the stone away.

19

This tile is stamped 'Tenth legion, Fretensis'. LE is short for legion, X is tenth and FR an abbreviation for Fretensis.

illustration on page 308). The verb 'stand firm' belongs to the language of war and means 'to take over' or 'hold a critical position in the battlefield'. The Christian is thus in a tactical hot spot in God's strategy against Satan. Such illustrations would have left the original readers of his letters in no doubt that the Christian life was not a picnic, but a call to fight mankind's oldest foe.

Abhorrence of warfare has influenced some Christians today to play down this aspect of the New Testament, but this is to misunderstand Paul's meaning.

Stone missiles flung into the fortress of Masada during the Roman siege in AD 74.

FOR FURTHER READING

Adcock, F.E., *The Roman Art of War* (Harvard, 1940).
Conteneau, G., *Everyday Life in Babylonia and Assyria* (Sidgwick and Jackson, 1954), pp.139–157.
Frye, R.N., *The Heritage of Persia*, chapter 3 (Weidenfeld and Nicholson, 1962).
Gordon, R.P., 'Armour and Weapons', *IBD*, 1 (IVP, 1980), pp.111–116.
Gordon, R.P., 'Legion', *IBD*, 2 (IVP, 1980), p.894.
Grant, M., *The Army of the Caesars* (Weidenfeld and Nicholson, 1974).
Madeline, S. and Miller, J. Lane, *Encyclopedia of Bible Life*, rev. ed. (A. and C. Black, 1979), pp.269–307.
Saggs. H.W.F., *The Might that was Assyria* (Sidgwick and Jackson, 1984), pp.243–268.
Vaux, R. de, *Ancient Israel: its Life and Institutions* (Darton, Longman and Todd, 1962. US ed. New York, McGraw-Hill, 1961), pp. 213–257. (New UK ed. 1973).
Wiseman, D.J., 'Assyria', *IBD*, 1 (IVP, 1980), pp.137–145.

19

King Hammurapi of Babylon (about 1792-1750 BC) in an attitude of prayer. This statue, well over 3,000 years old, is made of bronze and plated with gold. It is dedicated to the 'Amorite' god (Amurru).

SECTION VII:
Religion

The beliefs of Israel's neighbours

The emerging nation of Israel faced threats on two fronts. One was the military front, with native or invading peoples seeking to oust the twelve tribes. The other was the religious front. Whether by accident or design, the surrounding peoples were able to weaken Israel's political power by weakening its religious faith. The more Yahweh was seen to be like one of the many gods worshipped by the other nations, the less confidence Israel had in him and the less faithful it was to his laws.

Like Samson deprived of his Nazirite hair, Israel time and again woke up to find that its traditional spiritual strength had been cut away because it had succumbed to the nagging pressure of its neighbours to adopt their practices; not even people in the ancient world liked to think of themselves as 'different' or 'strange'.

Ancient man was confronted with all the deep questions about life and death which people of every age have had to face. The immediate need to find adequate food and shelter in a world where the regular patterns of the seasons were sometimes, it seemed, countered by inexplicable disasters, coupled with the built-in religious urge that every tribe and generation possesses even to the present day, led people to think of gods who controlled each area of human experience and the natural order.

A sun god who provided light and heat; a storm god who sent hail and rain; a fertility god who controlled reproduction of man, beast and plant: gods of every size and function took life out of man's hands, and sometimes they fought each other for supremacy

Bronze figurine of Syrian god from the late second millennium BC. It may represent the storm-god Hadad or Rimmon ('the thunderer').

Acts 17: 28 ▷

or vented their tempers on the poor helpless earthlings who were cowed into desperate submission. The fact that there might have been a single, supreme god 'in whom we live and move and have our being' does not seem to have entered the minds of people in the Near East until the Israelites brought their new and most unusual monotheism into the promised land. The God who revealed himself was to displace the old gods.

Joshua 24: 14 ▷▷

Ziggurat in Ur. Temples like this, dedicated to the sun and moon gods, would have been familiar to Abraham before he took his journey to the west.

PAGAN RELIGION IN PATRIARCHAL TIMES

Abraham, before he moved to Canaan, lived among Mesopotamian people who were polytheists . The religious practices of his people must have persisted for many centuries, because Joshua had to urge Israel to 'throw away the gods your forefathers worshipped beyond the River and in Egypt, and serve the Lord.' The Sumerian religion of the Mesopotamians had a pantheon: Utu, the sun god; Nana, the moon god; An, the god of heaven; Enlil, the god of the

ur; Enki, the god of water; Ninhursag, the mother goddess; and Inanna, the goddess of life and fertility. All vied for popularity.

But Abraham probably also had contact with Semitic people in Ur. From the Amorites he would have heard about gods such as El and his consort Asherah, Ashteroth, Anath, Melqart, and others whom we meet again among the Canaanites Israel encountered later in its history, such as Baal, Dagon and Shamash.

In the midst of this range of religious influences, Abraham became aware of the one true God, whom he knew as El Shaddai, God Almighty. Almost a centenarian, he one day had a fresh vision of God: '"I am God Almighty; walk before me and be blameless. I will confirm my covenant between me and you and will greatly increase your numbers."' But his great-great-grandchildren had to work out the implications of that vision in the very different religious atmosphere of Egypt, where they had become slaves.

Joseph married Asenath, the daughter of an Egyptian priest, and he, and later Moses who was brought up in the royal court, must have been familiar with contemporary religious beliefs and practices. The bulk of the Semitic slaves may have been ignored by the Egyptians and their priests, however, Moses' request to Pharaoh was 'Let my people go, so that they may worship me [the Lord].'

Some scholars have argued that there was a partial but eventually ineffective move towards monotheism in Egypt during the time of the heretic king Akhenaten (c. 1356-1340 BC) and perhaps even before in the days of his father, Amenhophis III (1386-1349 BC). The supreme universal sun god Amon-Re was divorced from his mythological trappings and was regarded as the only god, known as Aten (solar disc). A hymn addressed to

◁◁ Genesis 17: 1-2

Akhenaten, worshipper of the sun-disc, Aten. This wall painting is from Amarna and dates from about 1370 BC.

Amon-Re about 1400 BC contains some examples of how highly the god was regarded:

◁◁ Genesis 41: 45

Hail sundisc of the daytime,
Creator of all and maker of their
   living! ...
The fashioner of that which the soil
   produces ...
The sole lord who reaches to the
   ends of the lands everyday,

◁◁ Exodus 8: 1

Being the one who sees them that
   tread thereon ...
He makes the seasons by months.
Heat when he wishes and cold when
   he wishes ...
Every land makes utterance at his
   rising every day,
In order to praise him.

Another hymn, found at the tomb of Eye at Tell-el-Amarna, Akhenaten's capital, shows how the Pharaoh regarded the Aten:

20

Creator of seed in woman,
You who make fluid into man,
Who maintain the son in the womb
    of his mother ...
The world came into being by your
    hand,
According as you have made them.
When you have risen they live,
When you set they die,
You are lifetime your own self
For one lives only through you.

However, the Aten cult did not suit the national religion of Egypt, and the incipient monotheism soon died out. There was a strong reaction against it when Akhenaten died. Another attempt to construct a god had failed.

CANAANITE INFLUENCE

Documents discovered at Ugarit on the northern edge of Canaan have thrown light on the religious beliefs of people in the early days of Israel's occupancy of the land. There was a large pantheon of gods, and the supreme deity was called El, meaning 'god', who reigned as king 'at the source of the rivers'. He was 'father of the sons of the gods' and the 'father of mankind'. Sometimes he was called 'the bull', referring to his strength and procreative power. He was said to be the creator of all things, and also to be 'benevolent and merciful'. He was worshipped and sacrifices were offered to him, but nothing more of his nature is known.

The most prominent, and for Bible readers the best known of the gods, was Baal. The name means 'lord' or 'owner', and places were often named after him. He was known as 'he who rides on the clouds', that is, a storm or rain god, a name Israel gave to Yahweh. He was all-important in the growth of crops. When he withheld his power, drought withered them.

Several pictorial representations of

Exodus 34: 13▷▷

1 Kings 18: 19 ▷▷

2 Kings 21: 7 ▷▷

1 Samuel 31: 10▷▷

Jeremiah 7: 18; ▷▷
    44: 17-19

Psalm 18: 10f.▷

him have been found. He was often depicted as a god of thunder and lightning. He had a pointed beard, a helmet with horns, and he carried a club in one hand and a spear or symbol of lightning in the other.

In common with many ancient religions, Canaanite beliefs revolved around several gods. Besides El and Baal there were some important female deities. Many small female figurines, with their sexual details greatly exaggerated, have been found in excavations; the figurines were little images of the goddesses.

Asherah was the consort of El and chief goddess in the Ugaritic texts. She is often described as 'the lady, Asherah of the sea' and 'the creator or progenitor of the gods'. In the Old Testament the name Asherah is often given to a representaion of the goddess in the form of a wooden pole. The Israelites who approached Canaan under Moses' leadership were told before they entered the territory to 'cut down the Asherah poles' of the native inhabitants. The goddess was important in the days of Elijah: Queen Jezebel, who came from Sidon, had 400 prophets of Asherah and 450 of Baal. King Manasseh actually placed an image of Asherah in the Jerusalem temple.

The goddess Astarte was both benevolent and terrifying; she was the Canaanite goddess of both love and war. The Philistines worshipped her as Ashtoreth, a goddess of war to whom they dedicated the spoils of battle. She is probably the Queen of Heaven for whom apostate Israelites made cakes and poured out drink offerings, thus provoking the anger of the Almighty and his servant Jeremiah.

In the Ugaritic texts the goddess Anath was the most active, although she is not mentioned often in the Bible. Her name forms part of some place names such as Jeremiah's home town

A terracotta figure and mould probably representing Astarte or Ashtoreth. Worship of Ashtoreth was introduced by Solomon through the prompting of his Sidonian wives (1 Kings 11: 1-6).

of Anathoth, and the Canaanites sometimes regarded her as Baal's sister. They knew her as a virgin but also saw her involved in fertility rites; they emphasized her youthfulness and powers of life and generation. But she had a savage aspect to her nature and in the Ugarit texts is depicted fighting foes, wading through the blood of the slain, wearing a helmet and carrying a battle-axe and spear.

There was nothing secretive about Canaanite religion: it was practised in the open air, 'on every high hill and under every spreading tree'. Simple altars may well have been set up in rough enclosures on hill tops all over the region. On them Canaanites offered animal, possibly even human, sacrifices. They had feasts, perhaps including boiling of a goat kid in its mother's milk, a practice forbidden in the Mosaic law (see page 158). There were magic ceremonies and fertility rites.

Associated with the shrines were 'the holy ones', male and female cult prostitutes. It is not certain whether overt sexual acts took place at the

◁Exodus 23:19; Deuteronomy 14: 21

20

◁◁1 Kings 14: 23

The temple at Lachish described on this page. This model is in the Israel Museum.

Hosea 4: 14 ▷

shrines, but the prostitutes clearly played a central role in the fertility cult. This must have constituted part of the superficial attraction of pagan religion to the normally more virtuous, modest and chaste Israelites. The prophet Hosea complained of men who 'consort with harlots and sacrifice with temple prostitutes' and added that 'a people without understanding will come to ruin!' He and other prophets often speak of Israel having deserted God and gone after pagan deities as a man leaves his wife for a prostitute; there is reason to believe that 'playing the harlot' in a religious sense was sometimes literally as well as figuratively true.

Remains of Canaanite temples throw further light on religious practices. A temple at Lachish, the third on the same site and dating from about 1325 to 1260 BC, had a rectangular sanctuary with two rooms off it. There was no inner room or 'holy of holies'. The entrance was screened by a wall to prevent people seeing into it from outside. The shrine area had a hearth for a fire, and behind it was a platform which was probably an altar approached by three steps from the west side. Another platform behind the altar was probably where the cult statue stood. To the west of the altar was a bin for meal offerings. Around the sides were rows of benches on which worshippers put their votive (waved) gifts and offerings.

Outside were rubbish pits sunk into

the ground, and among the broken pots were found many animal bones. The animals would have been sacrificed, and they were all young sheep, goats, oxen and gazelles. Most of the bones were of the right foreleg, implying that the Canaanites had a similar practice to that of the Israelites: the right shoulder of a sacrificed animal was given to the priest to eat.

The worshippers at Lachish were polytheists. A small statuette thought to be the Syrian god Reshef has been found there, and the name of the goddess Elath was preserved on an inscription on a large jar.

Temples at Hazor have provided similar relics, including figurines, incense, libation and offering tables, seated figures of male deities cut in basalt, and many pottery and basalt vessels. One of the temples bore a close resemblance to Solomon's: it had a porch with two pillars near the inner entrance. This led into the main hall, which in turn led to the Holy of Holies which measured 13.5 m x 8.9 m (42.3 ft x 29.6 ft). At the back of this inner sanctuary was a niche for the cult figurine.

Stone pillars were common in pagan

Stone pillars were a common feature of Canaanite worship. These objects from Hazor form what is known as the 'Shrine of the Stelae'.

Canaanite shrines. The Israelites were commanded to break them down – and they were forbidden to erect them. Some of them represented Baal. Sacred pillars have been found in a Canaanite temple at Shechem, too. Abimelech was crowned king at a pillar at Shechem – long before the days of the kings – and a great white pillar found in the courtyard of the temple may have been the very stone. It may well have been this temple where the people 'prostituted themselves to the Baals' and 'set up Baal-Berith as their god' so soon after Gideon's great victory with a tiny army over the hordes of Midianites.

It is clear that there were close parallels between pagan and Israelite worship. Both religions had animal sacrifices with burnt and peace offerings; they both had grain and drink offerings. There was a priesthood and there were sacred buildings. It was therefore hardly surprising that some Israelites fused the two together, losing sight of the great spiritual difference between them and

◁Deuteronomy 16: 22

◁◁Leviticus 7: 32

◁Judges 9: 6

◁Judges 8: 33

◁◁1 Kings 7: 21

20

seeing only the similarity of the outward practices.

Some evidence of that fusion, or syncretism as it is called, comes from names used in the Bible. A true worshipper of Yahweh would give his children names which contained the element *Yahu*, as in Jermiyahu (Jeremiah), Yeshayahu (Isaiah), Eliyahu (Elijah) and Yehonatan (Jonathan). He would avoid names such as Jerubbaal, Merib-baal and Abi-baal. Yet in the collection of ostraca (broken pottery pieces with writing on them) found at Samaria and dating from the eighth century BC, there were eleven *Yahu* names and seven Baal names among a total of fifty-two. Clearly foreigners were bringing their religious ideas with them or Israelites were forsaking their true religion in Samaria.

1 Kings 11: 1-8 ▷▷

2 Kings 16: 3 ▷▷

Jeremiah 32: 35 ▷▷

Such paganism may have flourished in the very shadow of the Jerusalem temple. What is thought to have been an unauthorized shrine lay just outside the eastern wall of the Old Testament city. It had a small room with two pillars which were not needed to support the roof and which the excavator, Dr Kathleen Kenyon, suggested were Canaanite symbols for Baal. There was a small stone platform which could have been an altar on which libations were poured. The pottery there suggested that the shrine dated from about 700 BC.

Some Israelite leaders tried to reform the religious practices of their people and to outlaw Canaanite shrines. King Asa made a half-hearted attempt at reform; Elijah opposed Baal worship by his preaching; King Jehu killed many Canaanite priests; and King Hezekiah made a number of major reforms. The greatest reformer was King Josiah but his changes were short-lived and things soon went back to their former state. The power of 'folk religion' was not easily destroyed.

2 Kings 21: 3-6 ▷▷
2 Kings 23: 4-20 ▷

OTHER EARLY RELIGIOUS INFLUENCES

The Canaanites were the main but not the only influence on the beliefs of the Old Testament Israelites. Trade links and political alliances brought into the land non-Israelite people with their beliefs and customs. King Solomon married many foreign wives as he pursued political alliances and they introduced into the heart of Israel the worship of Ashtoreth, goddess of the Sidonians, Molech of Ammon, Chemosh of Moab, and gods of the Edomites, Hittites and Egyptians.

Molech (or Milcom) was especially significant – and detestable. King Ahaz 'even sacrificed his son in the fire', the book of Kings records. This was the central rite of Molech worship. 'They built high places for Baal in the Valley of Ben Hinnom to sacrifice their sons and daughters to Molech, though I never commanded, nor did it enter my mind, that they should do such a detestable thing and so make Judah sin' was God's lament through Jeremiah. The cult had survived possibly from pre-Israelite days, and it was practised during the time of the kings in countries east of Israel – Ammon, Syria and northern Mesopotamia. Further evidence of its existence is contained in the name of the gods honoured by Assyrian military colonists brought to Samaria after Israel's exile in 721 BC: Adrammelech and Anamelech. Both names contain the element *melech* and may be associated with Adad and Anu, ancient Babylonian gods.

Worship of astral deities – sun, moon and stars – was also known in Israel. Manasseh built altars for the hosts of heaven in the courts of the temple. He also burned his son as an offering, practised sorcery and divination, and consulted mediums and spiritists. Josiah destroyed Manasseh's cult shrines, including 'horses dedicated to the sun'. Figurines in the shape of horses, with a disc (the solar emblem) on their foreheads, have been discovered in Jerusalem and also in Hazor. Ezekiel also attests that a sun cult was practised in the temple and Jeremiah says it went on in everyone's home.

Other figurines found in Jerusalem include mother-goddesses with their hands clasped beneath their breasts. Their heads were square cut with wig-like hair and pinched bird-like features.

FROM BEL TO ZOROASTER

The syncretism which had begun early in Israel's history did not abate when the northern kingdom went into exile in 721 BC nor when Judah followed it in 587 BC. The promised punishment for spiritual adultery did not seem to drive all the people back to a pure version of Yahweh worship.

Not everyone went into exile, of course. The Assyrians claimed they deported 27,290 people from Samaria. But the Bible records that foreigners were imported to replace them: people from Babylon, Cuthah, Avva, Hamath and Sepharvaim were sent to Samaria and took their beliefs and gods with them. They were taught the law of God by a priest brought back from exile for the purpose, but they still set up their gods in the Samaritan shrines.

Without the restraints of a functioning temple and priesthood, many of the Israelites drifted further away from the faith of their forefathers. Some burned incense to the Queen of Heaven, although Jeremiah records that some faithful people also continued to bring gifts to the temple site.

In Babylon, the exiles were confronted with a new range of gods and beliefs. Isaiah mentions the gods

◁◁2 Kings 23: 11

◁◁Ezekiel 8: 16

◁Jeremiah 41: 5

Jewish exiles in Egypt settled at Elephantine. This papyrus, found there, is a copy of a letter from the local chief priest Yedoniah to the Persian viceroy of Judaea, Sanballat in 408 BC.

20

Isaiah 46: 1; ▷
40: 18-20

Malachi 1: 6-14▷▷

Bel and Nebo, and images of wood richly overlaid with gold and silver – impressive, but quite impotent. He ridicules the mentality of the person who makes an idol with his own hands, then worships it as if it had made him. Of course, some exiles maintained their faith and returned to

Jerusalem to rebuild the temple when they had opportunity, although a century after the return the prophet Malachi longed to see the temple closed down because of the contemptible worship which went on there.

Another group of Jews had probably fled to Egypt some time before the exile. At Elephantine Island, on the first cataract of the Nile, there was a

The supreme god, according to Zoroastrian belief, was Ahura Mazda. Here his symbol is portrayed on a relief in Persepolis.

temple for the worship of Yahu (Yahweh). It was destroyed by the Egyptians, but the conquering Persians allowed the Jews to rebuild it so long as they offered only incense, grain and drink, and did not make animal sacrifices. This restriction was probably made to avoid offending Egyptians, Persians, and the Jews back home in Jerusalem.

These people kept the sabbath and

the Passover, but documents from Elephantine show that they worshipped other gods beside Yahu. Ishembethel, Herem-bethel and Anath-bethel all received offerings in the temple. It is possible that these were different names for Yahu, but even so the worship at Elephantine was not orthodox Judaism.

Pagan influences were not removed from Palestine in the years after the exile. At Lachish a sun temple or solar shrine, dating from the Hellenistic times, has been found. Beneath it were the remains of an earlier Israelite 'high place' or pagan shrine, including a large upright stone, the trunk of an olive tree, and several pits containing broken stone inscriptions and votive objects. West of it was a small rectangular room with plastered benches along the walls and a raised platform in one corner. On the benches were cult vessels, an incense altar and four incense burners, chalices, bowls and lamps. The room had been destroyed in the tenth century BC.

The Hellenistic solar shrine was about 26 m x 17 m (88 ft x 56 ft). From the north-facing entrance worshippers entered a courtyard flanked on the east by five small rooms and on the west by the sacred area which was approached by five steps. At the top of these was a long ante-chamber leading to three more steps and the inner sanctuary which contained a small limestone altar, bearing the traces of a large hand and a large male figure with raised arms. A drain in the centre indicated that libation (drink) offerings were poured out on it. It was probably built in the fourth century BC.

The worship here would have been a challenge to the people of Judah at a time when Zoroastrianism from Persia was becoming known in western Asia. The Jewish sect at Qumran, where the Dead Sea scrolls were found, flourished in the last two centuries BC

20

and was certainly influenced by Zoroastrianism. It offered a plausible explanation for the evils of the world by teaching that there were two primeval spirits, the Holy Spirit and the Evil One, who were locked in conflict until the eventual future victory of the Holy Spirit.

This religion made much of the conflict of opposite forces – light and dark, good and evil. In later times the Holy Spirit was identified with Ahura Mazda, the supreme god. The monks at Qumran, who accepted some of this dualism, believed that the spirits of light and darkness were made by the supreme God and remained dependent on him.

Evidence from Marisa, once an important town in south-west Judaea, suggests that here at least people worshipped whatever god they chose. Paintings on tomb walls had Greek, Phoenician and Edomite religious symbols. Numerous lead figurines were found and are believed to have had some magical significance. Over fifty inscriptions on limestone fragments were prayers to various gods; the supplicants had Semitic, Roman, Egyptian and Edomite names.

FOR FURTHER READING

Aharoni, Y., *The Archaeology of the Land of Israel* (Philadelphia, Westminster, 1978).

Albright, W.F., *Archaeology and the Religion of Israel* (Baltimore, Johns Hopkins, 1955).

Davey, C.J., 'Temples of the Levant and the Buildings of Solomon', *Tyndale Bulletin*, 31 (1980), pp.107–146.

Gray, J., *The Legacy of Canaan, VT*, Supp. 1 (Leiden, E.J. Brill, 1965).

Kramer, S.N., *Mythologies of the Ancient World* (New York, Anchor Books, 1961).

Millard, A.R. and Wiseman, D.J. (eds), *Essays on the Patriarchal Narratives* (IVP, 1980).

Morenz, S., *Egyptian Religion* (Methuen, 1973).

Ringgren, H., *Religions of the Ancient Near East* (SPCK, 1973).

Shiloh, Y., 'Iron Age Sanctuaries and Cult Elements in Palestine', in *Symposia* (Massachusetts, ASOR, 1979).

Wiseman, D.J. (ed.), *Peoples of Old Testament Times* (OUP, 1973).

Wright, G.E., *The Old Testament against its Environment*, Studies in Biblical Theology, No. 2 (SCM, 1951).

Israel at worship

21

The Bible is shot through with references to and descriptions of Jewish religious practices. Even the newcomer to the New Testament is confronted with the subject after only a few verses in, say, Luke's Gospel. The father of John the Baptist is a priest and is chosen to burn incense in the temple in Jerusalem. Once John is born he is circumcised in a religious ritual; so too is Jesus just a chapter later, and his parents follow that by sacrificing a pair of pigeons.

Jesus' teaching and the letters of the apostles naturally assume familiarity with contemporary religious life. Jesus said on one occasion that he gave his life as a ransom for many, associating himself with the Old Testament sacrifices. Paul does the same thing when he speaks of Christians being 'justified by [Christ's] blood', and John uses similar imagery when he declares that Jesus is the atoning sacrifice for our sins. The life, death and resurrection of Jesus thus take on deeper significance as the underlying Old Testament thought is understood.

The Bible is a book of progressive revelation; God, it seems, did not reveal all his truths and requirements to his people at the very beginning. He allowed them to become familiar with one idea before progressing to the next. Hence Paul could explain to the Galatians that Jesus did not come into the world to deal with the effects of human sinfulness as soon as Adam and Eve took the law into their own hands, but 'when the time had fully come' – that is when God had prepared his people to receive and appreciate his ultimate act of love.

FIRST GLIMPSES OF GOD

The faith of the patriarchs, Abraham and his immediate descendants, appears to have had little formal organization. The Genesis records were written some time after the events took place; the name for God, Yahweh, used early in Genesis was not in fact revealed until the days of Moses, but the later author has put it into the patriarchal stories. However, the picture of patriarchal religion does not bear the marks of a mere projection back in time of a state of affairs which existed much later. There are no references to Baal, who was prominent later. There is a spontaneity, even an un-selfconscious sense of surprise, as the story unfolds of how Abraham and Jacob encountered God, for example.

Theirs was a God who revealed himself in dreams and to whom the patriarchs could relate easily in prayer. From time to time they built altars and offered animal sacrifices; often this was in response to some special revelation or blessing from God, as when the Lord told Abraham (then Abram) '"to your offspring I will give this land".' Abraham was familiar with the concept of offering tithes (a tenth of his produce) to God as a religious duty, and did so to the strange figure of Melchizedek, priest and king of Salem (Jerusalem) who appears as it were out of nowhere in the story, and promptly disappears from the sight of posterity

◁Exodus 6: 3

◁◁Mark 10: 45

◁◁Romans 5: 9

◁◁1 John 2: 2

◁Genesis 12: 7

◁Genesis 14: 18-20

◁◁Galatians 4: 4

WHAT THE TABERNACLE LOOKED LIKE

The tabernacle, the mobile worship centre used by the Israelites, was little more than a wooden-framed tent draped inside with colourful linen curtains. The violet, purple and scarlet tapestries were decorated with cherubim and were 12.7 m (42 ft) long by 2 m (6 ft) wide. They were sewn together into two sets of five curtains.

Outside, the walls of the tabernacle were made from eleven goats-hair curtains. The roof was made from tanned rams' skins. The upright wooden posts were plated with gold and stood in sockets of silver made from objects collected in the census tax.

The tabernacle, which must have been rather gloomy inside with the heavy coverings shutting out most of the light, was divided into two rooms – the pattern which was followed for all Israel's subsequent central places of worship. The outer room, or 'Holy Place', was 9 m (30 ft) long, twice the length of the inner room, the Holy of Holies. They were divided by a curtain or veil.

The ark of the covenant stood in the inner room. It was an acacia-wood box overlaid with pure gold plate. On top of it was the 'mercy seat', a slab of gold with a cherub at each end. The blood of the sacrifices was sprinkled on the top of the ark.

In the Holy Place there was an incense altar in front of the veil. It too was made of acacia-wood and overlaid with gold, and it had horns and an ornamental gold moulding on the top. Also in the Holy Place was a table for the Bread of the Presence and a seven-branched lampstand'.

The tabernacle was erected in a courtyard 45 m x 22.5 m (150 ft x 75 ft), the long sides running north and south. It was surrounded by a two-metre-high linen screen embroidered in violet, purple and scarlet. The posts supporting it were probably made from acacia-wood and stood in copper sockets. There was a gate 9 m (30 ft) wide in the eastern end of the screen. Within the courtyard was an altar made of acacia-wood and covered in copper, which was used for sacrifices. It had projecting horns at the top corners. A copper basin held water for the ritual washings of the priests, and was called the 'laver'.

When the Israelites pitched their camp the tabernacle was at the centre. It was surrounded by the priests' tents, beyond them were the Levites', and then round them the many tents of the twelve tribes. The Bible records that it

---

once he has received the tithes.

Once God had initiated a covenant relationship with Abraham, the patriarch willingly submitted himself and his family to the ritual act of male circumcision as a sign of the covenant. He and his descendants also seem to have acted in ways which were later frowned on by God himself. They planted trees at sacred spots and set up sacred pillars, practices which were forbidden in the later Mosaic law, another pointer to the antiquity of the early narratives of Genesis.

This may indicate that in earliest times these objects were not identified with actual deities, but were merely signs or symbols of God's intervention in the patriarchs' lives. Patriarchal religion is, perhaps surprisingly, free from the conflicts with other religions which, as we saw in the previous chapter, characterized most of the history of Israel. This may have been because they did not think of the Canaanite El as totally distinct from their own El Shaddai; they did not worship a different God but simply knew him better than the Canaanites, because of his special revelation.

THE FOUNDATIONS OF RITUAL

For many generations the faith of the patriarchs was kept alive in the hearts

Genesis 17: 9-14 ▷

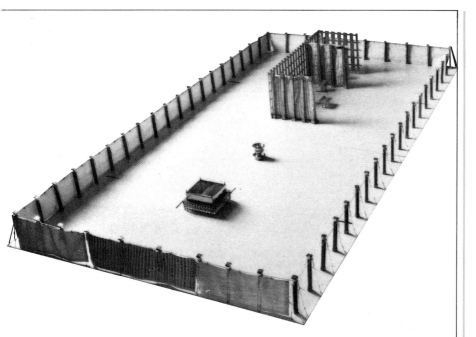

was erected at Shiloh soon after the entry into Canaan, and was moved to Nob and to Gibeon. Solomon brought it to the temple when his building was completed, but what happened to it afterwards is unknown.

The structure which stood at Shiloh during Samuel's lifetime sounds as if it was more solid than the original tabernacle. It is possible that part of the old tabernacle had perished through

A reconstruction of the tabernacle described in Exodus, showing, in the courtyard, the altar of burnt-offering and the laver and, behind the curtain, the incense-altar and the table for the bread of the Presence. The seven-branched lampstand and the ark of the covenant are not visible.

◁◁ 1 Kings 8: 1-9

age, and had been replaced by more enduring materials. It had doorposts and a door, and was called the 'temple of the LORD'.

◁◁ 1 Samuel 1: 9

and homes of the growing numbers of Israelites who were slaves in Egypt. Although there is no biblical description of corporate worship, Moses' excuse for leaving the country was so that the people could worship God together.

Once the fugitive Israelites were in the desert, they seem to have had a temporary meeting-place. 'Moses used to take a tent and pitch it outside the camp some distance away, calling it "the tent of meeting".' It seems to have been more of a counselling centre than a place of worship; people who needed to know God's will or purpose would go to the tent for an answer. Whenever Moses went into it the visible symbol

of God's presence, the pillar of cloud, descended on the tent. When that happened, everyone stood at his own tent door and worshipped God.

◁ Exodus 33: 10

The first central place of worship was the tabernacle, a much larger but still portable structure (see feature). Some scholars feel that the description of both the structure and the worship which took place within it is an idealized picture written long after the tabernacle gave way to the temple. The archaeologist W.F. Albright has suggested, however, that the spirit and much of the detail of the Exodus and Leviticus passages pre-dates the conquest of Canaan and goes back to Mosaic origins.

◁ Exodus 33: 7

21

Leviticus 3; 7: 11-21▷▷

Leviticus 1; 6: 8-13 ▷

Leviticus 4 - 5: 13; ▷▷
6: 24-30

Leviticus 2; 6: 14-23 ▷

Worship in the tabernacle centred on five offerings, the first of which was the burnt offering. The whole offering consisted of a ritually clean animal, a bull, ram, male goat or bird. Its blood was poured round the sides of the altar, and its inner organs and legs washed clean. Then it was cut into joints and every part, except the hide, was burned on the altar as an offering to God, 'an aroma pleasing to the Lord'. It was a symbol of a person's total dedication to God.

The grain offering was like a gift to God, an act of generosity prompted by love. It could be fine flour mixed with oil and offered cooked (without yeast) or uncooked. Part of the offering was burned on the altar, and the rest was given to the priests for food.

The peace or fellowship offering expressed friendship or communion between the worshipper and God. Part of the sacrifice, a male or female animal, was burned on the altar; inner fat, kidneys and liver were disposed of in this way. The right thigh and the breast were taken by the priests and the rest of the animal was eaten by the worshippers.

When a person discovered he had unwittingly broken God's law, he had to make a sin offering. It was a living animal or bird; if the offender was very poor it could be a portion of fine flour. If damage had been done or the victim

Israel's ritual was centred on one God, a God who commanded his people. The Sinai mountains were the chosen stage for God's revelation of the Ten Commandments to Moses.

Aerial view of the temple site in Jerusalem. Haram esh-Sherif.

suffered some loss, the guilt offering had to be made; the offender also had to compensate the victim fully and add 20% of the value to his payment. Once a year a 'Day of Atonement' was held at the tabernacle, in which an elaborate series of sacrifices was made to atone for all the sins of Israel committed over the past twelve months.

At home in the tent, the ordinary Israelite had regular opportunities for worship. Each week everyone observed the sabbath by resting from work. It was probably a day on which the priests taught the people about their relationship with God, but no details have survived concerning the nature of their sabbath worship.

Once a year the family celebrated the Passover feast. They killed and ate a lamb to commemorate the deliverance of Israel from Egypt in the exodus. It was celebrated in the spring, at the beginning of the barley harvest, and was followed the next day by the Feast of Unleavened Bread. Later, it seems, the two festivals were merged into one.

Other family festivals included the Feast of Weeks, or the Feast of Firstfruits, held at the time of the wheat harvest, and the Feast of Tabernacles, which recalled the Israelite wanderings in the desert, and which was also held at harvest time. How they were celebrated in the early days of Israel is unclear.

SOLOMON'S TEMPLE

From all accounts Solomon's temple was a place of grandeur and beauty, but no trace of it has been found. The construction of massive retaining walls for Herod's temple some 900 years later probably obliterated anything which remained from Solomon's day.

◁◁ Leviticus 5: 14-19; 7: 1-10

◁ Leviticus 23: 5-8

◁◁ Leviticus chapter 16

21

The temple stood on the east side of the Old City in an area now known as Haram esh-Sherif. The highest part of this rocky area, now covered by the golden-domed Moslem shrine, 'The Dome of the Rock', may have been the site of the inner sanctuary or the altar of burnt offering which stood outside the sanctuary itself.

1 Kings ▷ chapters 6 and 7

The two biblical accounts of the structure vary slightly, but the basic shape is clear. There were two rooms, the Holy Place and the Holy of Holies. There were two courtyards outside and at the entrance were two free-standing pillars called Jachin and Boaz. To explain these names it has been suggested that the pillars bore inscriptions and that the names are abbreviations of them. The inscriptions may have read: 'He will establish (Jachin) the throne of David

2 Chronicles ▷ chapters 3 and 4

and his kingdom to his seed for ever', and 'in the strength (Boaz) of Yahweh will the king rejoice'.

A pair of cypress-wood doors separated the entrance porch from the Holy Place, where lattice windows let in the daylight. The golden incense altar, the table for shew-bread and five pairs of lampstands stood in the Holy Place. Another pair of double doors led to the Holy of Holies and they were opened only for the high priest to enter once a year for the Day of Atonement ceremony. The ark of the covenant stood here, overshadowed by two olive-wood winged figures which touched both each other and the side walls.

Steven's reconstruction of the temple of Solomon described on this page shows clearly the twin pillars, vestibule, doors and side storage rooms.

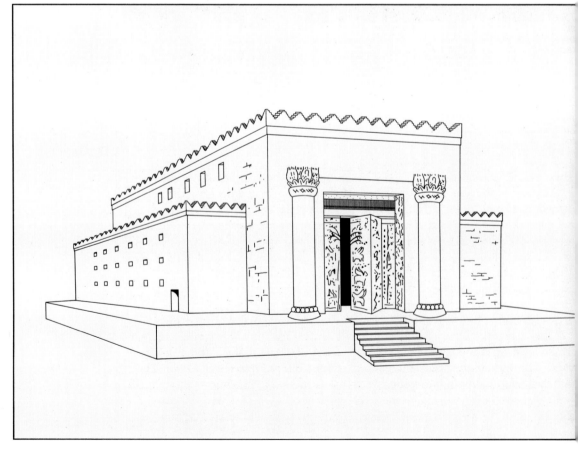

The 'ark of the covenant' has not survived but this cedar-wood chest belonging to Tutankhamun (about 1400 BC) may have been similar. Four carrying poles slide through bronze rings underneath the chest. It is 83 cm (about 32 in) long.

These ivory sphinxes (cherubim) are of Phoenician style and come from Nimrud (9th-8th centuries BC) but give an impression of what the cherubim in the temple may have looked like with their touching wings.

Both rooms were panelled with cedar-wood and the floor was planked with cypress. Walls and doors were decorated with carvings of flowers, palm trees and cherubim overlaid with gold. There was no visible stonework inside. Side rooms were built on to the temple, and the royal palace was close by – perhaps because Solomon believed that the Lord's anointed king should live close to the Lord's temple.

21

WHAT THE PRIESTS WORE

The robes of the high priest were almost royal in character. Dressed in gold, blue, purple and scarlet, the high priest would have been a conspicuous and splendid figure. The biblical details are not precise enough to draw a fully accurate picture of him, but they do enable us to get some idea of what he looked like.

Exodus 28: 1-43; ▷
39: 1-43

The first item listed is the ephod, made of multi-coloured material and fine twisted linen. It was supported by shoulder straps and could therefore have been a waistcoat, but, because it also had a band to girdle it, many commentators think it was a sort of kilt. Each shoulder strap had an onyx stone engraved with the names of six of the twelve tribes, so that the high priest carried them before God whenever he entered the tabernacle or temple.

A breastplate made of linen and gold, blue, purple and scarlet like the ephod, had four rows of stones each representing one of the twelve tribes. It was attached to the ephod shoulder straps by rings and gold chains. It was a double square, almost like an apron, into which could be placed the Urim and Thummim, sacred stones which were used to determine God's will. The high priest picked a stone from the pouch in answer to an enquiry; if it was Thummim, the answer was 'yes'; if Urim, it was 'no'.

Besides these main garments the high priest wore a blue or velvet robe under the ephod which had bells on its skirts. As he moved about the temple, people could follow his movements by the sound of the bells. He had a coat or tunic of fine linen, and a linen turban. On the turban was a plate of pure gold, which may have been shaped like a flower, on which was engraved 'Holy to the Lord'. It was fixed to the turban by a diadem of violet ribbon. He also wore linen breeches, the equivalent of · underwear.

Other priests wore much simpler clothes. They wore tunics, girdles or sashes, caps and linen breeches. These were almost commonplace clothes, and the main distinguishing mark would have been the sash which was decorated according to the priest's rank.

Modern replica of Aaron's breastpiece, showing the stones and symbols for each of the twelve tribes.

PRIESTS AND PROPHETS

Israel's worship at the time of the kings centred largely on the temple, but it depended also on the growing band of men who led the sacrifices and ceremonies. Chief among them were the priests, the descendants of Aaron, who alone were authorized to offer sacrifices to God. They were a conservative group who often needed reforming and rebuking by prophets and kings when Israel's worship became corrupt or compromised. Chief among them was the high priest who came to wield considerable power.

2 Chronicles 17: 7-9▷▷

The Levites were auxiliary ministers who began as labourers caring for the tabernacle but later assisted the priests in the temple services. Many of them were scattered through the villages of Israel rather than being centred on the temple, and they seem to have been teachers of the faith to people in remote areas.

The prophets were not primarily involved in the conduct of worship, but they were frequently critical of it. The first clear picture of their function comes in the days of Saul with Samuel, who was God's spokesman to the nation. The Hebrew word for prophet, *nabi*, probably means one who is called. The prophets preached wherever they could attract a hearing, often away from the temple in the

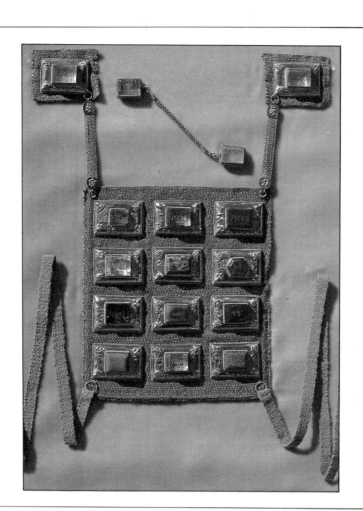

market places or on hillsides. Some were oddly dressed and they were invariably distinctive in behaviour. They were more numerous than the few who have left written records may suggest; occasional references to a 'man of God' reveal that other people with a prophetic ministry existed but they are rarely mentioned in the biblical account. In the days of Elijah and Elisha there were schools or communities of prophets, perhaps almost like religious orders.

Each of the prophets addressed specific needs or abuses in their own generation, but a common theme ran through all their messages. Worship which is pleasing to God has to come from the heart and be matched by a lifestyle which honours him.

> 'These people …
> … honour me with their lips,
> but their hearts are far from
>   me,'

records the book of Isaiah.

> 'Away with the noise of your
>   songs!
>   I will not listen to the music
>   of your harps.
> But let justice roll on like a
>   river,
>   righteousness like a
>   never-failing stream!'

recounts Amos.

◁◁ 2 Kings 6: 1

◁ Isaiah 29: 13

21

◁ Amos 5: 23f.

Another influential group of people was the wise men. Most nations had a body of teachers whose task was to pass on to their generation the collected wisdom of the past. It was often stated tersely in proverbs. The wise men were concerned with rules for practical godly living rather than with theology, but their basic concept was that 'the fear of the Lord is the beginning of knowledge'. In Egypt the wise men gathered together schools of younger men and passed on their sayings. Phrases such as 'Now then, my sons, listen to me' in the biblical texts suggest that a similar practice was prevalent in Israel. In post-exilic times the schools developed into training classes for scribes. Traditionally Solomon was the founder of Israel's wisdom movement.

Proverbs 1: 7 ▷

Proverbs 8: 32 ▷

WORSHIP IN THE COUNTRY

Travel was difficult – or at least inconvenient – in Old Testament times and people were not always inclined to walk or ride on donkeys for long distances in order to fulfil their religious duties. It is not surprising that unofficial shrines and temples were built in many parts of Israel. The books of Joshua, Judges and Samuel reveal that altars were set up at a time of need and in the place where they were needed; people did not wait to go to Jerusalem to make a thank offering or a guilt offering. Gideon, not a priest, built an altar on the site of a pagan shrine. Samuel, the travelling prophet, offered sacrifices at some of the towns on his itinerary. Only after David captured Jerusalem and Solomon, his son, had built the temple, was Jerusalem to become a 'national' religious centre.

Judges 6: 26 ▷

1 Samuel 9: 12: ▷
11: 15

One of the best preserved permanent shrines outside Jerusalem is at Arad, between Beer-sheba and the Dead Sea.

It had once been a flourishing town in a much earlier period, but was abandoned about 2700 BC and rebuilt as a fortress at the time of Solomon in the tenth century BC. At first there was only an enclosed, paved sacred area (a *temenos*) with a square stone altar on one side. Near the altar excavators discovered burnt bones and the burnt skeleton of a young lamb.

The Israelite sanctuary at Arad, described on this page.

In the second half of the tenth century BC a temple was erected on the north-west part of the pavement. It was 20 m (65 ft) long and 15 m (49 ft) broad, with an entrance on the east side. There was a large main room with a smaller room off it approached by three steps. On each side of the third step was a small altar with the charred remains of organic matter. Inside the smaller room was a paved platform, with a fallen rounded pillar beside it. Plastered benches round the walls were probably shelves for offerings and vessels. Outside in the centre of the court was an altar for burnt offerings, which was replaced some time in the eighth century BC by a floor and an oven, perhaps as a result of King Hezekiah's reforms. In the late seventh century BC the temple was demolished, perhaps in accordance with the reforms of Josiah. Names found on pottery fragments indicate

2

that the people of the area were worshippers of Yahweh.

Another shrine was believed to have existed at Beer-sheba, also in the south of Judah. It looks as if it had been destroyed (again possibly in the time of Hezekiah and the prophet Isaiah) but the smooth stones used for the altar had been used in other buildings; archaeologists collected them and reconstructed a horned altar for animal sacrifice. The blood of the sacrifice was traditionally sprinkled on the horns. The altar stood 157 cm (5 ft 3 in) high. One of the stones had a carved snake, an emblem which was significant in Moses' day when he put a model snake on a pole so that anyone who looked at it would not die after being bitten by a plague of poisonous snakes which invaded the Israelite camp. A bronze snake was kept in the temple until Hezekiah's day, when the king removed it because it had become an object of worship.

Numbers 21: 8 ▷

2 Kings 18: 4 ▷

At the opposite end of the country, at Dan in the north, there was a large sacred area with a horned altar. It was a rival shrine to the Jerusalem temple in the days of the kings.

At a sacred site in Kuntilet Ajrud, 50 km (31 miles) south of the large oasis of Kadesh Barnea, a wide variety of inscriptions in old Hebrew script was found on the rims of stone vessels. One said, 'Given by Obadiah, son of Adanah, may he be blessed by Yahweh.' Phrases on the plaster walls include 'blessed by Baal' and 'Yahweh favoured'; some even appear to refer to Yahweh and his Asherah. It may have been a wayside shrine used by travellers of different religions.

In order to regularize worship and to avoid the dangers of syncretism, successive kings reformed its structure and practices. Asa (*c.* 913–873 BC) removed some cult prostitutes and idols, but he did not destroy the high places; his reforms may have been restricted to Jerusalem.

Hezekiah's (715–687/6 BC) reform was more significant. His father Ahaz had sold the nation to Assyria and had compromised his faith by paying homage to Assyrian gods. A copy of a pagan altar was built in the temple precincts in Jerusalem. Hezekiah worked cautiously, perhaps out of fear of the Assyrians, but succeeded in removing high places and in destroying sacred pillars. His reforms met with only partial success and he did not manage to centralize all worship in Jerusalem.

Josiah (640–609 BC) undertook a more far-reaching reform. He purged foreign cults and killed their priests and religious prostitutes, and although king of Judah he was also able to extend his reforms to Israel in the north because the Assyrian presence there had grown weak. He also closed down the outlying shrines and invited rural priests to join the temple priests in Jerusalem.

It was a profound change, and one which bred resentment among the people. It led to a change in external patterns of worship but not to a wholesale spiritual revival in which the hearts of the people were changed. When Josiah died, his successor Jehoiakim lifted all restraints and the nation quickly fell back to its old ways of worship, to a fresh accommodation with pagan beliefs, and to fresh condemnation from God's prophet Jeremiah.

THE DEVELOPMENT OF RITUAL

It is a tragic but true fact of life that adversity often draws from people a degree of creativity and spiritual devotion which lie dormant or

Facing page: a 'horned altar'. This one is from Megiddo, 10th-9th centuries BC.

neglected in happier times. The period of the exiles of Israel and Judah did much to establish the Jewish pattern of worship which we meet half a millennium later in the life and times of Jesus Christ.

The people remaining in Judah, their temple ruined by Nebuchadrezzer's forces, were filled with despair. Out of their darkness emerged the moving poetry of Lamentations:

Jeremiah 41: 5▷▷

> How deserted lies the city,
>   once so full of people!
> How like a widow is she,
>   who once was great among the
>   nations!
> She who was queen among the
>   provinces
>   has now become a slave.
> Bitterly she weeps at night,
>   tears are upon her cheeks.
> Among all her lovers
>   there is none to comfort her.

Psalm 137: 1-2 ▷▷

Lamentations 1: 1-2▷

Leaderless, the Judaeans were prone to syncretism, chasing the 'lovers' who, because they were false gods, were powerless to comfort them. A few remained faithful to Yahweh, bringing gifts to the ruined temple site. Jeremiah records that eighty men, shaved and with torn clothes as a sign of mourning, brought offerings to the temple site from Shechem, Shiloh and Samaria.

Across the Fertile Crescent, in Babylon, the exiles shared a similar bitterness and sadness. Their captors tormented them, asking them to sing their national songs. Once more, the poetry of affliction flowed from their lips:

> By the rivers of Babylon we sat and
>   wept
>   when we remembered Zion.
> There on the poplars
>   we hung our harps…
> How can we sing the songs of the
>   LORD

Remains of the temple wall rebuilt by Nehemiah in the 6th century BC. Jerusalem.

while in a foreign land?
If I forget you, O Jerusalem,
    may my right hand forget its
    skill.

But sadness no doubt gave way to resignation, and resignation to hope. Some of the exiled Jews continued to observe the sabbaths and to circumcise their sons. They followed their food laws and practised their rituals of cleanness. On the eve of their release there was a profound reinterpretation of Israel's ancient faith, finding expression in Isaiah chapters 40 to 55, emphasizing that Yahweh is the one true God, the sovereign Lord of history who laid out the universe and gives breath to the people on earth.

The first thing the Jews did on their return to Jerusalem in 539 BC was to repair the altar and to begin the

sacrifices again. Then they set about rebuilding the temple, a long task hindered by opposition but finally encouraged by the prophets Haggai and Zechariah and completed in 515 BC. Nothing of this temple remains, except perhaps a section of wall foundations on the west side of the present enclosure joining the stonework of the Herodian wall. It was inferior to Solomon's grand building.

It contained a golden altar, a table for the Bread of the Presence (shew bread), and sacred cups, bowls and censers which were plundered by Antiochus Epiphanes in 175 BC. Instead of Solomon's ten lampstands there was only one seven-branched candelabrum in the holy place. The ark of the covenant seems to have disappeared completely and it is never mentioned in any post-exilic literature.

◁◁Psalm 137: 4-5

◁Ezra 6: 14-22

MUSIC IN WORSHIP

Music played an important part in worship in the temple and later in the synagogues. The Psalms in the Bible were clearly written to be sung, and many of them carry notes about tunes: 'To [the tune of] "The Doe of the Morning"'; and 'To [the tune of] "Lillies"'. Other terms may have been musical directions but are not understood; they include 'According to *gittith*' and 'According to *alamoth*'. The term *selah* occurs seventy-one times and probably indicated an interlude or change in the musical accompaniment.

The difficulty of identifying musical instruments was discussed in chapter 16, but some of the Psalms clearly envisage a full orchestral backing:

Praise him with the sounding of the
    trumpet,
    praise him with the harp and lyre,
praise him with tambourine and
    dancing,
    praise him with the strings and
    flute,
praise him with the clash of cymbals,
    praise him with resounding
    cymbals.

The tunes were probably simple, perhaps not dissimilar to the early Christian melodies preserved today in Gregorian, Armenian and Byzantine chants, and in the music of the Yemenite Jews. Some of the Psalms were written for processions to sing, perhaps in celebration of a victory or during a pilgrimage to the temple.

Your procession has come into view,
    O God,
    the procession of my God and
    King into the sanctuary.
In front are the singers, after them
    the musicians;
    with them are the maidens playing
    tambourines.

There is a group of Psalms (120-134) which are called 'songs of ascents', and were probably used by worshippers climbing the hill to Jerusalem.

The singing in the temple was led by the Levites, although other people may have joined in. David is credited with having organized the Levites as singers and musicians for temple worship.

◁◁ Psalm 22
◁ Psalms 69 and 45

◁◁ Psalms 8; 46; 81
and 84

◁Psalm 68: 24f.

◁1 Chronicles 15: 16;

◁2 Chronicles 7: 6
◁◁Psalm 150: 3-5

2

Ezra 6: 16-18 ▷

Despite the great rejoicing at the dedication of the second temple, accompanied by many sacrifices, the worship continued to be imperfect by the standards of the law. Imperfect Malachi 1: 7-8 ▷ animals were offered for sacrifice; foreigners were given room in the temple area; business was being Nehemiah 13: 4-9 ▷
Nehemiah 13: 10f ▷ transacted on the sabbath. The Levites had to go out to work because they were not paid their tithes. People Nehemiah 5: 1-5 ▷
Nehemiah 13: 23ff ▷ mortgaged their homes and were reduced to becoming slaves of their own countrymen, and Jews were once again marrying foreigners. The people made a new covenant with God when Nehemiah 9: 38 ▷ Ezra read the law (possibly the Pentateuch) to the nation at a special assembly.

FESTIVALS AND OBSERVANCES

In due course two new festivals were introduced. One was the Feast of Hanukkah, or Dedication, sometimes called the Feast of Lights. It was first celebrated in early December in 164 BC when Judas Maccabaeus purified the sanctuary after its defilement three years previously by Antiochus Epiphanes. Candles were lit on each of the eight days of this festival.

Esther 9: 18-28 ▷ The second was the Feast of Purim, associated with the book of Esther. It may have been an adaptation of a Persian festival. It took place in Acts 2: 5-12 ▷▷ February-March, and a day's fast preceded two days of feasting. In later centuries it virtually became a carnival, and participants wore masks and disguises. The celebration reached its climax in the public reading of the book of Esther, accompanied by boos or hisses whenever the wicked Haman's name occurred, and cheers at the mention of Mordecai.

The older festivals and observances continued, and were perhaps moulded into their final form during or shortly after the exile. The Passover became the foremost festival, celebrated in March-April (14 Nisan in the Jewish calendar). It was obligatory, and it celebrated Israel's deliverance from Egypt. An unblemished male lamb was killed, originally at home and later in the temple, and carefully prepared. The family or group of friends met for the meal at sundown, and the head of the house gave an opening prayer over the first cup of wine. Then they ate bitter herbs – a reminder of bitter times – and a second cup of wine was poured but not drunk. The meal was then served, but it was not eaten until the Passover liturgy was recited, beginning with a son's question to his father: 'How is this night different from all other nights?' Then Psalm 113, the *Hallel*, was sung, and the main meal was eaten after a prayer over the unleavened bread. A prayer over a third cup ended the feast, Psalms 114 to 118 were sung and a fourth cup was drunk. When the temple was destroyed in AD 70, the lambs could not be ritually slain and the Passover was observed without the lamb.

Fifty days later came the Feast of Pentecost, originally called the Feast of Weeks. This was observed at local sanctuaries as well as in Jerusalem, and was primarily an offering of the first-fruits of the land. It became a pilgrimage in Josiah's day, and remained so thereafter, which explains why Jews from many areas were in Jerusalem on the day the Holy Spirit was poured out on the first Christians. So they recognized the variety of languages the disciples were speaking.

The Feast of Booths (or Tabernacles) took place in the autumn. The people thanked God for the completed harvest. For seven days they camped out in tents or shelters made from tree branches to commemorate Israel's journey through the desert. After the destruction of Jerusalem the feast

The modern Jewish Passover celebration contains all the traditional elements described in this section.

ceased to be an occasion for pilgrimage to the capital but was celebrated in every town and village.

Finally the Day of Atonement (*Yom Kippur*) became very significant after the exile although it had been celebrated in the centuries before. Three animals were sacrificed, a bull for the sins of the priesthood and a goat for the sins of the people. The high priest laid hands on a second goat, the 'scapegoat', and sent it out to die in the wilderness, symbolically carrying the sins of the people away. Only the high priest could utter the name of God,

Yahweh; only he could enter the Holy of Holies, on only this day in the year.

The writer to the Hebrews in the New Testament takes up the picture of this ceremony and describes how through his death Jesus Christ has entered the real Holy of Holies, the presence of God, bearing his own shed blood to atone for the sins of the world.

◁ Hebrews chaper 9

BRINGING GOD TO THE PEOPLE

The exiled Jews in Babylon mourned the loss of their temple. But they needed somewhere to meet together, to hear the Scriptures being read and to pray. So it is likely that they opened the first 'synagogues'. The first ones for which we have clear evidence were in the third century BC, established by Jews who had been dispersed to Egypt.

From inscriptions it is clear that there were five synagogues in Lower Egypt and four in Middle Egypt.

There was a synagogue mentioned in the second century BC in Antioch,

SCRIBES AND PHARISEES

Jesus often encountered opposition from the Scribes and Pharisees. They formed the religious elite of the first century and were highly critical of the way Jesus seemed to ignore their traditions.

The scribes were originally people who kept records and wrote documents, and became public administrators of high standing. But over the centuries they became experts in the law of Moses. Ezra was described as a priest who 'had devoted himself to the study and observance of the Law of the LORD, and to teaching its decrees and laws in Israel'; he was a 'teacher, a man learned in matters concerning the commands and decrees of the LORD for Israel'.

Ezra 7: 10f.▷

Probably through the influence of Hellenistic thought, the old priestly instruction became insufficient, and the scribes adopted Greek methods of instruction using questions and counter-questions. Jewish scribes began to establish an honoured tradition, and were sometimes known as 'wise men'. They were called on to give legal and theological opinions, such as formulating how much work could be done on the sabbath and arranging for the purchase of a house.

A group of pupils gathered round a teacher and followed him wherever he went. Once a pupil completed his course of study he was declared a scholar and the scribe laid hands on him. He then had authority to answer questions and discuss the law of Moses independently as a teacher. He was called rabbi and could wear the long robe of a scholar.

There were two major schools of interpretation among the scribes at the time of Jesus. Hillel, who had come from Babylon, was milder and more generous than the rigorous Shammai. Paul's teacher Gamaliel came from the Hillel tradition, which was the dominant tradition in Judaism. The scribe was the only person apart from chief priests and members of the patrician families who could become a member of the Sanhedrin, the Jewish ruling authority.

The Pharisees (the name means 'separated ones') were one group of Jews among several who banded together to preserve the purity of their faith. There was widespread dissatisfaction with the Jerusalem priesthood, and various brotherhoods were formed to protect members against the encroachment of foreign influences and from any relaxing of their religious obligations. The Pharisees held themselves aloof from the world around them, but did not go to the extremes of the Essenes and the associated Qumran community who lived on the shores of the Dead Sea, forming an exclusive and monastic community.

The Pharisees originated in Maccabean times as the 'pious ones' (*hasidim*) and set out to follow the commands of the law exactly. They took the greatest care to observe the rituals concerning cleanliness. Some priests joined the group, but the members were mostly laymen, including craftsmen, farmers and merchants. They met together for meals. Some of them became scribes and enjoyed a prominent place in the Sanhedrin.

For all their piety, they placed great burdens of religious obligation on the ordinary people. They had lost the spirit of the law and turned devotion into a system. God became to them almost a machine, bound to bless the person who carried out the right rituals at the right time. Jesus' concept of God, however, was of a loving Father who cared for people and provided for their needs, and who asked to be loved and obeyed from the heart and not simply to be recognized by outward and often empty ritual.

and by the time of Jesus every town had at least one; larger cities such as Jerusalem, Rome, Alexandria and Antioch had several. 'Synagogue' means 'congregation' and later came to mean 'a place of assembly' in the same way as the word 'church' has changed its meaning. It brought God to the people. He was no longer remote in the worship of the distant temple; he was present in every place. The synagogue became the focus of an entirely new form of religious and social life, and it became a part of the Jewish scene down to the present day.

Reconstructed synagogue at Tell Hum (Capernaum), probably 4th-5th centuries AD.

21

The synagogue was usually built on a simple plan. There was a long room with two rows of columns supporting the roof. Seats were placed around the room at ground level and in a gallery. At the end of the room facing Jerusalem, there was a niche set in the wall where the Torah scrolls were kept. In time this became known as the 'ark'. In front of it was a platform where the scribe stood to read the law and to recite prayers and benedictions. The seats nearest to the reading desk were usually reserved for the more 'honourable' of the members, a practice which Jesus criticized. The scholars sat on 'the seat of Moses' with their backs to the ark and facing the congregation.

Matthew 23: 6▷▷

Artist's impression of a complete synagogue (based on the remains from the 3rd-4th centuries AD at Meiron). Many features of this cut-away drawing are similar to the building at Capernaum, illustrated on page 345.

A synagogue could be started wherever there were ten male Jews; women were not allowed to play any part in its organization or ministry. But each sabbath whole families would make their way to the synagogue, men sitting in one part and their wives in another, to listen to the Shema: 'Hear, O Israel: The LORD our God, the LORD is one. Love the LORD your God with all your heart and with all your soul and with all your strength.'

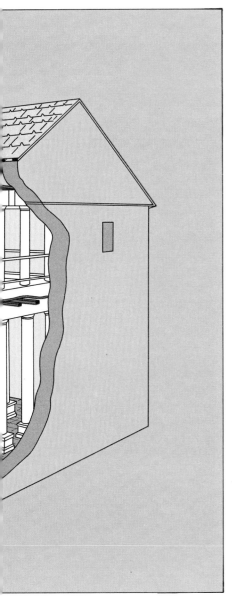

In the morning and in the evening this was preceded by two benedictions and was followed in the morning by one and in the evening by two more. These were all recited at the lectern. Other prayers were said in front of the ark; these were mostly praises to God, repeated by one person with the congregation saying 'Amen'. Then the Pentateuch (the law) was read, followed by a reading from the prophets. After a sermon or address the service closed with a benediction.

◁◁Deuteronomy 6: 4-5

Synagogue services would also be held on feast days, and in many places on Mondays and Thursdays as well, days on which people from outlying areas might come to market. But the synagogue was more than a centre for worship. It was a gathering place for friends, a school for boys, and the focus for local government. People in need were given gifts from the synagogue funds. Although it was subject to the law of the land, each synagogue had a group of elders to run it, and they were led by a 'ruler of the synagogue'; Nicodemus was a synagogue ruler. He came to Jesus by night and was told that learned as he was, he needed to be spiritually reborn.

◁John 3: 1

HEROD'S TEMPLE

The temple built by the returned exiles in the fifth century BC had suffered some damage during the Greek domination of Jerusalem. It had been a stronghold in the battle against the foreign garrison at the nearby citadel, and was further damaged when Herod and his Roman supporters attacked Jerusalem in 37 BC. Herod, always a prolific builder, decided to dismantle the old structure and rebuild it in the prevailing Hellenistic-Roman style. He was not of pure Jewish stock, being an Idumaean, and his apparently magnanimous act might have been a political gesture to reconcile the Jews

21

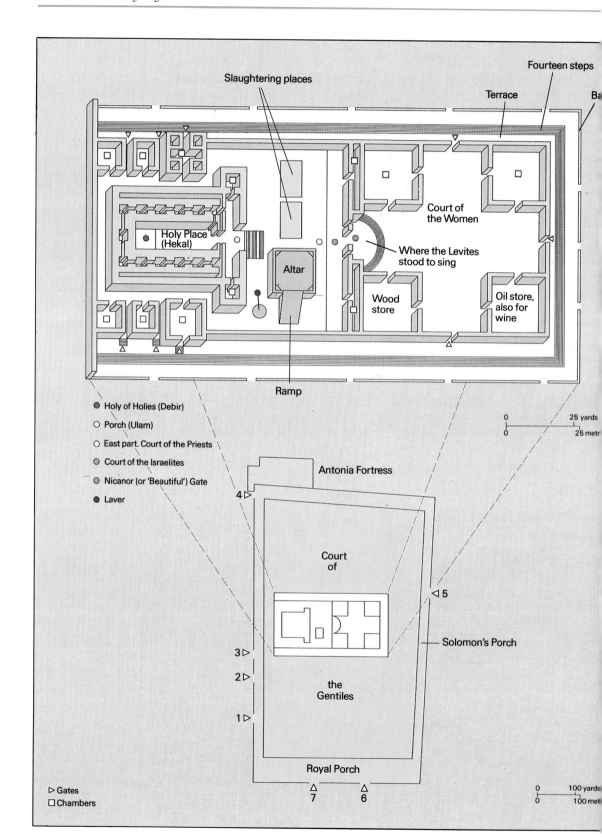

Slaughtering places

Fourteen steps

Terrace

Ba

Holy Place
(Hekal)

Court of
the Women

Where the Levites
stood to sing

Altar

Wood
store

Oil store,
also for
wine

Ramp

- Holy of Holies (Debir)
- Porch (Ulam)
- East part. Court of the Priests
- Court of the Israelites
- Nicanor (or 'Beautiful') Gate
- Laver

0   25 yards
0   25 metr

Antonia Fortress

4 ▷

Court
of

◁ 5

Solomon's Porch

3 ▷

2 ▷

the
Gentiles

1 ▷

Royal Porch

△   △
7   6

0   100 yards
0   100 met

▷ Gates
□ Chambers

ossible plan of Herod's temple. Compare the econstruction on pages 350–351 and the hotograph on page 331.

him. When the work began early in 9 BC Herod took great pains to respect he sacred area; he even trained 1,000 riests as masons to build the shrine self. Although the central part was ompleted within a year and a half, ome of the subsidiary buildings were till under construction half a century

later, according to Jews who misunderstood Jesus' comment about raising up the temple of his body in three days.

The temple was built on a huge platform about 450 m (1,476 ft) north–south and 300 m (984 ft) east–west. The land was levelled, with some rock

Jews praying at the Western Wall. The massive blocks of masonry are shown dramatically in this photograph.

◁John 2: 20

21

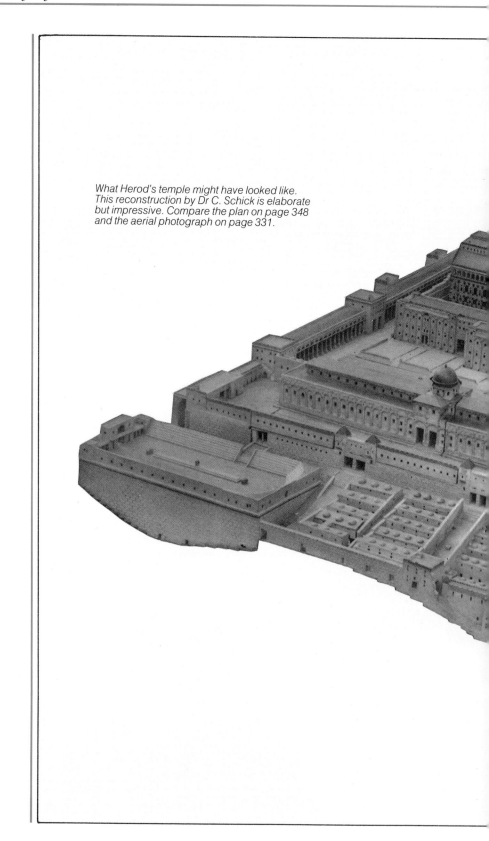

*What Herod's temple might have looked like.
This reconstruction by Dr C. Schick is elaborate
but impressive. Compare the plan on page 348
and the aerial photograph on page 331.*

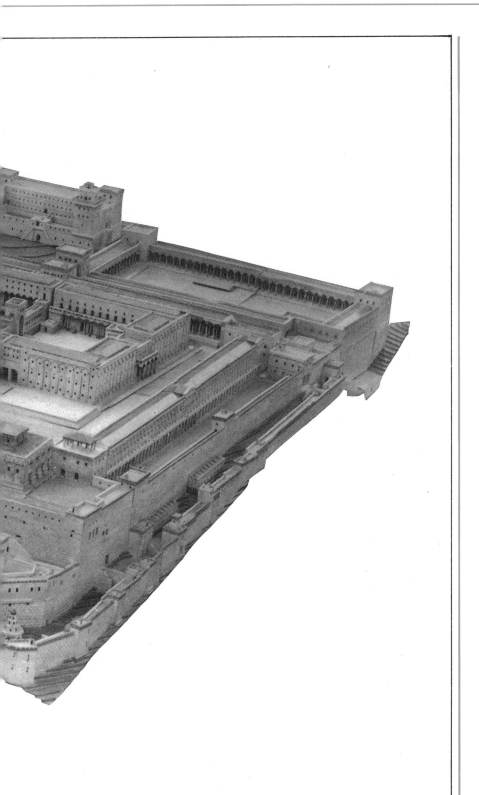

21

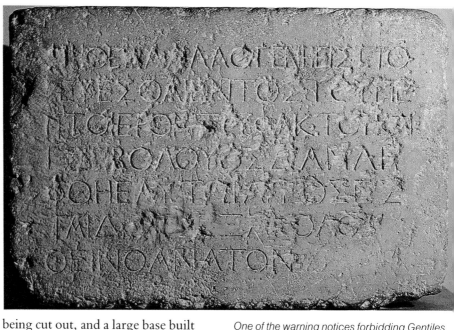

One of the warning notices forbidding Gentiles to enter the inner courtyard of the temple. This one is written in Greek capital letters.

being cut out, and a large base built where the hill sloped away. The massive enclosure wall was built of limestone blocks mostly a metre (3 ft) high and up to 5 m (16 ft) long. At the south–east corner, overlooking the Kidron Valley, the inner courtyard wall was about 45 m (148 ft) above the rock. It is thought that the parapet above this corner was the 'highest point of the temple' where Jesus was tempted, by the devil, to jump off in a spectacular demonstration of his divinity. Sections of this wall still remain standing, and much more has been revealed by excavations.

There were gates in each of the four walls, although the only gate on the north side, the Tadi Gate, was apparently never used. Traces of two gates on the south side are still visible in the area of the al-Aqsa Mosque, known as the Huldah Gates; one was double and the other triple, and they were approached by a monumental stairway. Ramps led from them up to the court. At the north–west corner of the enclosure lay the Fortress of Antonia, which was probably the residence of Roman procurators when

Matthew 4: 5▷

John 2: 14-16 ▷▷

they were in the city. The garrison stood ready to quell any disturbance in the temple area.

The outer courtyard, the Court of the Gentiles, was open to anyone and was surrounded by a portico inside the walls. The porch on the east side was known as Solomon's porch, and it was inside these colonnades that the scribes held their schools and debates. This would also have been where the money-changers and merchants had their stalls, which Jesus overturned.

The inner courtyard was on a slightly higher level and was surrounded by a balustrade. Notices in Greek and Latin warned Gentiles that if they entered the inner court they were liable to be executed. It was divided into three parts: the Women's Court, the Court of Israel (men only), and the Priests Court into which men could walk at the time of the Feast of Tabernacles.

The shrine itself was a copy of Solomon's. It was made of cream stone and had three storeys of chambers on the north, south and west sides to a height of 18 m (60 ft). Golden spikes were fixed to the roof to prevent birds from perching on it.

Of all the temples in Jerusalem, this one lasted for the shortest time. When Jerusalem was attacked in AD 70 the giant stones were demolished. Once again the sacrificial system of the Jewish religion ceased.

FOR FURTHER READING

Baker, J.P., 'Prophecy, Prophets', *IBD*, 3 (IVP, 1980), pp.1276–1287.
Davies, D. Henton, 'Tabernacle', *IDB*, 4 (New York, Abingdon, 1962), pp.498–506.
Ellison, H.L., 'Pharisees', *IBD*, 3 (IVP, 1980), pp.1209f.
Freeman, D., 'Feasts', *IBD*, 1 (IVP, 1980), pp.504f.
Gaster, T.H., 'Sacrifices and Offerings', *IDB*, 4 (New York, Abingdon, 1962), pp.147–159.
Gooding, D.W., 'Tabernacle', *IBD*, 3 (IVP, 1980), pp.1506–1511.
Millard, A.R. and McKelvey, R.J., 'Temple', *IBD*, 3 (IVP, 1980), pp.1522–1532.
Stewart, R.A., 'Passover', *IBD*, 3 (IVP, 1980), pp.1157f.
Stinesburg, W.E., 'Temple, Jerusalem', *IDB*, 4 (New York, Abingdon, 1962), pp.534–560.
Thompson, J.A., 'Sanhedrin', *IBD*, 3 (IVP, 1980), pp.1390–1391.
Thompson, R.J. and Beckwith, R.T., 'Sacrifice and Offering', *IBD*, 3 (IVP, 1980), pp.1358–1368.
Wenham, G.J., 'The Religion of the Patriarchs' in *Essays on the Patriarchal Narratives* (IVP, 1980), pp.157–188.

21

Jesus said, 'I am the good shepherd' (John 10:11). This photograph of sheep in the Kidron Valley shows Jerusalem in the background.

The life and worship of the first Christians

Throughout this book one thing above all others will have become clear: life in Bible times, compared to life in modern western society, was often hard and uncomfortable. It was socially and economically insecure; war and famine were constant threats. Duvets and double glazing for cold winter nights and days had not been thought of; there was no audio and video equipment to while away the silent hours of darkness.

It is important to recall these facts when reading the descriptions of early church life. Just as the harsh facts of first-century existence were not cushioned by modern comforts, so too the worship and fellowship of the first Christians was far from being easy or ideal; Paradise was not regained the day after Pentecost. The first Christians had to squeeze time for meetings out of a Roman pattern of work which allowed (grudgingly) the Jewish sabbath (Saturday) but not the Christian Sunday. They had no purpose-built meeting places, and had to make do with homes or hired halls. Their way of life soon attracted suspicion from people who variously regarded them as Jewish heretics to be persecuted, as traitors to Rome (because they acknowledged another king, Jesus) to be imprisoned, or as

barbaric cannibals (because they 'ate' the 'body and blood' of Jesus at their corporate meals) to be ostracized.

It is perhaps all the more remarkable that the New Testament is able to reflect an atmosphere of great and deep joy, despite the difficulties. 'They broke bread in their homes and ate together with glad and sincere hearts, praising God and enjoying the favour of all the people.'

◁ Acts 2: 46-47

PRESSURES ON BELIEVERS

Even in times of persecution there was a keynote of joy in the writings of the early church. Yet the first Christians in some respects faced even greater religious pressure than their Jewish ancestors. Whereas the Israelites of old had strayed from God's ways and willingly compromised their faith with pagan superstitions, sometimes the early Christians were forced at sword-point to take part in pagan worship as a test of their political loyalty.

EMPEROR-WORSHIP
Roman emperors had become revered as gods. Some hesitated to use the title, but Augustus (27 BC – AD 14) allowed temples to be erected in his honour, and men like Caligula (AD 37-41) and Nero (AD 54-68) had no qualms about

accepting and encouraging veneration. Domitian (AD 81-96) built a temple in Ephesus containing his own statue. Officials, who were appointed annually to act as priests of the provincial cult of 'Rome and the Emperor', were drawn from the chief citizens or Asiarchs.

Most of the ordinary Romans had no religious scruples about paying cultic reverence to the emperor, and the Jews had a long-standing exemption from such things because they followed an ancient religion. As long as Christians were regarded as Jews they too were exempt, but once they were seen to be separate the Christians lost their privileges and were counted with the mass of Roman citizens. Concerned to be good citizens who submitted 'to the governing authorities ... which God

Temples were erected in honour of the Roman emperor. This is Hadrian's temple in Ephesus, dating from the 2nd century AD.

has established' and to 'honour the king' (Romans 13: 1 and 1 Peter 2: 17), church members were faced with impossible demands. Although the rules were not always pressed, there were periods during the first four centuries when Christians had to choose between dying for Jesus or denying him. Only the conversion of the Emperor Constantine (AD 308-337) guaranteed that this pressure would be relieved for the duration of the Roman Empire.

PAGAN CEREMONIES

Polytheism was a fact of life in the first century, and because it was generally acceptable the Christians constantly came up against problems. When converts abandoned their old religions – and cut off their financial support – people with vested interests could become very angry. The account of the riot of Ephesus, sparked off by silversmiths annoyed at their loss of trade in models of the patron goddess Artemis (Diana), is one example of the problem.

Christians who were members of trade guilds were required to participate in pagan ceremonies related to the guilds' patron deities. Those who refused were likely to lose their ancient equivalent of a union card, and because the law allowed such 'closed shops', their livelihood too.

Even the relatively ordinary household duties of buying meat from the butcher or going out to dinner with friends were fraught with problems. Some butchers bought their produce wholesale from the pagan temples where it had been ritually slaughtered or partially offered as a sacrifice to idols. Christians in Corinth were unsure whether or not to buy such meat, or to eat it if it was set in front of them. Paul's advice was that as idols were not real gods anyway, the rituals were meaningless and the meat could

Head of the statue of Artemis from Ephesus, 2nd century AD. Note the signs of the Zodiac.

◁◁ Acts 19: 23-41

be eaten with a clear conscience. However, he also made allowances for those whose consciences were so sensitive, in that church of very mixed attitudes, that they would regard not only such food as 'unclean' but were also offended by fellow Christians whose scruples were, like Paul's, less rigorous. He suggested that it was a greater sin to cause a brother to be offended.

◁ 1 Corinthians 8: 4-13; 10: 25-33

All around the Christians would be the sights and sounds of pagan worship. The great temple of Artemis in Ephesus stood on a platform 127 m (418 ft) long by 73 m (239 ft) wide. A flight of steps led into the temple which contained 100 columns, some sculptured, each 2 m (over 6 ft) in diameter. The altar was 6 m (20 ft) square and stood in front of the huge statue of Artemis. The temple was

22

decorated with bright paintings and gold leaf.

This temple was not an ancient monument to be visited by tourists, but a functioning and very dominant centre of pagan ritual. The person who abandoned the brilliance of the worship and sacrifices and the social friendship of the temple for the simplicity of the Christian breaking of bread and fellowship, needed powerful convictions to make the change and to deal with the battery of questions such an act would prompt from the people among whom he lived.

SUPERSTITION, CULTS AND MAGIC

Apart from the overt pressures to conform to pagan religions, the early Christians also lived in a cultural atmosphere which reeked of superstition. People of the Near East in the first century AD were beset with deep anxieties and uncertainties about life. Ideas about fate, a yearning for miracles, and a fascination with astrology and magic pervaded daily life. People felt threatened by demons and they engaged in fearful searchings for ways of escape.

Some of the mystery religions offered them what they were looking for. Oriental cults originating from Egypt, Syria, Phrygia and Persia became fused with Greek religions. The initiate to the cult of Isis was instructed, given a purifying bath, then had to fast. On the day of initiation he was clothed in linen and led to a holy place for a ritual from which he was believed to emerge as a divine being filled with power and surrounded by radiant light.

In the cult of Attis and Cybele, which came from Phrygia, the initiate underwent a 'divine' experience of delirium and ecstasy to the accompaniment of music. Then he entered a deep pit covered with boards drilled with holes. A bull was killed on the platform and its blood flowed through the holes and drenched the initiate beneath. He drank some of the blood and, when he emerged, was

Mithras slaying the bull. Again the signs of the Zodiac are prominent. This marble relief from Sidon dates from about 400 AD.

greeted as a person who had been born again.

The cult of Mithras, which originated in Persia, had struggle and victory as its main themes. In Persian mythology Mithras, the god of light, killed a fierce bull and drove out the darkness. Only men could become members of the cult, and they were branded on the forehead by a hot iron, were baptized and ate a sacred meal. Believers were obliged to observe an ethical code, and the cult spread rapidly as Roman soldiers practised it on their expeditions. The spiritual conflict between Christianity and the Mithraic cult, which was fierce because some of the rites were similar, ended in the fourth century when Christianity was officially recognized. Some Christian churches were built over Mithraic shrines to symbolize the triumph.

Magic and sorcery were rife in New Testament times, and the apostles encountered them on their travels. In Ephesus magicians who became Christians made a bonfire of the papyri and parchments which detailed their magic spells. A number of magic scrolls have been preserved and can be seen today in museums in London, Paris and Leiden.

Another groups of teachers, called Gnostics, were responsible for what was really the first Christian heresy. They said that the truth was a secret hidden from ordinary mortals and would be revealed only to cult initiates. They regarded Jesus as a divine being among other divine beings, and the emphasis on the humanity and deity of Jesus Christ in 1 John is taken as evidence that Gnosticism was flexing its muscles at the close of the first century AD.

It was a century in which Christians needed not only a living dynamic faith, able to draw on the power of God to face persecution. They also needed to understand fully who it was they had trusted as their Lord and Saviour, and why. It was no place for spiritual babies; 'grow up in your salvation' was an apostolic command. And corporate church life was germane to that growth.

◁ 1 Peter 2: 2

EARLY CHRISTIAN WORSHIP

In the months following the death, resurrection and ascension of Jesus, the Christians continued to worship in the temple at Jerusalem. They met together 'in the temple courts' but they also 'broke bread in their homes'. Worship of Jesus had already begun to permeate their daily lives as they recalled his death and resurrection during their mealtimes.

◁ Acts 2: 46

Christians in the provinces clearly worshipped in their local synagogues. The commission of Saul of Tarsus in Damascus was to root out the Christians from the Jewish fellowship; his vision of Jesus stopped him in his tracks and sent him on his journey as a friend rather than a foe of the embryonic church. During his missionary journeys he went first to the Jewish synagogues to expound the fulfilment of the Scriptures in the life of Jesus. At Philippi there may not have been a synagogue; Paul found a place of prayer by the riverside where a few Jews – mostly women – gathered. No doubt the new converts from his first sermons stayed in the synagogues until a combination of Jewish opposition and personal dissatisfaction drove them out.

◁ Acts 9: 2

◁◁ Acts 19: 18-20

◁ Acts 16: 13

From the beginning the church seems to have been regarded not as a place, nor even a human association, but a divinely created institution: 'Paul … to the church of God in Corinth' was how he addressed both his letters to that tumultuous city, reminding the divided fellowship as he did so that 'You are not your own; you were

◁ 1 Corinthians 1: 1f.;
2 Corinthians 1: 1

22

Facing page: Roman homes had their household god or lares. This dancing figure, 21.5 cm (8½ in) high would have been one of a pair which flanked the household altar.

bought at a price.'

Sometimes, however, the word 'church', which means 'gathering', is given to groups at certain places. He wrote a letter to 'the churches in Galatia' and in it mentioned 'the churches of Judea'. This was an umbrella term for the smaller groups within a region. Most of them would have met in homes and kept loose links with each other for friendship and mutual support. Paul wrote greetings to Priscilla and Aquila in Rome, and 'also the church that meets at their house'. He implies in the phrase 'If the whole church comes together' that the home groups met in a larger gathering for worship from time to time.

The basic pattern for worship was probably set directly after Pentecost. 'They devoted themselves to the apostles' teaching and to the fellowship, to the breaking of bread and to prayer'. The 'fellowship' probably included discussion and counsel as well as sharing personal possessions, and was built around the common meal which in the course of time became known as the eucharist ('thanksgiving') or communion, when they recalled the death of Jesus by sharing in bread and wine. This may have been a separate gathering from the one in which the teaching of Jesus was passed on, the Old Testament Scriptures read, and corporate prayer offered. There were probably brief summaries of teaching which helped focus on the central facts of their faith: 'Christ died for our sins according to the Scriptures, that he was buried, that he was raised on the third day according to the Scriptures'.

◁◁ 1 Corinthians 6: 19f.

◁◁ Galatians 1: 2, 22
◁ 1 Corinthians 15: 3f.

The picture of developing worship in Corinth shows great spontaneity. People speak in tongues, prophesy or share a hymn or a prayer as they are led by the Holy Spirit working among them. Paul lays down guidelines for worship so that it can remain spontaneous without getting out of hand. 'Be eager to prophesy, and do not forbid speaking in tongues. But everything should be done in a fitting and orderly way.'

◁ 1 Corinthians 14: 26-40

◁◁ Romans 16: 3, 5
◁◁ 1 Corinthians 14: 23

The Lord's Supper, the communion, was a fellowship meal rather than a symbolic one as it usually is today. The words of Jesus over the bread and wine

◁◁ Acts 2: 42

A wall-painting from the Roman catacombs showing an early Christian ritual meal, recalling the 'Lord's Supper'.

22

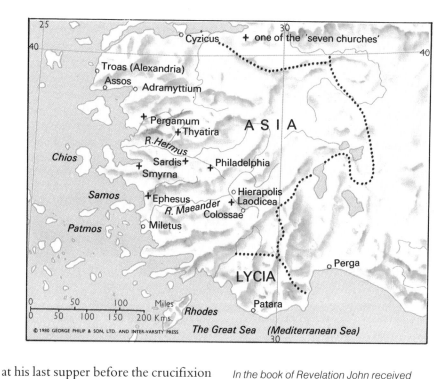

Map labels: Cyzicus, + one of the 'seven churches', Troas (Alexandria), Assos, Adramyttium, Pergamum, Thyatira, R.Hermus, ASIA, Chios, Sardis, Philadelphia, Smyrna, Samos, Ephesus, Hierapolis, Laodicea, R. Maeander, Colossae, Patmos, Miletus, LYCIA, Perga, 50 100 Miles, Rhodes, Patara, Patara, The Great Sea (Mediterranean Sea), © 1980 GEORGE PHILIP & SON, LTD. AND INTER-VARSITY PRESS

In the book of Revelation John received messages from God 'to the seven churches in the province of Asia'. This map shows the seven churches and the island of Patmos where the vision was given.

1 Corinthians 11: ▷
23-25

at his last supper before the crucifixion were preserved and repeated: 'The Lord Jesus, on the night he was betrayed, took bread, and when he had given thanks, he broke it and said, "This is my body, which is for you; do this in remembrance of me." In the same way, after supper he took the cup, saying, "This cup is the new covenant in my blood; do this, whenever you drink it, in remembrance of me."' The death of Jesus, through which the believer died to the world and his own sinful nature, was as central to the worship of the church as was Jesus' resurrection, through which they received new life and could confidently assert that 'Jesus is Lord'.

1 Corinthians 12: ▷▷
7-30;
Romans 12: 3-8

Acts 6: 1-7 ▷▷

Philippians 1: 1 ▷▷

EARLY CHURCH ORGANIZATION

At first there were no officers in the church, although the apostles were seen to carry great authority and no doubt the Jewish synagogue traditions of leadership carried over into the first house-churches. Paul's first letter to the Corinthians, as well as the later letter to the Romans, carries lists of functions performed by people within the church, who included prophets and teachers, but also helpers and administrators. The first churches saw themselves as the 'body' of Christ, with each member being an active part of it with a vital, even if small, role to play in its growth. People like Priscilla and Aquila must have been both organizers and pastors; and the apostles appointed 'deacons' to deal with practical matters.

In his later letters Paul speaks of elders and pastors – although when he addresses the Philippians he mentions the 'saints' before the overseers and deacons, and there is clearly no sense of hierarchy. In the pastoral Epistles (1 and 2 Timothy and Titus) the leadership structure is being formalized,

Two of the 'seven churches' had been established in Laodicea and Sardis. Corinth in Greece also had an established Christian congregation in the 1st century AD.

Corinth: temple of Apollo, 6th century BC.

with the apostolic delegate Timothy being instructed to appoint elders who are spiritually mature and of good character.

It was a far cry from the rigid structures of Old Testament religion. A new covenant had indeed been instituted, in which the law of God was written on his people's hearts. The promise of Jesus to be with his followers for ever was the first stage in restoring the personal fellowship between man and God lost in the mists of man's early history in Eden; his promise to return and take his followers into the heavenly presence of God for ever would complete that restorative process.

Meanwhile, having direct personal access to the living God without the need of elaborate ritual to approach him or of specially consecrated priests to intercede on their behalf, the first Christians soon learned that their new form of faith and worship was more demanding than the old. 'I urge you, brothers,' Paul wrote to the Christians in Rome under the lengthening

Laodicea: part of the remains of the gymnasium.

◁◁ Matthew 28: 20

22

Romans 12: 1-2 ▷▷

shadow of Nero's tyranny, 'in view of God's mercy, to offer your bodies as living sacrifices, holy and pleasing to God – which is your spiritual worship. Do not conform any longer to the pattern of this world, but be transformed by the renewing of your mind. Then you will be able to test and approve what God's will is – his good, pleasing and perfect will.'

It is a challenge which has echoed down the centuries. Times have changed; the cars have at last replaced the camels, the telephone has bridged

Sardis: temple of Artemis, AD *150, with later Byzantine chapel.*

Christian crosses carved on one of the columns of the temple of Aphrodite at Aphrodisias in Turkey (3rd-4th centuries AD).

the gaps between cities and nations. Today the land flows with canned milk and imported honey; the freezer brings the harvest forward; and glass and concrete insulate us from the cold of winter and the heat of summer. But the God of the Bible always maintains that 'I change not'. And the people he spoke to in times vastly different from our own knew just as we do what it was to laugh and cry, to love and to be alone, to hurt and to die. As we see them in the context of Bible times, we see a reflection of ourselves, and in the stories of their faith we can find hope and meaning for a new generation.

FOR FURTHER READING

Banks, R., *Going to Church in the First Century* (Sydney, Hexagon Press, 1980).

Banks, R., *Paul's Idea of Community: The Early House Churches in their Historical Setting* (Paternoster Press, 1981).

Edersheim, A., *Life and Times of Jesus the Messiah* (1901) Vols 1 & 2 (New ed. Pickering & Inglis, 1959).

Edersheim, A., *Sketches of Jewish Life in the Days of Christ* (reprint 1876. Grand Rapids, Eerdmans, 1967).

Lohse, E., *The New Testament Environment* (SCM, 1974).

Martin, R.P., 'The Lord's Supper', *IBD*, 2 (IVP, 1980), pp.912–915.

Martin, R.P., *Worship in the Early Church*, rev.ed. (Marshall, Morgan & Scott, 1974. US ed. Grand Rapids, Eerdmans, 1974).

Meeks, W.A., *The First Urban Christians*, rev.ed. (New Haven, Yale UP, 1984).

Reicke, B., *The New Testament Era: The World of the Bible from 500 BC to AD 100* (Black, 1969).

Schweizer, E., *Church Order in the New Testament* (SCM, 1961).

Schweizer, E., *the Lord's Supper according to the New Testament* (English Translation, Philadelphia, Fortress, 1967).

Walker, G.S.W., 'Church Government', *IBD*, 1 (IVP, 1980), pp.286–288.

22

Acknowledgments

ACKNOWLEDGMENT OF THE SOURCES OF ILLUSTRATIONS

The publishers have made every effort to trace the copyright holders of illustrations in this book. Should any have been inadvertently missed, copyright holders are asked to contact the publishers.

RELIEF MAPS

Relief maps © copyright George Philip and Sons Ltd. and Inter-Varsity Press appear on pages: 207, 218, 305 and 362.

DIAGRAMS, CHARTS, ILLUSTRATIONS AND PLANS

All diagrams, charts, line drawings, colour illustrations and town plans have been specially prepared for Inter-Varsity Press, some of them for *The Illustrated Bible Dictionary* (1980) and the *New Bible Atlas* (1985). The publishers are glad to acknowledge their indebtedness to the sources indicated below:

Plan of Tel Beersheba, p.44
After Y. Aharoni, 'The Beersheba Excavations' in *Tel Aviv* 2 (1975), p.148.

Plan of Marisa, p.49
After A. R. Millard, *Treasures from Bible Times* (Lion Publishing, 1985), p.153.

Drawing of door and lintel, p.60
After material supplied by A. R. Millard.

Israelite four-roomed house, p.61
After material supplied by C. J. Davey.

Plan of house excavated at Shechem, p.63
Based on G.E. Wright, *Shechem* (Gerald Duckworth, 1964), fig. 76.

Reconstruction of the 'Mansion', p.66 and plan of the 'Burnt House', p.68
After N. Avigad, *Discovering Jerusalem, Recent Archaeological Excavations in the Upper City* (Blackwell, 1984), pages 99 and 126 respectively.

Drawing of a cistern, p.115
After *Bulletin of the American Schools of Oriental Research* 185, 1967, p.24.

Cross-section of water system, pages 120-121
Based on W. G. Dever and S. M. Paul, *Biblical Archaeology* (Keter Publishing House, Jerusalem, 1973), p.132, fig.b.

Reconstruction of a copper-smelting furnace, p.185
After material provided by C. J. Davey.

Bow-drill, p.196
After material provided by A. R. Millard.

Alphabets chart, pages 236-237
After material provided by A. R. Millard.

Town walls, p.286
After W. G. Dever and S. M. Paul, *Biblical Archaeology* (Keter Publishing House, Jerusalem, 1973), p.85.

Defensive town gates, p.288
Gate plan, after M. Avi-Yonah (ed.), *Encyclopaedia of Archaeological Excavations in the Holy Land*, vol.2, p.437. Reconstruction after material supplied by C. J. Davey.

Artist's impression of synagogue, pages 346-347
After E. M. and C. L. Meyers and J. F. Strange, *Annual of the American Schools of Oriental Research*, vol.43, p.87.

Plan of Herod's temple, p.348
Based on information from J. Wilkinson, *Jerusalem as Jesus knew it* (Thames and Hudson, 1978), pages 71 and 84.

PHOTOGRAPHS

The photographs in the *Handbook of Life in Bible Times* are reproduced by

EDITORIAL AND
PRODUCTION:

Derek Wood (organizing editor)
Michael Sims (production)
Caroline Masom (picture research)
Katy Coutts and Brenda Gooday
    (editorial)
Ann Ward and Marie Palmer (index)

DESIGN AND
TYPESETTING:

Swanston Graphics Limited:
Andrew Bright, Tony Hoyle,
Sue Paling, Jeanne Radford,
Ivan Sendall, Malcolm Swanston and
Neil Walker

Index

INTRODUCTION

THREE INDEXES

The index has been divided into three
parts for ease of reference, basically
places, people and general.

Locations with names are listed in
the first index. Buildings will be found
in the general index where their
locations are indicated, *e.g.*

Antonia fortress (Jerusalem)

The personal names index includes
peoples, deities and names of God but
buildings named after people will be
found in the general index, *e.g.*

Apollo, temple of (Corinth)

ALPHABETICAL ORDER

Entries are listed on a letter-by-letter
basis, not word-by-word, *e.g.*

Bethany
Beth Ashbea
Beth-eden
Bethel
Bethesda
Beth Horon...

REFERENCE SYSTEM

Page references. Ordinary figures
indicate a reference in the text. Italic
figures refer to illustrations or maps,
e.g.

Aegean Sea   42, 78; *302*

Reference is made in the text to the
Aegean Sea on pages 42 and 78, and
there is either an illustration or a map
locating the Aegean Sea on page 302.

An asterisk indicates 'see' or 'see
also', cross-referring to a related entry.

f. indicates 'and the page following';
ff., 'and the two following pages'.

Index of places

Index of people

General index